FEMINIST
INTERPRETATIONS
OF
AYN RAND

NANCY TUANA, GENERAL EDITOR

This series consists of edited collections of essays, some
original and some previously published, offering feminist re-
interpretations of the writings of major figures in the Western philosophical tradition. Devoted to the work of a single
philosopher, each volume contains essays covering the full
range of the philosopher's thought and representing the diversity of approaches now being used by feminist critics.

Already published:

Nancy Tuana, ed., *Feminist Interpretations of Plato* (1994)

Margaret A. Simons, ed., *Feminist Interpretations of Simone
de Beauvoir* (1995)

Bonnie Honig, ed., *Feminist Interpretations of Hannah Arendt*
(1995)

Patricia Jagentowicz Mills, ed., *Feminist Interpretations of
G. W. F. Hegel* (1996)

Maria J. Falco, ed., *Feminist Interpretations of Mary
Wollstonecraft* (1996)

Susan J. Hekman, ed., *Feminist Interpretations of Michel
Foucault* (1996)

Nancy J. Holland, ed., *Feminist Interpretations of Jacques
Derrida* (1997)

Robin May Schott, ed., *Feminist Interpretations of Immanuel
Kant* (1997)

Céline Léon and Sylvia Walsh, eds., *Feminist Interpretations
of Søren Kierkegaard* (1997)

Cynthia Freeland, ed., *Feminist Interpretations of Aristotle*
(1998)

Kelly Oliver and Marilyn Pearsall, eds., *Feminist
Interpretations of Friedrich Nietzsche* (1998)

FEMINIST INTERPRETATIONS OF AYN RAND

EDITED BY
MIMI REISEL GLADSTEIN
AND
CHRIS MATTHEW SCIABARRA

THE PENNSYLVANIA STATE UNIVERSITY PRESS
UNIVERSITY PARK, PENNSYLVANIA

Library of Congress Cataloging-in-Publication Data

Feminist interpretations of Ayn Rand / edited by Mimi Reisel Gladstein
and Chris Matthew Sciabarra.
    p.   cm.—(Re-reading the canon)
    Includes bibliographical references and index.
    ISBN 0-271-01830-5 (cloth : alk. paper)
    ISBN 0-271-01831-3 (pbk. : alk. paper)
    1. Rand, Ayn—Criticism and interpretation. 2. Feminism and
literature—United States—History—20th century. 3. Women and
literature—United States—History—20th century. 4. Canon
(Literature) I. Gladstein, Mimi Reisel. II. Sciabarra, Chris
Matthew, 1960– . III. Series.
PS3535.A547Z66 1999   98-16939
                                   CIP

It is the policy of The Pennsylvania State University Press to use acid-free paper for the
first printing of all clothbound books. Publications on uncoated stock satisfy the minimum requirements of American National Standard for Information Sciences—
Permanence of Paper for Printed Library Materials, ANSI Z39.48–1992.

Contents

Part Two: Feminist Rereadings of Rand's Fiction

Part Three: Toward a Randian Feminism?

Preface

Take into your hands any history-of-philosophy text. You will find compiled therein the "classics" of modern philosophy. Since these texts are often designed for use in undergraduate classes, the editor is likely to offer an introduction in which the reader is informed that these selections represent the perennial questions of philosophy. The student is to assume that she or he is about to explore the timeless wisdom of the greatest minds of Western philosophy. No one calls attention to the fact that the philosophers are all men.

Though women are omitted from the canons of philosophy, these texts inscribe the nature of woman. Sometimes the philosopher speaks directly about woman, delineating her proper role, her abilities and inabilities, her desires. Other times the message is indirect—a passing remark hinting at women's emotionality, irrationality, unreliability.

This process of definition occurs in far more subtle ways when the central concepts of philosophy—reason and justice, those characteristics that are taken to define us as human—are associated with traits historically identified with masculinity. If the "man" of reason must learn to control or overcome traits identified as feminine—the body, the emotions, the passions—then the realm of rationality will be one reserved primarily for men,[1] with grudging entrance to those few women who are capable of transcending their femininity.

Feminist philosophers have begun to look critically at the canonized texts of philosophy and have concluded that the discourses of philosophy are not gender-neutral. Philosophical narratives do not offer a universal perspective, but rather privilege some experiences and beliefs over others. These experiences and beliefs permeate all philosophical theories whether they be aesthetic or epistemological, moral or metaphysical. Yet this fact has often been neglected by those studying the traditions of philosophy. Given the history of canon formation in Western philosophy, the perspective most likely to be privileged is that of upper-class white males. Thus, to be fully aware of the impact of gender biases, it is imperative that we re-read the canon with attention to the ways in which philosophers' assumptions concerning gender are embedded within their theories.

This new series, Re-Reading the Canon, is designed to foster this process of reevaluation. Each volume will offer feminist analyses of the theories of a selected philosopher. Since feminist philosophy is not monolithic in method or content, the essays are also selected to illustrate the variety of perspectives within feminist criticism and highlight some of the controversies within feminist scholarship.

In this series, feminist lenses will be focused on the canonical texts of Western philosophy, both those authors who have been part of the traditional canon, as well as those philosophers whose writings have more recently gained attention within the philosophical community. A glance at the list of volumes in the series will reveal an immediate gender bias of the canon: Arendt, Aristotle, de Beauvoir, Derrida, Descartes, Foucault, Hegel, Hume, Kant, Locke, Marx, Mill, Nietzsche, Plato, Rousseau, Wittgenstein, Wollstonecraft. There are all too few women included, and those few who do appear have been added only recently. In creating this series, it is not my intention to reify the current canon of philosophical thought. What is and is not included within the canon during a particular historical period is a result of many factors. Although no canonization of texts will include all philosophers, no canonization of texts that excludes all but a few women can offer an accurate representation of the history of the discipline, as women have been philosophers since the ancient period.[2]

I share with many feminist philosophers and other philosophers writing from the margins of philosophy the concern that the current canonization of philosophy be transformed. Although I do not accept the position that the current canon has been formed exclusively by power relations, I do believe that this canon represents only a selective history of the tradition. I share the view of Michael Bérubé that "canons are at once the location, the index, and the record of the struggle for cultural representation; like any other hegemonic formation, they must be continually reproduced anew and are continually contested."[3]

The process of canon transformation will require the recovery of "lost" texts and a careful examination of the reasons such voices have been silenced. Along with the process of uncovering women's philosophical history, we must also begin to analyze the impact of gender ideologies upon the process of canonization. This process of recovery and examination must occur in conjunction with careful attention to the concept of a canon of authorized texts. Are we to dispense with the notion of a tradition of excellence embodied in a canon of authorized texts? Or, rather than abandon the whole idea of a canon, do we instead encourage a reconstruction of a canon of those texts that inform a common culture?

This series is designed to contribute to this process of canon transformation by offering a re-reading of the current philosophical canon. Such a re-reading shifts our attention to the ways in which woman and the role of the feminine is constructed within the texts of philosophy. A question we must keep in front of us during this process of re-reading is whether a philosopher's socially inherited prejudices concerning woman's nature and role are independent of her or his larger philosophical framework. In asking this question attention must be paid to the ways in which the definitions of central philosophical concepts implicitly include or exclude gendered traits.

This type of reading strategy is not limited to the canon, but can be applied to all texts. It is my desire that this series reveal the importance of this type of critical reading. Paying attention to the workings of gender within the texts of philosophy will make visible the complexities of the inscription of gender ideologies.

Notes

1. More properly, it is a realm reserved for a group of privileged males, since the texts also inscribe race and class biases that thereby omit certain males from participation.

2. Mary Ellen Waithe's multivolume series, A History of Women Philosophers (Boston: M. Nijhoff, 1987), attests to this presence of women.

3. Michael Bérubé, Marginal Forces/Cultural Centers: Tolson, Pynchon, and the Politics of the Canon (Ithaca: Cornell University Press, 1992), 4–5.

Acknowledgments

It is impossible to thank all the individuals who have made contributions—large and small—to this volume. You know who you are. However, the Penn State Press family, its director, Sandy Thatcher, the Re-Reading the Canon series editor, Nancy Tuana, and two anonymous readers who recommended publication were involved with the development of the volume in its entirety. And we are deeply appreciative of their support.

Thanks also to Cherene Holland and Keith Monley for production and copyediting, respectively. Finally, our appreciation to all of our authors, for their perseverance, cooperation, and commitment to this project.

Below is full citation information for all reprinted material in this volume:

"Ayn Rand and Feminism: An Unlikely Alliance," by Mimi Gladstein, is reprinted, with permission, from *College English* 39, no. 6 (1978): 680–85, a publication of the National Council of Teachers of English.

"On *Atlas Shrugged*," by Judith Wilt, is reprinted, with permission, from *College English* 40, no. 3 (1978): 333–36, a publication of the National Council of Teachers of English.

"Ayn Rand: A Traitor to Her Own Sex," by Susan Brownmiller, is excerpted and reprinted with the permission of Simon & Schuster and Curtis Brown Group Ltd., London, from *Against Our Will: Men, Women, and Rape*, by Susan Brownmiller. Copyright 1975 by Susan Brownmiller. The excerpts from *The Fountainhead*, by Ayn Rand, are reprinted with the permission of Simon & Schuster. Copyright 1943 by The Bobbs-Merrill Company; copyright renewed 1970 by Ayn Rand.

"Psyching Out Ayn Rand," by Barbara Grizzuti Harrison, is reprinted by permission of Georges Borchardt, Inc., for the author. Originally appeared in *Ms.*, September 1978. Copyright 1978 by Barbara Grizzuti Harrison.

"Reflections on Ayn Rand," by Camille Paglia, is excerpted from "Interview with the Vamp," by Virginia Postrel. Reprinted, with permission, from the August/September 1995 issue of *Reason* magazine. Copyright 1995 by the Reason Foundation, 3415 S. Sepulveda Blvd., Suite 400, Los Angeles, Calif. 90034.

In the Introduction, the section "The Philosophy of Objectivism" is an adaptation of an excerpt from Chris Matthew Sciabarra, "Ayn Rand." Used by permission of Charles Scribner's Sons Reference Books, an imprint of Simon & Schuster Macmillan, from *American Writers: A Collection of Literary Biographies, Supplement IV, Part 2: Susan Howe to Gore Vidal*, A. Walton Litz, editor in chief, Molly Wiegel, assistant editor, 517–35. Copyright 1996 by Charles Scribner's Sons.

Introduction

Mimi Reisel Gladstein
and
Chris Matthew Sciabarra

Feminism is not a monolith. It is composed of a variety of approaches in both method and content. This volume reflects that proposition on two fundamental levels: First, it brings into focus disparate ideological trends within feminism. Second, it brings into sharp relief the thought of a twentieth-century woman philosopher and novelist whose iconoclastic man worship and individualism has been both praised and criticized, sometimes scorned, by feminists of all stripes.

Given the fact, however, that Ayn Rand's work has been an inspiration to many women, some of them feminists, and not a few men as well, it was inevitable, perhaps, that our call for papers fell upon the ears of those who were most affected by Rand. Whereas many of the approaches within this volume might be characterized as critically sympathetic, we have made every effort to achieve an intellectual and ideological balance under highly charged circumstances. Then again, it seems that anything related to Ayn Rand is, by definition, highly charged. That is as it should be.

Analogous to the diversity of feminist approaches is the variety of interpretations Rand's philosophy—Objectivism—has inspired. Like feminism, Objectivism is not a monolith. Its developing impact on Western culture has prompted a new generation of scholars to grapple with the implications of Rand's thought. Publications motivated by critical assessment of her work have grown exponentially since her death. Her philosophy is a major inspiration to libertarian politics worldwide, her name virtually synonymous with individualism and free-market capitalism.

The Philosophy of Objectivism

For those who are acquainted with Rand only as a novelist, the author of *The Fountainhead* and *Atlas Shrugged*, it may come as a surprise that she developed an integrated system of thought with implications for every major branch of philosophy.[1] In metaphysics, Rand argued in favor of an "objective reality."[2] In epistemology, she accepted the validity of sensory perception and the efficacy of human reason. In aesthetics, she examined the conceptual basis of art and its role in human life. In ethics, she advocated "rational self-interest." And in politics, she favored individualism and laissez-faire capitalism.

In contrast to some of the more nominalist approaches in contemporary feminism, Rand's system is founded on the principles of philosophical realism.[3] She believed that an objective reality exists, that it is what it is, independent of what human beings think or feel about it. But "existence" is not merely an abstract category. To exist is to be something specific; everything that exists has a definite nature. Consciousness is the means of grasping the identity of the elements that exist.

In her *Introduction to Objectivist Epistemology*, Rand (1990) developed her view of consciousness and presented her theory of concept formation and definition. She regarded consciousness as an active faculty, involving three interactive levels: the sensational, the perceptual, and the conceptual. Because the mind cannot retain isolated sensations in memory, Rand argued, the foundation of human knowledge is sensory perception.

She maintained that the "form," or way, in which we perceive objects is a product of the means by which we perceive.[4]

Absent here is any notion of a peculiarly "feminist" epistemology. For many contemporary feminists, Rand might be viewed as "masculinist" in her exaltation of the role of consciousness and reason in human life. In Rand's view ([1957] 1992, 1016), reason "perceives, identifies and integrates the material provided by man's senses"; it is not just a logical capacity but one that has application to practical living. Rand's concept of reason is profoundly expansive. It is the distinctive and defining element of the human, conceptual level of consciousness. It entails moments of perception, differentiation, identification, abstraction, and integration. As an integrative faculty, it combines analysis with synthesis and applies logic to experience. And it constitutes volitional activity. Indeed, volition is at the base of human cognition, in Rand's view, for the primary act of free will lies in our ability to focus, to move to a higher degree of awareness—which Rand expressed epigrammatically as the choice "to think or not to think" (1012). Since each of us has the capacity to evade thought, this fundamental choice is the root of all human rationality and morality.

It is Rand's basic conviction that human knowledge is valid, and that concepts constitute an objective *relation* between consciousness and existence. They are neither "intrinsic" (that is, existent in reality apart from consciousness) nor "subjective" inventions (that is, purely of the mind, having no relation to the external world).[5] The task of epistemology is to elucidate the "rules of cognition," rules deriving from the nature of both existence and consciousness.

Rand maintained that for human beings the mind is the "basic tool of survival." But the mind is not an exclusively analytical faculty; it is inclusive of subconscious, emotional components as well as conscious, reasoning ones. The mind is also interdependent with the body. Such an understanding of mind-body unity led Rand to reject as false many derivative alternatives, including the materialist-idealist dichotomy. As Leonard Peikoff (1991, 35) explains in his *Objectivism: The Philosophy of Ayn Rand,* Rand repudiated monism *and* dualism: "A philosophy that rejects the monism of idealism or materialism does not thereby become 'dualist.' This term is associated with a Platonic or Cartesian metaphysics; it suggests the belief in two realities, in the mind-body opposition, and in the soul's independence of the body—all of which Ayn Rand denies."

By implication, Rand rejected the belief in an inherent antagonism between reason and emotion. She acknowledged the importance of emotion to a fully integrated existence. She viewed emotions as responses emanating from a subconscious estimate "of that which furthers man's values or threatens them, that which is *for* him or *against* him." She argued that "emotions are not tools of cognition"; that is, they cannot, in themselves, guarantee the validity of one's subconscious evaluations (Rand 1964, 27).

Central to Rand's understanding of emotion was her conviction that the subconscious mind was a mechanism for the spontaneous integration of experience. This conception was primarily an outgrowth of Rand's essays on the nature and function of art, anthologized in her book *The Romantic Manifesto*.[6] According to Rand (1975b, 17), "the source of art lies in the fact that man's cognitive faculty is *conceptual*." All art—painting, sculpture, literature, music, and their related performing arts—is the means by which one brings into conscious awareness a view of oneself and of the nature of existence. Rand explained that "*[a]rt brings man's concepts to the perceptual level of his consciousness and allows him to grasp them directly, as if they were percepts*" (20).[7]

Rand defined art as "*a selective re-creation of reality according to an artist's metaphysical value-judgments*" (19). "Metaphysical value-judgments" are estimates of the world that are relevant to human life. In art, such "metaphysical value-judgments" are often held implicitly or subconsciously, in the form of a "sense of life"—which Rand characterized as "an emotional, subconsciously integrated appraisal of man and of existence" (25). "Sense of life" is crucially important to both artistic creation and aesthetic response. The artist translates a broad abstraction into concrete form, whereas the responder grasps the abstraction through a perception of the concrete form in which it is expressed (35).

Grasping the integrated function of the conscious and subconscious dimensions of mind in art, and in life, Rand argued that no person could escape from the need to analyze and understand the beliefs underlying thoughts, emotions, actions, and institutions. Since people are rational and conceptual beings by nature, they must be guided, ultimately, by conscious convictions and values chosen and validated by their minds. Rand stressed the relationship between values and facts, morality and prudence. According to Rand, the concept of value is implied in the concept of life because values are not possible without life and because the sustenance of genuinely *human* life is not possible without the rational pursuit of values. What human beings are—rational animals—

determines what they ought to do (Rand 1964, 17). If they choose to live and to flourish as efficacious beings, they must articulate and act on philosophical and moral principles that have practical significance for their survival.[8]

Thus, according to Rand, ethics is "an *objective, metaphysical necessity of man's survival.*" And since the identity of each life-form dictates the means of sustenance, human life—that is, "man's survival qua man"—is the standard of moral values. In Rand's view, "that which is proper to the life of a rational being is the good; that which negates, opposes or destroys it is the evil" (23).

In her essay "The Objectivist Ethics," Rand details the fundamental ethical principles of Objectivism: "*Value* is that which one acts to gain and/or keep—*virtue* is the act by which one gains and/or keeps it. The three cardinal values of the Objectivist ethics—the three values which, together, are the means to and the realization of one's ultimate value, one's own life—are: Reason, Purpose, Self-Esteem, with their three corresponding virtues: Rationality, Productiveness, Pride" (25).

For Rand, these values and virtues are different aspects of a single ethical totality. Recognizing the integration of mind and body, she argued that the rational, purposeful, and creative character of human action is manifested in the act of material production.[9] "Production," Rand (1967, 15) emphasized, "is the application of reason to the problem of survival." And because human survival is not merely physical, people must also act to achieve "the values of character that make [their lives] worth sustaining." Just "as man is a being of self-made wealth, so he is a being of self-made soul" (Rand [1957] 1992, 1020). In Rand's usage, the "soul" refers not to a mystic endowment but to human consciousness in all of its complexity.

Rand advocated an ethic of rational, benevolent selfishness.[10] She argued that if human life is the standard of value, then each person must be the beneficiary of his or her own moral actions (Rand 1964, ix). Rand held that "man must live for his own sake, neither sacrificing himself to others nor sacrificing others to himself. To live for his own sake means that *the achievement of his own happiness is man's highest moral purpose*" (27).

Rand's concept of egoism rejects both altruistic self-sacrifice and conventional notions of selfishness. Altruism is not a compassionate morality; its implicit premise is that individuals are not ends in themselves but must serve as means to the welfare of others. Such a prescription for self-abnegation undermines an individual's independence, integrity, and honesty—Rand argued—and leads not to social justice but to a rationale for exploitation.

Rand equally opposed "brute" selfishness, which posits the sacrifice of others to one's own ends. As Ellsworth Toohey, Rand's arch villain in *The Fountainhead*, asserts: "Every system of ethics that preached sacrifice grew into a world power and ruled millions of men. . . . The man who speaks to you of sacrifice, speaks of slaves and masters. And intends to be the master" (Rand [1943] 1993, 637–38).[11]

Rand identified voluntary trade as the only rational, just, and moral principle for all adult human relationships. All forms of human interaction—material exchanges, communication, friendship, and romantic love—ought to be nonexploitative and nonsacrificial. Individuals should act as "independent equals" trading value for value, neither seeking nor granting the unearned (Rand 1964, 31).[12]

Rand's political project is the concluding aspect of her systematic philosophy. It aims for the establishment of an ideal society that enables individuals to actualize their unique potentialities. For Rand, individual growth and creativity depend upon appropriate social conditions. Toward that end, she advocated a free society based upon the principle of individual rights. Because individuals must pursue their own rational self-interest in order to sustain their lives, they require a society that protects their ability to do so. Rand opposed the initiation of physical force, because it interferes with an individual's capacity to act on his or her own rational judgment. Individual rights—the rights to life, liberty, property, and the pursuit of happiness—ensure individual freedom in a social context. Rand (1964, 94) maintained: "The right to life is the source of all rights—and the right to property is their only implementation. Without property rights, no other rights are possible. Since man has to sustain his life by his own effort, the man who has no right to the product of his effort has no means to sustain his life. The man who produces while others dispose of his product, is a slave."[13]

The principle of individual rights entails a defense against any state intrusions on freedom of contract *or* conscience, full respect for economic *and* civil liberties, and, moreover, a commitment to a woman's right to choose an abortion. So important was Rand's pro-choice stance that, like many feminists, she opposed the election of Ronald Reagan due to his antiabortion politics; "anyone who takes that attitude has no right to claim that he is a defender of human rights," she asserted (in Schwartz 1980, 2).

Unlike many feminists on the left, however, Rand (1967) viewed capitalism as the only *"social system based on the recognition of individual rights"* (19). She referred to capitalism as "an unknown ideal" because she believed that it had never existed in pure form and that it had always been undercut by various degrees of government intervention. In Rand's view, such intervention was the fundamental cause of socioeconomic injustice and instability, including militarism, monopolies, business cycles, inflation, unemployment, racism, social fragmentation, and the emergence of "tribal" groupism. Under such a system, only the state can dispense privileges that benefit some groups at the expense of others. Rand held that a pure capitalism, with a voluntarily financed government, could end such injustice. She embraced an enriched conception of a free society, far beyond the typical neoliberal emphasis on the strictly political. She wrote: *"Intellectual* freedom cannot exist without *political* freedom; political freedom cannot exist without *economic* freedom; *a free mind and a free market are corollaries"* (Rand 1961, 25).

According to Rand, the emergence of capitalism was the logical culmination of a secular Aristotelian worldview. She emphasized that whereas the Industrial Revolution irrefutably demonstrated the practical efficacy of reason, the emergent capitalist system was hampered from its earliest moments not only by a predatory state but also by an altruist culture that implicitly condoned human sacrifice. The fundamental "inner contradiction" of modern capitalism, Rand (1964, 95) maintained, has been the attempt to synthesize the pursuit of individual happiness with an altruist moral code. Capitalism cannot survive on such a cultural base, she argued; it requires a fully rational, secular ethos untainted by religious mysticism or altruism.

Rand refused to accept the status quo as unalterable. All human institutions, in her view, must be critically assessed and "then accepted or rejected and changed when necessary" (Rand 1982, 33). She envisioned a radically new politics that transcended the limitations of Left and Right. Ultimately, she considered Objectivism to be the necessary precondition of a full philosophical and cultural renaissance.

The Hermeneutics of Rand Scholarship

While many of Rand's followers reject the very notion that Objectivism includes anything beyond the published, carefully edited words of its creator, Rand's system of thought undergoes a continuing metamorphosis. W. W. Bartley (1985, 27) suggests that, in the evolution of an idea,

> [w]hen we produce and affirm a theory, we also propose its logical implications. . . . That is, we affirm all those statements that follow from it—as well as further implications which result from combining this theory with other theories which we also propose or assume. But this means that the informative content of any idea includes an *infinity* of *unforeseeable* nontrivial statements. Thus the content of an idea is far from identical with some particular person's thoughts about it. For there are infinitely many situations, themselves infinitely varied, to which the theory may be applicable. Yet many of these situations have not only not even been imagined at the time the theory is proposed; they are also, literally, unimaginable then, in terms of the information then available.

Bartley's insights suggest that this hermeneutic is unavoidable. Indeed, Bartley's argument is a reminder to the editors of this very collection that our own work on Rand can be employed by other authors in ways that are unforeseeable to either of us.

Herein, the feminist interpretations brought to bear on the Randian canon illustrate our conviction that Rand's philosophy—much like feminism itself—is not monolithic. The very dynamics of rereading the Randian canon make for provocative applications and modifications in the collision of ideas. In this volume, feminism is both the context of—and the basis for—that collision. What results, however, is as provocative in its implications for Rand's system as it is for feminism.

This whole enterprise, as challenging in its conception as in its execution, has been both educational and joyous. The multitudinous responses from feminist scholars in a variety of disciplines and their impressive credentials made our job the gratifying one of dealing with a surplus of assets. Our contributors include academics from such disciplines as philosophy, art, English, linguistics, anthropology, political science, and psychology, as well as nonacademic professionals, including writers, scholars, and commentators of international repute.[14] Their works have provided us many hours of intellectual stimulation and challenge. While we could not agree with all the conclusions of our authors, we were anxious to provide a forum for a continuing discussion. We trust our readers will share our enthusiasm for the enterprise.

Though our emphasis is on canonical rereading, we have made every effort to represent Rand's perspective fairly by addressing our call for submissions to many of those associated with Randian study. Two of Rand's early close associates submitted pieces for this volume. Barbara Branden, author of the only authorized biographical essay published in Rand's lifetime and of the full-length independent biography *The Passion of Ayn Rand* (1986), contributes "Ayn Rand: The Reluctant Feminist."[15] This article is not simply a condensed version of her previous works. Rather, it contextualizes Rand's life as a paean to feminism, complete with both triumph and tragedy. Nathaniel Branden, father of the modern self-esteem movement and author of *Judgment Day: My Years with Ayn Rand* (1989), attempts to answer the question "Was Ayn Rand a feminist?" To some extent, however, every article in this volume attempts to answer the same question.

The participation of Barbara Branden and Nathaniel Branden in this collection may have been made easier by Rand's public split from them in a notoriously bitter schism of 1968. The details of that split are explored briefly in Barbara Branden's essay. By contrast, several individuals who remain within the Randian circle and who can be characterized as "orthodox" Objectivists were not willing to contribute to any volume whose premise is feminism. Leonard Peikoff, Rand's designated heir, declined to participate, as did Michael S. Berliner, the executive director of the Ayn Rand Institute. For these individuals, "feminism" as such is an invalid concept. It is a derivative of what the Austrian economist Ludwig von Mises (1963) once called "polylogism," that is, the view that the mind's logical structure varies among the members of different social groups, defined by class, race, sex, gender, or any other conceivable orientation (75).[16] For Mises, Marxists and racists are typical polylogists because they view all members of a specific social class or race as endowed with logical and cognitive structures peculiar to that class or race. Each group is said to think in a manner distinctive to, derived from, and dictated by that group's inherent "logic." While Mises opposed the idea of disparate logics within the human species, he suggested that polylogism, as an intellectual doctrine, was a typical by-product of the fragmenting power of the state, insofar as it created a clash of group interests vying for special privileges at one another's expense. These interests, in seeking to establish dominance, often employ spurious notions of collectivist ideol-

ogy to rationalize their achievement of political power. For various Objectivists who take Mises's lead, "feminism" is but one more manifestation
of the polylogist mentality.[17]

The view that "feminism" as such is an invalid concept is represented
in this volume by the Objectivist philosopher David Kelley, founder of
the Institute for Objectivist Studies. In Part Three, Joan Kennedy Taylor's
interview with Kelley provides one Objectivist reading of the Randian
perspective on the epistemic validity of "feminism."[18] But Taylor rejects
the view that feminism is an invalid concept. She argues that Rand's own
premises can help feminists to develop a tenable definition of "feminism."

Feminist Interpretations of Ayn Rand

Our volume is divided into three parts. Part One, which we have called,
"Looking Back," opens with Barbara Branden's biographical sketch of
Ayn Rand. Since many readers may be unfamiliar with Rand's life and
work, Branden's essay provides a useful introduction. Viewing Rand as
the "reluctant feminist," Branden suggests that the contradictions in
Rand's life are rooted in her very definition of femininity as "hero worship." However, Branden argues that this "contradiction to feminism"
should not tarnish our appreciation of Rand's legacy for women.

Following Branden's contribution is Mimi Reisel Gladstein's original
and path-breaking article "Ayn Rand and Feminism: An Unlikely Alliance," first published in 1978 in the journal *College English*. This piece
and its companion piece, a reply from Judith Wilt, have for over two
decades remained among the only published studies in mainstream academic journals of Rand's relevance to feminism. We are happy to bring
them to a wider audience. Gladstein and Wilt, who have both chaired
English departments at major universities, argue, with qualifications, that
much in Rand is applicable to feminism, and both would include *Atlas
Shrugged* on their reading lists for women's studies courses.

The first part continues with an excerpt from Susan Brownmiller's
Against Our Will: Men, Women, and Rape. Brownmiller (1975) turns to
the notorious "rape" scene in *The Fountainhead*. For Brownmiller, the
"philosophy of rape" on display in the confrontation of Howard Roark
and Dominique Francon qualifies Ayn Rand as a "traitor to her own sex."

As will become apparent, this characterization of Rand has inspired many of our authors in their rereading of the Randian canon on sex and gender. Brownmiller's oft-cited remarks are followed by reprinted selections from two important but disparate feminist voices: Barbara Grizzuti Harrison and Camille Paglia. Harrison's article, "Psyching Out Ayn Rand," originally appeared in the September 1978 issue of *Ms.* magazine. Harrison opposes Rand as "the high priestess of the acute Right," and articulates the concerns of many feminists who are not enamored by the masochistic fantasies portrayed in Rand's works of fiction. And yet, noting the philosopher-novelist's influence, particularly on what she calls "her man who once worked in the White House," Harrison concludes, "I am afraid of Ayn Rand."[19]

This fear is not on display in "Reflections on Ayn Rand," an excerpt from *Reason* magazine's interview with Camille Paglia, "Interview with the Vamp." Claudia Roth Pierpont (1995, 81) has remarked that "Camille Paglia's brightly belligerent spirit and her Victoria's Secret Nietzscheanism" are derivative of *Atlas Shrugged*'s Dagny Taggart. Indeed, Paglia recognizes herself as a kind of spiritual progeny of Ayn Rand. Though she differs with Rand on many important issues, Paglia argues that Rand should be included in the feminist canon.

In Part Two of this volume, "Feminist Rereadings of Rand's Fiction," we turn to a chronological consideration of the works of Rand the artist, the novelist, the dramatist. The first two articles in this part are linked thematically in their consideration of the notion that Rand manifests an inherent bias toward Instrumentalist rationalism, at odds with the "organic," "Synthesist," or "dialectical" view that is central to many feminist approaches. Susan Brownmiller has claimed, for instance, that Rand's reason-centered philosophy is "spiritually male." This suggestion has found more detailed articulation in Lynda Glennon's work *Women and Dualism:*

> Instrumentalism . . . is the ideal type feminists are least likely to identify with . . . Instrumentalism is the embodiment of the extremes of modern consciousness: rationalistic, self-interested, emotionally managed. It stresses the work orientation of human activity. The individual is most human when doing productive work—efficient, rational, assertive, and ambitious. . . . Instrumentalism includes the rational, progressive ethos of technocratic society; the exchange ethos of capitalism; the

individualistic, objectivistic ethos of Ayn Rand; the modernistic outlook of the middle class; and the assertive self-interestedness of the archetypical male. (Glennon 1979, 46–47)

For Glennon, such Instrumentalism is "one response to the fragmentation of the self." It aims to resolve the modernist dualistic dilemmas that it confronts—mind versus body, fact versus value, reason versus emotion—by adopting a kind of monism, by "deemphasizing, if not eliminating, the expressive, emotional side of human beings and society." Instrumentalism promotes a one-sided, partial view of human beings as "rational, productive, . . . objective, self-assertive, self-oriented, [and] aggressive," while downplaying the emotional, the intuitive, the aesthetic, the creative (48).[20]

Glennon recognizes the Instrumentalist model as an ideal type, a definition by essentials, and that no thinker embodies these characteristics in "pure" form. But for Glennon, Rand's expression of "functional rationality" to the detriment of emotion qualifies her as a predominantly Instrumentalist thinker.

Glennon is correct that feminists would least likely identify with the Instrumentalist model. While a case can be made for Rand's affinity with this model, several authors have rejected this contention. Chris Matthew Sciabarra, in his *Ayn Rand: The Russian Radical* (1995), has argued that Rand was a superior dialectician who rejected modernist dualities as the embodiment of false alternatives. He hypothesizes that Rand inherited this dialectical approach—with its emphasis on contextuality as applied to the systemic and dynamic relations within an organic unity—from her Silver Age Russian roots.

In direct engagement with Glennon's work, the French scholar Valérie Loiret-Prunet extends Sciabarra's thesis in her analysis of *We the Living*. Using the linguistic theories of Emile Beveniste and Dany-Robert Dufour, Loiret-Prunet argues that Kira Argounova, the protagonist of *We the Living*, exhibits the essential ternary patterns of feminist Synthesism. Kira *is* "synthesis and seamless unity," in contrast to her two male counterparts, Leo Kovalensky and Andrei Taganov, fragmented selves in a fractured social universe. In Loiret-Prunet's view, Rand's approach is a direct challenge to radical feminists on the left because it aims for a nondualistic integration that is libertarian in its political implications. Loiret-Prunet suggests that Rand's work may constitute an unexpected resource for fem-

inist scholarship on the social preconditions and destructive consequences of dualism.

The dialectical and organicist aspects of Rand's project are also addressed by Barry Vacker, whose analysis of *The Fountainhead* reveals a
Third Wave feminist "aesthos." Through a comparative study of Naomi
Wolf and Ayn Rand, Vacker argues that Rand's expressions of masculinist
linearity often overshadow a set of underlying assumptions that acts "like
a dialectical critique of the prevailing aesthetic forms which are central
to the power of the existing social and moral order." In Roark's buildings
especially, Vacker sees a relational organicity expressed in "strange attractors" symbolizing "the formal realization of individuality." For
Vacker, feminists should appreciate Rand's cultural aesthetics, which are
in harmony with the kaleidic aesthos of an emerging postindustrial
epoch.

The next authors then turn to the important issues raised by Brownmiller in her examination of the "rape" in *The Fountainhead*. Ulrike
Heider, echoing Brownmiller's concerns in her book *Anarchism: Left,
Right, and Green* (1994), has suggested that the "love story between su-
perpeople Howard Roark and Dominique Francon reveals Rand's . . .
ultimately reactionary concept of women. The beautiful blond heroine is
intelligent, independent, professionally successful, and—fitting a misogynist stereotype—frigid and unsensual. . . . Rand, the strong woman, shares
the patriarchal view of sexuality's violent nature and of women enjoying
subjugation and rape" (106–7).

Wendy McElroy, author of *XXX: A Woman's Right to Pornography*
(1995) and *Sexual Correctness: The Gender-Feminist Attack on Women*
(1996), admits some discomfort with Rand's sexual depictions, but she
rejects such characterizations entirely. For McElroy, a rereading of Rand's
scenes as "rough sex" reveals an element of consent. In her view, Rand
provides an alternative to those who embrace either traditionalist or
"rape culture" paradigms of sexuality. Her women are strong, independent, and sexually self-defining.

Judith Wilt, noting the "persistent subcurricular hum" of Rand's romances of female agency and self-making, finds need for a stricter reading
of their appeal. This she provides, in the context of the ongoing debate
in feminist and cultural theory about the formulas for classic and popular
romances. Hers is an exploration of the paradoxes and liminality of
Rand's works, both in the worlds of romance and philosophy. Tracing
Rand's romantic triangles, sexual violence, and homosocial desire

through the glamour and clamor of what she views as Rand's "voluptuous call for the cleansing apocalypse," Wilt sees Rand's works as "hew[ing] closely to the Fraserian synthesis of Western myth."

Premyth, the realm of the mother goddess, the archetypal feminine, is the engendering realm for Karen Michalson's analysis of Dagny Taggart's role in contemporary fiction. Michalson answers her title question, "Who is Dagny Taggart?," by tracing Dagny's story as that of a female epic hero, a paradigm unrecognized because, in these times, the goddess walks unrecognized as Athena-like; she "hides herself in armor."

Part Three, "Toward a Randian Feminism?" is posed in the form of a question precisely because it elicits a variety of answers. The authors in this part consider the interplay of Objectivism and feminism, through explorations of Rand's epistemology, philosophical psychology, ethics, politics, aesthetics, and attitudes toward sex and gender.

Nathaniel Branden brings to the examination of Rand and feminism the unique perspective of the evolving stages of his close relationship with her. While he notes certain ambiguities in Rand's positions, Branden cautions against too literal a reading. He reminds readers of the role of fantasy in creativity, and he explains that in the poetry of Rand's ideal romances, what her heroines worship is not any man or men in general, but "man at his highest, man the abstraction—the masculine principle." Branden suggests that there is no inequality in the relationships in Rand's fiction, for her "heroes treat the women they love with unreserved respect, admiration, adoration, and 'worship.'"

Joan Kennedy Taylor, author of *Reclaiming the Mainstream: Individualist Feminism Rediscovered* (1992), confronts the epistemological issues raised by the Randian canon as they pertain to the very concept of "feminism." Taylor examines, too, how many of Rand's followers have tended to "package-deal" the ideological movements that they oppose. Peikoff defines "package-dealing" as "the fallacy of failing to discriminate crucial differences. It consists of treating together, as parts of a single conceptual whole or 'package,' elements which differ essentially in nature, truth-status, importance or value" (in Rand 1982, 30n).

Taylor's interview with Objectivist philosopher David Kelley suggests that Rand herself did not fully appreciate those aspects of the women's movement that are consistent with individualism. For Rand, the modern women's movement, like modern welfare liberalism, had undermined the individualism of its classical liberal predecessor. In her essay "The Age of

Envy," Rand (1975a, 173) writes: "Just as the egalitarians ride on the historical prestige of those who fought for political equality, and struggle to achieve the opposite—so their special sorority, Women's Lib, rides on the historical prestige of women who fought for individual rights against government power, and struggles to get special privileges by means of government power."

But whereas Rand sought to disown the women's movement in its entirety, Taylor seeks to reaffirm individualism in the feminist battle for political and social change. In reclaiming feminism in the name of individualism, Taylor suggests, too, that liberalism itself may be in need of reclamation, against those who have corrupted *its* meaning.

The whole issue of individualism versus collectivism, with its polylogistic implications, undergirds the current dialectic in a number of "rights" movements. There is conflict in the ranks of African-American scholars about the detrimental consequences of victim mentality and the internalization of collective stereotypes. Important national leaders question the wisdom of a collective political stance, of the ghettoization to groupthink. Conflicts within the ranks are inherent in revolutions. And it is a historical commonplace that those whose ideas create the philosophical revolution that necessarily precedes the political and cultural ones, are not those in power after the revolution. This situation may provide us with one way of understanding the lack of attention shown Rand by feminists. A major obstacle to the development of feminist scholarship on Rand has been political. It is not just that Rand has been summarily dismissed as simply conservative or reactionary. It is that she has been condemned as quasi-fascistic and elitist too. Ulrike Heider (1994) has stressed that Rand, the "radical rationalist" and "Queen of Reason," was actually "influenced by Nietzsche's ontology of power and his disdain for weakness and compassion. In Rand's theoretical and literary writings, social Darwinism, the Nietzschean superman, and laissez-faire take on a quasi-fascistic taint" (104).[21]

Estelle C. Jelinek (1978), too, has expressed fundamental concern with Rand's perceived elitism. Jelinek argued that Rand projects a "personal vision of the creative artist as a superior human being and, concomitantly the inferiority of the masses in *The Fountainhead*." This individualism is "carried to the fascistic extremes that Ayn Rand articulated in her later books and in her philosophy of [O]bjectivism." Jelinek asked: "How can feminists and radicals of all types accept uncritically

this elitism and miss the incompatibility with the rest of their lives?"
(317).

Sharon Presley's essay goes to the heart of these issues. Presley, a feminist psychologist, examines Rand's philosophy of individualism by surveying the literature on egoism and altruism and by contrasting Carol Gilligan's "ethics of care" with Rand's ethics of "rational selfishness." Presley concludes that Rand can contribute to a humane feminist ethic that preserves the moral autonomy and integrity of the self.

Susan Love Brown delves into what she perceives as contradictions in Rand's philosophical positions and the mixed messages of her rhetoric. For Brown, Rand's work exhibits certain cognitive dissonances. Brown hypothesizes their root in a "cultural model of gender that dichotomizes human characteristics in such a way as to cause people to choose between their sexual identity and their human identity." In "Ayn Rand: The Woman Who Would *Not* Be President," Brown offers an explanation for one of Rand's most controversial positions, a strategy that allowed Rand to integrate a powerful intellect with her femininity. Robert Sheaffer contributes his assessment of an illogical mathematics that he sees at the base of Rand's position on the same issue. Sheaffer takes a Paglian position on the necessity for feminists to confront the darker aspects of sexuality. For Sheaffer, the ghosts of Friedrich Nietzsche and the Marquis de Sade are hovering over the Randian corpus. And though he believes Rand's reading of the appeal of "dominance" is convincing, he finds contradictions in her later positions that equate sexual attraction and reason. Sheaffer argues that Rand's stress upon the constant quest for the "hardest to conquer" creates too many romantic limitations for men and women.

More Brandian than Randian, Diana Mertz Brickell employs the analyses of the cultural ideals of femininity and masculinity in Susan Brownmiller's *Femininity* and Warren Farrell's *Myth of Male Power*. Brickell enunciates a position consonant with the egoistic standard of value found in Rand's ethics. She concludes that despite some antifeminist tendencies, Objectivism is a philosophy "capable of liberating men and women from the harmful and destructive gender roles which have existed throughout most of human history." Her essay, "Sex and Gender Through an Egoist Lens: Masculinity and Femininity in the Philosophy of Ayn Rand," sets forth a paradigm for authenticity in the expression of our sexual selves, in our reading of gender.

Our volume concludes with essays from Norway and Australia, a further telling illustration of the worldwide impact of Rand's ideas. From the far north comes "The Female Hero: A Randian-Feminist Synthesis," Thomas Gramstad's visionary conception of a postandrogynous ideal. Gramstad uses Rand's own premises to dispute her "Platonic" view of gender. Looking beyond androgyny, and in concert with such feminist anthropologists as Riane Eisler, Gramstad reclaims an ancient archetype of female power: the Amazon. He argues for a mutuality, equality, and symmetry that translates into freedom and gender individualism.

From postandrogyny to poststructuralism, our volume concludes with Melissa Jane Hardie's singular and witty strategy for a feminist reading of Rand through the perspective of camp aesthetics. As she deconstructs the "camp appeal and paradoxical readability" of Rand's works, Hardie focuses mainly on the cinematic version of The Fountainhead and on Mary Gaitskill's 1991 fictional vamp on Rand and her followers. Her essay, "Fluff and Granite: Rereading Ayn Rand's Camp Feminist Aesthetics," takes its multiconnotative title both from Anna Granite, the Rand figure in Gaitskill's Two Girls, Fat and Thin, and "Fluff," Frank O'Connor's improbable nickname for his wife, Ayn Rand. Hardie provides many surprising interpretive turns in her rearticulation of the debate over Rand's relevance to feminism. She uses the works of such authors as Deleuze, Eco, Mouffe, Sontag, and Sedgwick in exploring such issues as the sadomasochistic and the homosocial in Rand's representations of sexuality.

Jenny A. Heyl (1995), in her discussion of Ayn Rand in Contemporary Women Philosophers, observed: "Perhaps because she so eschewed academic philosophy, and because her works are widely considered to be works of literature, Objectivist philosophy is regularly omitted from academic philosophy. Yet, throughout literary academia, Ayn Rand is considered a philosopher. Her works merit consideration as works of philosophy in their own right" (223).[22]

As co-editors of this volume, we hope to have contributed to a critical rereading of Rand's works "as works of philosophy in their own right." That this discussion of an influential woman thinker of the Western canon takes place in the context of feminism is both appropriate and long overdue.

Notes

1. This introduction to the philosophy of Objectivism is adapted from Sciabarra 1996, especially 528–33. See our Acknowledgments for permissions information.

2. By "metaphysics," Rand meant ontology, not a cosmological investigation of the ultimate constituents of reality.

3. "Constructivism" is another term that might be used to describe contemporary approaches within feminist epistemology. This usage is not to be confused with Hayek's definition of "constructivism" as a form of rationalism.

4. Kelley (1986) develops a realist theory of perception heavily informed by Rand's approach.

5. Rand uses the word "intrinsicism" to describe the tradition of classical objectivism (lowercase o), which viewed concepts as corresponding to inherent properties of the object. Her own use of the concept "objective" in a relational sense precludes the more common usage of the "objective" (which, in Rand's parlance, is the "intrinsic") in contrast to the "subjective." Thus, Rand's "Objectivism" (uppercase O) constitutes her resolution of the "false alternatives" of intrinsicism and subjectivism.

6. On Rand's aesthetics, see Torres and Kamhi 1999.

7. All italics appear in the original unless otherwise indicated.

8. The close affinity between Rand and the Aristotelian-eudaimonistic tradition is noted by Den Uyl and Rasmussen (1984), in their essay "Life, Teleology, and Eudaimonia in the Ethics of Ayn Rand."

9. For a comparative analysis of the quasi-Aristotelian praxis orientation in the Randian and Marxian conceptions of productive work, see Sciabarra 1995, 246–48.

10. Sciabarra (1995, 230–36) argues that in the development of her ethics, Rand draws from a constellation of Aristotelian and Nietzschean ideas on the "great-souled man." Shelton (1995) suggests ties between Rand and Epicurus.

11. The similarities here, to Hegel's master-slave duality, are examined by Sciabarra (1995, 300–311).

12. The psychological aspects of Rand's theory are explored in Branden 1969, composed mainly of his writings while he was associated with Rand. Though still heavily influenced by Rand's Objectivism, Branden (1994) departs from some of his earlier formulations.

13. Den Uyl and Rasmussen (1984, 181 n. 25) suggest that this proposed relationship between the individual and his or her property bears some resemblance to Hegel's conception. Sciabarra (1995) expands this notion considerably in his exploration of Rand's dialectical sensibility and its possible roots in the Silver Age culture of her Russian youth.

14. A note about our contributors and their strategies for rereading: We have left it to our authors to decide which editions they would use in their articles. Some chose original editions of Rand's works, while others chose anniversary or recent editions, some of which contain selections from Rand's philosophical journals. We have also left it to our authors to decide on such nominal issues as whether to call the young Ayn Rand Alice, Alisa, Alyssa, or Alissa Rosenbaum, whether to call Rand's father Fronz or Zinovy Rosenbaum. Finally, our authors have alternately chosen to characterize left-of-center feminists, in or out of the "mainstream," as "collectivist," "equality," "leftist," "radical," "socialist," and so forth.

15. See also Barbara Branden's "Who Is Ayn Rand?" in Branden and Branden 1962.

16. Peikoff (1982, 60–62) discusses the influence of "polylogism" in Nazism.

17. Of course, there is immense variety within feminism and Marxism. Unlike some Objectivists, Mises himself realized that feminism did not consist of one uniform position and/or method. Indeed, while Mises opposed the "socialist" and "radical wing of Feminism," he supported the individualists within feminism. Mises (1951, 101) writes:

"So far as Feminism seeks to adjust the legal position of woman to that of man, so far as it seeks to offer her legal and economic freedom to develop and act in accordance with her inclinations, desires, and economic circumstances—so far it is nothing more than a branch of the great liberal movement, which advocates peaceful and free evolution." Mises's wife adds that "Lu was a great defender of women. . . . I would not be astonished if one day 'Women's Lib' would discover Lu—once

19

the activists have overcome their anxiety problems concerning equality of sex and consider politics and economics their most important tasks. If they do, they may well declare my husband one of their heroes" (Mises 1984, 140). For further discussion on Mises and feminism, see McElroy 1997.

18. Kelley seems to have qualified his thinking on this issue. At the "Atlas and the World" conference on 4 October 1997, celebrating the fortieth anniversary of the publication of *Atlas Shrugged*, Kelley, in response to a comment from the floor, called Rand the first feminist, or, at least, the first in her generation.

19. Harrison's fears seem to have been unfounded. Alan Greenspan, then an economic adviser to President Ford, later became chairman of the Federal Reserve Board, and has served under both Republican and Democratic administrations. It is questionable just how consistently Greenspan has applied Rand's principles. On this issue, see Bradford 1997.

20. Glennon contrasts the Instrumentalist ideal type with three others: the monistic "Expressionist" type, with its one-sided emphasis on feelings; the pure dualistic type, "Polarist"; and the dialectical alternative to monism and dualism, "Synthesist." See Loiret-Prunet in this volume for a lengthier discussion of Glennon's taxonomy.

21. On the connection between Rand and Nietzsche, see especially Rand 1997. Peikoff, in his foreword, confirms that in Rand's earliest notes one can detect the "influence of Nietzsche, in the form of droplets of subjectivism, and of the idea that the heroes among men are innately great, as against the inherently corrupted masses, who deserve only bitterness and domination from their superiors" (ix). Peikoff argues that these "droplets . . . evaporate[d] without residue" as Rand grew to intellectual maturity. Still, some view Nietzsche's impact as decisive to Rand's evolution. For example, Merrill (1991, 21–40) suggests that Rand went through a bona fide Nietzschean "phase" reflected in the first edition of *We the Living*, while Sciabarra (1995, 31–40, 100–112) argues that the influence of Nietzsche can be found even in *The Fountainhead*. Sciabarra views these Nietzschean vestiges as an outgrowth of Rand's Russian years, including her acquaintance with the Russian Symbolists, who were also heavily influenced by Nietzsche.

22. In this passage, Heyl is referring, of course, to the fact that many literary scholars view Rand as a philosophical thinker but that philosophy professors often dismiss her as a novelist. Interestingly, Rand saw herself as *both* a novelist *and* a philosopher, with no implicit dichotomy between these functions. See Rand 1961, vii.

References

Bartley, W. W., III. 1985. Knowledge is a product not fully known to its producer. In *The Political Economy of Freedom: Essays in Honor of F. A. Hayek*, edited by Kurt R. Leube and Albert H. Zlabinger. Munich: Philosophia Verlag.

Bradford, R. W. 1997. Greenspan: Deep-cover radical for capitalism? *Liberty* 11, no. 2:37–42.

Branden, Barbara. 1986. *The Passion of Ayn Rand*. Garden City, N.Y.: Doubleday.

Branden, Nathaniel. 1969. *The Psychology of Self-Esteem: A New Concept of Man's Psychological Nature*. Los Angeles: Nash Publishing.

———. 1989. *Judgment Day: My Years with Ayn Rand*. Boston: Houghton Mifflin.

———. 1994. *The Six Pillars of Self-Esteem*. New York: Bantam.

Branden, Nathaniel, and Barbara Branden. 1962. *Who Is Ayn Rand? An Analysis of the Novels of Ayn Rand*. New York: Random House.

Brownmiller, Susan. 1975. *Against Our Will: Men, Women, and Rape*. New York: Simon & Schuster.

Den Uyl, Douglas J., and Douglas B. Rasmussen, eds. 1984. *The Philosophic Thought of Ayn Rand*. Urbana: University of Illinois Press.
Glennon, Lynda M. 1979. *Women and Dualism: A Sociology of Knowledge Analysis*. New York: Longman.
Heider, Ulrike. 1994. *Anarchism: Left, Right, and Green*. Translated by Danny Lewis and Ulrike Bode. San Francisco: City Lights Books.
Heyl, Jenny A. 1995. Ayn Rand (1905–1982). In *Contemporary Women Philosophers*, vol. 4, edited by Mary Ellen Waithe. Boston: Kluwer Academic Publishers.
Jelinek, Estelle C. 1978. Anaïs Nin: A critical evaluation. In *Feminist Criticism: Essays on Theory, Poetry, and Prose*, edited by Cheryl L. Brown and Karen Olson. Metuchen, N.J.: Scarecrow Press.
Kelley, David. 1986. *The Evidence of the Senses: A Realist Theory of Perception*. Baton Rouge: Louisiana State University Press.
McElroy, Wendy. 1995. *XXX: A Woman's Right to Pornography*. New York: St. Martin's Press.
———. 1996. *Sexual Correctness: The Gender-Feminist Attack on Women*. Jefferson, N.C.: McFarland.
———. 1997. Mises's legacy for feminists. *Freeman* 47, no. 9:558–63.
Merrill, Ronald E. 1991. *The Ideas of Ayn Rand*. LaSalle, Ill.: Open Court.
Mises, Ludwig von. 1951. *Socialism: An Economic and Sociological Analysis*. Translated by J. Kahane. London: Jonathan Cape.
———. 1963. *Human Action: A Treatise on Economics*. 3d rev. ed. Chicago: Henry Regnery.
Mises, Margarit von. 1984. *My Years with Ludwig von Mises*. 2d enl. ed. Cedar Falls, Iowa: Center for Futures Education.
Peikoff, Leonard. 1982. *The Ominous Parallels: The End of Freedom in America*. New York: Stein & Day.
———. 1991. *Objectivism: The Philosophy of Ayn Rand*. New York: Dutton.
Pierpont, Claudia Roth. 1995. A critic at large: Twilight of the goddess. *New Yorker*, 24 July, 70–81.
Rand, Ayn. [1943] 1993. *The Fountainhead*. 50th anniversary ed. New York: Dutton.
———. [1957] 1992. *Atlas Shrugged*. New York: New American Library.
———. 1961. *For the New Intellectual: The Philosophy of Ayn Rand*. New York: New American Library.
———. 1964. *The Virtue of Selfishness: A New Concept of Egoism*. New York: New American Library.
———. 1967. *Capitalism: The Unknown Ideal*. New York: New American Library.
———. 1975a. *The New Left: The Anti-Industrial Revolution*. 2d rev. ed. New York: New American Library.
———. 1975b. *The Romantic Manifesto: A Philosophy of Literature*. 2d rev. ed. New York: New American Library.
———. 1982. *Philosophy: Who Needs It*. New York: Bobbs-Merrill.
———. 1990. *Introduction to Objectivist Epistemology*. 2d enl. ed. Edited by Harry Binswanger and Leonard Peikoff. New York: New American Library.
———. 1997. *Journals of Ayn Rand*. Edited by David Harriman. New York: Penguin Dutton.
Schwartz, Jerry. 1980. Interview with Ayn Rand. *Objectivist Forum* 1, no. 3:1–6.
Sciabarra, Chris Matthew. 1995. *Ayn Rand: The Russian Radical*. University Park: Pennsylvania State University Press.
———. 1996. Ayn Rand. In *American Writers: A Collection of Literary Biographies, Supple-*

ment IV, Part 2: Susan Howe to Gore Vidal, edited by A. Walton Litz and Molly Wiegel. New York: Charles Scribner's Sons.

Shelton, Ray. 1995. Epicurus and Rand. *Objectivity* 2, no. 3:1–47.

Taylor, Joan Kennedy. 1992. *Reclaiming the Mainstream: Individualist Feminism Rediscovered.* Buffalo, N.Y.: Prometheus Books.

Torres, Louis, and Michelle Marder Kamhi. 1999. *What Art Is: The Esthetic Theory of Ayn Rand.* LaSalle, Ill.: Open Court.

Part One

Looking Back

1

Ayn Rand:
The Reluctant Feminist

Barbara Branden

Ayn Rand's life and work, in most aspects, was a feminist manifesto.

In 1963, she read and admired Betty Friedan's *Feminist Mystique*. But as the '60s progressed, she failed to recognize that every new movement has its lunatic fringe—certainly her own Objectivist movement did—and she quickly became disgusted with women's shrilly raucous demonstrations, their hatred of men, the "bra-burning" and its accouterments that had become the most evident and highly publicized manifestation of the new feminism. As the most vocal feminists began demanding that government, through an endless series of laws—through quotas, laws forbidding pornography, laws granting special status to women—enforce their causes throughout the land, Ayn Rand turned ever more violently against feminism. She seemed unaware of the growing pro-individualist concept of feminism—of which her own books were a significant source.

From her own individualist, free-enterprise viewpoint, she said that "Woman's Lib," as she insisted on calling it, was irrational and depraved. She once told me, "Nobody ever helped me, and I never asked for help— and *certainly* not from the government." She was convinced that being a woman had never been a factor in her own long and painful struggle. This viewpoint—that women had fought their lonely battles to the top of their professions on their own, unaffected by being women, and that any woman need only be sufficiently determined in order to rise to the limit of her capacities—is a concept I have heard very often from highly accomplished women in middle age. Like Ayn Rand, they seem unable to believe that the fact of being women had any negative relevance to their careers.

Ayn Rand was in fact greatly hindered by being a woman. In the '30s, '40s, and '50s, when she wrote *We the Living, The Fountainhead,* and *Atlas Shrugged,* she was writing not just as a novelist but as a philosopher: through these books and through her later nonfiction work, she was presenting a philosophical system that was substantially new and that challenged every culturally prevalent school of thought.

It is relevant to the issue of feminism that the reviews of her books, with a few rare exceptions, were startlingly savage and accusatory, and ignored what she had actually written. Discussing the political philosophy presented in *Atlas Shrugged,* Patricia Donegan (1957, 155) wrote in the *Commonweal,* "Miss Rand is all for the survival of the fittest, dog-eat-dog. . . . The destruction of the weak to the advantage of the strong is applauded." "Ayn Rand's philosophy is nearly perfect in its immorality," said Gore Vidal (1961).

The worst of all the reviews of *Atlas Shrugged* appeared in William F. Buckley's conservative *National Review.* The review was written about a woman who had unswervingly and vehemently opposed the initiation of physical force, who viewed "force and mind [as] opposites," who crusaded for the absolutism of reason and its corollary, the rejection of faith. Buckley had assigned the review to Whittaker Chambers, a former Communist spy who had reembraced religion. In an article entitled "Big Sister Is Watching You," Chambers (1957, 595–96) wrote: "*Atlas Shrugged* . . . is a forthright philosophical materialism. . . . It is when a system of materialist ideas presumes to give positive answers to real problems of our real life that mischief starts . . . a temptation sets in to let some species of Big Brother solve and supervise them. . . . Miss Rand . . . calls in a Big Brother of her own . . . she plumps for a technocratic elite. . . . And this can only lead to a dictatorship. . . . From almost any page of *Atlas Shrugged*, a voice can be heard, from painful necessity, commanding: 'to a gas chamber—go!' "

It is interesting to note that the most vituperative and inaccurate reviews of *Atlas Shrugged* were written by men, although a few women joined them. And the most enthusiastic review of *The Fountainhead* was written by a woman, Lorine Pruette, in the Sunday *New York Times Book Review*. Pruette (1943) stated: "This is the only novel of ideas written by an American woman that I can recall. . . . You will not be able to read this masterful work without thinking through some of the basic concepts of our time."

Can one doubt that, had Ayn Rand been a man, she would at least have been taken seriously as a philosopher, however much her reviewers might have disagreed with her ideas? Can one doubt that the respectful, sober attention given to male writers on philosophy, however erroneous the reviewer might consider the content of that philosophy, would have been given to Ayn Rand had she been a man? It is as if most male reviewers said to themselves, "I dislike her ideas on reason, individualism, and free enterprise. Besides, whoever heard of a *woman* philosopher? Therefore, I am free to dismiss her ideas as 'execrable claptrap,' as 'crackbrained ratiocination' [Rolo 1957]. Who will defend a woman who presumes to tell men how and by what principles they should lead their lives? Philosophy is 'man's work.' "

One would have thought that many women reviewers would have rushed to defend her. They did not. Her politics blinded them to the heroic feminism of her female protagonists. Feminists on the left, many believing that every human ill can be cured only by government, have not recognized the feminist models Ayn Rand gave them and have attacked her angrily. They would do well to study her further. She gave to women, particularly in her portrait of Kira in *We the Living* and Dagny in *Atlas Shrugged*, a vision of the female potential more uplifting and more truly feminist than had ever before been presented in literature. Countless young women have said that Ayn Rand's work changed their lives and encouraged them to choose and excel in careers they had wanted but had not dared pursue. The heroines in her novels—and the courageous life of Ayn Rand—have profoundly influenced generations of women and continue to do so. They are role models of transcendent intellectual and emotional power.

Kira is a young woman who wants to build glass skyscrapers and aluminum bridges and—in that most male-dominated culture of Russia—never accepts the idea that being a woman requires her to choose, if not marriage and motherhood, then at least a "gentler" profession. She keeps her spine straight, her values intact, and her mind intensely active under the horrors of the new Soviet Russia. She defies the collectivist regime. She makes her own decisions, and she loves as passionately as she lives.

In the end, all alone, she attempts to escape over the Latvian border, walking for hours through a white, frozen world of snow, not knowing that her fragile body is also beginning to freeze. Then a shot rings out, fired by a Soviet soldier who thinks he has seen "something" moving in the snow, far away.

Kira lies very still in the snow, watching a red spot widening under her. After a long time, she rises slowly to her knees, then she stands and staggers on, reeling, stumbling, faltering, falling, and painfully rising again. "There, in that world across the border, a life was awaiting her to which she had been faithful her every living hour, her only banner that had never been lowered, that she had held high and straight, a life she could not betray, that she would not betray now by stopping while she was still living, a life she could still serve by walking, by walking forward a little longer, just a little longer" (Rand 1959, 445). At dawn, she falls again and knows she will not rise. "She smiled, her last smile, to so much that had been possible" (446).

Although Kira dies—her death one of the means by which Ayn Rand demonstrated that under collectivism the worst of human beings prospered and the best were inevitably destroyed—the nobility of her life and the exalted nature of her death gave to young women in America, and now all over the world, the sense of "so much that [was] possible."

Dagny is the apotheosis of the Ayn Rand female ideal. She is a beautiful woman of prodigious intellect who runs a major transcontinental railroad. She is free of inner conflict, serene in her basic relationship to existence, passionately ambitious and creative. She is the woman thought to be impossible in the conventional view of life—the woman engineer, dealing with the material world of metal rails and freight cars and diesel engines, who is, simultaneously, consummately feminine.

The theme of *Atlas Shrugged*, the greatest of Ayn Rand's works, is "the mind on strike." All across the country, the most brilliant creators—in industry, science, literature, philosophy, commerce, medicine, banking, and invention—are vanishing, for reasons no one understands; people see only that their collectivist society is economically disintegrating at a headlong rate.

When Dagny learns that the "men of the mind" are on strike against a society that tortures and expropriates the creative intellect, and that they have escaped to the mountains of Colorado to create a free society, she refuses to join them. It seems to her monstrously wrong to leave the world to the "looters," and unbearable to think of abandoning her beloved railroad. She will endure anything in order to work and produce. She continues her tortured, doomed struggle to save her railroad until, in the end, she understands that people of reason and persuasion *are* doomed in a world run by people of faith and force. She joins the strikers. She utters the vow that is their banner and their symbol, her voice confident and steady: "I swear—by my life and my love of it—that I will never live for the sake of another man, nor ask another man to live for mine" (Rand 1957, 731). She and the other strikers will return to the collapsing world when the code of the looters has collapsed.

Dagny is the symbol and reality of the producer—a role not given to a woman in fiction before *Atlas Shrugged*. And, like Kira, she is the symbol and reality of the woman of powerful emotion, who loves passionately. She loves both her work and, ultimately, John Galt, the hero of *Atlas Shrugged*. She will give up neither value without struggling to the limit of her strength, endurance, and intellect to serve and protect them. If one wished to show a young woman what an individualist feminism could mean, one need only point to the figure of Dagny.

Yet, despite her masterful portrayal of heroic women, despite the fact that she saw women as properly being independent, active, and productive, there is a contradiction to feminism that threads through Ayn Rand's life and through her work. To understand the nature and the source of this contradiction, one must look to the experiences of her life, especially to her experiences with men and with the world around her, and to the conclusions she drew from those experiences.

Ayn Rand was born in St. Petersburg in 1905, the eldest of three sisters in a Jewish middle-class family. Her name, until she chose a pen name years later in America, was Alice Rosenbaum. It was immediately apparent to the adults around her that, from her earliest years, she was a brilliant, endlessly questioning child. But she was a lonely child, unable to relate to other girls in her school classes, who often turned to her for help with their assignments but, intimidated by her intellect and her interest in little but reading and thinking, did not include her in their activities. Nor did her parents alleviate her essential aloneness; her mother wished her to be involved in "feminine" activities, to play with dolls, to be con-cerned with her appearance, to be gay and frivolous, to gossip with girl-friends—all of which was impossible to Ayn; her father, a severe, silent man, showed little interest in her, although she loved and respected him.

Intelligence, then and throughout her life, was the quality she most admired. She always expected, even demanded, that her own intellectual qualities be perceived and respected; she would react with pleasure and bewilderment if any other aspect of her character or personality were understood or loved.

Through her reading (particularly her beloved books by Victor Hugo, which she read in adolescence), she became convinced that what was most interesting and important—in fiction and in life—was the battle between good and evil. That battle was to engage her ever after; it was a major element in her own literature; it was the perspective from which she viewed the world. When she was nine years old, the idea of writing stories began to intrigue her. It soon became more absorbing than any-thing else. She would sit in school, barricaded behind a book, scribbling furiously at her latest adventure. It was not work to her; it was a pure, ecstatic pleasure.

Soon after, Ayn discovered her first feminine ideal. She and her family were vacationing in the Crimea, and one day, gazing at the tennis court—which had been built to accommodate the many foreign visitors in the area—she saw a slender, graceful young English girl racing effort-lessly after a ball and decisively smashing it across the net. Ayn stared, fascinated by this "sophisticated, foreign figure—doing something no Russian girl was allowed to do and doing it with consummate grace. . . . It was a creature out of a different world, my idea of what a woman should be," she would tell me glowingly many years later. "She was a symbol of the independent woman from abroad."[1] The girl served for Ayn as a focus, a projection, an image that she was to use in creating her feminine heroes.

Yet, in blatant contradiction to the qualities she admired in the young English girl, she, even before adolescence, was what she later called an antifeminist. "I regard man as a superior value," she said. She never thought that "woman's place was in the home," and she strongly believed that women should pursue demanding careers and that they were the intellectual and moral equals of men. But the human qualities she most cared about, she said, were "specifically masculine attributes; above all, purposefulness and strength." It is almost inconceivable that she would say this, when *she* had created Kira and Dagny, among whose salient characteristics were purposefulness and strength. But in her novels, she would *define* femininity as "hero worship." And she would say to me that a man was defined by his relationship to reality, while a woman was defined by her relationship to man.

In her adult writing, she was to present a concept she believed justified this view. Nathaniel Branden ([1969] 1971) briefly summarized her theory in *The Psychology of Self-Esteem:*

> The difference in the male and female sexual roles proceeds from differences in man's and woman's respective anatomy and physiology. Physically, man is the bigger and stronger of the two sexes; his system produces and uses more energy, and he tends . . . to be physically more active. Sexually, his is the more active and dominant role; he has the greater measure of control over his own pleasure and that of his partner; it is he who penetrates and the woman who is penetrated. . . . While a healthy aggressiveness and self-assertiveness is proper and desirable for both sexes, man experiences the essence of his masculinity in the act of romantic dominance; woman experiences the essence of her femininity in the act of romantic surrender. (208)

Thus, sex, for a man, is conquest. For a woman, it is submission; it is hero worship.

It was during the summer of 1914, at the age of nine, that Ayn fell in love. His name was Cyrus; he was the hero of an adventure story she discovered in a French boys' magazine. He was a man of enormous audaciousness and defiant independence. The spirit of Cyrus became the spirit of all the fictional heroes she would create. As an adult, she would translate Cyrus's courage and daring into intellectual terms; but the basic nature of "the heroic man" was never to alter. And it even influenced her depiction of the heroic woman—the name of the central protagonist in *We the Living*, Kira, is the Russian feminine version of "Cyrus."

By the day of Ayn's twelfth birthday, a million Russian troops had deserted the World War I lines and were looting and clogging the starving, inflation-ravaged cities. Enraged demonstrators clogged the broad avenues of St. Petersburg, shouting, "Down with the monarchy!" Ayn stood on the balcony of her apartment, and witnessed the first shots of the Russian Revolution.

In the midst of the revolution, Ayn found her first love, a love who did not exist only in books and in her imagination: Alexander Kerensky, now prime minister, who was, she then believed, a man who stood for freedom and the individual. "My infatuation with Kerensky," she was later to tell me, "had a very important influence on me in one respect. I decided that I could never be in love with an ordinary man; I could never be in love with anyone but a hero." But soon Kerensky was removed from power, and the Bolsheviks, within a few blood-soaked days, took over the helpless city. The terror began.

After her father's pharmacy was nationalized, Ayn went with her family to the Crimea, where she attended and graduated from high school and where she immediately became an intellectual leader in her class. And because she came from the sophisticated North, she "was forgiven for [her] intelligence."

Now an adolescent, she decided that it was time to learn about sex. The other girls were talking about boys, and some of them were going out on dates. One day, she heard a girl explaining to an eager group of schoolmates that sexual desire is very different from spiritual love—that it is a desire unrelated to one's spiritual choices. Ayn was appalled by this idea. She was convinced that she could never respond sexually to good looks in the absence of an unusual mind and character—and that her kind of man would respond in the same way. Her conviction, in essence, was that romantic-sexual love is a response to one's highest values, whether those values are held consciously or subconsciously.

It is interesting to note that Ayn was not invited on dates. This was a phenomenon that was to follow her for the rest of her life: that men found her intellectually fascinating, but did not see her as a woman. In America, I often would see her at social gatherings, at parties, at discussions in her home, surrounded by men who wanted to talk with her, to hear her ideas, to ask her philosophical questions, but who made no overtures of a romantic nature. They appeared to sense that she was too strong, too brilliant, and too serious for them to be "comfortable" with romantically. She existed for them only as an intellect; they did not see the feminine body, or the feminine soul that was so basic and so starved a part of her. Thus she wrote of Dagny's need to find a man stronger and wiser than she, a man she could learn from as everyone learned from her, a man as passionately sexual as she, a man she could fully admire as everyone admired her. Ayn never found such a man. But she would create him in her novels, and in her sex scenes. She gave to Dagny her own longing to find in a man the masculine power, the audaciousness, the wisdom, the power greater than her own that she herself never found. It was Ayn Rand speaking when she wrote of Dagny's need to find the courage, the will, and the strength in a man that would bring her help-lessly to her knees.

By the summer of 1921, the civil war had ended. Russia lay crushed under the Bolshevik heel, helpless, angry, and hopeless. The Rosenbaums returned to Communist Petrograd, and, as former bourgeoisie, endured semistarvation and terror. In the fall, Ayn entered the University of Pe-trograd, free to all students, to major in history.

During these years, Ayn experienced her first real romantic relation-ship, with a young man named Leo. She had met him at a party, and soon was seeing him regularly. Ayn knew that she was too openly showing her violent, almost painful passion for him. Leo began to withdraw. When he stopped seeing her, Ayn endured the most prolonged period of pain in her life. But she was determined not to let pain win a permanent victory; she saw joy as the meaning of human existence. "Life is ahead," she told herself ferociously.

Ayn graduated in the spring of 1924. And in the beginning of 1925, the unimaginable happened. Through her family's contact with relatives living in Chicago, Ayn was able to begin the process of securing the necessary papers for passage to the United States. She knew that if she went to visit her American relatives, she would never return to Russia. It did not occur to her that a young girl might be afraid to leave her home and family and everything familiar to her and set out for a strange new land with the expectation of conquering that land by means of words on paper.

In February of 1926, at the age of twenty-one, speaking almost no English, with fifty dollars in her pocket and an old typewriter clutched in her arms, Ayn stood on a pier at the Hudson River. She was setting out on a path that would require a single-tracked, courageous, passionate devotion to her career, a refusal to be stopped or turned aside by the worst of obstacles, by years of rejection, by the unconscionable distortion of her ideas, by hatred and endless attacks, and by deep romantic disappointment. As she stood on the pier, she did not know that, while *We the Living*, *The Fountainhead*, and *Atlas Shrugged* were struggling inside her to be born, three years later she would write, on her wedding license, under the category of profession: "Waitress." She did not know the pain—and the triumphs—that awaited her. Had she known the worst that was to come, she would have accepted it willingly. Her career was an absolute. The presentation of her philosophy in the form of exciting action stories—and most especially the creation of her "ideal man"—was an absolute. And although female worship of this "ideal man" was the feminist contradiction in her work, and became a disastrous contradiction in her life, there were no contradictions in her conduct of her career. Here, she was at least the equal of Kira and Dagny, and a role model without peer.

After arriving in the United States, Ayn went to movies regularly, watching intently with a professional interest in the art of film writing and in order to improve her English. In midsummer 1926, Ayn set out for the world of motion pictures. In Los Angeles, she stayed at the famous Hollywood Studio Club, a haven for young women in any branch of film, a home full of energy and good-fellowship. Through a remarkable series of events, Cecil B. DeMille took her under his wing, allowed her to watch the shooting of *The King of Kings*, and discussed with her the craft of screen writing.

Ayn worked as an extra for several months. During her second week in Hollywood, she was sitting on the streetcar, on her way to work, when, as she told me years later, "I suddenly caught sight of his face—and that was it." He was tall and slender. The skin of his face was taut against high cheekbones. His mouth was long and thin. His eyes were a cold, clear blue. His body was relaxed with the boneless elegance of a cat. "His manner suggested an aloof, confident self-sufficiency. . . . Don't let them tell me about love at first sight," she said. "It *was* love at first sight."

It was indeed. Contrary to her dictum that love is a response to a person's values, she fell in love, at sight, with a man she knew nothing about, believing that his character and spirit were conveyed by his face and manner. She spent much of the rest of her life trying to convince herself and others that he was what she wanted him to be. She was to love Frank O'Connor more than anyone else in her life, with a love that never wavered. He was the one love who never betrayed her; he was the rock against whom she could lean; he was the one person who was always on her side and stood by her unflinchingly, who understood her context, her values, her dedication to her work. Frank was not an intellectual. He did not have the ambition or the drive of an Ayn Rand hero. But he was a man of infinite generosity of spirit, a quiet, handsome, elegant gentleman of great kindness and warmth, deeply loved by all those who came to know him.

Ayn Rand always spoke of Frank as "her kind of hero," just as, not long after we met her in 1950, she spoke of Nathaniel and of me. There was in her a deep need to see us as she did. She had allowed herself to care deeply for the three of us—most particularly, of course, for Frank—to admit us into "her world," to accept us without reservation. It followed from this that we—a gentle, sensitive, passive man and a boy and girl just out of their teens—*had* to be giants in order to be worthy of her world.

Discovering that Frank had a bit part on the set of *The King of Kings*, Ayn desperately tried to find a way to meet him. She solved the problem by walking toward him, stepping directly into the path she knew he had to follow—and sticking her foot out. He stumbled and almost fell, and they began talking. They were married three years later, on 15 April 1929.

Ayn later became a junior writer at the DeMille studio. But once the studio closed, Ayn scrambled for whatever jobs she could find. She stuffed envelopes, sold newspaper subscriptions, and worked as a waitress. During one month, unemployed, she lived on thirty cents a day. Finally she found work as a filing clerk in the wardrobe department of RKO; within a year, she was head of the department. And Frank was working steadily.

In 1930, Ayn began outlining her first novel, *We the Living*, a ringing protest against collectivism that was set in Soviet Russia and was the closest to an autobiography she would ever write. In 1932, Universal Studios made her an offer for a screen original she had written entitled *Red Pawn*. With the money she received, Ayn immediately quit her job at RKO to devote full time to writing. *Red Pawn*, a brilliantly original work, was placed on a shelf. It has never been produced.

Early in the marriage, Frank became unhappy with the progress of his career, and his interest in acting waned. As Ayn grew more fired with ambition and purpose, Frank sank deeper into quiet defeat. By 1933, money was again running short, and Ayn took time from *We the Living* to write a stage play, *Penthouse Legend*, later entitled *Night of January 16th*. It was to have a reasonably successful run in Los Angeles and, under the directorship of Al Woods, to run on Broadway with considerable success—and to bring Ayn and Frank back to the city she loved. It was a most unusual role reversal for the time: a man moving for the sake of his wife's career. Indeed, Ayn always lived her life contrary to the traditional gender roles of the time.

When she again saw New York City's gleaming skyscrapers, she felt she was home at last. But a disaster struck shortly after their arrival. Al Woods had not been able to arrange financial backing for the immediate production he had planned. The Great Depression was at its height, and unemployment was rampant. Frank searched desperately for any kind of work; for a while, he was a clerk in a cigar store—and then . . . nothing. Ayn secured a job as a freelance reader for movie studios. They struggled to buy enough food to survive. "I'd buy one lamb chop for dinner for Frank," Ayn would later recall. "I had to diet anyway, so I would do without. One day, we had fifty cents between us, and our only food was the remains of a box of oatmeal. . . . It was slightly Russian."

We the Living had been completed, and was published by the Macmillan Company. Ayn's advance was two hundred and fifty dollars. And with her substantial royalties from the play, Ayn and Frank were able to live in relative comfort. But We the Living was published in the middle of America's Red Decade, a period of national infatuation with the "noble experiment" in Soviet Russia. Macmillan gave the book a minimum of publicity and advertising, and the few reviews that appeared announced that it was blatant propaganda and not illustrative of the reality of the Russian experiment. Ayn earned one hundred dollars in royalties before We the Living went out of print. When it was reissued in 1959, at the height of her success, it went on to sell many millions of copies.

The concept of "the ideal man," originating early in Ayn's childhood, had come to fruition in her mind during her twenties. The ideal man became architect Howard Roark, who was to represent the creative principle in man. His universe was The Fountainhead. The novel's theme was individualism versus collectivism, not in the realm of politics, but on the battlefield of the human soul.

It was late in 1935 when Ayn felt she could spend all of her time systematically planning The Fountainhead. For the first time, it seemed possible that she could complete a project of her own without the need to interrupt her work to earn a living. She had set herself a unique literary goal. She intended to present a new moral theory, the morality of rational self-interest, and to dramatize it in a novel. She had rejected the conventional view of morality as self-sacrifice, in favor of an unprecedented concept of good and evil, a radical view of man—and intended to present it not in the form of a treatise, but concretized and illustrated in human action, in the character of Howard Roark, in the events of a story. It was an assignment of stunning intellectual audacity.

She once said, "If all philosophers were required to present their ideas in novels, to dramatize the exact meaning and consequences of their philosophies in human life, there would be far fewer philosophers—and far better ones."

But as she labored on the manuscript, the writing was once again threatened by financial worries. Frank was not working—a fact that Ayn never appeared to resent, as if she saw their financial support to be wholly her responsibility. This caused Frank great suffering, as he continued vainly to search for work. Once again, Ayn had to interrupt her novel to engage in writing that she did not want to do but hoped would bring her the money she needed. By the fall of 1940, Ayn's savings had dwindled to seven hundred dollars. She took a job as a reader for Paramount Pictures in New York, working twelve or more hours a day, seven days a week.

Despite rejections from twelve prospective publishers, *The Fountainhead* was finally published in May 1943, by Bobbs-Merrill. Sales at first were ominously slow, due to what Ayn called "vague, noncommittal, and meaningless" advertisements—and the fact that reviewers, even those few who praised it, did not mention its theme. For all practical purposes, it was as if the press were under censorship; "individualism" seemed to be the forbidden word. To make the situation still worse, wartime paper rationing began. Bobbs-Merrill kept issuing small editions, which quickly went out of print. It seemed as if *The Fountainhead* would follow *We the Living* into oblivion. Yet, two years after publication, solely on the strength of word of mouth, *The Fountainhead* had sold 100,000 copies.

In *The Fountainhead*, Ayn defined love as "a command to rise." In the characters of Kira and Dagny, and in the life of Ayn Rand, women have found a similar command to rise. But aspects of the relationship of Dominique Francon and Howard Roark in *The Fountainhead* have troubled many feminists. In the notorious "rape scene," Roark takes Dominique by force. She resists him with all her strength, despite her clearly expressed passionate sexual desire for Roark. Ayn later remarked, "If it's rape, it's rape by engraved invitation."

This much is true: Without exception, in every sex scene Ayn Rand wrote, the woman resists, and the man physically forces her submission.

But in each case, the woman has, through words or actions or manner, issued her "engraved invitation." Thus, in psychological fact, there are no literal "rape scenes" in Ayn's work. No feminist loathed rape more than she.

Ayn was to live a life marked by the imposition of iron controls on her emotions, control of her disappointments at the reactions her work received and at her inability to find in life the people and the world she was creating in her novels. But in the area of romantic love, if sex were initiated, even forced, by the man, then she could, for once, drop the controls. She could allow the softer, more womanly part of herself to emerge. She could be wholly a woman, without emotional restraint, and reveal without fear that in her which was soft, loving, greedy for sex and for life.

In the fall of 1943, Ayn received word that Warner Brothers was interested in the movie rights to *The Fountainhead* and wanted to know her price. She demanded fifty thousand dollars, a fantastic amount to ask for in those years. "This book is going to be worth much more than fifty thousand dollars," Ayn told her agent. "But for now, that's a good price. I know the value of the book. I'll take the chance of losing the deal."

Ten days passed. Arriving home from lunch one day, she saw Frank standing in the living room, an odd look on his face. "Well, darling," he said, "while you were at lunch you earned fifty thousand dollars."

Her contract required that Ayn come to Hollywood to write the preliminary script. She hoped that if Warner Brothers liked her work, they might hire her to do the final script. They did so—but not until 1947; the wartime shortages of materials for the many sets the film would require made it impossible to consider production any sooner.

While waiting, Ayn and Frank bought a house, a small ranch, in the San Fernando Valley, thirteen acres of land and a modern home of steel and glass designed by Richard Neutra. Frank, for the first time in years, was happy. He managed the ranch, reconditioned the land, landscaped the grounds, and grew acres of flowers and citrus trees for commercial sale. On one section of the land were cages of exquisite peacocks, cages that Frank, typically, had built without tops so that the peacocks were free to fly. He often worked eighteen hours a day. To work with beautiful things—his flowers and his peacocks—and to work with his hands, to make things grow, to be engaged in activities that were *his*, not Ayn's, gave him a deep contentment. But Ayn was not happy in California. She missed the activity and excitement of New York.

While waiting for production of the movie, Ayn began working for Hal Wallis, producer of *Jezebel*, *Dark Victory*, and *Casablanca*. She wrote movie scripts, such as the highly successful *Love Letters* and *You Came Along*. At last, Ayn received word that *The Fountainhead* was shortly to begin production. The producer was Henry Blanke. The director was King Vidor. She was to write the final script. But Ayn had to wage a ferocious war to protect the integrity of her script; Vidor constantly demanded that she dilute her philosophy. Ultimately, Vidor—intimidated and/or captivated by the firebrand that was Ayn Rand and by the forceful logic of her arguments—made concessions to her that were astonishing in Hollywood. Her script was shot almost exactly as she wrote it.

Nevertheless, Ayn would say years later that she was never completely happy with the finished movie; she disliked a great deal about both the acting and the directing. But the movie brought her large numbers of new readers and put the novel back on the best-seller lists.

Just as Ayn's professional life was ravaged by conflicts, her emotional life, due to her growing disillusion and disappointment in people and an equally growing bitterness, was buried ever deeper in the underground of her spirit. Her life as a woman, despite her love for Frank, despite her insistence that he was her ideal man, was painfully unfulfilled, and sometimes their marriage, marked by growing silences between them and growing irritation, seemed to be decaying. But Ayn held tight to whatever was golden in her soul, carrying it untouched and unaltered through the years. That store of gold led her to the work that united and integrated all the separate threads of her life: the creation of *Atlas Shrugged*.

In *Atlas*, she was to write of Dagny's first encounter with John Galt, the creator and leader of the strike. Looking at his face, Dagny thought, "[I]n all the years behind her, *this* was what she would have given her life to see: a face that bore no mark of pain or fear or guilt . . . This was her world, . . . this was the way men were meant to be and to face their existence—and all the rest of it, all the years of ugliness and struggle, were only someone's senseless joke. . . . 'We never had to take any of it seriously, did we?' she whispered" (Rand 1957, 701–2).

In this meeting, two women are in love: Dagny and Ayn. The years of painful struggle and disappointment would come to an end for Dagny, through the living reality of John Galt. They were not to end for Ayn. Galt could never return her impassioned hero worship; like all the men she loved who lived and breathed in the real world—like her father, like Leo, like Frank, like the man who soon was to enter her life—he could never return the overwhelming intensity of her love. He sentenced her to a lifetime of unrequited love.

In March 1950, while working on *Atlas Shrugged*, Ayn Rand agreed to meet two young fans of *The Fountainhead*. Nathaniel Branden had written her a letter, posing philosophical questions that intrigued her with their perceptiveness, and she agreed to meet him. On their second meeting, with her consent, I joined him. Nathaniel and I were students at UCLA, he in psychology, I in philosophy. We had both read *The Fountainhead* at fifteen, and had been profoundly influenced by it. Our meeting with Ayn was a never-to-be-forgotten landmark in our lives. We talked until dawn, about all the philosophical questions Nathaniel and I had been struggling with since we had met two years earlier; we talked about metaphysics, politics, religion, the nature of knowledge, aesthetics, morality, free will, the absolutism of reason. In the clarity with which she explained issues, in the irresistible logic of her arguments, we felt as if she were weaving a personal miracle for us. As our friendship developed, Ayn shared with us her work in progress. It was an unrepeatable intellectual and emotional experience.

In the summer of 1951, Nathaniel and I left California and enrolled at New York University. Our parting with Ayn and Frank was difficult, but it did not last long. In the fall, Ayn phoned to announce happily that she and Frank would arrive in New York in three weeks. On their arrival, Ayn told us that she had come to New York partially because of us. "It was an enormous contributing factor," she said. "I followed you across a continent."

Rand followed her own desires, but the move was an agonizing one for Frank. There is little doubt that Ayn's discussions with him consisted in her telling him that she *had* to return to New York and that she knew he wanted to also. And there is no doubt that Frank did *not* want it, although he did not tell her so. The return to New York ended a way of life that was precious to him, a way of life he lacked the strength to fight for. Once again, Ayn exhibited behavior that was at the heart of her contradiction to feminism: her willingness to reconfigure reality to fit her psychological needs.

In January of 1953, Ayn and Frank were matron of honor and best man at Nathaniel's and my marriage.

We began to introduce to Ayn young people, friends of ours, who were eagerly interested in her ideas. During the next several years, they attended regular Saturday-evening discussions at Ayn's home. As a private joke—it soon was not private—we referred to ourselves as "the Collective" because the term was so absurdly the opposite of what her philosophy represented.

In the fall of 1954, a year and a half after our marriage, I realized Ayn and Nathaniel were not just loving friends. I knew, beyond question or argument, that they had fallen in love. When I confronted him, frantic with rage and pain, he stared at me with a look of stunned disbelief, as if I had suddenly gone mad. "For God's sake, I love *you!*" he replied, his eyes suddenly wet. "She—she's twenty-five years older than I am!" I stood my ground.

The next day, Ayn telephoned Nathaniel. She had to see him at once, she said. The nightmare that was to last fourteen years, and was finally to smash hundreds of lives, had begun.

I have discussed, in great detail, the affair between Ayn Rand and Nathaniel Branden in my biography, *The Passion of Ayn Rand*. Given the scope of this paper, I cannot provide an exhaustive account of the circumstances surrounding the affair. Ayn had argued that an inexorable logic had brought Nathaniel and her to the point of romantic love. She had claimed that the affair did not threaten either marriage. She had assured us that the age difference between Nathaniel and her would preclude any long-term commitment. Frank and I had intellectually accepted Ayn's theory of love; we could not deny it now. But the underlying reasons for our acceptance of this situation are too complex to summarize in the space of an article.

Ayn could not, after all, be content with reality. She struggled to turn base metals—the painful, unsatisfactory fact of having an adulterous affair with the too young husband of her closest woman friend—into the gold of a great and exalted romance. She succeeded in her fiction. She did not succeed in her life.

The initial timing of the affair could not have been more unfortunate. Ayn was writing John Galt's climactic philosophical speech in *Atlas Shrugged*. The speech required two nerve-racking years to complete, and the unremitting effort and tension of this work profoundly exacerbated Ayn's insensitivity to the context of others, her lack of human empathy, her need for control, her judgmental explosiveness, her tendency to self-aggrandizement. The bitterness and pain in her personality began to take ascendancy over the lighter, gayer aspects. Innumerable times, her shocked friends witnessed her verbal flaying of people whom she felt had failed her and failed her standards, with an indifference to their feelings that was appalling—and immensely damaging to her victims.

On an evening in March 1957, Ayn walked out of her study in a state of dazed numbness and exaltation, and handed Frank the last page of her manuscript to let him see the words "The End." *Atlas Shrugged* was published by Random House in October of 1957.

And then it was over—over forever in Ayn's life—that happy period of excitement and hope and expectation that had preceded publication. And with it seemed to go almost the last of her fragile capacity to live in the world. The reviews of *Atlas* were savage, and sales began slowly. As always in Ayn's career, it was predominantly word of mouth that caused sales to skyrocket. Within little more than a year after publication, Ayn was on her way to world fame. She was becoming wealthy, and she was passionately admired by many thousands, finally millions, of devoted readers. She had written the novel she had been moving toward all her life—and then she sank into a profound depression that was to last for more than two years.

It was not the bad reviews, she said; it was not the outpouring of hatred directed against her; it was not the initial slow sales. It was that there was no one to protest the attacks, no one with a public name, reputation, or voice to speak or fight for her, to name the nature and the stature of her accomplishment. "I no longer know to whom I'm addressing myself when I write. I feel paralyzed by disgust and contempt. What sense does it make to continue writing?"

Ayn's depression brought to an end, with a number of unplanned exceptions, her sexual relationship with Nathaniel. She did not intend the ending to be permanent, she told him. She knew she would recover emotionally, but now she had nothing to give or to want. Their romance was put "on hold."

In January of 1958, a few months after the publication of *Atlas*, Nathaniel conceived the idea of organizing an institute in response to the tidal wave of mail Ayn was receiving. He prepared a course of twenty lectures entitled "Basic Principles of Objectivism," a detailed, systematic presentation of Ayn Rand's philosophy. Soon, Nathaniel Branden Institute (NBI) was successfully offering a variety of courses in eighty cities, from Los Angeles to Toronto to Clear, Alaska, and a stream of requests began arriving from Europe, Africa, Asia, and Australia. Our purpose, in which we succeeded, was to make Ayn Rand known not merely as a novelist, but as an important philosopher. The intellectual level of the students was exceptional. Ayn Rand Clubs began springing up on college campuses, and increasing requests for material arrived from teachers and professors who wished to include a discussion of Objectivism in their classes. The influence of Ayn Rand as a philosopher was spreading, and has, today, spread across the globe. Ayn received invitations to speak at universities, where her appearances attracted unprecedented audiences. She was a strangely powerful speaker; this small, unprepossessing woman with the heavy Russian accent had the charismatic power of certainty.

She turned to the writing of nonfiction, discovering that she immensely enjoyed it. She began to write articles for a monthly journal, later called *The Objectivist*, that she and Nathaniel formed. I served as the journal's managing editor. Many of these articles were later published in book form, and, as anthologies, they contributed substantially to the dissemination of her ideas and to her fame. In her professional life, she was what feminists have long sought, a model of the woman intellectual whose ideas on a variety of broad cultural and philosophical issues have made a serious impact.

In 1964, Ayn turned once more to her personal life and to Nathaniel. She was ready to resume their sexual affair. She did not know that it was much too late. Nathaniel had fallen in love with Patrecia Gullison, a beautiful young NBI student. He was having an affair with her, and he could not bring himself to tell Ayn. He had accepted—he was teaching it in classes all over the country, as he taught it to his therapeutic clients and his friends inside and outside of "the Collective"—Ayn's theory that romantic love is one's response to one's highest, most exalted values, and that to choose a lesser value over a greater one was an act of spiritual and moral depravity. Now he was in love, but not with Ayn Rand, not with the woman who he believed exemplified all that was best and noblest in the human spirit.

I asked Nathaniel for a divorce in the summer of 1965. Toward the end of 1966, Nathaniel told me what was happening with Ayn, with Patrecia, and with himself. I was horrified, and frightened for both Ayn and Nathaniel.

My worst presentiments came true. The ensuing events, detailed in *The Passion of Ayn Rand* (1986), ended in denouncements and disaster. When the break was complete and NBI was liquidated, Ayn gave her own interpretation to the events, leaving our students bewildered about what *really* had happened. She wrote an article for *The Objectivist*, saying that she had broken with Nathaniel and with me. She accused Nathaniel of a host of sins, including a wholly invented charge of financial dishonesty—accused him of everything but the truth.

During the next few years, the influence of Ayn's ideas grew enormously. But the organized, official movement vanished with NBI, and with it, much of the true believer mentality that had begun severely to damage it. (In contrast to such fine organizations as the Institute for Objectivist Studies, the Ayn Rand Institute is, sadly, a remnant of this true-believer approach to Objectivism and Ayn Rand.) Ayn's influence now takes its appropriate form, as each new generation reads her works, profits from them, learns from them, and goes on to lead independent lives of their own choosing.

In her final years, Ayn continued writing, but she made only a few public appearances. Alan Greenspan, a member of the former Collective, entered the federal government as chairman of the Council of Economic Advisers under President Ford, and Ayn was delighted with his success. When he was sworn in, she and Frank traveled to Washington to attend the ceremony and to meet the president. Not long thereafter, they traveled to Washington again, to attend a state dinner for Malcolm Fraser, prime minister of Australia. Fraser had asked that she be invited; she was his favorite author.

It had been a long, hard journey from starvation and terror in Soviet Russia to attendance at the White House as the welcome and respected guest of an American president and an Australian prime minister. It was a sanction that she needed and had earned.

In the summer of 1981, Ayn, no longer well, accepted an invitation to address the National Committee for Monetary Reform, an organization dedicated to the reestablishment of a gold standard and to educating the public in free-market economics. More than four thousand cheering people rose to their feet to give her a standing ovation. But the trip to New Orleans took its toll. Ayn was desperately ill. In February 1982, she was hospitalized with cardiopulmonary problems. On the morning of 6 March 1982, Ayn Rand died.

A service was held for Ayn in New York. Then she was buried beside Frank (who had died in 1979) in a private ceremony held outside New York City in a town named Valhalla.

In the introduction to *The Passion of Ayn Rand*, I wrote: "Her person encompassed the grandeur of the heroes of her novels, their iron determination, their vast powers of intellect and imagination, their impassioned pursuit of their goals, their worship of achievement, their courage, their pride and their love of life—as well as the terrors, the self-doubts, the lack of emotional balance, the private agonies that are so alien to an Ayn Rand hero. Her virtues were larger than life—and so were her shortcomings" (1986, ix).

I have suggested in this article that in Ayn Rand's pursuit of her career, and in her female heroines, one finds a superb feminist manifesto. Even though her life was flawed by her own mistakes, even though her fictional characterizations were affected by the contradiction to feminism—her concept of femininity as "hero worship"—they continue to represent a standard and an ideal that are worthy of emulation by women everywhere. Unless one demands that a role model be a goddess. I do not.

Note

1. Unless otherwise indicated, the quotes herein are derived from interviews with Ayn Rand conducted by this author in the early 1960s. See Branden 1986.

References

Branden, Barbara. 1986. *The Passion of Ayn Rand*. Garden City, N.Y.: Doubleday.
Branden, Nathaniel. [1969] 1971. *The Psychology of Self-Esteem: A New Concept of Man's Psychological Nature*. New York: Bantam.
Chambers, Whittaker. 1957. Big sister is watching you. *National Review*, 28 December, 594–96.
Donegan, Patricia. 1957. A point of view. *Commonweal* 67 (8 November).
Pruette, Lorine. 1943. Battle against evil: Review of *The Fountainhead*. *New York Times Book Review*, 16 May, 7ff.
Rand, Ayn. 1957. *Atlas Shrugged*. New York: Random House.
———. 1959. *We the Living*. New York: New American Library.
Rolo, Charles. 1957. Comes the revolution. *Atlantic Monthly* (November): 249–50.
Vidal, Gore. 1961. Comment. *Esquire*, July, 24–27, 67.

2

Ayn Rand and Feminism: An Unlikely Alliance

Mimi Reisel Gladstein

In a field as new as women's studies, to protest the traditional reading list or approach may seem premature. However, after several traumatic semesters one might argue convincingly for a reevaluation. Whereas generally the task of choosing texts for women's studies courses in literature is an exciting experience because of the anticipation of introducing students to many writers who are left out of their regular curricula, it also posits the difficulty of achieving a balanced representation of the various images of women. The particular difficulty in point is finding sufficient

In this selection, and in the Wilt, Brownmiller, Harrison, and Paglia reprints that follow, the editors of this volume have attempted to provide citation information for references that were undocumented in these articles as they first appeared. In all such cases, our notes are in brackets. We have also standardized reference forms, and created corresponding reference lists throughout.

representations for that section of the course that should be entitled "The Liberated Woman" or "She Who Succeeds." In American literature, the shortage is acute.

Having made a study of the dearth of self-actualized, positive heroines in works by American male novelists for the Educational Resources Information Center, the problem was not unexpected. Nor has this deficiency gone without critical comment. Caroline Heilbrun discussed the implications of this problem in her article for *Saturday Review*, "The Masculine Wilderness of the American Novel." Wendy Martin's conclusion in "Seduced and Abandoned in the New World" is that "as daughters of Eve, American heroines are destined to lives of dependency and servitude as well as to painful and sorrowful childbirth because, like their predecessor, they have dared to disregard authority or tradition in search of wisdom or happiness" [Martin (1971) 1972, 329]. The problem is not limited to fiction. Studies abound that lament the lack of positive female role models in everything from the "Dick and Jane" primary readers to high school history books.

Adding women writers to the reading lists, whether they be writers newly discovered or resurrected by feminist criticism or already acclaimed writers, does little to alleviate the problem. The resultant mood created by the reading material in women's studies courses in American literature is rage or despair. This is true though there are several excellent short story and poetry anthologies that can be used in combination with any number of novels. The same is true, though to a lesser extent, in a course that focuses on biography or autobiography. After going mad with *Zelda*, attempting suicide in *The Bell Jar*, and agonizing through an early Anaïs Nin *Diary*, not to mention any of the *Marilyn* biographies, the student is convinced that women can't possibly win. In the fiction courses, reading *Play It As It Lays*, *Diary of a Mad Housewife*, and *Memoirs of an Ex–Prom Queen* produces the same conclusion. The neurotic, manipulated, or exploited female continues to be the mainstay of American fiction. Not that one owes one's students a happy ending, but after several semesters of depression (especially strong because of the intense personal identification such courses develop), a touch of positivism is in order, and one feels the need to search for a novel with a female protagonist who is active, independent, professionally successful, sexually emancipated, and doesn't pay for it by dying in childbirth, going mad, compromising, or giving it all up for the man she loves.

Examination of my reading experience led to the realization that my own move toward independence and liberation had been inspired by a popular novel. Pre-Friedan and pre-Millett, nascent feminism had been nurtured by the reading of Atlas Shrugged, published in 1957. Atlas Shrugged, written by Ayn Rand, is not generally considered to be philosophically feminist. In fact, it may not be on anyone's reading list for women's courses, except mine. But close analysis of the book's themes and theories will prove that it should be. Much that Rand says is relevant to feminist issues. Best of all, the novel has a protagonist who is a good example of a woman who is active, assertive, successful, and still retains the love and sexual admiration of three heroic men. Though the situation is highly romantic, and science fiction to boot, how refreshing it is to find a female protagonist in American fiction who emerges triumphantly.

Students, though groaning about the 1100-some-odd pages of the novel, are very favorable in their responses and find the book's messages relevant to feminism in many ways. The positive influence of the book on women was recently validated by yet another feminist from a nonacademic field. In a Playboy interview early in 1976, Billie Jean King discussed how Atlas Shrugged had affected her life. Ms. King, who did not read the book until the spring of 1972, commented:

> The book really turned me around, because, at the time, I was going through a bad period in tennis and thinking about quitting. People were constantly calling me and making me feel rotten if I didn't play in their tournament or help them out. I realized then that people were beginning to use my strength as a weakness— that they were using me as a pawn to help their own ends and if I wasn't careful, I'd end up losing myself. So, like Dagny Taggart, I had to learn how to be selfish, although selfish has the wrong connotation. As I see it, being selfish is really doing your own thing. Now I know that if I can make myself happy, I can make other people happy—and if that's being selfish, so be it. That's what I am. [King 1976]

By nourishing her individual strength, King was able to accomplish much for the cause of women in sports. Similarly, there are many ways that Atlas Shrugged, though not written for that purpose, can be of benefit to other feminists. Paradoxically, the book is viewed suspiciously by most liberal feminists who see it as a criticism of collectivism, which it is, but somehow miss the positive implications it holds for women.

Since all of the current rights movements owe much of their impetus to the black civil rights struggle, it may be instructive for feminists to view the issue of collectivism in that camp. Many black commentators, Ralph Ellison and Albert Murray among the most prominent, have pointed out the shortcomings of black collectivism, namely that collectivism can stifle self-actualization by emphasizing reaction rather than encouraging positive self-determination. In "The World and the Jug," Ellison [1995, 185] reminds us that beyond all the politics there is the essential aloneness of the individual "even as he shares the suffering of his group." Further, he makes the point that the individual writer must take what he needs from wherever he finds it and that, for Ellison, Ernest Hemingway, regardless of his political views, is more valuable, more of a "relative" than is Richard Wright.[1] In *Omni Americans*, Murray's recurrent theme is that while black reaction may indeed give a movement its initial energy, that energy will dissipate without attention to individual development.

In a parallel manner, the individual woman must be receptive to resources of all kinds. The old bromide that a chain is only as strong as its weakest link holds true for the women's movement. In order to contribute effectively to sisterhood, the individual must develop strength of self. In a state of the movement article in *Ms.* (September 1975), radical feminist Robin Morgan underlined the necessity to accept any and all paths toward individual liberation. Morgan notes that "the early excesses of collective tyranny have shifted" and that the concept of individuality is to be cherished [78].[2] Both Betty Friedan and Gloria Steinem, in private conversation and published articles, have indicated the need to withdraw periodically from collective action in order to rekindle inner reserves. They feel that at times the drain of organization reduces their effectiveness. It is at this level—beyond the armies, the races, the movements— that Ayn Rand speaks to us all. What benefit is winning the battle if we lose ourselves in the process?

The refrain of *Atlas Shrugged* is John Galt's oath, "I swear by my life and my love of it that I will never live for the sake of another man [person], nor ask another man [person] to live for mine" [Rand 1957, 731]. (For purposes of this paper, I will feminize or neuter all masculine nouns and pronouns. Though Ms. Rand refers to men and mankind, she obviously means humankind, as evidenced in the rest of this study.) While the context of the oath is economic, the message is the same one advanced by feminists, that no woman should live her life for or through others, as women have traditionally been encouraged to do. Typical of the studies that touch upon this issue is Edith de Rham's *Love Fraud*. In her attack on "the staggering waste of education and talent among American Women," de Rham [1965, 110] argues that by persuading women to concentrate their lives on men who in turn concentrate on work, "Women become victims of a kind of fraud in which their love is exploited and in which they are somehow persuaded that they are involved in legitimate action." It is just this kind of exploitation that Ayn Rand deplores.

Whereas de Rham calls it "the love fraud," Rand calls it self-sacrifice or altruism. Rand's attack on altruism, which is defined as an ethical principle that "holds that one must make the welfare of others one's primary moral concern and must place their interests above one's own . . . that service to others is the moral justification of one's existence, that self-sacrifice is one's foremost duty and highest virtue," is essentially relevant to women because they have been the chief internalizers of this concept. This concept of self-sacrifice has encouraged women to view themselves as sacrificial animals whose desires and talents are forfeited for the good of children, family, and society. This negative behavior produces looters, moochers, leeches, and parasites, in Rand's vernacular. Women have been socialized to feel guilty if they fail to carry out the practice of sacrificing their careers for the advancement of others, whether it be husband, family, or simply a matter of vacating a position to a more needy male. And this sacrificing of a woman's abilities and potential is not viewed with horror or outrage, but rather with acceptance, while a similar male sacrifice is seen as a great tragedy or waste. Of course, Rand rejects any sacrifice as negative because she sees it as the surrender of a greater value for the sake of a lesser one or for the sake of a nonvalue.

John Galt's climactic speech, which is the distillation of the novel's message, emphasizes Rand's exhortation against self-immolation. The morality John Galt speaks out against is the same one women have been trying to crawl out from under. As Galt explains it, "virtue, to you, consists of sacrifice. . . . You have sacrificed independence to unity . . . sacrificed reason to faith . . . sacrificed self-esteem to self-denial . . . sacrificed happiness to duty" [Rand 1957, 1010]. Galt is abjuring that same behavior which has been fostered in women by society and religion. As Galt sees it, (such) "morality demands the surrender of your self-interest and of your mind" [1012]. The typical image of the submissive woman is one with no interest or mind of her own. She lives only for her husband and, according to Galt, "to serve God's purpose or her neighbor's welfare, to please an authority beyond the grave or else next door—but not to serve *her* life or pleasure" [1011]. According to traditional morality, Galt proclaims, "Woman's good is to give up her personal desires, to deny herself, renounce herself, surrender." And women have lived by this standard; they have even fed it to their daughters with statements such as "It is for your own happiness, you must serve the happiness of others, the only way to achieve your joy is to give it up to others" [1031]. Galt, Rand's spokesperson, does not believe happiness is to be achieved through the sacrifice of one's values; he believes instead that "Woman has to be woman . . . she has to hold her life as a value . . . she has to learn to sustain it . . . she has to discover the values it requires and practice her virtues. . . . Happiness is that state of consciousness which proceeds from the achievement of one's values" [1013–14]. What could be more relevant to feminism?

The nature of male/female relationships is another important area of philosophical exploration for Rand. Through Dagny's associations with Francisco d'Anconia, Hank Rearden, and John Galt, Rand illustrates what a relationship between two self-actualized, equal human beings can be. In such relationships, Rand denies the existence of a split between the physical and the mental, the desires of the flesh and the longings of the spirit.

This concept is very important for human liberation because the body/mind and sex/love dichotomies have been detrimental to human potentiality. Women have been encouraged to develop their physical attributes at the expense of their mental abilities, and men have been taught to seek women who admire them (men) rather than women they admire. Rand sees such activity as counterproductive. In a nonfiction work, *The Virtue of Selfishness*, her definition of romantic love is a combination of pride and admiration. Pride she defines as pleasure in one's own achievement, and admiration as the pleasure one takes in the character and achievement of others [Rand 1964, 65]. [Rand's colleague, Nathaniel Branden, writing on "the psychology of pleasure," in *The Virtue of Selfishness*, states]: "The highest expression of the most intense union of these two responses—pride and admiration—is romantic love. Its celebration is sex" [65]. According to this philosophy, the object of a person's desire is a reflection of one's image of self. In the novel, Dagny—our positive protagonist—uses this fact as a standard of measuring others. Since Hank Rearden is capable of wanting her, he must be worthy of her. As she puts it, "I feel that others live up to me, if they want me" [Rand 1957, 375]. In this context, also, if one desires a person, one also prizes everything that person is and stands for. Dagny makes this point quite clear when she speaks of her sexual relationship with Rearden during a radio broadcast. She says, "It was the ultimate form of our admiration of each other, with full knowledge of the values by which we made our choice. We are those who do not disconnect the values of their minds from the actions of their bodies" [853]. Within this framework, the act of sexual intercourse possesses special meaning. It is a joyous affirmation of one's life, of one's beliefs, of all that one is. Dagny realizes this after her first sexual encounter with Francisco, when she thinks "of the times when she had wanted to express, but found no way to do it . . . the feeling of being in love with the fact that one exists . . . she thought that the act she had learned was the way one expressed it" [108]. Dagny picks sexual partners who affirm her and affirm life.

Rand has written specifically about her concept of people who use sex as conquest, or proof of masculinity, amelioration of despair, or escape from boredom. She feels that a man's romantic-sexual responses are psychologically revealing. [As Nathaniel Branden puts it:]

> A man of self-esteem, a man in love with himself and with life, feels an intense need to find human beings he can admire—to find a spiritual equal he can love. The quality that will attract him most is self-esteem. . . . To such a man sex is an act of celebration, its meaning a tribute to himself and to the woman he has chosen. . . . But if a man lacks self-esteem, he attempts to fake it—and he chooses his partner (subconsciously) by the standard of her ability to help him fake it, to give him the illusion of a self-value he does not possess. [in Rand 1964, 66]

The message of such a philosophy is a positive one for women as it encourages the development of full potential and strong self-esteem, rather than depreciation and inhibition, as the medium to fulfillment in male/ female alliances. This attitude also inspires men in the direction of liberated women, for, [Branden] explains, "if a man is attracted to a woman of intelligence, confidence and strength, if he is attracted to a heroine, he reveals one kind of soul; if, instead, he is attracted to an irresponsible, helpless scatterbrain, whose weakness enables him to feel masculine, he reveals another kind of soul" [66]. Examples abound, throughout the novel, in which through character or situation the message is either sub-liminally or overtly applicable to positive female existence.

Though Rand stresses the primacy of individual action and responsi-bility, she does not exclude the importance of sisterhood. It is simply that Rand sees the development of *individual* strength as primary. When Cherryl Taggart, in desperation, turns to Dagny for help, Dagny's re-sponse to Cherryl's uncertain approach is the affirmative, "We're sisters, aren't we?" [Rand 1957, 888]. Thinking Dagny is referring to their legal status (Cherryl is married to Dagny's brother), Cherryl turns away. Dagny assures her that the sisterhood is through choice, not law. They are sisters because they value the same things. Dagny stresses the fact that her offer of help is not a charitable act, but a recognition of Cherryl's essential worth. She invites Cherryl to stay with her and even elicits a promise that Cherryl will return. Still, though the sisterhood is warming, it is not enough to save Cherryl, for she has not developed enough strength to cope with the horror of her situation.

The utopia of the novel, Galt's Gulch, is inhabited by people whose behavior and ideals Ayn Rand admires. They are people who are engaged in positive and productive endeavors, and the woman who chooses moth-erhood is deliberately included. Dagny reflects on the joyous results of such choice, two eager and friendly children.

But domestic duties are not solely the realm of women in Galt's Gulch. Various of the male inhabitants are seen cooking, cleaning, and serving. When Dagny does housework, she is paid for her contribution.

In full honesty, there are attitudes toward women and femininity in the novel that are offensive, but they are few and are heavily outweighed by the positive aspects. Most significantly, for our purposes, Dagny Tag-gart is an affirmative role model. She is the head of a railroad. She has sexual relationships with three men and retains their love and respect. She is not demeaned or punished for her emancipation, sexual or profes-sional. She has no intention of giving up her railroad for the man she loves. She retains them both. She behaves according to her code of ethics and is not punished by God or society. She is that rarity in American fiction—a heroine who not only survives, but prevails.

Notes

1. Ed. note: Actually, what Ellison rejects is categorization with Richard Wright solely on the basis of their common "racial identity"; that is, he rejects "polylogism." See our Introduction. Ellison

says that Hemingway was more important to him than Wright because "he appreciated the thing of this earth which I love." In other words, they shared a sense of life.

2. Ed. note: Interestingly enough, Morgan defines "radical" in the same way as Rand defines it when she calls herself a "radical for capitalism." A "radical," for Morgan (1975, 77), is "one who goes to the root."

References

de Rham, Edith. 1965. *The Love Fraud: A Direct Attack on the Staggering Waste of Education and Talent Among American Women.* New York: Pegasus.

Ellison, Ralph. 1995. The world and the jug. *The Collected Essays of Ralph Ellison.* New York: Modern Library.

King, Billie Jean. 1976. Interview. *Playboy*, March, 55–70, 194–96.

Martin, Wendy. [1971] 1972. Seduced and abandoned in the new world: The image of woman in American fiction. In *Woman in Sexist Society*, edited by Vivian Gornick and Barbara K. Moran. New York: New American Library.

Morgan, Robin. 1975. Forum: Rights of passage. *Ms.*, September, 75–78, 98–103.

Rand, Ayn. 1957. *Atlas Shrugged.* New York: Random House.

———. 1964. *The Virtue of Selfishness: A New Concept of Egoism.* New York: New American Library.

3

On *Atlas Shrugged*

Judith Wilt

I *could* wish that the cancer-causing cigarette were not the ultimate symbol of glowing mind-controlling matter in the book; I could wish that the rails which reflect the self-assertion of the heroine were not envisioned running to the hands of a man invisible beyond the horizon— most of all I wish the author had resisted the temptation to have her hero trace the Sign of the Dollar over the devastated earth before his Second Coming. But yes, I agree with Mimi Gladstein, there is a feminist element in Ayn Rand's *Atlas Shrugged* [1957], and it's on my ideal women's studies reading list too.

It made a deep impression on me at nineteen, and now I can see at least two feminist reasons why. First, the book's opening sections on Dagny Taggart's childhood and adolescence depict with great power the most shattering discovery the awakening womanmind makes—this world is not the one the vigorous confident girlchild expected to find and to help run when she "grew up." And second, the book's middle and final sections depict with still greater power, nay satisfaction, the destruction of that false usurpers' world.

Rand's extended invocation of catastrophe feels astonishingly like the 1970s: "On the morning of September 2, a copper wire broke in California, between two telephone poles. . . . On the evening of September 7, a copper wire broke in Montana, stopping the motor of a loading crane. . . . On the afternoon of September 11, a copper wire broke in Minnesota, stopping the belts of a grain elevator. . . . On the night of October 15, a copper wire broke in New York City, . . . extinguishing the lights" [909, 925, 936, 943]. In fact, *Atlas Shrugged* partakes of the general post–nuclear apocalypticism of the 1950s. But there is also a special quality of *feminine* rage discernible not only in the analysis of the Originating Sin behind the usurping world—"altruism," selflessness, the worship of "the other" and his need before one's own—but in the nature of the destruction.

According to her vision of the great age of progress (the nineteenth century, that is—not, I admit, perfectly recognizable to the historian in Rand's form), humanity civilized, indeed organicized, material nature by infusing it with its own purposeful creativity—metal plus mind equals the living copper wire, the bridges and motors and lights which are, so to speak, the mystical body of the human mind, the "material shapes of desire," as Rand phrases it. When mind goes astray or is withdrawn, the enterprise collapses upon itself, and the plot of *Atlas Shrugged* is predicated upon the desire of the best minds in the world to "go on strike," to destroy the old shapes of desire because they have been appropriated, usurped. Thus in the novel destruction of what is outside the self becomes the measure of greatness, purposefulness, authenticity, even more than construction or preservation of what is inside the self. The heroine's adolescent lover, Francisco d'Anconia, devotes his life to "destroying d'Anconia Copper in plain sight of the world" [765]. The hero, John Galt, who organizes the strike and convinces the suppliers of oil, then coal, then steel, to withdraw just as the national economy, swinging wildly about in its search for a savior, needs them most, is the hated "Destroyer" to Dagny before she actually meets him. Even after she meets him and knows him, complicatedly, as the full shape of her desire, that desire remains destructive to the measure of its authenticity. Before entering his

Atlantis she understands that she would have destroyed the Destroyer if she could—but not until she had made love to him; after she leaves it to go back and try to halt the world's self-destruction, she goes to see him in his hideout in New York despite the risk that she will lead his enemies to him. He describes, to her horror, the trap she has probably enclosed them both in, and urges:

> "It's our time and our life, not theirs. Don't struggle not to be happy. You are."
> "At the risk of destroying you?" she whispered.
> "You won't. But—yes, even that. ... Was it indifference that broke you and brought you here?"
> "I—" And then the violence of the truth made her pull his mouth down to hers, then throw the words at his face: "I didn't care whether either one of us lived afterwards, just to see you this once!" [1092]

This subterranean commitment to a cleansing violence, an ethic of destruction, is evident in Rand's vision of both work and sex, is indeed what makes the two functions of the same desire. What attracts Rand, and Dagny, to the industrial barons of the nineteenth century is unmistakably the sense of their successful smashing of opposition. What brings Dagny back to her job after one early frustration is the disastrous train wreck which destroyed the Taggart tunnel through the Rockies—she cannot accept that destruction and wants to mitigate it. The test of ethical adulthood at the end of the novel is her willing desertion of the railroad she runs, just as the Taggart bridge across the Mississippi, the last link to the West, is destroyed. Leaving, she sanctions this and all following destruction. Dagny first comes to John Galt by crashing her plane into his private mountain retreat; when they return to the city, he follows her, running, into the dark tunnel of the terminal, and they share a love scene not easily distinguishable from mutual rape: "she felt her teeth sinking into the flesh of his arm, she felt the sweep of his elbow knocking her head aside and his mouth seizing her lips with a pressure more viciously painful than hers" [957].

At the root of all this eager violence is an equivocal passion for the display of *will* in a world where will seems to Rand's heroine to have either utterly rotted away or else become so devious in its operations as to be unrecognizable, a world "feminized" in the worst sense of the word.

"Oh, don't ask me—do it!" she prays at seventeen when Francisco, too, "seizes" her, and she receives his violence thankfully as an anodyne for the disappointment of the formal debut party months before, where "there wasn't a man . . . I couldn't squash ten of" [108, 104]. What she doesn't realize then, what Francisco and Galt are about to learn, is that the power to create *or* to squash that comes from will is not in fact equal to the power to expropriate or squash that comes from will-lessness, not only because there is more of the latter than the former in the world, but more because the people of will have accepted the chains of certain moral systems which short-circuit or diffuse their desires.

Dagny suffers from the quantity of will-lessness opposed to her will. Gaining the position she requires, operating vice-president of the Taggart railroad, was "like advancing through a succession of empty rooms," deathly exhausting but productive of no violence, cleansing or otherwise. Her disgust and near despair are in this respect interestingly like that of an ambitious *man*. Indeed, at the wedding of her wealthy brother and the energetic little shopgirl he marries, the bride challenges the sister-in-law she has heard of as a cold and unfeminine executive: "I'm the woman in this family now," and Dagny replies, "That's quite all right, I'm the man" [396]. At the same party Francisco, the self-proclaimed womanizer who is actually one of the Destroyers, answers Hank Rearden's contemptuous "Found any conquests?" with "Yes—what I think is going to be my best and greatest" [416]. Rearden is himself the conquest Francisco is after; Dagny's first lover wants her second lover not for explicitly sexual purposes, of course, but for the Cause. And yet, in several scenes Rearden is the female to Francisco and Dagny in the novel:

> "I'm saying that I didn't know what it meant, to like a man, I didn't know how much I'd missed it—until I met him."
> "Good God, Hank, you've fallen for him!"
> "Yes, I think I have." [427]

This is more than the love of one man for another, though it is certainly that too, and eloquently described by Rand, and welcome. It is the love of one being whose desire has been short-circuited, "hooked to torment instead of reward," as Rand describes it, for another whose desire is direct and confident of its ends. And it is this kind of frustration, desire short-circuited, will "contravened," as Lawrence would say, that makes Rearden a kind of female icon. It is the archetypal female plight that Rand explores in his story, displacing it cleverly from her heroine, whom she values too much to subject to it, to her middle-rank hero, whom she loves and pities.

Rearden's existence at book's opening is a schizophrenic shuttling between an unendurable dead family and marriage, and a profoundly satisfying work life whose very satisfaction is a guilty torment because all his love is concentrated there among the machines, mill schedules, and metals, which are, inexplicably and "shamefully" to the usurpers of altruism, alive and lovable to him. He makes the classic "female" adjustment: he accepts the world's definition of his work life, love, and productivity as guilt and his withdrawal of pure love from his family as shame. He hates and tries to eliminate the sexual desire which is at the heart of the corrupt world of marriage and family and relies on sheer strength, doubled and redoubled, to support both sides of his existence and the conflicts between them. "Well, then, go on with your hands tied, he thought, go on in chains. Go on. It must not stop you." When he finds himself desiring Dagny Taggart, the mind and spirit his working soul most admires, it is a catastrophe to his split self—"the lowest of my desires—as my answer to the highest I've met. . . . it's depravity, and I accept it as such" [255]. Dagny does not challenge his definition, knowing that their living experience as lovers will teach him the truth, but it is Francisco who actually tells him the truth. In this novel it is still true that women, even the heroine, mainly exist and demonstrate, while men develop and articulate. "Only the man who extols the purity of a love devoid of desire, is capable of a depravity of a desire without love," Francisco argues [491]; only "the man who is convinced of his own worthlessness will be drawn to a woman he despises" [490]. Led by Francisco and Dagny, Rearden emerges from the schizophrenia, reconnects the circuits of his sexual and productive desire to his sense of self-worth, and achieves in the end, like Dagny, that act of abandonment-destruction which, again, is Rand's rite of passage from the usurpers' world to the "real" one. Only it is not just the mills which, like Dagny's railroad, must be destroyed: it is also Rearden's family—mate, mother, brother—which, deprived of his coerced strength, must be let slide into poverty and degradation and madness before the new beginning is possible.

Finally, interestingly, Rearden's reward for making his passage does not include a mate, as Dagny's does. Discovering that Francisco, whom he loves, was Dagny's first lover, Rearden "seized" the woman (again) and consummated an act of love that included, through the woman's body, "the act of victory over his rival and of his surrender to him," just as Dagny too "felt Francisco's presence through Rearden's mind." When Dagny chooses John Galt, the purest shape of her desire and the full expression of her sense of self-worth, Rearden is left, as Francisco was before him, with only his maturity, his recaptured sense of being. Solitary, but not alone, for all three men and the woman are "in love—with the same thing, no matter what its forms." And in Rand's world, which is above all Aristotle's and Euclid's world, "A is A," as the title of her last section proclaims, all movement arises from the unmoved mover of legitimate self-love, and four people who are equal to the same first principle are equal to each other, as long as they live.

Essentially, Rand's novel portrays the victory of Aristotelian and Euclidean thought over Platonic and Planckian relativism. For them, as for John Galt, "reality" stays put and yields its truths to human observation. Only the villains celebrate, only the psychotic accept, the message of much twentieth-century physics and psychology, that matter is not solid or perfectly predictable and that the mind is at some level simply "a collection of switches without shape." In this respect, in addition to being, as Mimi Gladstein argues, both a science fiction romance and a feminist model, *Atlas Shrugged* is genuinely a "novel of ideas," and it belongs, all 1100 pages of it, on that reading list too.

References

Rand, Ayn. 1957. *Atlas Shrugged*. New York: Random House.

4

Ayn Rand:
A Traitor to Her Own Sex

Susan Brownmiller

[T]he victim of rape . . . is romanticized by Ayn Rand in *The Fountainhead*, the story of Dominique Francon and Howard Roark.

I had not looked at *The Fountainhead* [1943] for more than twenty years (it has remained in print for three decades), and when I requested it at the library, I was faintly anxious that the search for Dominique's undoing amid the more than seven hundred pages of Rand's opus might take more time than I cared to spend. I seriously underestimated the universality of my interest. The library's copy of *The Fountainhead* opened itself to Dominique's rape. Hundreds of other readers had, in effect, indexed it for me. And I must say, the two-and-a-half-page scene was as torrid as I had remembered it—all the more remarkable in the light of present-day fiction, since the genitals of the two antagonists are not even mentioned.

The vivid picture I had carried in my memory for more than twenty years was surprisingly accurate: architect Roark in work clothes, a stranger from the stone quarry, climbing through aristocrat Dominique's window late at night. The two of them locked in silent struggle. His victory, her defeat, and then his silent departure through the French windows. Not a word has been exchanged, but clearly this has been a coupling of heroes, a flashing signal of superior passion, a harbinger of the superior marriage that finally takes place offstage along about page 700.

And now, with the book before me, I can report verbatim Ayn Rand's philosophy of rape, as posited by Dominique, after the nocturnal visit of Roark:

> It was an act that could be performed in tenderness, as a seal of love, or in contempt, as a symbol of humiliation and conquest. It could be the act of a lover or the act of a soldier violating an enemy woman. He did it as an act of scorn. Not as love, but as defilement. And this made her lie still and submit. One gesture of tenderness from him—and she would have remained cold, untouched by the thing done to her body. But the act of a master taking shameful, contemptuous possession of her was the kind of rapture she had wanted. [231]

A week later Dominique is still mooning:

> I've been raped. . . . I've been raped by some redheaded hoodlum from a stone quarry. . . . I, Dominique Francon. . . . Through the fierce sense of humiliation, the words gave her the same kind of pleasure she had felt in his arms.
> . . . She wanted to scream it to the hearing of all. [233]

So this was grand passion! A masochistic wish by a superior woman for humiliation at the hands of a superior man! *The Fountainhead* heated my virgin blood more than twenty years ago and may still be performing that service for schoolgirls today.

Ayn Rand is the chief ideologue of a philosophy she calls Objectivism, essentially a cult of rugged individualism, vaguely right-wing, and what I would call spiritually male. She is an example of the ways in which a strong, male-directed woman accommodates herself to what she considers to be superior male thought. Roark is Rand's philosophic hero; Dominique is merely an attendant jewel, a prize of prizes. But if rape for Roark is an act of individual heroism, of manhood, of challenge met and coolly dispatched, then rape for Dominique must embody similar values. When superman rapes superwoman, superwoman has got to enjoy it—that is the bind Rand has gotten herself into. Rand becomes . . . a traitor to her own sex.

References

Rand, Ayn. 1943. The Fountainhead. Indianapolis: Bobbs-Merrill.

5

Psyching Out Ayn Rand

Barbara Grizzuti Harrison

Her idealized portrait stares, all bones and angles, intensity and reproach, from the covers of her novels: dark, avenging eyes, a sensual, implacable mouth, a cap of dark, sleek hair. (No smile.) She looks like one of (*all of*) her heroines. She has—this is how she writes about the faces of her heroes and her heroines—the incorruptible face of an executioner, or a saint.

The portrait is drawn by an artist named *Ilona*. She likes names like Ilona—and Dagny, and Dominique—exotic names that suggest heroism, names that manage to evoke both fragility and discipline, an excess of femininity and controlled strength. *She* would never write a novel about a woman called Joan or Barbara or Rose.

A lot of people think she's awfully silly. Some people think she's dangerous. There are those who adore her, with a fervor bordering on hysteria. She has inspired a cult.

Ayn Rand is the high priestess of the acute Right.

Born seventy-three years ago in St. Petersburg (now Leningrad),[1] Russia, Rand labored in the vineyards of make-believe before she found her true vocation. She was first a movie extra and a junior screenwriter for Cecil B. DeMille. After DeMille closed his studio, she worked as a waitress in a roadside cafe, then as an office worker in the wardrobe department of RKO, and finally as a scriptwriter for Hal Wallis Productions. After a short stint as a typist in the New York offices of architect Eli Jacques Kahn, she wrote *The Fountainhead*, the novel for which she became famous. If the sales figures of three decades are any indication, it is a novel which probably will never go out of print.

She is, she says, "virtually the only novelist who has declared that *her* soul is *not* a sewer, and neither are the souls of her characters, and neither is the soul of man" [Rand (1963) 1975, 172]. The only contemporary novels she admires—other than her own—are detective stories, and for years the one writer she regarded as an island of Romanticism in a sea of aesthetic boredom and moral depravity was Mickey Spillane. (Oh, I do wish I had invented her; she is truly *sui generis*, superbly perverse.)

She leaves any room that William F. Buckley, Jr., enters; having concluded at the age of thirteen that the concept of God is "morally evil," she regards Roman Catholic Buckley as a traitor to the cause of "full, pure, uncontrolled, unregulated laissez-faire capitalism" [Rand (1961) 1964, 33], which she espouses with a passion usually reserved for saints. Buckley is said to have presided over her excommunication from the "respectable" Right. Rand wonders why he should have troubled to do so, since she claims never to have been associated with him or his "followers"; "I abhor them," she says.

Fired by the conviction that the world is being destroyed by altruists, collectivists, communists, liberals, mystics, and "the mob" (words she frequently applies to those who don't march to a capitalist-atheist utopia in her footsteps), she no longer grants interviews. Nothing can convince her that interviewers are not soppy, unreasoning "looters" who derive exquisite pleasure from distorting her views.

Issuing broadsides in her newsletter, *The Objectivist*, she declares herself to be unalterably opposed to the "grotesque phenomenon" of Women's Liberation, and to the monstrous regiment of "sloppy, bedraggled, unfocused females" who are undertaking "to surpass the futile sordidness of a class war by instituting a sex war" [Rand (1971) 1975, 175].

She is also opposed to Medicare, public-housing projects, free abortions, free child-care centers, the progressive income tax, and any other kind of government aid.

She believes that liberal intellectuals are "frightened zombies" who are bent on destroying heroic industrialists; she declares that it is "moral cannibalism" to accept the premise that we are our brothers' keeper. She calls her "philosophy"—"the concept of man as a heroic being, with his own happiness as the moral purpose of his life, with productive achievement as his noblest activity, and reason as his only absolute"— Objectivism [Rand 1957, About the Author].

And she has had her "man in the White House." Rand disciple Alan Greenspan, a Nixon appointee, served as an economic adviser to President Ford. A conservative with a quasi-religious dedication to free enterprise, Greenspan says that she convinced him, through hours and hours of nocturnal argument, that capitalism is the only moral system.

In spite of their length, and in spite of their flat-footed, inelegant style, Ayn Rand's Fountainhead (1943) and Atlas Shrugged (1957) have sold more than 100,000 copies a year since their publication. Her monthly four-page Objectivist tract no longer exists. So little of her advice had been followed, she says, that she intends to return full-time to writing books: "The state of today's culture is so low that I do not care to spend my time . . . discussing it. I am haunted by a quotation from Nietzsche: 'It is not my function to be a flyswatter' " [Rand 1975, 2].

Rand may not be a flyswatter, but she certainly is a door-slammer. She maintains a stony silence about psychologist Nathaniel Branden, once primary promulgator of the Objectivist faith, which he sought to apply to psychotherapy. Branden acted in some way to incur Rand's wrath; but Rand will say no more than that he is "no longer associated with me or with my philosophy" [Rand 1968, 1]. In the sixties, Branden's effective proselytizing spawned a school of Objectivist therapists. The Nathaniel Branden Institute sponsored weekly lectures on Objectivism. (Rand is said to have had no financial interest in the institute.) At one lecture, according to writer Nora Sayre [1966], Branden rasped while Rand sat around like an eminence grise until her ire was sufficiently aroused. When someone demanded to know why non-Objectivists were unwelcome at lectures, "Miss Rand explained," Sayre says, "that anyone who disagrees with Objectivism is despicable and self-destructive; she then shouted, 'Let him go to hell his own way!' "

The literary establishment has never really taken Ayn Rand seriously. She couldn't care less. She has the imperturbable arrogance of one who knows she has The Truth. "There are very few guideposts to find," she says. "*The Fountainhead* is one of them." Those who reject the ideas set forth in *The Fountainhead* "are of no concern of mine; it is not me or *The Fountainhead* that they will betray; it is their own souls" [Rand 1968, xi].

She is not adorable. But she can't be shrugged off. Although it requires inordinate patience and devotion to turgid prose to read Rand's books— and although her sex scenes reek with sadomasochism—the lady speaks (as they say) to a lot of women; it's interesting to consider why.

The 1949 movie version of *The Fountainhead*—Rand adapted it for the screen—does little to explain the success or the appeal of the novel. A posturing Patricia Neal kept doing these jerky things—like throwing her favorite sculpture down an air shaft because it was too beautiful to exist in a world of commies and mystics and parasites and crowds of insipid people who resembled "soft shivering aspic"; she kept getting married a lot to men she didn't love, while resolutely refusing to marry the man she *did* love—because the thought of his perfection in an imperfect world drove her bonkers. ("Dominique," says Rand, "is myself in a bad mood" [in Branden and Branden 1962, 155]).

Gary Cooper, Neal's hero-lover, an architect rebuked and scorned for his excellence in a world of "second-handers," had to make a lot of speeches about man's spirit and skyscrapers and the virtues of selfishness, looking all the while as if he profoundly wished for a six-gun and a horse—which would have enlivened the proceedings considerably, inasmuch as Cooper looked about as comfortable at a drawing board as Frank Lloyd Wright would have looked on Trigger. The movie was not even fun-bad enough to be resurrected as camp.

The book, on the other hand, *is* fun-bad, though no less pretentious. *The Fountainhead* is a ripe and fanciful mixture of politics and sex. In case anybody can possibly have forgotten, Rand's architectural genius hero Howard Roark is thwarted (up to page 757) by liberals and mystics from building New York in his own image. Rand's novels end happily (which is to say, in *her* image); on page 758, the victorious Roark (a man with cruel eyes and hair "the exact color of ripe orange rind") is united atop New York with Rand's Dominique Francon (a woman with "an exquisitely vicious mouth," long legs, and emerald bracelets too heavy for her fragile wrists). The lovers deny themselves the right to marry until all of New York capitulates to Roark's architecture and his ego. In the closing scene, a windblown Dominique ascends in an open elevator to Roark, who is standing atop one of his buildings, blotting out the ocean and the sky. Heady stuff.

Rand [(1963) 1975, 167] describes herself as a Romantic Realist. Romantic? Yes—if one's ideas of romance derive from gothic novels and forties movies ("Nothing but your body, that mouth of yours, and the way your eyes would look at me if . . ."). A Realist? She says that her purpose is the "presentation of an ideal man." Well, if you're going to create heroes, you must, in conscience, give them real worlds to conquer. Rand, instead, sets up straw figures for her heroes and her heroines to knock down: her villains have names like Wesley Mouch and Ellsworth Toohey—and execrable physiques to match.

Rand's knowledge of the real world approximates that of one who has been hermetically sealed in the Chrysler Building since birth. (Anyone who can write a sentence like *Plato was the transmission belt by which Oriental mysticism infiltrated into Western culture* does not, to put it kindly, live anywhere but in her own head.) On the evidence of her novels, Rand appears to believe that the very poor have a terrific time because they can buy radios on the installment plan and do not mind "the feel and smell of one another's flesh on public beaches and public dance floors." And in *Atlas Shrugged,* she implies that American economic intervention in the "pestholes of Asia" and in the underdeveloped countries of Latin America is motivated by demented, savagely liberal altruists who wish wrongheadedly to lend a hand to the undeserving poor. (Now *you* didn't know that's what United Fruit was doing in the banana republics, did you?) Unreal.

Well, about those heroes of hers. I happen to think that women who devoured *The Fountainhead* and *Atlas Shrugged* were attracted, not to them, but to Rand's *heroines;* but we might as well get the gents out of the way first.

In Ayn Rand's tidy, black-and-white universe, all reasonable, rational men are also inordinately good-looking—and fast on the draw. In *The Fountainhead* [1943], Roark and Dominique *don't* waste any time talking before their first sexual encounter—which consists, as it happens, of Roark's raping Dominique. Roark's physical presence hits Dominique like "a slap in the face" [217]. She sees him working in a stone quarry, "his long fingers continuing the straight lines of the tendons that spread in a fan from his wrist to his knuckles," and she's a goner, longing to be "broken . . . weak with pleasure," all before she knows whether . . . he has passed third-grade math [218]. (Rand's assembly-line heroes all have pitiless eyes and scornful mouths; they discourse on the joys of oil derricks and power plants and the Industrial Revolution while they're unzipping their flies.)

There are three heroes in *Atlas Shrugged,* all in love with the same woman, and all remarkable examples of male bonding. Neither of the losers in the sweepstakes for Dagny Taggart's affections minds at all, when, after a lumbering Pilgrim's Progress, she chooses the most heroic of the heroes in the valley of the heroes. (They're like the Seven Dwarfs in their devotion to one another and to her.) One of the heroes distinguishes himself by destroying his own nationalized copper mine, in order to prove that the world cannot exist without unfettered capitalists to make things work.

In spite of their bizarre activities, justified by the Objectivist premise that it is moral to put one's own profit and achievement first, all Rand's heroes are given to the utterance of bromides, which they deliver as if they were unfurling defiant banners: "If one doesn't respect oneself, one can have neither love nor respect for others." Rand may lay claim to eminence and singularity, but platitudes like that are just as likely to crop up in assertiveness-training manuals or pop-psychology books—and just as likely to be accepted as gospel by needy people with low self-esteem.

One thing can be said about Rand's heroes: they don't take any crap. I suppose it's possible that women who cohabit with wishy-washy, effete, ineffectual men—men who wield worldly power, but who have little authentic authority—have been drawn to Rand's juggernaut heroes because they are able to take the reins so firmly and make the world work for them, and for their women.

Maybe. But I'm inclined to believe that the women who love Rand's books are seduced by an age-old formula: they identify themselves, in fantasy, with a strong, dominant woman who is subdued by an even stronger, more dominant male; with the independent woman who must, to preserve her integrity, capitulate to a more powerful man. Rand gave women romantic heroines who managed to combine hothouse femininity with stern military precision of thought and action.

Rand told women what their experience had unhappily prepared them to believe—that man was the life force and woman could respond to nothing else, that man had the "will" of life, and prime power. Then she added a thrilling kicker: she placed these men at the feet of her heroines. " 'Kiss my hand, Roark.' He would kneel and kiss her ankle. . . . she felt herself owned more than ever, by a man who could . . . still remain controlled and controlling—as she wanted him to remain" [331]. Rand gave women haughty, indomitable, fierce heroines—who sang in their chains and found ecstasy in surrender.

There is—provided one lobotomizes the political-feminist part of one's brain—a certain amount of delicious, randy fun to be found in this stuff. Rand knows how to push the atavistic dream-machine buttons. Her "delicately austere" heroines move serenely and aristocratically through crowds of overblown, overdressed women, standouts and knockouts in their chaste severe costumes (which are usually your basic black with lots of diamonds and shoulder bones showing, or dresses "the color of ice" melded to bodies that have never heard of cellulite). And nobody ever *telephones* anybody in her novels. The heroes make Superman-dramatic unannounced visits to the always immaculate penthouse apartments of their waiting perfumed heroines. They come bearing crude bracelets made of some new revolutionary steel they've just invented.

There are some yummy visual set pieces in *The Fountainhead*. Dominique dines in solitary splendor: "A shallow crystal bowl stood in a pool of light in the center of the long table, with a single water lily spreading white petals about a heart yellow like a drop of candle fire." She bathes in a sunken bathtub, "the hyacinth odor of her bath salts, the aquamarine tiles polished, shining under her feet, the huge towels spread out like snowdrifts to swallow her body" [215]. Ah, shades of Cecil B.—Rand's apprenticeship in Hollywood served her well.

She said it before Gloria Vanderbilt did: you can't be too skinny or too rich.

Executive women were hardly popular in the fiction of the forties and fifties. Rand—who says, somewhat obscurely, that men are "metaphysically the dominant sex"—created imperious women who melted at superheroes' touch. She never made the mistake of scaring traditional women off with shoulder-padded Joan Crawford types. She gave us women who were capable of running the world—but who rejoiced in being "a luxury object" for "the amusement" of a powerful man; Dagny Taggart can make transcontinental trains run on time, but she is never happier than when she is sewing buttons on the stained and sweaty work clothes of her man.

Rand gave us women who were ruthless with those they perceived to be their inferiors, but who blissfully received "dark satisfaction in pain" from the men they adored.

From there, of course, it's a skip and a jump to sadomasochism.

The question of whether women's oppression has so damaged us that we enjoy wallowing in masochistic fantasies is a vexing one (and I don't propose to try to resolve it). But if women want S-M dream trips, they have only to read Ayn Rand.

On Dominique's second meeting with Roark, she, on horseback, slashes him across the face with a branch . . . because she hates herself for longing to be "defiled" by him. Next thing you know, there he is in her hyacinth-scented bedroom, "austere in cruelty, ascetic in passion." And he rapes her. And she loves it, purple bruises (which go well with emeralds) and all. "He did it as an act of scorn. Not as love, but as defilement. And this made her lie still and submit. One gesture of tenderness from him—and she would have remained cold, untouched by the thing done to her body. But the act of a master taking shameful, contemptuous possession of her was the kind of rapture she had wanted" [231–33].

After that first fine careless rapture, D. discovers that Roark is not just a common laborer but an architect whose buildings are so beautiful they give her multiple orgasms. Precisely because his buildings are so beautiful, she decides to destroy him. She cannot bear the thought of his buildings, in a world of neoclassical architecture and tenements, being desecrated by such plebeian artifacts as "family photographs . . . dirty socks . . . and grapefruit rinds." (And I thought the rich *lived* on grapefruit.)

"I hate you, Roark," Dominique says, ". . . for what you are, for wanting you, for having to want you. . . . I want to be owned, not by a lover, but by an adversary who will destroy my victory over him, not with honorable blows, but with the touch of his body on mine" [290]. After this extraordinary speech, Roark says—and under the circumstances, it's hard to think what else he could say—"Take your clothes off." Sex is all "clenched teeth and hatred" from there on in, till Roark and Dominique blow up a public-housing project in a final act of cathartic violence that paves the way for them to marry and raise little skyscrapers in their gladiatorial image.

Rand says that she appeals to "rational egoists." I think, on the contrary, that she appeals both to narcissism and to self-hatred, traits which are apparently mutually exclusive but which in fact often coexist in one fragmented personality: scratch a narcissist, and you often find, beneath the veneer of braggadocio, a frightened self-loather.

One way to bolster weak egos is to tell people that they're better than all those other poor slobs they see around them. It isn't rational—but it can be ego-enhancing for people with terminally poor self-images.

In Rand's books, the sick and the unemployed are the victims of their own incompetence—all poor slobs. When children appear in her novels, they are sniveling, squalling, soggy, ugly brats, given to writing dirty words on sidewalks and grotesquely in need of orthodontics. Villains are likely to be "mama's boys." "Breeders" (mothers) are overprotective, corseted, squashy women with fat ankles and bullying personalities. Rand's idea of polar opposites is "a starving genius" and "a pregnant slut."

I hate to think that women hold themselves in such low esteem that they'll buy this horseshit; I'm bound to conclude, however, that for many women, traditional wife/mother roles are so unrewarding that they'll lap up fantasies of a pure, clean, competent, radiant life that most definitely does not include damp babies and runny noses. (In a 1964 *Playboy* interview with Alvin Toffler, Rand allowed as how it was okay for a woman to have as her vocation the raising of a family provided it was done with "science" and without "emotional indulgence.")

I guess by now it's obvious that I'm straining hard to find a charitable explanation for Rand's continuing appeal to women. Basically, I think the appeal to women who have spent so much energy—with so little return—on gaining the approval of others, and the appeal to women who have led sacrificial lives, is Rand's clarion call to selfishness. If you've spent a lifetime being "nice"—and not being rewarded for being nice—it must feel very good when someone comes along and makes a virtue of selfishness. It certainly short-circuits political analysis; it also puts women right back, masochistically, into thinking that *they* are the cause of their own oppression, and hooks them with the less-than-novel idea that all oppressed people can pull themselves up by their own bootstraps.

Rand allows women to have their sacrificial cake and eat it too: she would, she says, step in front of a bullet aimed at her husband, not because she is altruistic (heaven forbid!), but because he is an objective value she cannot live without. That's what's known as being *selfishly* sacrificial. (Rand's husband, to whom she's been married for forty-eight years, is Frank O'Connor, an artist whose work has decorated her book jackets.)

I've been writing as if only women buy and read and follow Ayn Rand. That's unfair and untrue. Men love Rand too. They are people who enjoy a measure of economic comfort but suffer from the pervasive fear that "welfare looters" and Third World "bums" will take it all away from them. Rand panders to the fears of the middle class; she does so with phony equations: give housing to the unemployed, she says, and people who work to earn a modest living will go homeless. Government bureaucrats are inept, she says (and she's not going to find many who will contradict her); so the answer is not to regulate industry at all.

And since so many Americans are indeed overtaxed and underrewarded, Rand's false and pernicious equations—which refuse to name our real enemies—exert an enormous appeal. She flourishes in a climate of despair.

I think of her man who once worked in the White House; and I am afraid of Ayn Rand.[2]

Notes

1. Ed. note: This article was published in 1978, when Rand was seventy-three years old.
2. Ed. note: Harrison, here, speaks again of Alan Greenspan, who subsequently became chairman of the Federal Reserve Board. See our Introduction.

References

Branden, Nathaniel, and Barbara Branden. 1962. *Who Is Ayn Rand? An Analysis of the Novels of Ayn Rand.* New York: Random House.
Rand, Ayn. 1943. *The Fountainhead.* Indianapolis: Bobbs-Merrill.
———. 1957. *Atlas Shrugged.* New York: Random House.
———. [1961] 1964. The Objectivist ethics. In *The Virtue of Selfishness: A New Concept of Egoism.* New York: New American Library.
———. [1963] 1975. The goal of my writing. In *The Romantic Manifesto: A Philosophy of Literature,* 2d rev. ed. New York: New American Library. Originally published in *The Objectivist Newsletter,* October–November 1963.
———. 1968. To whom it may concern. *The Objectivist,* May.
———. [1968] 1993. Introduction to the 25th anniversary ed. of *The Fountainhead.* In *The Fountainhead,* 50th anniversary ed. New York: New American Library.
———. [1971] 1975. The age of envy. In *The New Left: The Anti-Industrial Revolution,* 2d rev. ed. New York: New American Library. Originally published in *The Objectivist,* July–August 1971.
———. 1975. A last survey, part 1. *Ayn Rand Letter* 4, no. 2.
Sayre, Nora. 1966. The cult of Ayn Rand. *New Statesman* 11 (March): 332.

6

Reflections on Ayn Rand

Camille Paglia

REASON MAGAZINE: Somebody once described you as "Ayn Rand on mushrooms." I'm curious whether at some point in your life you've had any encounter with Ayn Rand's work or people influenced by her.

PAGLIA: Ayn Rand was an enormous figure for people who were intellectuals in college in the mid-'50s and late '50s. I entered college in '64, so I never heard her name in college. She was just gone.

I never read Ayn Rand until people started to compare me to her. Since I came on the scene, it has come up repeatedly—people have asked me about Ayn Rand, followers of Ayn Rand. I might be on a call-in show; they always asked. Because I was being asked so much, I went out and I read some of Ayn Rand. And I was struck. I could see what the parallels are.

That is, she was influenced by many of the same works that I was. She was reading Romantic thinkers and Nietzsche and so on. There are certain passages in her where I went, "Oh my God, that sounds like a passage from *Sexual Personae*." So I was really struck.

At the same time, I saw the differences. First of all, she's a libertarian or a radical individualist as I am, but she is very—like Simone de Beauvoir—contemptuous of religion. I am an atheist, but I *respect* religion. I respect all the world religions, and I regard them as these symbol systems, belief systems that are like poetry. I *love* these great mythological systems. I feel that mystical and religious thinking tells you more about the universe in many ways than ordinary prose, or even science, does.

So I'm uncomfortable with that. For both de Beauvoir and Ayn Rand religion is symptomatic of an infantile mind, or of an overemotional mind. I believe in mystery; I believe in both Apollo *and* Dionysus. So I think that my system is more complete.

And what else? I find both Simone de Beauvoir and Ayn Rand deficient in humor. Comedy is my attitude toward life, and I feel that comedy is the spirit of the last half of the twentieth century. The first half of the twentieth century would have been the age of Beckett and *Waiting for Godot* and that whole bleak, nihilistic attitude toward the world that Susan Sontag is still carrying around with her like a big black hat. The attitude of the last fifty years is like that of rock and roll—energy, comedy, exuberance, the pleasure principle, improvisation, spontaneity. These are my principles. So I think I have a kind of childlike quality and playfulness that are missing from the dour adulthood of both Simone de Beauvoir and Ayn Rand.

Also I am a little bit uneasy, OK, with the politics. I don't think that Ayn Rand is a fascist particularly, but I think there is a kind of contempt for ordinary people in Ayn Rand—a little bit. I love the high achiever. I am a great worshiper of the high achiever. But I also feel at home with people of the working class. And I think that in Rand there's a little bit of a kind of snobbish elitism about those vulgar masses out there. That makes me a little uncomfortable with her.

But I think if one is looking for parallels, there is no doubt that there are a lot. I'm very happy to be considered one of her successors, even if not influenced by her directly. And I think there is no doubt that my impact on many people is exactly like her impact on many people. That is, we came as a kind of a fresh breeze into a period of conformism. She and I say to people, "Think for yourself! Don't be such a toadie! Stop going along with the group! Don't be such a sheep, just going along passively with other people!"

One would think that women's studies, if it really obeyed its mission, would make her part of the agenda. But no, of course not! Women's studies has been oriented toward rediscovering the mediocre thinker, or the writer who talks about her victimization, rather than someone who preaches individualism and independence as Ayn Rand does.

Part Two

Feminist Rereadings of Rand's Fiction

7

Ayn Rand and Feminist Synthesis: Rereading *We the Living*

Valérie Loiret-Prunet

Women and Dualism

In her book *Women and Dualism: A Sociology of Knowledge Analysis*, Lynda Glennon (1979) confronts the feminist responses to the mind-body dualities of modernism. Glennon tells us that modern dualism tends to dichotomize "emotionality and functionality [as] polar opposites" (2), granting to women the sphere of emotion, and to men the sphere of reason (3).[1] For Glennon, today's "feminists are questioning the logic of duality," even though they sometimes reproduce the polarities they seek to transcend.

Glennon identifies four ways in which feminists have dealt with dualism in humanity and society. These Weberian "ideal types" within feminism are Instrumentalism, Expressivism, Polarism, and Synthesism (5).

The Instrumentalist model views people as most authentic when they are rational, productive, and self-interested. It solves the dualism between emotional women and rational men by urging women to eliminate their expressive tendencies and to embrace a technocratic instrumental monism. It is the model that feminists least identify with, but it is prevalent among middle-class career women, and is expressed, Glennon says, in the "individualistic, objectivistic ethos of Ayn Rand" (47).

By contrast, the Expressivist model embraces an emotionalist monism. It maximizes "typical" femininity by fully embracing communal, spontaneous, nonmanipulative social relations (8). It elevates female expressivity to a position of superiority.

Whereas Instrumentalism and Expressivism embrace monism as a response to modern dualities, Polarism maintains the dualities and asks women and men simply to pursue their true gender selves.

Synthesism, for Glennon, is the most dialectical alternative. It aims for a fusion of reason and emotion, "feminine" and "masculine" characteristics, and rejects the divisions of self as dehumanizing. Glennon suggests that in contrast to the dyadic presumptions of Instrumentalist, Expressivist, and Polarist types, the Synthesist model echoes the triadic organizations in Hegelian "logic" (100), in which the transcendence of polar opposites is achieved through a higher synthesis. This conjunction of synthesis and triadic identity has been well noted by a generation of post-Hegelian philosophers, including Karl Marx, and many feminists, including the American psychologist Lillian Rubin. Rubin (1983), who worked on the theories of Nancy Chodorow, the author of *The Reproduction of Mothering* (1978), argues that there is a tendency for men to reproduce dyadic structures, while women embrace triadic ones. These distinctions are dysfunctional, in Rubin's view, for they are supported and enhanced by social institutions in ways that fragment the development of boys and girls.

Interestingly, this very focus on the institutional roots of dyadic fragmentation is a hallmark of radical feminist critique.[2] Glennon (1979) reminds us that the advocates of triadic Synthesism are almost always "[f]eminists of a more radical persuasion" who assume that *capitalism* engenders both dualism and "masculinist" Instrumentalism, and that such dysfunctionality can only be conquered through socialist or communist transformation (21). Indeed, the "Synthesist world-view resembles what Marx had in mind for utopian communism" (114).[3]

But Glennon suggests that radical feminists are mistaken to

> assume that if socialism or communism replaced capitalism, the "woman problem" would vanish. Capitalism does contain the most advanced form of dualism in evidence today, but any society that operates on technocratic premises dooms women to unhappiness. . . . Soviet women (and men) also must face the problems of dualism that are built into technocracy. The issue is not capitalism per se. Technocracy creates and nourishes the dualism in our lives, and as a particular form of this dualism, the modern version of the gulf between men and women. (21)

Given these distinctions between Instrumentalist, Expressivist, Polarist, and Synthesist ideal types, it is understandable that Glennon would characterize Rand as a fully Instrumentalist thinker. Rand, after all, believed in the supreme moral and practical efficacy of reason. She was a profound individualist who emphasized self-motivation, objective standards, production, and *capitalism* as key factors in the sustenance of human life. Rand seems to be, at first glance, a paradigmatic case of the Instrumentalist model.

And Glennon is not alone in her characterization. In suggesting Rand's affinity with a rationalistic, "emotionally managed" model of human identity, Glennon would agree with the assessments of such critics as Albert Ellis (1968) and Hazel Barnes (1967), who both lament what they view as Rand's one-sided, monistic emphasis on reason to the detriment of emotion. Norman Barry (1987, 112) has argued further that Rand's philosophy is an exercise in linear, "deductive reasoning from first principles." And even some followers of Ayn Rand, like James G. Lennox (1996, 13), would agree with critics such as William O'Neill (1971, 83), who sees in Objectivism an operational dualism between the self and the world.

To examine and qualify each of these differing conceptions is beyond the scope of this paper.[4] My aim here is somewhat different. I believe that while there may be Instrumentalist aspects to Rand's work, she is *primarily* a theorist of synthesis. While proving such a contention would require an examination of the full Randian canon, I focus here on the triadic patterns of synthesis present in Rand's first, most Russian novel—*We the Living*.[5] Among its unique features, the novel's central protagonist is a woman, Kira Argounova, who—more than Dominique Francon in *The Fountainhead*, more than Dagny Taggart in *Atlas Shrugged*—is Ayn Rand. Rand (1995b, xviii–xix) tells us that this novel

> is as near to an autobiography as I will ever write. It is not an autobiography in the literal, but only in the intellectual, sense. . . . It is only in this sense that *We the Living* is my autobiography and that Kira, the heroine, is me. I was born in Russia, I was educated under the Soviets, I have seen the conditions of existence that I describe. The particulars of Kira's story were not mine; I did not study engineering, as she did—I studied history; I did not want to build bridges—I wanted to write; her physical appearance bears no resemblance to mine, neither does her family. The specific events of Kira's life were not mine; her ideas, her convictions, her values were and are.

By focusing on Rand's alter ego, Kira, as a model of synthesis and seamless unity, and by tracing the elements of triadic organization throughout, I believe that we can uncover an unexpected resource for feminist scholarship on dualism. What is most remarkable here is that Rand's patterns of synthesis center on her female protagonist, rather than the two male characters—Leo Kovalensky and Andrei Taganov—who remain dyadic and fractured. What distinguishes Rand from other radical feminist Synthesists, however, is her rejection of their Marxist political ideal. Whereas Glennon questions the exclusive connections between capitalism and dualism, Rand goes a step further: she sees statism and collectivism as among the institutional sources of modern dualities and social fragmentation.

Hence, while radical feminists have attacked masculinist and capitalist social conditions in their revolt against dualism, it is doubly ironic that Rand, a woman philosopher, grasps the inextricable link between the personal and the political, advocating *both* synthesis *and* libertarian capitalism.[6] By examining the patterns of synthesis in Rand's most anti-Communist novel, *We the Living*, feminists might reengage the Randian canon in a manner that is productive of important theoretical consequences. Indeed, Rand's unusual integration might challenge some radical feminists to reconsider the very nature of modern dualism and its links to the growth of collectivist ideology and state power.

Rand's synthesis takes place in virtually every aspect of her novel: stylistically, substantively, and philosophically. The very fabric of Rand's literary style is organically linked to her philosophical substance. Rand (1975b, 40) herself said: "The theme of an art work is the link uniting its subject and its style. 'Style' is a particular, distinctive, or characteristic mode of execution. An artist's style is the product of his own psycho-epistemology [method of awareness]—and, by implication, a projection of his view of man's consciousness."

What must be remembered too, is that Rand's style is deliberate; she once remarked "that there was not a single word in her novels whose purpose she could not explain" (in Branden 1962, 135). And she often viewed her own descriptions as written on four interconnected levels, such that there were many integrated layers of meaning: the literal, the connotative, the symbolic, and the emotional (136). This is not to say that Rand wrote in a self-conscious manner; her own conception of the process of creative writing suggests a literary craft heavily informed by introspection and the tacit dimensions of the subconscious (Sciabarra 1995, 204–10). But Rand seems to know what she is doing, even if she does not grasp it in the terms I employ in this paper.

Rand's style in We the Living ranges from simple images of three and ternary rhythms to quite complex triadic sentences reflecting a deep trinitary style-thought integration. By "ternary," I mean that Rand's literary rhythm often encompasses a succession of three terms. By "triadic," I mean a logical relation between three terms. And by "trinitary," I mean a synchronic whole of three points. By extension, "binary" means a simple construction in two, a combination of two; "dyadic" means a logical, or more organized, relation between two terms, whereas "dualism" refers to the theory that recognizes two independent—if not opposed—principles or ideas.[7] In using each of these techniques, Rand exhibits, in We the Living, a high level of artistic integration between style and subject.

Synthesis in Style

We the Living is extraordinarily rich in images of three, ternary rhythms, and triadic patterns of style. According to their philosophical importance, it is possible to classify these images, ranging from the simplest, which appear as mere clues or hints, to ternary rhythms in the construction of sentences (a succession of three tempos or a group of three sentences) and, finally, to triadic sentences (a construction in three points) (see Diagram 1).

Diagram 1

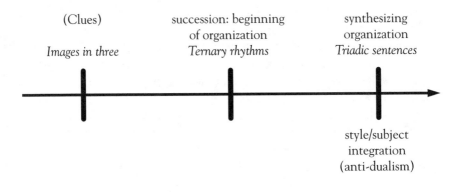

Images in Three and Ternary Rhythms: From Repetition to Unity

Images in three are numerous in the whole book. Let us consider the following:

- By 1922, "[i]t had taken two weeks to make a three days' trip—from the Crimea to Petrograd" (Rand 1995b, 3). It is possible that Rand's observation is the result of experience, and that during the czarist period she had traveled from the Crimea to Petrograd in a more timely fashion. But there are other images of three that cannot be dismissed so easily. For instance:
- Lydia, Kira's sister, tells the other train passengers that she is not used to "such mode of traveling." She does not "condescend to hide outward signs of social superiority, of which she proudly displayed three: a jabot of tarnished gold lace on her faded velvet suit, a pair of meticulously darned silk gloves, and a bottle of eau-de-cologne" (5). This imagery in three could still be seen as coincidence. Yet the imagery is repeated in other small, unimportant details:

- When Maria Petrovna counts out logs to put in the fire, at their arrival in Petrograd, she painfully counts out three logs (22).
- When Kira calls Leo's name, she repeats it three times: "repeating . . . a name as a drug: 'Leo . . . Leo . . . Leo . . .' " (338).[8]

The purpose here is not simply to catalogue the instances of such imagery, or to read too much symbolism into simple facts. Yet such signs, which may not have deep philosophical significance, might be a subconscious resurgence of Rand's own concerns with triadic synthesis, traces of the molding of her thought, of ironical *clins d'oeil,* or of an instinctive choice by the author of the number three. Moreover, such imagery appears in more complex ways, accompanied by a ternary leitmotif in the rhythm and grouping of sentences. For example:

> [1] The smell of carbolic acid rose higher than all the rest. [2] Station buildings were disinfected against the diseases that poured into the city on every train. [3] Like a breath from a hospital window, the odor hung in the air as a warning and a grim reminder. (14)

In this group of three sentences, in which the length of each sentence increases, Rand creates a ponderous, painfully heavy rhythm, reinforced by the semantic field of threat, menace, and sickness—"acid," "disinfected," "hospital," "odor," "warning," "grim." These sentences are grouped in a single paragraph that is cut off from the rest of the text. As a unit, they offer a meaningful, illustrative pause, a reflection on the atmosphere of Petrograd. At least ten times in the first part of her novel, whenever she wishes to highlight such special meaning, Rand uses this literary technique, a grouping of three sentences. Even when Kira describes Andrei for the first time, Rand writes: "She watched his tall figure walking on hurriedly, his shoulders erect in his leather jacket, his feet steady on the ice" (62).

Here the repetitive pattern focuses on Andrei's physical self-assurance, which Kira admires. The rhythm, or grouping, in three is Rand's technique of laying stress on a particular atmosphere or feeling. These patterns in three do not express a triple meaning, that is, three differently expressed ideas, but one meaning (sickness or disease in the sentences describing Petrograd, and self-confidence in the ones describing Andrei). The device is accumulative and repetitive.

Triadic Patterns: Synthesis in Style

Triadic Sentences: The Beginning of Synthesizing Organization

More complex than the above examples, in both their organization and significance, are sentences Rand constructs that are not merely ternary but triadic. These triadic sentences can be found very frequently throughout the novel. By triadic, I mean a whole, an organic unity of three points, whose structuring is not linear but an implication of transcendence. At the very least, it is a real triangular relation. Such sentences are all organized the same way and have a common point: the triadic relation is based on the repetition of one of the points, which appears common to the two others. This pattern is similar in every instance in which it is used, and the rhythm is always ternary. The first example is to be found at the beginning of the novel (4): "Kira Argounova had not started the journey in a box car. At the start, she had a choice seat: the little table at the window of a third-class passenger coach [1]; the little table was the center of the compartment [2], and Kira—the center of the passengers' [3] attention." "Center" is the term common to the two other elements, and the whole structuring is based on this mutual link (see Diagram 2).

Diagram 2

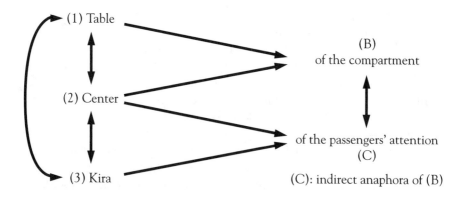

Stylistically, the impression given is a typically Russian one: that of opening a kind of nest of dolls, one after the other.[9] Yet upon closer inspection, we see the perfect interweaving of a system that is undoubtedly the result of a deeply organized and synthesizing mode of thought: the woman, Kira, is literally and figuratively at the center of things. The triadic relation—table/center/Kira—by the way it is constructed, expresses more than an accumulation, or an insistence on a feeling. It deals with, and reveals, an essential concept of Rand's thought: the synthesizing value of the individual standing at the center of everything. Indeed, the individual stands at the very center of Rand's Objectivist philosophy. And it is noteworthy that, in this context, the center is an individual *woman*, Rand's self-acknowledged alter ego.

Thus we see here two types of ternary rhythms: simple ones, organized on a linear sequence, whose effect is repetition or insistence; and more complex ones, such as the above example, which, through a very specific pattern of "pivot" terms, contains a triadic organization that is, in each instance, philosophically meaningful. Many more examples of this can be found. In the very last sentence of the novel, when Kira dies, thinking of her life abroad with Leo, one can find a ternary rhythm (433): [1] "She smiled, [2] her last smile, [3] to so much that had been possible."

The Style of Communism: Ternary Patterns

The sentence structure that Rand uses for Andrei Taganov, the misguided, idealistic Communist in *We the Living*, shows, ironically, similar ternary patterns. In keeping with Glennon's suggestion of an identity between Synthesism and communism, Sciabarra (1995) has remarked that Marxism, at least in its origins, expressed a genuine yearning for synthesis (37–40). But Rand loathed the Marxist synthesis in praxis, and materialism that abolished the value of the individual. Yet, consciously or not, through the character of Andrei, Rand (1995b) acknowledges the fact that Kira's and Andrei's modes of thought are similar, even though they culminate in antagonistic, antithetical ideals. Let us consider one example, in which Andrei speaks of the Communist movement of his day:

> Still if I had a choice, I'd want to be born when I was born [. . .] because now [1] we don't sit and dream, [2] we don't moan, [3] we don't wish—[1] we do, [2] we act, [3] we build! (72)

Here we have a perfect example of a double antithetical ternary sequence, whose effect is to condemn the indecisive, impractical, wait-and-see policy of czarist times, and to glorify the Marxist philosophy of praxis through the masses: "We." With Andrei, as with Kira, one concept (action) is repeated three times, with the final manifestation its concretization: "we build!" But it is not only in Andrei's political statements that ternary rhythms can be found; even when he speaks to Kira, the pattern is similar (309): [1] "Kira, the highest thing in a man is not his god. [2] It's that in him which knows the reverence due a god. [3] And you, Kira, are my highest reverence. . . ."

It is not surprising to find this rhythm here, since Andrei transfers his highest reverence from Communism to Kira. But even with a change in ideal, the mode of thought remains. In these three sentences, there is a dialectical movement (it is not his god, it is that which knows the reverence due a god) culminating in synthesis (Kira). The mode is not only ternary, but triadic as well. It also illustrates stylistically Kira's instinct that she and Andrei function in the same mode: "[Y]ou see, if we had souls [. . .] and if our souls met—yours and mine—they'd fight to the death. But after they had torn each other to pieces, to the very bottom, they'd see that they had the same root" (97).

It is worth noticing that these ternary rhythms and triadic organizations belong quite exclusively to Andrei.[10] Some other sentences, not expressed by him, illustrate a dualistic pattern: "Red letters announced: LONG LIVE THE DICTATORSHIP OF THE PROLETARIAT! WHO IS NOT WITH US—IS AGAINST US!" (13). Exemplified in Rand's style, the very slogan of the Communist Party expresses a profound dualism. Thus, despite its yearning for synthesis, Communism, in Rand's view, created a dualistic antagonism between the individual and the community.

Rand's view is consistent with Glennon's own acknowledgment that "Soviet women (and men) also must face the problems of dualism" (1979, 21). But as Sciabarra (1995) suggests, for Rand, "Communism both constituted and perpetuated a social dichotomy between the individual and the masses. . . . In such a system the individual has no alternative but conflict with the society at large" (104). Thus, we see how communism, at its best, symbolized by the idealistic Andrei, functions principally in a ternary mode of thought, even as it rapidly descends into dualism, opposing the individual to society, divorcing value and fact, forcing the individual to adopt attitudes of conflict.

Some feminist critics and writers, such as Carol Gilligan (1987), Sara Ruddick (1986), and Cynthia Hampton (1994), have suggested that the separation and opposition in dualist thinking leads to alienation and violence. For in seeking to close the vast gulf between fragmented spheres in a dualistic world, alienated people often resort to brutality, rather than genuine synthesis and integration. Many radical feminists typically view the communist ideal as the essential means of conquering such dualism. Hence, Rand's indictment of communism as an expression of dualist alienation and violence runs counter to the assumptions of her socialist feminist adversaries. That she aims in *We the Living* for synthesis rather than Instrumentalism is, then, both startling and provocative.

According to Emile Beveniste (1966, 1:325), the famous French linguist, we find the notion of rhythm in its linguistic expression, that is, "a spatial configuration defined by the arranging and distinctive proportion of elements." Ternary and binary rhythms, linguistic manifestations of very old and essential modes of thought, are the two basic rhythms used in literature; their alternation and interpenetration always create meaningful patterns. In this sense, one might say that Rand's predominating choice of ternary rhythms in her fiction is proof of a style (ternary rhythms and sentences, triadic structures) and subject (antidualism and synthesis) integration.

Rand also seems to have an instinctive and essential understanding of rhetoric, of the very nature of language. She expresses an affinity for rhetoric in that she wrote fiction in order to explain, to convince, and to denote, rather than simply to describe or imagine. But she was also a passionate disciple of Aristotle, who reestablished the value of rhetoric, while Plato, whom Rand detested, had denounced it as pure sophism. Aristotle's *On Rhetoric*, which Rand must have read, abounds with ternary notions and images. Moreover, she must have agreed with Aristotle's theory of logical, formal literary criticism, which centered on the text rather than on its historical or religious context. As Holman and Harmann (1992, 339) remark, "Aristotle's chief contribution is closely reasoned argument in favor of the complex relation—cause and effect, means and end, form and matter." This integrative view of the text could be a definition of Rand's theory of fiction as exemplified in *We the Living*. She seems to refute binary rhythms and sentences (when she did not use them on purpose to illustrate their negative effects and meaning) as expressive of the style of dualism. In Rand's work, such dualism was a polemical style concerned primarily with opposition, offering no resolution in synthesis. Thus, for Rand, the style-subject integration was clear: Communism had engendered dualism and opposition; its "airtight" environment crushed any prospects for the emergence of human synthesis.

Synthesis in Thought

The Plot of We The Living: The Triangle Pattern as Formal Trinity

It has been said of the plot of *We The Living* that the triangular relationship between the characters Kira, Leo, and Andrei is a classic literary pattern of "one woman between two men." Rand supposedly found inspiration for the triangular relationship in one of her favorite plays, *Monna Vanna*, by Maurice Maeterlinck. Such triangles can be found in many other narratives. Ronald Merrill (1991) observes: "As Nathaniel Branden has pointed out, this ancient cliche provides the plot for Tosca and many other stories" (34). *We the Living*, in its triangular structure and narrative, is thus an example of an archetypal plot.

But this triangular structure is far more interesting and complex than it seems to be: it is not only a triangle but a perfect example of a formal trinity. The French linguist and philosopher Dany-Robert Dufour suggests that, at the heart of all great and classic forms or patterns of narration, we are likely to find at least a tertiary or triadic preoccupation or structure, and at best an instance of what he calls a "formal" or "radical" trinity. According to Dufour (1990), every great narrative (be it an odyssey, an epic, or the Bible) or classic pattern of narration, being rooted in language, reproduces literally or figuratively the original and natural trinity of language found in the process of speech and thought based on *je* (I), *tu* (you), and *il* (it or him) (141–42).

In speech, there is always an "I," a subject, or what linguists call an "addresser," who speaks to a "you," the "addressee," about an "it" or "him," a referent or "referred-to." The particularity of this "it," according to Dufour (and Beveniste as well),[11] is that "it," "the third" person, is not necessarily present. "It" can be present or absent, or present in its absence (as referred to). Dufour sees this "it" as the metaphoric and symbolic "empty place" at the core of each individual's future, and life, that is to say, death. In the interplay of personal pronouns, "it" or "him" is capital: "it brings into relation the first 'I' and the second 'you'" (141). A third one is needed to have a first and second one, "and this relationship in three cannot be fragmented in dyadic relations" (142).

In Dufour's view, all the trichotomies, triads, tertiary sequences are anamorphoses of the most basic and simple trine pattern: the form *je* (I)–*tu* (you)–*il* (it-him).[12] In my view, the triangular relationship between

Kira, Leo, and Andrei expresses an anamorphosis of the trine pattern of language. Kira is the principal narrative voice (and the author's voice), and can be seen as the "I," or first-person subject of the triangle. Moreover, Kira stands for "I," the self, the individual in the story and in Rand's philosophy. Leo can be seen as the second person, the "you" to whom Kira speaks in her heart and life, her prime "addressee." And Andrei, who comes third in the story (Kira meets him after Leo), is the "it-him," or the "third" person. Some illuminating ideas emerge from this organization of the characters (see Diagram 3).

Diagram 3

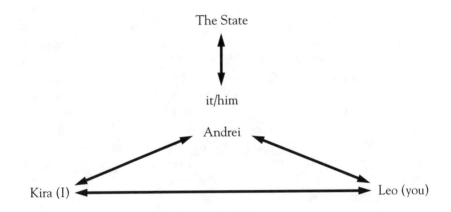

As Dufour says, the "third person," present or absent, is what permits the two other persons to be. It is true that Kira meets and establishes a relationship with Leo before meeting Andrei. Yet this relationship could not continue without Andrei, since it is through Andrei that an ailing Leo is sent to the Crimea for medical treatment. Thus, metaphorically, Andrei, the third person, is both present (in his meetings with Kira and in the story) and absent (from Kira and Leo's relationship). Kira does not tell Leo about Andrei, and Leo does not know that Andrei is Kira's lover, or that Andrei is giving money to Kira to sustain Leo's life.

Andrei can also be viewed, at the beginning of the novel, as the physical and moral embodiment of the ideal of Communism, the Collective One that Kira calls an "entity." Andrei's cause is "to bring the millions up to where I want them" (Rand 1995b, 71). For the first two-thirds of the novel, he is married to Communism, to the ideal of the Collective with which he is One. This Collective One is organized and dominated by the State, which is also, through Andrei, the third person, the "it" that forces Kira, as Sciabarra (1995) observes, "to see the world dualistically, in terms of herself versus everyone else" (105). Unlike those feminists who see capitalism as the source of dualities, Rand sees the State as evil here, for it perpetuates a social dualism in people's lives and thoughts.[13]

But the "it," the State through Andrei, is also both "present" (in its everyday-life manifestations—the banners, the slogans, the squalor, the terrible living conditions of the people) and "absent" as a whole, an entity, towering invisibly, like Big Brother, above the masses. In this "empty place" of the third person, we have the symbolic place of what is both present and absent as the Law (be it the God of the Christian Trinity,[14] or the State in Marxism, or the Name of the Father in the Lacanian Oedipus organization of identity).[15]

Thus, an apparently simple, classic triangular relationship between Kira, Leo, and Andrei functions as a trinity, an anamorphosis of the trine pattern of speech contained at the core of each narrative. It is perhaps because this triangle plot system, "woman–two men," exemplifies the trine pattern rooted in language and the transmission of the narrative that it is so classic in literature. We also find this trine pattern in the written language of the author, or the narrator, as "I," the reader as "you," and the book, or text, as "it": according to Dufour, we see it in almost any transmission of the narrative. What defines Kira and Leo's existence, their very relationship, is the "absent," the State, even if it is the State that also prevents them in the end from having a life together. The "State" is an overwhelming "Absence," which finds its existence in the death of the individual—death in life for Leo, real death for Kira, and suicide for Andrei, who has represented the State until the moment he realizes its destructive effect on the individual. Andrei is at first what "is not," and at the end, he is that which "cannot be." As Rand argued, spiritual and physical death are the essential by-products of totalitarianism.[16]

Dualism and Synthesis in the Characters

The three main characters in *We the Living*, Kira, Leo, and Andrei, exemplify Rand's Russian literary penchant for creating characters as embodiments of ideas that stand as "negative" examples of dualism (Leo) and "positive" examples of the revolt against dualism (Kira and, in a certain unexpected way, Andrei) (see Diagram 4).[17] The ideas that emerge "victorious" are certainly antidualism and synthesis. Yet it is interesting to note that the perfect "radical" pattern in three is very rare (we saw an instance of it with the triangle as trinity). Here the synthesis (Kira) is obtained through a dialectical literary method and its philosophical-psychological preoccupation with integration (Sciabarra 1995, 102).

Diagram 4

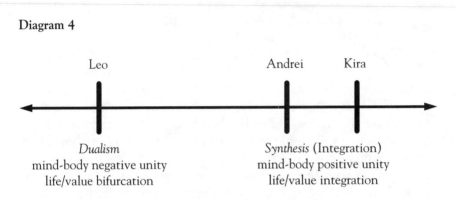

Leo

Andrei   Kira

Dualism
mind-body negative unity
life/value bifurcation

Synthesis (Integration)
mind-body positive unity
life/value integration

Leo as a Divided Character: Life/Value Bifurcation

It is quite difficult to analyze the character of Leo without reference to Rand's alleged "Nietzschean phase."[18] Sciabarra (1995) explains: "The impact of Nietzschean philosophy on Russian Symbolism was significant. . . . Nietzsche's thought also influenced the Marxism of the Silver Age" (34). Rand had read Nietzsche on her own, and may have studied his works while in attendance at the University of Petrograd. She also cites Aleksandr Blok, a Russian Symbolist writer, as among her favorite poets (33). But what we find in the character of Leo are some simplified, almost caricatured, aspects of Nietzschean philosophy. Sciabarra suggests that Rand may have absorbed the peculiarly Russian Symbolist interpretation of Nietzsche, with its emphasis on the Dionysian. By reproducing these schematic interpretations of Nietzsche in the character of Leo, Rand does not give full tribute to the complexity of Nietzsche's philosophy. But Leo, despite his Nietzschean undertones, cannot be described as a superman or a Master. Rather, Leo stands as a "poetic metaphor" of the unreconciled Apollo/Dionysus duality, and a final surrendering to the Dionysian.[19]

In the novel, Leo quotes Nietzsche (and Spinoza) (Rand 1995b, 117). His physical beauty, with his hard, clean-cut features, evokes the old aristocratic model with which Rand was still fascinated.[20] His face, and especially his mouth, show his open scorn and contempt for the masses, and for the Collective: his mouth is a "scornful arc," "calm, severe, contemptuous . . . that of an ancient chieftain who could order men to die, and his eyes were such as could watch it" (43). The object Kira associates with Leo, metaphorically, is the whip. It is an image that is also associated with her, and that establishes her connection to Leo.[21]

In Nietzsche's *Birth of Tragedy*, it is the Apollonian principle that is "the art of appearance, indeed is appearance" (Tanner 1994, 9). It also corresponds to the principle of individuation, and in this regard, Leo exemplifies some Apollonian qualities: solitary, physically clean-cut and hard, apparently and thus morally so, not lacking in courage and nobility. Rand (1975a) saw "Apollo as the symbol of beauty, order, efficacy . . . i.e. the symbol of reason" (58). But Leo is not an integrated person: his apparent qualities do not correspond to his essence, his true inner self. We do not find a positive correspondence between his body (his physical appearance conveying impressions of contempt, strength, nobility, and courage) and his mind, or his actions. On the contrary, as Merrill (1991) notes, "his courage, like his beauty, is of the delicate sort. Just as his god-like beauty is that of a consumptive, so his arrogant soul cracks easily under prolonged pressure" (96). The only mind-body unity Leo exhibits is based on weakness, despite apparent strength. He is the image of negative mind-body unity.

However, we find a true dualism/duality in Leo in that he has no real value on which to base his life. When Kira tries to convince him that he must desire something, look up to something in his life, he answers: "It's a curse, you know, to be able to look higher than you're allowed to reach. One's safer looking down, the farther down the safest—these days." And when Kira says, "One can also fight," he just answers, "Fight what?" and concludes: "I don't want to believe anything. I don't want to see too much" (Rand 1995b, 65).

What we have here is a life/value bifurcation, a duality in ethics that makes Leo a "diseased ego."[22]

According to Sciabarra (1995, 236), Rand traced an internal relationship between life and value, such that neither phenomenon was possible in the absence of the other. For Rand, "the choice to live necessitated" a guiding code of values (240). "Life *is* the ultimate value. It entails value in its very identity. . . . One can no more refer to life without value, than to value without life," and Sciabarra insists that, for Rand, their bifurcation is "worse than a contradiction" (242).

Yet this bifurcation is at the heart of the character of Leo. And to demonstrate the (negative) link between antilife, nonvalue, and nonaction, Leo's conduct is gradually dominated by the Dionysian principle. He indulges in black-market activities, but does not save the money to go abroad. He drinks more frequently, and jokes about being a "gigolo," before becoming a real one at novel's end, when he leaves Kira for Tonia, a rich, much older woman he met at the sanitarium: "Well, I'm through with it. . . . I'm going to have champagne, and white bread, and silk shirts, and limousines, and no thoughts of any kind, and long live the Dictatorship of the Proletariat! . . . Leo Kovalensky, the great gigolo of the U.S.S.R.!" (Rand 1995b, 239, 410–11). He blames Kira for having disappointed him, she who "represented his last hold on . . . self-esteem," when he discovers the truth about her and Andrei. But he had abdicated his self-esteem long before knowing of Kira's "unfaithfulness." Moreover, in Randian terms, self-esteem is not a value somebody else represents for you, but something you build internally. Leo, because of his initial bifurcation of life and value, surrenders himself to an intoxicating, Dionysian loss of self. In this destiny, we see Rand's condemnation of the Dionysian aspect of Nietzsche's thought as glorified by the Russian Symbolists.

Nietzsche (1956, 19) had originally viewed the Apollonian-Dionysian opposition as one in which "these two very different tendencies walk side by side, usually in violent opposition to one another, inciting one another to ever more powerful births" until they seem at last "to beget the work of Art that is as Dionysiac as it is Apolline-Attic Tragedy." It is also true that, becoming more and more conscious of pain and suffering as *au fond* eternally destructive of the individual, Nietzsche seemed to move more in the direction of the Dionysian principle and to abandon the individuation and separateness of the Apollonian. It is against this duality that Rand reacted violently, and the character of Leo exemplifies both the working of dualism and the author's revolt against it. What awaits Leo at the end of the novel is nothing else but death in life.

Interestingly, Leo's dualism, his mind-body negative unity and his life/value bifurcation, is a kind of a dyadic functioning that is antithetical to Kira's synthesis. For Rand, as for many feminists, such dysfunctional, dyadic patterns can be traced to oppressive social conditions. But in contrast to radical feminists on the left, Rand argues that it is statist and collectivist social conditions that are the causal factors in Leo's dualism.

Andrei's Death as Ultimate Fight Against Dualism

In many ways, Andrei is a more interesting character than Leo. As Merrill (1991, 36) puts it, Andrei is "an authentic hero, a true soldier, a man of strict integrity and true courage . . . in many ways he steals the show."[23] In contrast to Leo, Andrei is an "integrated" character in that he exhibits a real mind-body, life-value unity, based on strength, and not weakness. In Andrei, there is not the duality of Leo's bifurcation. This is all the more surprising because Andrei is meant to stand for the evil that is Communism. But Andrei represents Communism at its best—similar, perhaps, to the Synthesist, communitarian ideal of radical feminism— before that ideal was soured by the corruption and hypocrisy of the Soviet regime.[24] The sailor Timoshenko, who, like Andrei, is a true authentic soldier of the Red cause, tells us: "All I know is that we've done it. We made a revolution. We had red banners. The banners said that we made it for the world proletariat. We had fools who thought in their doomed hearts that we made it for all those downtrodden ones who suffer on this earth. But you and me, Comrade Morozov, we have a secret. We know, but we won't tell. Why tell? The world does not want to hear it. We know that the revolution—it was made for you, Comrade Morozov, and hats off to you!"[25] (Rand 1995b, 344).

Rand suggests that Andrei's dedication to a supreme value is similar to Kira's own dedication, despite their antithetical ideals. Andrei has a deep mind-body unity. When Comrade Sonia describes him as "the saint that sleeps with Red flags" (85), we feel Andrei's noble character, his purity, and his intense loyalty to the Communist ideal. Despite her sneering use of the word "sleeps," Comrade Sonia unwittingly introduces a sexual and physical connotation that highlights Andrei's marriage of body and soul to Communism. Andrei physically enacts the sanctity of the ideal in which he believes. Likewise, in the physical descriptions of Andrei, we find the same mind-body synthesis: "In the year 1915, Andrei stood at the machine, and his eyes were colder than its steel, his hands steadier than its levers, *his nerves colder and steadier than both*" (87, emphasis added). We find in this sentence a transcendence through Andrei's mind and body ("his nerves colder and steadier") of two linked principles ("than both," that is, the steel and the levers of the machine, the principle in which "it" [the steel] and what "it" does [the levers] depend on the will of man).[26] In the next sentence, Rand writes: "His skin was tanned by the fire of furnace; his muscles and the will behind his muscles were tempered like the metal he had handled." Rand enriches this mind-body unity by emphasizing the will behind Andrei's muscles and the triadic relation of the "muscles," the "will," and the "metal handled."

Like Kira, in contrast to Leo, Andrei embodies a life/value integration. Like Kira, he believes in life as the supreme value, and in the supreme value of making his life.[27] He tells Kira: "You remember, you said once that we had the same root somewhere in both of us, because we both believed in life? It's a rare capacity, and it can't be taught. And it can't be explained to those in whom that word—life—doesn't awaken the kind of feeling that a temple does, or a military march, or the statue of a perfect body" (255).[28] For Andrei, Communism, until he meets Kira, is like "the very heart of life condensed" (204).

But even when he is still very "Red," at the beginning of the novel, Andrei's own explanation of his commitment to the cause already intro-duces the importance of the "I," despite the Communist submission of the "I" to the Collective One. When Kira tells him: "I thought that Communists never did anything except what they had to do; that they never believed in doing anything but what they had to do," he answers: "That's strange . . . I must be a very poor Communist. I've always done only what I wanted to do." And he adds: "There is no such thing as a duty. If you know that a thing is right, you want to do it. If you don't want to do it, it isn't right. If it's right and you don't want to do it—you don't know what right is and you're not a man" (70). Here we still find in Andrei's words the life/value, mind-value-action, integration and syn-thesis. In Rand's words, the result of this "is a fully integrated personality, a man whose mind and emotions are in harmony, whose sense of life matches his conscious convictions" (1975c, 29). And we see in Andrei a condemnation of dualism/duality in man ("if it's right and you don't want to do it"), showing the divorce between value and reason, value and action, which culminates in the absence of value ("you don't know what right is") and the absence of "life" ("you're not a man"). It is clear that even if Andrei has dedicated himself to a false ideal, he is, and remains, a man.

By contrast, Leo, whose character is based on a life/value bifurcation, is not a man, in the sense defined by Andrei. Even when Andrei speaks of his dedication to the Communist cause, we already hear Rand's "Roarkian" accents. When Kira asks him if "he hadn't ever wanted a thing for no reason save one, that he wanted it" (Rand 1995b, 71), he answers: "Certainly. That's always been my only reason. I've never wanted things unless they could help my cause. For, you see, it is my cause." Though he has not yet accepted Kira's view "that there is something in us which must not be touched by any state, by any collective, by any number of millions" (80), his constant use of the personal pronoun "I" and of the possessive adjective "my" already provides hints of the virtue of selfishness that resides in his heart. Gradually, he perceives that the Red State means not synthesis for the living, but death for the individual. As that ideal deteriorates before his eyes, he understands the regime's corruption, its political cynicism, greed, and quest for power. As Stepan Timoshenko tells him: "Look at our Party! . . . we are not red enough for them. We're not revolutionaries. We're kicked out as traitors. We're kicked out . . . because we yelled to them that they've lost the battle, strangled the revolution, sold out the people, and there's nothing left now but power, brute power. They don't want us. Not me, not you. There's no place for men like you, Andrei, not anywhere on this earth" (297). Grasping this truth, Andrei confronts the party officials, whose cynicism and self-aggrandizement he has unveiled, and in a memorable speech, akin to Roark's courtroom speech in *The Fountainhead*, he enunciates his final credo:

> "Comrades! Brothers! Listen to me! Listen, you consecrated warriors of a new life! Are we sure we know what we are doing? No one can tell men what they must live for. No one can take that right because there are things in men, in the best of us, which are above all states, above all collectives! Do you ask: what things? Man's minds and his values. . . . Every honest man lives for himself . . . the one who doesn't—doesn't live at all. . . . No laws, no Party, no G.P.U. will ever kill that thing in man which knows how to say 'I.' You cannot enslave man's mind, you can only destroy it." (380)

As Andrei's Communist ideal collapses (and even before it collapses, to be exact), he transfers his "highest reverence" to Kira. His love for Kira obeys perfectly his new life/value of the sanctity of the individual. He says: "Because no matter what human wreckage I see around me, I still have you. And—in you—I still know what a human being can be" (309).

But Andrei understands that his ideal is not transferable. Kira is and will always be Leo's, and he does not question her loyalty. Faithful to his life/value integration, Andrei, without a highest reverence, cannot live, and he kills himself. The Red State does not permit him to live in accordance with his "new life." He chooses "not to be," because he knows that under such conditions of statist brutality, he cannot fully be himself. Here, he exemplifies perfectly his definition of what being a "man" has meant for him. Caught in a duality—he knows his "new life/value" is right, but he can't live in Russia in accordance with this principle— Andrei reaches for a new life/value unity in death.

As Dufour (1990) explains, there are in fact two kinds of men: the binary man and the trinitary man. The one who functions with a binary mode of thought wants in fact to eradicate the "empty place," the "it," the third person. He wants purely and simply to eradicate death. For Dufour, the binary mode of thought is an illusory way to conquer mortality.[29] By contrast, the man whose mode of thought favors integration, and not differentiation, trinities instead of binaries, accepts death and "sees the representation of death in life as the basis of his symbolic order and social place." Dufour concludes: "We must understand the history of culture as the place of a very ancient struggle between two irreducible modes of dealing with the most important human issue: death" (349).

In choosing death, Andrei functions as a man whose mode of thought is essentially, and deeply, "trinitary." Death is in fact what permits him to be by not being anymore. Through—and by—death, which gives him back his symbolic order as a man and as an individual, he transcends the divorce of facts and values and of the individual and the State that collectivism perpetuates. For Andrei, synthesis becomes a kind of death-life circularity and permeation. For Andrei, as for the Russian woman novelist Nina Berberova (1991, 20), "death is life." What awaits Leo at the end of the novel is death in life. What awaits Andrei is life in death.

Kira as Synthesis and Seamless Unity

Kira, the female character, is not only closer to Andrei than to Leo (even if she remains loyal to the latter), she is also a synthesis of both. As an integrated character, she displays, like Andrei, a deep mind-body unity and life/value integration. For Kira, her life is her love for Leo, and her love is her life. Kira's mind-body unity is expressed in Rand's description: "It seemed that the words she said were ruled by the will of her body and that her sharp movements were the unconscious reflection of a dancing, laughing soul. So that her spirit seemed physical and her body spiritual" (1995b, 27).

Kira's unity is even more complete than Andrei's; it is a total, deep correspondence, interpenetration, *fusion* of mind and body. Likewise, Kira believes in life as the sanctity of the individual. Just as Andrei holds Communism in highest reverence, so Kira holds Leo in "highest reverence." When she looks at Leo, her face is "a mirror for the beauty of his" and reflects "no admiration, but an incredulous, reverent awe" (44–45). When she begs a party official to find a place for Leo in a State sanitarium, she says: "Don't you see why he can't die? I love him. We all have to suffer. We all have things we want, which are taken away from us. It's all right. But because we are living beings—there's something in each of us, something like the very heart of life condensed—and *that* should not be touched" (204). The terms are interesting, for the connecting and key image is the heart: the "heart" not only permits the human body to live (the life principle) but also symbolizes the siege of love and affections (the love-as-value principle). Thus we see how, through the image of the heart, Rand expresses the complete life/value integration of Kira in a single word.

Kira is not only interesting as the perfect embodiment of unity and integration, she is also in a way the synthesis of both men. This synthesis is quite complex. Kira is the synthesis (C) of two principles (A, Leo, and B, Andrei) that are both right and wrong. As Sciabarra (1995, 17) explains: "It must be emphasized, however, that Rand does not literally *construct* a synthesis out of the debris of false alternatives. Rather, she aims to *transcend* the limitations that, she believes, traditional dichotomies embody. In some instances, Rand sees each of the opposing points of view as being half-right and half-wrong. Consequently, at times, her resolution contains elements from each of the two rejected positions."

Which principle in Leo does Kira both share and transcend? I think, mainly, the contempt for the masses. As I suggested earlier, the image connecting Leo and Kira is the whip. Kira knows that it is "an old and ugly fact that the masses exist and make their existence felt" (Rand 1995b, 41). And much has been said about the passage in which Kira clearly expresses this contempt to Andrei (a passage that was revised and "softened" here, by Rand, in a later edition of *We the Living*, seemingly because of its explicit Nietzschean tones): "What *are* your masses but millions of dull, shriveled, stagnant souls that have no thoughts of their own, no dreams of their own, no will of their own, who eat and sleep and chew helplessly the words others put into their brains. I loathe your ideals because I know no worse injustice than the giving of the undeserved. Because men are not equal in ability and one can't treat them as if they were. And because I loathe most of them" (71–72). So in a way this contempt is right, because the masses stand for, and submit to, the Collective One. They stand opposed to individualism. But it is also "wrong," because Rand herself did not despise the common man. Her biographer, Barbara Branden (1986, 32–33, 161), points out: "In fact, in the years I knew her, she often spoke of her deep respect for the 'common man,' saying that in many ways . . . the American common man had a greater intelligence [and] commitment to reason and individualism than was generally understood."

Moreover, as Sciabarra (1995, 104) observes, when Kira "is able to remove herself briefly from this context [the deadly duality between the individual and the community engendered by Communism], she exclaims that indeed, she does not wish to fight for or against the people. She wants only 'to be left alone.' " In a sense, Kira both shares and transcends the limitations of Leo's contempt for the masses.

With Andrei, Kira shares his capacity for highest reverence, his purity and idealism. But she does not share the "limitations" of his ideal, Communism. If she shares Andrei's principle of life/value integration, she simultaneously refuses the false ideal of the Collective. She stands as the synthesis of both men because she unites what is right in each, even as she transcends the limitations of each.

Of course, it may be said that Kira expresses a mind-body duality in loving Leo and being Andrei's mistress. Yet, this duality is a consequence of statism; it is the State that causes her to behave this way, since it forces her to pay a price in order to save the man she loves. But even here, Rand handles Kira's sexual encounter with Andrei in a way that focuses on their common belief. Despite Kira's hatred of sex with Andrei, their common belief in "highest reverence" is validated in the act. Despite the obvious antagonism between Kira and Andrei, their affair shows a possibility for synthesis and integration. The sexual attraction Andrei feels for Kira is an outgrowth of their mutual values.[30] And even if Kira tells Andrei that their relationship was motivated only by her interest in saving Leo, she almost tells him that she loves him when he comes to see her for the last time with the news of Leo's liberation.[31]

Thus, Kira appears, in this trinity, as the central, key element that transcends and synthesizes what is half-right and half-wrong in each man, both men being psychologically, philosophically, and even socially complete antagonists. Rand makes it clear that this concern for synthesis took root early in Kira's life. The story of the Viking that Kira read when she was only a small girl already exhibits the refusal of duality: the Viking standing over the tower of the city he has conquered (transcendence), laughing at kings (rulers and states, thus also statism), laughing at priests (religions, gods, and mysticism), and giving full tribute to a life, "which is a reason unto itself" (Rand 1995b, 32).

It is true that despite this synthesis, Kira dies in the end, shot by the State's representative when she tries to escape from Russia. But Kira remains loyal to life, to the life that could have been for her and Leo. In contrast to Andrei, who, at the end, does not even believe in the ideal of Communism, Kira yearns for the life that might have been, that should be: it is abroad. She is one step beyond Andrei: "She was calling him, the Leo that could have been, that would have been had he lived there. . . . There, in that world, across the border, a life was awaiting her to which she had been faithful her every living hour . . . a life she could not betray" (432).

As with Andrei, we find the permeation of life and death that roots Kira at the heart of the trinitary process: "Life had been, if only because she had known it could be, and she felt it now as a hymn without sound, deep under the little hole that dripped red drops into the snow, deeper than that from which the red drops came" (433). The hymn without sound is both death, the empty, soundless place, and life, anterior, deeper than the wound of death itself, which still exists because it has existed. Even if the State is victorious, "life, undefeated, existed and could exist" (433).

Kira, as a character, is a truly feminist hero. She is profoundly feminist in her concern for synthesis, embodying a deep life/value integration and a fusion of Leo's and Andrei's positive principles. Ultimately, such synthesis is fundamental not to *female* identity, but to *human* identity. And for Rand, such *human* existence cannot be realized under the collectivist social conditions envisioned by Synthesist feminists.

Ironically, the revolt against dualism—exemplified in the character of Kira, the author's soul mate—most probably took root in Rand's psyche in the days of her Russian youth. Sciabarra (1995) argues persuasively that Rand repudiated traditional Russian modes of resolution that culminated in the State (Marxism) or in God (religion). Like the Russian writer Nina Berberova, Rand celebrates individual integration and synthesis. In her autobiography, *The Italics are Mine*, Berberova (1991) paints a self-portrait of a young Russian girl who is astonishingly similar to Kira/Rand. Triadic, tertiary images abound in Berberova's book.[32] Her first memories date back to when she was "almost three" (7). Like Rand's Kira, what Berberova wants as a child is to stay alone (20) and to enjoy her solitude. She sees her family as the "nest," which is repulsive to her. She rejects religion, with its "emotional overtones," its "twilight, icon-lamps, candles and chants for the dead," as a "smoke screen over life" (23). She sees three possibilities in life: "living for the future life, living for future generations, or living for the present moment" (3). Like Kira, who does not want to die or fight for life, but just to live it, young Nina chooses the third way—for her, "the most ferocious immanence." But all these tertiary images are anamorphoses of Berberova's instinctive and deep hatred for dualism:

> All dualism is painful for me, all splitting or bisecting contrary to my nature. When Lenin speaks about matter in opposition to energy, when Berdyaev speaks about material principle (reaction) and spiritual principle (revolution), when idealist philosophers speak about spirit and flesh, I am jarred, as by a false note. . . . My whole life has been the reconciliation within myself of the old dichotomy. . . . Long ago I stopped thinking of myself as being composed of two halves. I feel physically, that a *seam*, not a *cut*, passes through me, that I myself am a seam . . . that I am not living in vain, but there is sense in that I am as I am, an example of synthesis in a world of antitheses. (23–24)

Later, Berberova reflects further on her growth to individuality: "[T]hen came the day when suddenly the fog around me lifted: I understood that what I had thought were factions in me were a union, that contradictions within myself were an organized system, my individual counterpoint. The personality supposedly divided in two was actually a personality that in itself, in its closed quintessence, connected the two in one process. This was the great day of my life . . . and the beginning of calmness and moderation in my knowing and organizing myself" (36).

The similarities to Rand's thoughts and philosophy are striking here. Rand (1997) suggested in her journals that she, herself, represented "the proper integration of a complete human being" (480). And this desire for synthesis permeates *We the Living*, the rhythm of its sentences, its style, its plot, and its characters. Rand's later novels, *The Fountainhead* and *Atlas Shrugged*, perpetuate many of the same stylistic elements and imagery.[33] Indeed, this leitmotif can be found in all of Rand's fiction, though it remains most prevalent in her earliest, most Russian novel.

Berberova provides us with an understanding of the complex historical context that has shaped the yearning for synthesis that informs her own writings—and those of Ayn Rand. Berberova (1991) tells us that she

> responded to the life of [her] generation, a generation that lived in two worlds, one moving towards an end, the other hardly be-ginning. It brought peace and fullness of existence into a shat-tered, distorted, and troubled world. At that junction of the <u>old</u> and the <u>new</u>, the <u>dying</u> of one epoch and the <u>birth</u> of another, a process that has lasted fifty years, *we* fuse the two. And, in a certain sense we even feel we are a *privileged class* because we breathe freely in both the old and the new. . . . On the <u>symbolic</u> plane we will probably later come to *stand for something*, like the sign for a <u>bridge</u> or a <u>curve</u>. (37, underlined emphasis added, ital-ics in the original)

I think these words capture the historical context within which Rand constructed her Objectivist synthesis. Berberova's words provide the per-fect validation of Dufour's idea that the trinitary mode of thought, exhib-ited in forms or patterns in each narrative because it echoes the first trinity, is one that symbolically acknowledges the issue of death. It sees a life/death permeation, not to say fusion, in its original manifestations (<u>old</u> and <u>new</u>, <u>dying</u> and <u>birth</u>).

The thinkers and writers who were at the junction of two worlds—old Imperial Russia and the new Russia—who anticipated and felt the death of the first world without knowing what the new one had in store for them, were thus doubly rooted in the trinitary mode of thought. Not only did they have a natural intimation of death, but they saw the individual as the answer, the synthesis of the worlds in opposition. Their individual-ity was order restored at the heart of disorder. It is not, therefore, surpris-ing to see that two Russian-born women writers, Ayn Rand and Nina Berberova, insisted so much upon synthesis, trinitarism, and fusion.

The issue is even deeper, however. In Rand's *We the Living* and in Berberova's *Italics are Mine*, it is the woman who permits the reestablishment of unity and fusion, triumphing over masculinist-modernist dichotomies, division, disorder, and violence. As we have seen, in the world of *We the Living* there is, at times, a gendered dualism, with its atmosphere of death, war, squalor, estrangement, and brutality, condensed in the slogans and actions of the Red party. The world of the novel is very *masculinist*. Aside from its two main male protagonists, it is a world populated by men commissars and party officials who represent the rigid, technocratic, and totalitarian forms of Communism. Even the most important female Red, Comrade Sonia, is decidedly unfeminine.

The radical feminist concern for synthesis, stemming from its affinity with triangular psychic organization, provides one answer to this fractured, dualist world and its fragmented, dualist way of thinking. Like the radical feminists, Rand grasps that such dualism is rooted in—and reproduced by—prevailing social conditions and institutions, though she differs in her view of the actual nature of this context. In *We the Living* especially, Rand recognizes the power of social conditions to shape and fracture the lives of individuals (Sciabarra 1997, 29). Without an understanding of this context, "there *is no* story. It is the background that creates the characters and their tragedy. It is the background that makes them do the things they do. If one does not understand the background— one cannot understand them" (Rand to Jean Wick, 27 October 1934, in Rand 1995a, 17).[34] For Rand, the answer for women—and for men—is not to be found in the Communist-collectivist political ideals of radical feminism; it is to be sought in the free interactions of individuals who trade value for value in voluntary, equitable, nonexploitative social relations. In Rand's view, only capitalism—the "unknown ideal"—can provide these social conditions (Sciabarra 1995, 365–79).

As the first female character to take center stage in all of Rand's novels, Kira repudiates dualism—both personally and politically. Rand has created in Kira an emotionally powerful monument to the feminist concern for synthesis. In the style and substance of *We the Living*, perhaps more directly than in her other works of fiction, Rand has provided us with a model of the integrated female hero, who seeks a triumph over dualities and who yearns for *human* synthesis that ultimately transcends gender.

Of course, simply because one rejects dualism does not mean that one's work is necessarily feminist or a resource for feminism. What this essay suggests, however, is that Rand's affinity with the feminist concern for synthesis, as expressed in her most autobiographical novel, might become the basis for a fruitful reengagement, by the feminist academy, with the very nature of dualism and its requisite social conditions. Rand's grasp of dualism as incompatible with human existence is something that radical feminists can—and should—appreciate. But she remains the first, and perhaps the only, woman novelist and philosopher who has severed the connection between such synthesis and the typically collectivist political ideals of radical feminism. Ultimately, Rand challenges her leftist feminist adversaries to rethink their political premises. Her work may yet become a surprising resource for future feminist scholarship on this most important issue.

Notes

Dedicated to Ludivine.

1. My discussion in this section specifically—and throughout—is heavily informed by the work of Chris Matthew Sciabarra.

2. In this context, and throughout the essay, I use the term "radical feminism" in the same way that Lynda Glennon uses it, to refer to a feminism that adheres to a Marxist or quasi-Marxist framework and a socialist political agenda.

3. Glennon suggests, too, that Synthesists have an affinity with androgyny as a utopian sexual model. In the current volume, Thomas Gramstad attempts a provocative Randian defense of a post-androgynous ideal.

4. The reader seeking a comprehensive critique of such views of Rand should consult Sciabarra 1995. Sciabarra presents a strong case for Rand as a dialectical thinker in revolt against dualism. His book is a useful resource for feminists seeking a fruitful, dialectical rereading of the Randian canon. It was he, too, who first suggested "surprising" parallels between Objectivism and the Synthesist-feminist work of Lynda Glennon. See Sciabarra 1995, 199–200.

5. All page references to We the Living refer to Rand 1995b. I recognize distinctions between the original 1936 edition of We the Living and Rand's edited, post–Atlas Shrugged editions, but these distinctions are beyond the scope of this paper. See Sciabarra 1995, 99–106.

6. Sciabarra (1995) was the first theorist to grasp this connection. He states: "Objectivism is a seamless conjunction of method and content—of a dialectical method and a realist-egoist-individualist-libertarian content. This synthesis is Rand's most important contribution to twentieth-century radical social theory" (380–81). Interestingly, whereas I trace triadic organization in Rand's We the Living, Sciabarra reconstructs Rand's critique of statism as a tri-level model, in which she examines relations of power on personal, cultural, and structural levels of generality. One might say that such triadic patterns are prolific in Rand, in her literary craft, philosophy, and social theory.

7. "Dyadic" is used when I speak of a psychological—or, rather, psychoanalytical—construction in two (as in the "masculine" identity), whereas "dualism" and "duality" are especially used for the character of Leo, who is illustrative of Rand's philosophical refutation, or condemnation, of dualism as alienation or bifurcation.

8. Due to space considerations, I cannot consider all the images of three throughout the novel. Suffice it to say, these images are too numerous to catalogue.

9. The nest-of-dolls image refers to the real Russian painted dolls in which successively smaller dolls nest one inside another, from the biggest to the smallest.

10. Actually, Andrei speaks mainly in ternary rhythms. Yet one of the sentences analyzed above ("we don't . . . we build") functions also on a dualistic principle, an opposition.

11. Beveniste (1966, I and II) writes: " 'It or him' can be an infinity of subjects, or nothing" (chap. 18).

12. We find exactly the same idea in the works of the Anglo-Saxon linguist Peirce, who speaks of a "firstness," a "secondness," and a "thirdness" in language and thought. Austin (1962) sees also illocutionary and prelocutionary acts in speech.

13. Rand's critique of Communism and dualism is of primary significance in We the Living, but she had not yet offered any defense of capitalism as nondualistic. This was one of the by-products of her later fiction and nonfiction. See especially Sciabarra 1995, 283–94.

14. Or rather, the Holy Spirit in the Christian Trinity of the Father, the Son, and the Holy Spirit. See Dufour 1990.

15. See Lacan 1973, 1981.

16. See especially Rand in lecture 8 of Peikoff's taped lecture course "The Philosophy of Objectivism." Quoted by Sciabarra 1995, 100.

17. Sciabarra (1995, 35) writes: "Each of Dostoyevsky's characters embodies particular ideas. In their interplay, collisions, and encounters, certain of these ideas emerge victorious. It is this literary method that deeply influenced Rand."

18. See especially Merrill 1991, 21–40. On the relationship between Rand and Nietzsche, see the fascinating material in Rand 1997. Peikoff discusses the influence of Nietzsche on Rand's early work in his foreword, and one can detect that influence throughout Rand's early journals. The Journals also contains a very small section of notes on We the Living—less than twenty pages. Harriman suggests that the scarcity of notes is due to the fact that Rand's "research" for the novel derived mainly from her own experiences in Russia.

19. The term "poetic metaphor" is David Oyerly's. See Sciabarra 1995, 400 n. 22.

20. Merrill (1991, 35) states: "Rand, a daughter of the Russian bourgeoisie, throughout her life retained an admiration for the aristocracy, or at least the aristocratic manner."

21. On this connection between Kira and Leo, see the third section below. Rand (1995b, 29) writes that young men noticed Kira, "the slim girl who strode down streets swinging a twig like a whip." She also writes that Kira watched "in ecstasy" a play in which "the whip [was] cracking expertly in the hand of a tall, young, overseer" (31).

22. This is Rand's term when speaking of characters who are "second-handers." See Sciabarra 1995, 209.

23. Peikoff writes in his introduction to We the Living that in constructing the plot, Rand thought, "Wouldn't it be interesting if 'the man to whom [the girl] sells herself is not a villain but a hero—and the man for whom she makes her sacrifice is the villain in the end'? With this twist, the heroine's conflict deepens immeasurably, while the final tragedy becomes in a sense even greater for the 'villain' than for the other two" (in Rand 1995b, viii). This is interesting as yet another dialectical theme, in which there is an inversion of the "hero" and "villain" roles that permeate each of the fragmented male characters to whom Kira relates.

24. It should be noted that while many radical feminists would repudiate Soviet realities as antithetical to the genuine communist ideal, Rand was critical not only of the reality but of the ideal itself. So it is incorrect to claim, as some might, that Rand was criticizing a social system that no truly radical feminists would have sanctioned. For Rand, the communist ideal of collectivism made the Soviet reality possible.

25. Comrade Morozov is the perfect example of the party official organizing black-market activities for his own profit. We see in this speech that Rand denounces the bifurcation between the value (a revolution for the world proletariat) and fact (a revolution for the looters) of Communism.

26. We find here anticipations of Rearden's domination of metal in Atlas Shrugged. In the case of Andrei, the domination is more direct and physical.

27. In Rand's *Journals*, Andrei's affinity with Kira is made more apparent. In her notes for *We the Living* from 1930, Rand writes of Andrei that he was

> a born individualist and leader who never discovered it. A great mind and a profound honesty. An iron will and unconquerable strength. . . . his tragedy is the same as Kira's. Both are superior individuals. Both have in their souls the sensitivity, the understanding, the hunger for the real life, as few men see it. Both rise to fight for their rights to that life; and both face the same enemy: society, the state, the mass. She is stronger, in that she realizes the fight and the enemy. He is more tragic, because his fight is unconscious. (1997, 51–52)

28. It is interesting to note here how Andrei's style (his triadic definition of life as evoking the feeling of [1] a temple, [2] a military march, and [3] a statue of a perfect body) echoes his integrative thought and personality, which is the deepest common attribute he will share with Kira.

29. See the very interesting chapter entitled "Le pythagorisme: Binarité et immortalité" (Pythagorism: Duality and immortality), in Dufour 1990, 349.

30. This love-sex, life-value integration announces the relation between Hank Rearden and Dagny Taggart in *Atlas Shrugged*, where Rearden understands that his sexual response to Dagny corresponds to their sharing the same values.

31. There is at least one textual reference to validate the idea that Kira, though staying fiercely in love with Leo, may also have loved Andrei, in some way. When they see each other for the last time, she runs after him and meets him in the street: "She raised her hand, and her fingers brushed his cheek slowly, barely touching it, from the scar on his temple to his chin, as if her trembling finger tips would tell him something she could not say" (Rand 1995b, 394). Of course, "could not" is quite ambiguous: it may express Kira's refusal or inability to tell Andrei she loves him. Kira wants to stay faithful to the conception, and the reality, of her love for Leo. She may also not be fully aware of the nature of her feeling, and may not wish to recognize it as love. It should be noted too that Kira's feelings in her last scenes with Andrei are dramatized well in the unauthorized but faithful Italian film version of the novel released during World War II. On the film version, see Sciabarra 1995, 399–400 n. 17; 1996, 520.

32. Sciabarra (1995) was the first to emphasize these similarities between Berberova and Rand; I merely develop this idea.

33. In *The Fountainhead*, for instance, many sentences are constructed on ternary rhythms. A triangular form is expressed in Roark's organic concept of architecture (see Vacker's essay in this volume), and in the relation of Roark, Dominique, and Wynand. *Atlas Shrugged* is divided into three parts. The references in both novels are numerous.

34. Quoted in Sciabarra 1997, 29.

References

Austin, James Langshaw. 1962. *How to Do Things with Words*. Cambridge, Mass.: Harvard University Press.
Barnes, Hazel. 1967. *An Existentialist Ethics*. New York: Alfred A. Knopf.
Barry, Norman. 1987. *On Classical Liberalism and Libertarianism*. New York: St. Martin's Press.
Berberova, Nina. 1991. *The Italics are Mine*. New York: Alfred A. Knopf.
Beveniste, Emile. 1966. *Problèmes de linguistique générale*. Paris: Gallimard.
Branden, Barbara. 1986. *The Passion of Ayn Rand*. Garden City, N.Y.: Doubleday.
Branden, Nathaniel. 1962. The literary method of Ayn Rand. In *Who Is Ayn Rand? An*

Analysis of the Novels of Ayn Rand, by Nathaniel Branden and Barbara Branden. New York: Random House.

Chodorow, Nancy J. 1978. *The Reproduction of Mothering: Psychoanalysis and the Sociology of Gender.* Berkeley and Los Angeles: University of California Press.

Dufour, Dany-Robert. 1990. *Le mystère de la Trinité.* Paris: Gallimard.

Ellis, Albert. 1968. *Is Objectivism a Religion?* New York: Lyle Stuart.

Gilligan, Carol. 1987. Moral orientation and moral development. In *Women and Moral Theory,* edited by Eva F. Kittay and Diana T. Meyers. Totowa, N.J.: Rowman & Littlefield.

Glennon, Lynda M. 1979. *Women and Dualism: A Sociology of Knowledge Analysis.* New York: Longman.

Hampton, Cynthia. 1994. Overcoming dualism: The importance of the intermediate in Plato's *Philebus.* In *Feminist Interpretations of Plato,* edited by Nancy Tuana. University Park: Pennsylvania State University Press.

Holman, C. Hugh, and W. Harmann. 1992. *A Handbook of Literature.* New York: Macmillan.

Lacan, Jacques. 1973. *Les quatre concepts fondamentaux de la psychanalyse.* Paris: La Seuil.

———. 1981. *Le séminaire.* Paris: Le Seuil.

Lennox, James G. 1996. Reply. *Reason,* May.

Merrill, Ronald E. 1991. *The Ideas of Ayn Rand.* La Salle, Ill.: Open Court.

Nietzsche, Friedrich. 1956. *The Birth of Tragedy.* New York: Doubleday Anchor Books.

O'Neill, William F. 1971. *With Charity Toward None: An Analysis of Ayn Rand's Philosophy.* Totowa, N.J.: Littlefield, Adams.

Rand, Ayn. 1975a. Apollo and Dionysus. In *The New Left: The Anti-Industrial Revolution,* 2d rev. ed. New York: New American Library.

———. 1975b. Art and sense of life. In *The Romantic Manifesto: A Philosophy of Literature,* 2d rev. ed. New York: New American Library.

———. 1975c. Philosophy and sense of life. In *The Romantic Manifesto: A Philosophy of Literature,* 2d rev. ed. New York: New American Library.

———. 1995a. *Letters of Ayn Rand,* edited by Michael S. Berliner. New York: Penguin.

———. 1995b. *We the Living.* 60th anniversary ed., with a new introduction by Leonard Peikoff. New York: Dutton.

———. 1997. *Journals of Ayn Rand.* Edited by David Harriman New York: Dutton.

Rubin, Lillian B. 1983. *Intimate Strangers: Men and Women Together.* New York: Harper & Row.

Ruddick, Sara. 1986. Maternal thinking. In *Women and Values,* edited by Marilyn Pearsall. Belmont, Calif.: Wadsworth Publishing.

Sciabarra, Chris Matthew. 1995. *Ayn Rand: The Russian Radical.* University Park: Pennsylvania State University Press.

———. 1996. Ayn Rand. In *American Writers: A Collection of Literary Biographies, Supplement IV, Part 2: Susan Howe to Gore Vidal,* edited by A. Walton Litz and Molly Wiegel. New York: Charles Scribner's Sons.

———. 1997. Reply to critics: *Ayn Rand: The Russian Radical*—a work in progress. *Reason Papers,* fall, 25–38.

Tanner, Michael. 1994. *Nietzsche.* New York: Oxford University Press.

8

Skyscrapers, Supermodels, and Strange Attractors: Ayn Rand, Naomi Wolf, and the Third Wave Aesthos

Barry Vacker

Beauty—ah, Beauty is a compelling goddess to all artists, be it in the shape of a lovely woman or a building.
—from a speech by architect Guy Francon, in *The Fountainhead*

There is no excellent beauty that hath not some strangeness in the proportion.
—Francis Bacon

Both tall and slender and beheld as beautiful, the skyscraper and the supermodel are two of the most visible symbolic representations of "beauty" in modern industrial culture, both embodying the linear Newtonian aesthetic style of industrialism while simultaneously representing widely divergent symbolic and cultural meanings.

For Ayn Rand, the skyscraper represented the aesthetic culmination of the capitalist industrial worldview, symbolizing the triumph of reason, science, egoism, and, not least importantly, beauty. In the skyscraper, form and function come together as beauty not merely to symbolize integrity and truth, but to *be* truth. The "objective" beauty of the skyscrapers that make up the New York City skyline *is* the truth of industrial capitalism.

For Naomi Wolf, the supermodel represents the aesthetic culmination of the patriarchal capitalist industrial worldview, symbolizing the triumph of image, deceit, greed, and, not least importantly, the beauty myth. In the supermodel, form deceives function in a beauty whose glittering allure not merely symbolizes deception and falsehood, but comes to *be* falsehood. The "subjective" beauty of the fashion and cosmetics industries, guided from the skyscrapers of Fifth Avenue and Madison Avenue, *is* the falsehood of industrial capitalism.

According to Rand, art is a "barometer" of culture, wherein the prevailing artistic practices provide insight into the state of the culture. Libertarian philosophy, with which Rand has become associated, has virtually ignored her aesthetic-cultural vision in a self-induced blindness expressed through endless arid visions of *homo economicus*, becoming little more than an apology for a fading Industrial Age.[1] Perhaps because of Rand's praise of egoism and capitalist industrialism, feminist scholars may tend to overlook the insights of her cultural aesthetics, as presented by Rand in *The Fountainhead* ([1943] 1968). While in certain respects a metaphor for industrial culture, *The Fountainhead* actually suggests a humane aesthetic in harmony with the new nonlinear worldview of the emerging Information Age, what futurist Alvin Toffler (1980) refers to as "The Third Wave."

While libertarian philosophy has produced hardly any cultural vision for the Third Wave, Naomi Wolf, a leading feminist scholar on cultural aesthetics and author of the best-selling book *The Beauty Myth* (1991), explicitly calls for women to move beyond patriarchal industrialism and create a "Feminist Third Wave" (277–83). Wolf presents a polemical cultural critique of the female imagery found in mass media, focusing her criticisms on the role of ideal beauty and the supermodel. She passionately exhorts women to turn away from the cultural image of the supermodel, a Platonic ideal designed to enslave women through superficial physical appearances that prescribe normative behaviors. By contrast, in *The Fountainhead*, Rand presents a theme of artistic and spiritual integrity expressed through the character of Howard Roark, an atheistic architect whose aesthetic vision is revealed through buildings that exhibit revolutionary structure and form. Such structures produce a strange new beauty that explodes the classical and traditional aesthetic forms, themselves premised in timeless Platonism, Newtonian linearity, and the Cartesian division of mind and matter.[2]

As such, *The Fountainhead*'s vision can be embraced by feminists in an effort to define a new Third Wave "aesthos," a new set of beliefs and assumptions interrelating science, ethics, and politics through an aesthetic worldview.[3] Rand's aesthetic transcends Church and State, culture and gender, industry and nature; its organicity entails a much deeper complexity than the linearity of the skyscraper or the symmetry of the *Cosmopolitan* supermodel. It operates like a dialectical critique of the prevailing aesthetic forms, which are central to the power of the existing social and moral order.[4] The classical forms of pure symmetry are destroyed, as if Euclidean geometry met violent rupture on the turbulent edge of "order and chaos," where new structures emerge in the form of what scientists call "strange attractors"—unique and seemingly chaotic nonlinear patterns, shapes, and structures that are often strikingly beautiful. Through Roark's buildings, the natural world, and the faces and bodies of Roark and his lover Dominique, Rand depicts a lawful nature where final and formal nonlinear causality are integrated in the realization of an organic and kaleidic aesthos, demanding new forms that may seem strange in their structure, yet attractive in their beauty. Such "strange attractors" are symbols for the highest and most demanding expression of human spirit and freedom—the formal realization of individuality.

This essay will contrast the cultural aesthetics of Ayn Rand with the radically different views of Naomi Wolf, placing them in the context of the emerging postindustrial era. *The Fountainhead* is a novel set during the first half of the twentieth-century, an era when the culture of industrialism fully developed in the United States; *The Beauty Myth* is a nonfiction polemic critiquing a highly visible component of the aesthos of industrial capitalism. While neither *The Fountainhead* nor *The Beauty Myth* present complete theories of beauty, they do present important concepts regarding the cultural aesthetics of industrialism. Hopefully this essay will strike chords of resonance and discord in an attempt to break the symmetrical confines of much aesthetic thought, stimulating new ideas for the kaleidic aesthos of a postindustrial epoch.[5]

Transition to the Third Wave

What seems like chaos is actually a massive realignment of power to accommodate the new civilization.

—Alvin Toffler

It is no coincidence that *The Fountainhead* was published in 1943, during the middle of World War II, and *Atlas Shrugged* in 1957, during the height of the Cold War; both wars were fought over the structure of civil society in the Industrial Age. Industrialism promised a utopia of rational, scientific, efficient, materially abundant social order, superior to the primitive feudalism of the Agricultural Age. World War II represented the culmination of the industrial war; large industrialized nation-states used mass factory technologies to produce war machines and mass death. The war was fought not over "industrialism," but rather over the structure of industrialism, to determine whether it should be capitalist or socialist (communist international socialism or fascist national socialism). Both communism and fascism had similar visions of industrial order: a state-controlled top-down linear centralization of production, media, and society; mass political movements led by charismatic leaders; a heroic ruling class, be they proletarians or Aryans, who purged society of cultural enemies such as capitalist exploiters or inferior races; and the imposition of collectivism on bourgeois individuals in the desire for uniform social order. These aesthetic visions were conveyed in the mass art of "socialist realism" or "fascist idealism." With fascism annihilated in World War II, the Cold War was a struggle between Communism and capitalism.

On the Cold War military stage, masses of machines and men lined up on both sides of an Iron Curtain. On the Cold War media stage, masses of images and artists lined up behind an Aesthetic Curtain, drawn to reveal the battle between the socialist realism of Communist propaganda and the "capitalist realism" of consumer advertising.[6] Two visions of an ideal cultural aesthetic engaged in battle—the alienated human united with self and society through the state in the centralized linear Communist industrial order versus the material human contented with self and world through commodities in the capitalist industrial order. While Wolf is repulsed by the aesthetics of patriarchal capitalist industrialism, Rand is repulsed by the ethics of communist industrialism, seeing in capitalist industrialism an aesthetic vision of beauty realized through reason, purpose, and egoism.[7]

Atlas Shrugged was published as the Industrial Age was being eclipsed by the Information Age, for 1957 was approximately the first year information-knowledge workers outnumbered industrial-manufacturing workers in the United States (Poret 1980).[8] While *Atlas Shrugged* gazed back on the achievements of capitalism in the Industrial Age, its vision of the future projected inhumane socialistic collapse. And while *The Fountainhead* gazed back on the dogma of classicism and the rise of modern architecture, its vision of the future projected aesthetic triumph. If *Atlas*

Shrugged is a paean to industrial capitalism, symbolized by the heroic industrialist and the factory, then *The Fountainhead* can be considered a paean to postindustrial aestheticism, symbolized not only by the heroic architect and the skyscraper, but also by the complex organic forms of strange attractors. *The Fountainhead* is an intuitive anticipation of a non-linear postindustrial aesthetic, as if Rand, the insightful philosopher, gazing back on the ethos of capitalist industrialism, was overwhelmed by Rand the intuitive artist, expressing the aesthos of postindustrialism.

The Third Wave Aesthos

The flowing life which comes from the sense of order in chaos . . .
—Gordon L. Prescott, architect in *The Fountainhead*

There is a brief passage in *The Fountainhead* that contains a deep insight into culture and civilization, the importance of which can easily be overlooked. Through the words of Ellsworth Toohey, a socialist journalist and architecture critic, Rand suggested that each "soul" and each "civilization" had its own distinct "style." The style of the soul, an individual's inner spirit, was often expressed through the physical qualities and expressions of the face. Rand used the faces of her characters to great metaphorical effect, as they each symbolized certain worldviews. Rand also suggested that each civilization had its own style, which was expressed through some underlying fundamental principle. Even though Toohey is the archvillain of the novel, Rand often used his words to convey what she believed to be important truths about the world. Regarding the style of a civilization, Toohey muses: "Do you remember the famous philosopher who spoke of the style of a civilization? He called it 'style.' He said it was the nearest word he could find for it. He said that every civilization has its one basic principle, one single, supreme, determining conception, and every endeavor within that civilization is true, unconsciously and irrevocably to that one principle" (Rand [1943] 1968, 270). While it may be somewhat reductionist to condense into one principle the ideas of a civilization, Rand's suggestion contains an insight into different cultures and the conflicts between them. Simply put, each civilization has its own unique aesthos—a vision of science, ethics, and politics interrelated through an aesthetic worldview. Perhaps better than anyone, futurist

Alvin Toffler has grasped this fundamental precept. Interestingly, it was Toffler who interviewed Rand for *Playboy* in 1964.[9]

Toffler coined the term "Third Wave" in his seminal historical synthesis, which outlined the sociocultural transformations that ripple across the planet as technological advances are implemented around the world, creating entirely new forms of civilization. He outlined three broad "waves" that have shaped human civilizations: the First Wave of the Agricultural Revolution, the Second Wave of the Industrial Revolution, and the emerging Third Wave and its Information Revolution. Toffler shows how the prevalent scientific, communication, and production technologies led to dramatic sociocultural transformations precisely because the new forms of technology demanded new forms of art, science, media, social organization, family structure, economic production, currency, government, transportation, and other lifestyle changes.

The First Wave had the plow as its key tool, speech as its key media, and the feudal village as its social structure; the Second Wave had the factory, the printing press, and the nation-state; and the Third Wave will have biotechnology, nanotechnology, the Internet, and new social structures. While the First Wave sought to satisfy physical needs through food production and the Second Wave sought to satisfy physio-material needs through the abundance of mass production, the Third Wave will move up the hierarchy and satisfy cognitive needs with abundant information, knowledge, and experiences. While the Second Wave was fueled somewhat by liberal individualism, its guiding production principle was undifferentiated mass production created through machines and mass labor, targeted for mass markets, sold through mass merchandising, and managed through mass media. This massification of society is often overlooked in Rand's praise of industrialism. The economic structures embodied in capitalism and communism were geared toward mass production for masses of consumer-citizens. Similarly, there emerged mass political movements, which took on liberal and socialist forms, both of which required mass nation-states. Surely there are differences between totalitarian communism and market-oriented capitalism; however, both systems were geared toward Second Wave industrial mass production. Permeating this Second Wave was a misapplied Newtonianism, where factory and society served as deterministic clockwork machines, and homogeneous individuals and nuclear families could be produced through the crushing pursuit of social order.

In the Third Wave, new forms of art, living, and social life will emerge to replace the technologically outmoded forms of the Second Wave. The essential source of Third Wave social value will be in the production and organization of information, knowledge, ideas, and aesthetic experiences. Mass customization supersedes industrial mass production, as emerging technologies allow both scale and individualization. Biotechnology and nanotechnology may render scarcity obsolete, requiring new economic models. Genetics will extend human life dramatically and alter reproductive behavior. In combination with the growing kaleidicity of aesthetic and sexual preferences, asymmetric family structures will emerge that seem just as scientifically "natural" as the Second Wave nuclear model.

The Second Wave traditional mass media are quickly being "demassified" (Toffler 1970, 144–56). The personal computer is integrating all previous communication media into one machine linked to fluid and plastic global networks. Broadcasting, with its passive audience, will eventually be obsolete, as computers and the embryonic Internet merge to create interactive, networked communication and economic systems. Computers will become as ubiquitous as the telephone or television, and the Internet will work like electricity—one simply plugs in via air or wire. Spanning national borders, the Internet is already accelerating the global spread of ideas and capital, creating a nonlinear horizontalization of power and knowledge that will eventually render the age of centralization, mass politics, and nation-states extinct. Unlike the fears of critics mired in Second Wave ideology, people will not be isolated behind computer screens, living sterile antisocial lives. Along with much more social mobility, community life will simply develop in a greater variety of forms not limited by place, nation, or outmoded social norms.

The ethic of collectivism, which was necessary to ensure conformity, is slowly being challenged by an embryonic ethic that could be termed "edgism" or "nonlinear individualism." Whereas collectivism herds the masses to the center, nonlinear individualism embraces asymmetric turbulence and individuality on the *edges* of the social order. In breaking outmoded norms, such individuals and organizations defy authority, ignore tradition, seek innovation, expand horizons, go "beyond the limit," and see virtue in living "on the edge." This ethic delights in kaleidic variation, cherishes organic experiences, and takes pleasure in continual processes rather than the pursuit of linear final ends. Much to the chagrin of State and Church, this ethic seems to pursue neither pure stability nor purified salvation, preferring to create its own organic social structures.

The emerging age will create an unrivaled potential for liberation and cultural variation, all of which are feared by those mired in Second Wave thought. In their own challenge to the simple mechanistic linearity of Newtonianism, many feminists welcome the emerging Third Wave and its new nonlinear sciences. Aided by the astounding leaps in computing power, these nonlinear sciences are producing a radical new view of natural processes.[10] "Complexity theory," or "chaos theory," does not challenge causality or the possibility of knowledge, but suggests a complex nonlinear causality that subsumes and transcends Newtonian linearity. While scientists have better understanding of overall systems and structures, they are not omniscient in specific or general prediction. Simple lawful systems emerge from complex and seemingly random phenomena, and from simple laws emerge complex and organic systems. Evolutionary processes undergo structural transformation when the system borders on the "edge of order and chaos" (Kauffman 1995, 23–28). "Fractals" are the form for seemingly chaotic or "strange attractors," which guide formal structuring through nonlinear causality and iteration, producing organic systems of self-similarity with open-ended variation. Fractals are replacing Euclideanism as the new geometry of nature, and are being discovered across the universe, from the microscopic to the intergalactic to the social.[11]

These new sciences have political implications; they undermine the notion of central planning, which is not merely impossible but also productive of chaos proportionate to the imposition of order. With the devolution of the nation-state, social structures will reflect kaleidic variation and chaotic coordination in fractal networks, bound by local geography or the nature of the social exchange. Because of their basis in knowledge flow, such structures will "attract" toward decentralization: voluntary social arrangements, private arbitration, restitutive justice, structural plasticity, and fluid media networks requiring freedom of expression. In their First and Second Wave stupor, Church and State may attempt violent suppression, but can only fail.

The Second Wave aesthos can be expressed, then, in several broad concepts: linearity, determinism, symmetry, uniformity, centralization, hierarchy, stability, collectivism, unity, and, above all, order. In contrast, the emerging Third Wave aesthos can be expressed in different concepts: nonlinearity, autonomy, asymmetry, diversity, decentralization, horizontalization, turbulence, edgism, individuality, and, above all, chaos.

While Randians cast their gaze back upon the age of capitalist industrialism, and Wolf casts her scorn upon it, advanced societies sit astride the emergence of a new epoch. Neither Rand nor Wolf seems to realize that, as with the other waves, the Third Wave will require radically different conceptions of value and social structure. The Third Wave portends fractal-like anarchism as the next utopia, sympathetic to Rand's libertarian separation of state from the realm of ideas, media, science, sexuality, religion, and economics. While Rand denounced anarchism,[12] her ideal of the industrial capitalist nation-state seems inapplicable to the new Third Wave context. Despite her libertarian social views, Rand's politics is essentially Second Wave.

But as Sciabarra (1995, 297–329) points out, Rand's philosophical system exhibits a deep systemic organicity. In my view, Rand's "dialectical sensibility," as Sciabarra calls it, anticipates the ideas of the new sciences. For in her aesthetics and theory of concepts, we can find a complex beauty, a Third Wave aesthos.

By contrast, while Wolf is right to call for a "Feminist Third Wave," it must be a Third Wave that is free from Second Wave ideology. To understand Wolf's clarion call, it is necessary to understand first her critique of the cultural aesthetics of capitalist industrialism, thus setting the stage for a transition to the Third Wave aesthos of *The Fountainhead*.

Supermodels and Slaves of Beauty

[Four hundred and fifty] full-time American fashion models . . . constitute the elite corps deployed in a way that keeps 150 million women in line.

An economy that depends on slavery needs to promote images of slaves that "justify" the institution of slavery.
—Naomi Wolf, *The Beauty Myth*

Naomi Wolf's purpose in *The Beauty Myth* is to present "a new way to see" the ideal woman in capitalist industrial society, and thereby to free women from a cultural ideal necessarily imposed on women by men since the Industrial Revolution (1991, 15, 19). Wolf sees capitalist industrialism as creating and perpetuating a Platonic vision of beauty, where the unattainable ideal of formal beauty tyrannizes female moral purpose, prescribing not only appearance but also behavior, operating as a form of "social coercion" that protects patriarchal institutions of power (13–14).

According to Wolf, the mass media present a "beauty myth" in which form deceives function, splitting women apart from their true selves and each other, leaving them as divided and powerless objects of aesthetic contemplation. Facing the false alternative of being sexual or serious (273), women pursue cosmetic appearance as a substitute for cultural assertiveness in an endless quest for social approval according to aesthetic norms created by men who desire to possess the "virtuous beauty" of external appearance, but not internal spirituality (12, 18). Permeating media, culture, work, economics, sexuality, dietary habits, and even law, the beauty myth is ultimately a fictive "totalitarian" tool of "social control" used by the male "power elite" to deceive, dominate, exploit, and enslave women in capitalist industrial society.

According to Wolf, the "beauty myth" has developed in response to expanding female liberation in capitalist industrial societies. While the Industrial Age has helped liberate women from material constraints that previously limited their autonomy, fearful capitalist patriarchy has sought a new form of social control precisely because the material constraints have been dangerously loosened. The "beauty myth" is this form of social control, responsible for all kinds of cultural phenomena, from the deeply disturbing (eating disorders, pornography, rape, gender discrimination, plastic surgery) to the highly aesthetic (advertising, photography, high fashion). For Wolf, the highly aesthetic is responsible for the deeply disturbing.

Before the development of the visual technologies of mass media, women were exposed to few images of female beauty, and those were mostly under Church control. According to Wolf, industrial capitalism seized upon these tools of imagery to create a changeless "Platonic Ideal Woman," a modern religion complete with its own Rites of Beauty (12, 86–130). Created and perpetuated in the mass media to replace the Feminine Mystique,[13] this beauty ideal is both inhuman, dividing women from their true selves and from each other, and impossible, creating an endless, enslaving quest for unattainable beauty (66). Real women are censored from the cultural scene by a capitalist media dependent on the economics of advertising and its high-fashion beauty myth (61–85). Thus, women have become powerless objects of aesthetic contemplation, competitively contemplated by women (14, 284), possessively contemplated by men (12). They live an illusory freedom in which aesthetic form deceives moral function (273). Cosmetic beauty subtly prescribes cultural behaviors, undermining not only individuality, identity, and self-esteem but also preventing women from true liberation (14, 16). For Wolf, the beauty myth is social coercion in the form of a "culturally imposed physical standard" that expresses the power relations of patriarchal industrial capitalism and strengthens male control "a hundredfold" (12, 16). The beauty myth perpetuates an inhumane industrial social order where the most deeply affected are like political prisoners in a prison camp. Wolf states: "Women must claim anorexia as political damage done to us by a social order that considers our destruction insignificant because of what we are—less. . . . a disgrace that is not our own, but that of an inhumane social order. Anorexia is a prison camp. One fifth of well-educated American young women are inmates. . . . To be anorexic or bulimic *is* to be a political prisoner" (208). Tall, overly slender, elegantly attired, features accentuated through airbrushing and eye shadow, plastered throughout the pages of patriarchal culture, the Platonic supermodel is, in effect, a high-fashion SS guard overseeing the concentration camp of capitalist industrialism from the runways and catwalks of its capital, the skyscrapers of Manhattan (31, 41).

Constituting the essence of the beauty myth is a changeless "Platonic Ideal Woman," which all women must forever strive to be, if they are to be valuable women. It is a myth perpetuated throughout the Western canon and in all of Western civilization, but it is fully transformed and exploited by capitalist mass production of visual imagery. For Wolf, not only is the beauty myth false, but it is inhumanely destructive. Wolf summarizes the beauty myth as follows:

> The beauty myth tells a story: The quality called "beauty" objectively and universally exists. Women must want to embody it and men must want to possess women who embody it. This embodiment is an imperative for women and not for men, which situation is necessary and natural because it is biological, sexual and evolutionary: Strong men battle for beautiful women, and beautiful women are more reproductively successful. Women's beauty must correlate to their fertility, and since this system is based on sexual selection, it is inevitable and changeless. (12)

Perhaps many biologists or cultural theorists interpret Darwin's evolution as meaning "changeless" beauty and "survival of the fittest," implying that only the "master" species will survive. A more accurate interpretation, however, is that species survive by varying fitness to serve functions for adaptive and coevolutionary living. This is more consistent with the flourishing diversity of life on earth (Kauffman 1993, 29–32). Hence, while she is right to call on women to reject a misguided Darwinism and a timeless Platonic ideal, Wolf unfortunately accepts many of the Platonic-Kantian assumptions that permeate contemporary culture and that cause many of the problems with which she is concerned.

According to Wolf, "ideal" beauty is presented in the media as objective and attainable, yet it is actually impossible because no one can attain such ideal beauty. Such beauty is not merely unattainable; Wolf (1991, 176) follows Plato in claiming that "ideal beauty is ideal because it does not exist." Women are deceived and coerced by the illusory and the impossible, a glittering veneer produced by the airbrushing and computer-imaging illusionists of capitalist media. In critiquing mass-media ideals, Wolf actually adopts the stance of Plato with regard to what she sees as the illusory qualities of beauty in the marketplace. She claims that beauty is determined by politics, specifically an industrial political economy that perpetuates patriarchal power and profits. She writes: "None of this is true. 'Beauty' is a currency system like the gold standard. Like any economy it is determined by politics, and in the modern age it is the last, best belief system that keeps male dominance intact" (12).[14] From the commonsense observation that the particulars of beauty have varied over time and across cultures, Wolf adopts a more modernist position, concluding that beauty is neither objective nor universal, but determined by industrial political economy (12, 36). Wolf's argument is that patriarchal industrial capitalism perpetuates the myth of "objective" and "universal" ideal female beauty, whereas beauty is actually subjective and culturally relative. For Wolf, this myth of objectivity keeps women enslaved. The mass media and advertisers remove physical "flaws" through illusion, thus censoring the true reality and identity of women. This identity is more truthfully expressed, according to Wolf, through aesthetic egalitarianism (83). But Wolf encourages women to jettison the Platonism and politicization of cultural aesthetics, the cause of deleterious consequences for women, while accepting the very assumptions that produced the consequences. To grasp this thesis fully, we must look beneath this veneer of relativism and understand Wolf's deep affinity with Plato, Kant, and Marx.[15]

In Plato's theory of beauty, perhaps the most poetically powerful ever, he argued that truth and beauty reside in a world of "ideal forms" external to both the object and the perceiving mind, thus requiring for their grasp some form of divine intuition. In attempting to create a philosophical system to render knowledge "objective," Plato (1956, 247) thought that the physical world of particulars revealed to the senses was not true "reality" but an imitation or reflection of ideal forms that constitute the true reality. Truth is to be found apart from any particulars of the physical world. Particulars are one step removed from truth (Plato 1989, 210). Lovers of true beauty should go beyond the unimportant physical world available to the senses, the source of neither real knowledge nor real things, and ascend the ladder of wisdom in the world of ideals, to seek beauty "in itself by itself with itself" (210–11). Thus, the beauty of physical objects is but a deceptive "image" luring us away from real truth into a waking dream (Plato 1956, 248–50; 1974, 601; 1984, 236). This illusion is compounded by art, an imitation of an imitation of reality that leaves citizens thrice removed from truth. For Plato (1980, 817), such deceptive illusion required that artists not be permitted to enter the market.

Kant transformed Platonism into modern subjectivism and relativism by claiming that subjective consciousness imposed form on reality and therefore human reason could know only appearances but not "the thing in itself." Kant sought to bridge noumena and phenomena, freedom and nature, through transcendental aesthetic judgment, which mediated between the two worlds. Ultimately, aesthetic judgment, as with all judgment, is concerned with subject-supplied formal appearances serving no material purpose. For Plato and Kant, true reality was something unavailable to the physical world of the senses. Thus, the form and beauty of real objects are illusory appearances—the origins of such notions as, "beauty is skin deep," "beauty is mere appearances," and "beauty is in the eye of the beholder."

Marx (1967) transposed such illusory-dependent formalism into the realm of political economy. Value, the amount of labor and production in the commodity, is the underlying essence of a commodity expressed in the equivalent form of use-value (38, 41). Under capitalist forms of production, the use-value of commodities is concealed by the illusion of exchange-value, which is but a surface appearance creating a surplus value for capitalists in the form of profit (36). Exchange-value is a one-sided depiction of a relation that masks coercion and exploitation. With the camera aiding mass production of aesthetic imagery in advertising and merchandising, exchange-value becomes "commodity aesthetic." In *The Aesthetic Dimension*, Marcuse (1968, 62) argued that "the Establishment has created and effectively sold beauty in the form of plastic purity and loveliness—an extension of exchange values to the aesthetic-erotic dimension." Like Plato's conception of art, the illusion of exchange-value is itself transformed into the illusion of commodity aesthetic, and is thus thrice removed from the true economic value. While such aesthetic is presented in a "free press," commodity aesthetic transforms free speech into falsehood and force. Thus, "commodity aesthetic is one of the most powerful forces in capitalist society" (Haug [1971] 1986, 10). Integrating these themes, Wolf views beauty under capitalism as illusory formal aesthetic dependent upon exchange-value as expressed in totalitarian market forces. *The Beauty Myth* is a popularized Marxist critique of commodity aesthetic premised in a contemporary Platonic-Kantian philosophy of beauty.

In arguing against the objective timeless Platonic ideal, Wolf follows the reasoning of most modern aestheticians and assumes that "objective" beauty is unchanging. And since there are cultural differences and aesthetic disagreements regarding objects and standards of beauty, as Wolf illustrates, beauty must then be purely subjective and culturally relative. Interestingly, the classical conception of "objective" beauty, that which resulted in dogmatic tradition and rigid cultural conservatism, was also rejected by Rand. However, Rand embraced a contextually objective nonlinear conception of beauty. Wolf follows the modernist, relativist aesthetic tradition, with its Kantian roots.

In my view, however, modernism rightly rejected the dogmatic traditionalism of classicism but mistakenly accepted the relativism of pure subjectivity that seeks to explode "objective" classical forms and to express inner emotion in nonrepresentational forms. The classical conception of "objective" beauty implied that everyone must agree, thus (seemingly) reducing the subjective freedom of both the artist and the beholder. Similarly, any aesthetic that served an objective form or commercial purpose seemingly limited the freedom of the artist. Aesthetics serving ends in a market are viewed, therefore, as not truly free. Here, Kant, Marx, and Wolf are conjoined in the realm of commodity aesthetics, where the "ideal beauty" promised as exchange-value is dependent on the capitalist industrial market, rendering beauty deceptive, coercive, and totalitarian.

Although Wolf (1991, 282) admits that the market would be powerless if women did not enforce it against each other, the industrial mass media still manipulate (what she sees as) the world of Kantian appearances through the aesthetics of ideal beauty to enslave women. Wolf's conclusions have serious implications for the meaning of free speech. According to Wolf, mass-media advertising works as censorship in two ways: first, women's magazines and other media refrain from criticizing the beauty myth for fear of losing advertising revenues from major advertisers in the apparel, health, and cosmetic industries; second, and more sinister, airbrushing and computer imaging censor the real nature of woman and create the illusory Platonic ideal that is the beauty myth (82). For Wolf, the marketplace is coercive and not open to "consciousness raising"; it works to censor, not expand, free speech, thus requiring a coercive state through which liberty, free speech, and truth are realized (79, 82, 277–78).

Wolf believes individualist feminist efforts are not enough to overcome patriarchal industrial imagery and media control. Women, in their "natural solidarity," should adopt a communal collective way of thinking and unite in a "woman-centered political activism" that defines their "self-esteem as political," part of a process Wolf calls renewing "democracy" (280–82, 289). Importantly, Wolf also champions a "Feminist Third Wave," a set of political and cultural proposals for renewing the spirit of feminism. Unfortunately, her Third Wave political proposals have the flavor of Second Wave statism, an ideology that, in my view, will be impotent and irrelevant in a fully Third Wave society. Wolf's political proposals include the unionization of women's jobs, lawsuits, enforced dress codes, antidiscrimination laws, parental leave, and fair compensation. Reproductive rights are also recommended, and presumably, this means freedom from the State, especially when it is guided by the Church.

However, in her nonstatist, more voluntarist cultural recommendations, Wolf suggests that feminists construct their own counterculture, become analytical, find alternative images in films, create feminist art and better rituals, find feminist heroines, have more intergenerational contact, look directly at one another, seek communal nakedness, modify their behavior toward each other, and develop a sexuality free from violence (277–83). It would seem that these cultural recommendations would be more likely to succeed in the kaleidic culture of the Third Wave, precisely because Wolf's suggestions are nonstatist, seeking to create culture, rather than to impose it.

There is no doubt Wolf is addressing a very real phenomenon, that of overconcern with media-saturated "appearances" and the resulting forms

of psycho-cultural neuroses—from mere superficialism to the more destructive compulsive-eating disorders. Misunderstanding beauty will always result in negative psychological and cultural consequences. Wolf's
call for a new definition of beauty that is noncompetitive, nonhierarchical, and nonviolent has the flavor of a Third Wave aesthos, wherein
women can celebrate their individuality and take pleasure in their bodies
(285–86). But Wolf's real target is not *beauty*; it is the post-Kantian
modern *superficiality* in understanding beauty, which spread during the
nineteenth-century at the very same time as capitalist industrial mass
production. Though modern culture is saturated with the idea that
beauty is "unattainable," "skin deep," or "in the eye of the beholder,"
these ideas are not only incorrect, they also lead to the psychological and
cultural consequences that Wolf deplores. Similarly, Rand celebrated the
body while being very critical of how physical beauty or ostentatious
ornamentation could be used to superficially mask an ugly or vacuous
spirit.[16] However, as we will see, Rand did not view fashion or ornament
as necessarily superficial; this is in direct contrast to the almost pathological desire of the many philosophers who denounce fashion as if it were
an assault on some timeless Platonic truth.[17]

There are complex reciprocal interactions between aesthetics, technology, and philosophy. But it would be difficult to conclude that nine-
teenth- and twentieth-century industrialism necessitated the
dissemination of post-Kantian aesthetics. Superficiality is the hand-
maiden to subjectivism because both excuse the need for deeper critical
thought. Aesthetic superficiality cannot be rejected by thinking superficially about aesthetics.[18]

This analysis, of course, does not mean that subjectivity has nothing
to do with aesthetics, for it does, but it operates in complex nonlinear
reciprocal relations between artist, object, and subject, requiring that the
subject's own aesthetic judgment bear some responsibility in the aesthetic
experience and its consequences. If, after visiting a museum, a person
tried to mimic the appearance of an individual portrayed in a painting,
then she or he would seem disturbed and superficial. But there would be
no need to condemn the painter for the behavior of the viewer. Similarly,
then, why assign to industrial mass media the responsibility for the same
behavior among citizen-consumers, especially since not everyone exposed
to the media imagery becomes alienated, develops eating disorders, opts
for plastic surgery, or emulates supermodels and celebrities? Seeing
beauty, especially the human beauty presented in the media, as "appear-

ance" or purely physical, will necessarily create a vicious circle from which escape is impossible. The consequences include a culturewide de-contextualization of beauty manifested in a neurotic desire for *unnatural* physical perfection, preoccupation with youth, and decharacterization of the human face.[19]

A deeper view of human beauty would see between body and mind a reciprocity that, properly understood, is expressed through a natural phys-ical-spiritual perfection in which human faces express the character of their souls and human bodies express their sexuality, in all its pleasure, free from guilt. Such a view of beauty would be more in harmony with nature, for it has the possibility of unifying the devastating duality be-tween *beauty* and *purpose*—placing universality and individuality, form and function, style and substance, subjectivity and objectivity in their proper contexts. While Rand does not present a complete aesthetic phi-losophy in *The Fountainhead*, she does suggest a foundation for a deeper understanding of beauty and purpose.

Skyscrapers and Strange Attractors

> I have not spoken of the aesthetic appeal of strange attractors . . . a
> realm lies here to be explored and harmonies to be discovered.
> —physicist David Ruelle

Since Rand's stated purpose in writing *The Fountainhead* was to present "an ideal man," one might well conclude, from a feminist perspective, that her aesthetics must therefore express linear masculinity. Both sup-porters and critics of Rand usually begin their discussions of her cultural ideas by focusing on the ethical and economic *content* of individual and social actions, not on the aesthetic *forms* of such actions. However, in *The Fountainhead*, there exists beneath the industrial metaphors an aesthetic vision of deep complexity and organicity, unlike typical industrial aes-theticism. Rand created an aesthetic vision in which humans and nature exist harmoniously, not in a static symmetrical world of timeless tradition and classical forms, but in a turbulent world of chaotic organicity and strange attractors, much like the aesthetics of the Third Wave. In hu-mans, beauty and purpose are united as aesthetic form and spiritual func-tion, expressed not in spiritless symmetry, but in an individuality that is both natural and strangely beautiful. For Rand, the beautiful is not a sterile object of aesthetic contemplation; it is the guide and end for virtuous action—egoistic integrity as the means, aesthetic beauty as the end. Form and function come together in an organic relation, with the ideal form being the natural individuality inherent in all potentiality. This is not merely "form following function," but the full realization of the organic reciprocity that exists in the nonlinear relation between form and function.

In the famed opening passage of *The Fountainhead*, a nude Roark is poised at the edge of a cliff above a lake. Laughing at the aesthetic conformists in society, he dives "down into the sky."

> He stood naked at the edge of a cliff. The lake lay far below him. A frozen explosion of granite burst in flight to the sky over the motionless water. The water seemed immovable, the stone flowing. The stone had the stillness of one brief moment in battle when thrust meets thrust and the currents are held in a pause more dynamic than motion. The stone glowed, wet with sunrays.
>
> The lake below was only a thin steel ring that cut the rocks in half. The rocks went on into the depth, unchanged. They began and ended in the sky. So that the world seemed suspended in space, an island floating on nothing, anchored to the feet of the man on the cliff.
>
> His body leaned against the sky. It was a body of long straight lines and angles, each curve broken into planes. He stood, rigid, his hands hanging at his sides, palms out. He felt his shoulder blades drawn tight together, the curve of his neck, the weight of the blood in his hands. He felt the wind behind him, in the hollow of his spine. The wind waved his hair against the sky. His hair was neither blond nor red, but the exact color of a ripe orange rind.
>
> . . . His face was like a law of nature—a thing one could not question, alter or implore. It had high cheekbones over gaunt hollow cheeks; gray eyes, cold and steady; a contemptuous mouth, shut tight, the mouth of an executioner or a saint.
>
> He looked at the granite. To be cut, he thought, and made into walls. He looked at a tree. To be split and made into rafters. He looked at a streak of rust on the stone and thought of iron

ore under the ground. To be melted and to emerge as girders against the sky. ([1943] 1968, 3–4)

There are many things that could be said about this passage, but here the focus will be on the aesthetic metaphors. There are no doubt strong industrial metaphors represented in the final paragraph. In the beauty of nature, Roark sees granite to be cut into walls, trees to be split into lumber for rafters, ore to be mined and melted into girders for skyscrapers. Similarly, the lake was "only a thin steel ring." A metaphoric Newtonian linearity and Euclidean geometry is expressed in Roark's rigid body of straight lines and angles. Perhaps there is an expression of industrial dominative masculinity, a seemingly sterile objectivity, in Roark's face, with its cold, steady, gray eyes, and tightly shut "contemptuous mouth." It would be easy to dismiss this passage as the expression of a fading Second Wave of Euclidean Industrial Humans. However, there is much more to the visually arresting imagery.

Roark could also be seen as representing the beauty of humans in a harmonious state of nature, in contrast to a simplistic Hobbesian-Darwinian state of nature, where warlike death struggles prevail. For Rand, the state of nature reflects the nonlinear relations between the objects and forces of nature. Her description contains frozen explosions of granite, immovable water cutting through flowing stones, reciprocal thrusts and currents held "in a pause more dynamic than motion," all seemingly suspended in space and floating on nothing, anchored to the feet of Roark on the cliff. Rand's words express the visual forms of strange attractors, the formal causality of chaotic natural forces modeled in the nonlinear phase spaces of physics.[20] Rand captures the essence of such visual modeling when she states, through Roark, that "[w]e live in our minds, and existence is the attempt to bring that life into physical reality, to state it in gesture and form" (541).

Awaiting Roark, as he stood against the sky, was New York City, Rand's capital of industrialism and of the greatest human-made structures, the skyscrapers, themselves standing against the sky. From the perspective of the Industrial Age, Roark could be seen as the heroic architect who tamed the materials of nature through the logic of science and technology, and who created great works of beauty. Here the aesthetic stress is upon the linear and the geometric, a purely dominative effort subjectively to fit reality into predetermined patterns.[21] However, Rand's cultural aesthetic does not separate mind from body, or spirit from science.

Her seemingly Euclidean geometry actually expresses nonlinear processes of turbulence that produce complex structures revealed in fractal-like forms. We find these new forms in Rand's descriptions—of Roark and Dominique's physical characteristics, of nature, and, most importantly, of Roark's buildings.

As the opening passage illustrates, Roark is far from the classical male ideal, especially with regard to his face. Roark's face is a study of unusual contrasts. One might argue that his gray eyes are metaphors for industrial steel and his orange hair a metaphor for Industrial Age electricity, or perhaps for the sun that gives life to nature. Yet, it is a strange face that Dominique knew "was the most beautiful face she would ever see, because it was the abstraction of strength made visible" (207). So, too, in the visual descriptions of Dominique, there is a mixing of industrial and post-industrial forms that challenges the classical ideal.

Some of Dominique's specific physical characteristics often take on industrial forms. For example, her hair is not described as soft and feminine, in the traditional sense. In one of her more visually descriptive phrases, Rand describes Dominique's hair as a "straight mass . . . stirred in a heavy ripple, like a wave through a half-liquid pool of mercury" (142). Later, Rand states that Dominique's hair was "like a pale helmet of polished metal" (522). Both descriptions are clear metaphors for the Industrial Human. Rand also gives Dominique's hair Euclidean form when she writes that it "slanted in a flat curve across her forehead and fell in a straight line" (138). Industrial-Euclidean forms are found, too, in Dominique's body, in the "inflexible precision of her legs" (216) and in "the elegance of line you'll find in a good yacht" (457). But these descriptions also suggest a metaphorical recognition of turbulence and fluidity that occurs in "waves" in both the social and natural world.

Dominique's physical being is a complex mixture of Platonic, industrial, and postindustrial features that explodes classical forms in its "strangely elegant" beauty. Rand describes her as follows:

> Her slender body seemed out of all scale in relation to a normal human body; its lines were so long, so fragile, so exaggerated that she looked like a stylized drawing of a woman and made the correct proportions of a normal being appear heavy and awkward beside her. She wore a plain gray suit; the contrast between its tailored severity and her appearance was deliberately exorbitant—and strangely elegant. . . . She had gray eyes that were not

ovals, but two long, rectangular cuts edged by parallel lines of lashes; she had an air of cold serenity and an exquisitely vicious mouth. Her face, her pale gold hair, her suit seemed to have no color, but only a hint, just on the verge of the reality of color, making the full reality seem vulgar. Keating stood still, because he understood for the first time what it was that artists spoke about when they spoke of beauty. (105)

As I will discuss later in more detail, Dominique has a strong Platonic streak in her personality, for she believes that beauty and greatness have no real chance in this world because they will be defiled or destroyed by the tasteless masses. Rand symbolizes this Platonism by describing Dominique's face, hair, and suit as having only a hint of color, existing "just on the verge of the reality of color, making the full reality seem vulgar." It would seem fair to conclude that such aesthetic symbolism has ethical implications, for Rand clearly believed Dominique more virtuous than the vulgar masses. The industrial metaphors include the long lines of her body, the rectangular gray eyes with parallel lines of lashes, the severe tailoring of the plain gray suit, and the "cold serenity" of Dominique.

In the context of Wolf's beauty myth, Dominique's "slender body," which "seemed out of all scale in relation to a normal human body," could be construed as a literary metaphor for the overly slender supermodel that Wolf derides. But such a conclusion neglects the full context in which Dominique resides and the symbolic meaning of her character. On one level, Dominique is obviously a Euclidean metaphor, her aesthetic form reflecting her ethical virtue, her stylized long lines perhaps resembling an avant-garde Art Deco fashion model. However, the obvious masculinity residing in the industrial forms and her "exquisitely vicious mouth" give Dominique an androgyny that explodes any notion of her being a vision of conservative classicism. In the context of the cultural aesthetics symbolized by Roark's buildings, by Roark's own physical features, and by being Roark's lover, Dominique's physical forms are symbolic of a cultural aesthetic that suggests nonlinearity. Dominique's exaggerated disproportionalities reflect the chaotic characteristics of strange attractors that exist on the edges of transitions between order and chaos.[22] Dominique's color, on the "verge" of full reality, could also be seen, in a very abstract sense, as a metaphor for existence on the edge of order and chaos. Dominique seems not real, yet reflects the essence of nature's structural forms and processes in a new beauty Rand describes as "strangely elegant."[23]

The battle between the ideal and the real harks back to Plato and Aristotle and rages in our culture wars today, setting the context for Wolf's beauty myth, in which aesthetic "idealism" is denounced in the name of egalitarian aesthetic "naturalism." Ideals are most misunderstood in the media. Contemporary social psychologists offer pronouncements about the impact of beauty ideals while showing little knowledge of aesthetic philosophy. It would seem that if "ideals" are transposed to a different context, one in which they represent nonlinear forms revealed through individuality, then there would be no need to reject them wholesale.

Rand saw no necessary conflict between the ideal and the real. She claimed to follow Aristotle, for whom the purpose of art was to objectify the essential and the universal.[24] In conveying aesthetic ideals, the artist should imitate reality, not slavishly present what has happened, but represent what might happen or what is possible according to the essential and universal truths of nature. Free from contradiction, the moral and aesthetic are integrated in art and nature—art objectifying the real, fiction expressing truth.[25] This gives the aesthetic, especially the ideal of beauty, a powerful role in filling human cognitive needs.

For Rand, knowledge begins with concrete particulars, grasped through the senses, from which nonlinear mental abstractions are derived inductively and integrated into cognitive units retained as concepts, themselves applied to reality deductively. Concepts are organized into complex nonlinear networks and mental hierarchies that embody the widest of abstractions, often in the form of an aesthos, which serves as the basis for our evaluations about the world around us, creating the natural need to "see" such abstractions directly. According to Rand (1971, 45), "Art fulfills this need: by means of a selective re-creation, it concretizes man's fundamental view of himself and of existence. It tells man, in effect, which aspects of his experience are to be regarded as essential, significant, important. In this sense, art teaches man how to use his consciousness. It conditions or stylizes man's consciousness by conveying to him a certain way of looking at existence." Art fills this need by stylizing consciousness in conveying a certain view of existence through abstract concepts concretized as organic wholes. Instead of faking reality, the artist stylizes reality. The artist omits the accidentals and selects the "essentials" that she regards as metaphysically important. By

emphasizing and stylizing these "essentials," the artist subjectively objec-
tifies her view of existence. Aesthetic forms are not divorced from reality,
but, properly, should integrate the facts of reality. Through a nonlinear
process of abstraction and concretization, aesthetic forms provide a metaphysical evaluation of the facts, in the form of a concept that can be
grasped directly at the perceptual level, as if the concept were a percept
(36). According to Rand, "the artist starts with a broad abstraction which
he has to concretize, to bring into reality by means of the appropriate
particulars; the viewer perceives the particulars, integrates them and
grasps the abstractions from which they came, thus completing the circle" (35). Via aesthetic abstractions in form, an aesthos is brought to
one's perceptual level in a nonlinear process involving artist, subject,
and the aesthetic object. This process gives aesthetics substantial emotive
power. Thus the aesthetic is the subjective objectification of universal
ideals, through the individual particulars of organic wholes, which are
grasped and integrated subjectively by artists and subjects. Aesthetic concepts are identified inductively and applied deductively.

For both Aristotle and Rand, to present the flawed or the imperfect is
to represent falsehood rather than "truth," because the "essentials" are
the real truth found in nature, which itself is always striving toward a
realization of the better or best. This viewpoint is in direct conflict with
aesthetic "naturalism," which assumes that aesthetic idealism is inherently Platonic and impossible. Naturalism opts for a representation of the
flawed and the imperfect as representative of "nature" in the form of
aesthetic egalitarianism.

At times, Dominique seems to be the pale, hazy unrealized Platonic
vision who believes that beauty has no chance to exist in a real world in
which ideal beauty is brought down to reality and ultimately destroyed
by the tasteless masses and the aesthetic egalitarianism of collectivist
intellectuals (Rand [1943] 1968, 294, 299, 462–63, 493, 508, 510, 528).
Dominique's Platonism is best symbolized when she drops the Greek
statue of Helios down the airshaft of her high-rise because, even though
she loves the statue of a naked man, she thinks it should be destroyed,
since no one should see such beauty (142). It is Roark, the Aristotelian,
who must make the sometime Platonist Dominique realize that beauty
can exist in *this* world. This task requires, in part, that Dominique be the
model for an object of great art. Roark, in designing the Stoddard Temple
of the Human Spirit, commissions a statue of Dominique to stand as the
solitary symbol of the human spirit in the temple. The sculptor Steven

Mallory has Dominique standing, nude, with her arms by her side, palms out, head thrown back in exaltation, an object of art expressing simultaneously the aspiration and fulfillment of the human spirit (341, 344–45). "The statue of a naked woman. . . . Uplifted in its quest—and uplifting by its own essence. Seeking God—and finding itself. Showing that there is no higher reach beyond its own form" (341). Against the backdrop of the temple's large windows open to the city skyline, the strangely elegant beauty of Dominique, the strangely attractive Third Wave supermodel, is brought down from the Platonic heavens to the real existence of this world through an inherently nonlinear process wherein form and essence exist in a reciprocal organic relation. Rand presented not an impossible idealism or a sterile industrialism, but a natural and kaleidic aestheticism found in the laws of nature, not in the might of a State or in the mysticism of a God. Purposeful individuality and nonlinear nature are symbolized by strangely beautiful faces, bodies, and buildings, existing far beyond the confines of a sterile industrial aesthetic, yet much deeper than a superficial Platonic impossibility.

The Organic Relation Between Beauty and Purpose

> [T]he beauty of the human body is that it hasn't a single muscle which doesn't serve its purpose; that there's not a line wasted; that every detail of it fits one idea, the idea of a man and the life of a man.
> —Ayn Rand, *The Fountainhead*

An unfortunate legacy of post-Kantian aesthetics is the idea that beauty is not related to any purpose, creating an aesthetic duality that ripples throughout culture. Thus, the fine arts are alleged superior to the utilitarian arts, the aesthetic is tarnished by the commercial, aesthetic freedom is limited by market demand, the surface obscures substance, and human sexuality is separate from human virtue. The last three of these dualities underlie much of Wolf's beauty myth. She sees market demand as limiting artistic and human freedom, image as suffocating substance, and beauty as being separate from sexuality. Rand clearly rejected the idea of beauty as apart from purpose, seeing instead an organic relation between the aesthetic, the ethical, the cultural, and the sexual.

While the relation between beauty and purpose can have several variable yet similar meanings, it is best represented by modern organic architecture, which sees beauty as the result of harmony between form and function (Osborne 1970, 46–53; Banham 1960, 320–30). Unfortunately, this is often mistakenly expressed as "form follows function." This mistake usually leads to a sterile formalism devoid of human spirit. Rand ([1943] 1968, 35) herself entertained the same idea when she had architect Henry Cameron, Roark's early mentor, state that "the form of a building must follow its function." Some elements of modern architecture and industrial design took "form follows function" also to mean "function apart from form," usually in the name of practical efficiency as a mask for aesthetic inadequacy. The most integrated interpretation is expressed by architect Frank Lloyd Wright (1977, 38) as follows: "[F]orm and function become one in design and execution, if the nature of the materials and method and purpose are all in unison." Wright, perhaps the greatest architect of this century, was not only a prolific designer but was also a prolific writer, authoring numerous essays and books detailing his philosophy of "organic" architecture (Wright 1960, 282–326). Wright is important because Rand (1995, 108–19) considered him a great artist, one of the few men of integrity of the twentieth century, the only man she believed could really "understand" the ideas of *The Fountainhead*. Rand corresponded with Wright several times in letters during the years she was working on *The Fountainhead*. Interestingly, in a letter dated 12 December 1937, Rand used Wright's own words to describe the theme of *The Fountainhead*, which would deal with the declining belief in the "organic" and "natural way" and the prevalence of vicarious forms of living and culture (109).[26] Wright (1958, 81–116) himself was quite critical of the effects of linear industrialism on society, especially that of centralization.

Despite her possibly inaccurate formulation of form following function, Rand suggests some additional components that give her conception of beauty a Wrightian organic flavor. Through Roark, she states: "The purpose, the site, the material determine the shape. Nothing can be reasonable or beautiful unless it's made by one central idea, and the idea sets every detail. A building is alive, like a man. Its integrity is to follow its own truth, its one single theme, and to serve its own single purpose" ([1943] 1968, 12).

While one could see a sterile linearity in Rand's expression of "a single theme," such a reading would be an oversimplification. Several points are crucial here in Wright's and Rand's formulations. First, the concept of "purposeful" beauty was never meant to provide an intellectual license for mundane, unimaginative industrial design, or the spiritless uniform glass rectangles that numb many of the world's skylines. Second, such beauty does not mean that ornament is superfluous, but that ornament should be determined by the theme of the structure. As Roark's mentor, Henry Cameron, said: "A building creates its own beauty, and its ornament is derived from the rules of its theme and its structure" (492). The very same principles could be applied in interpreting apparel and personal adornment, with these representing an expression of the inner theme of the person, not a superficial layer masking the lack of substance. Of course, as the consequences of "the beauty myth" indicate, there exists an abundance of shallow post-Kantian citizens. Unfortunately, however, too often in contemporary culture a person's concern with fine design or apparel is viewed as an expression of superficiality. In reality, however, some critics project their own aesthetic superficiality onto others. Even Rand, the rational philosopher, overlooked Rand, the intuitive artist, when she seemingly trivialized the importance of "decorative" arts in comparison to the "fine" arts (Rand 1971, 74–75). With their roots in Newtonian linearity and Kantian aesthetics, such unwarranted distinctions continue to haunt culture.[27] Understanding the nonlinear organic relation between structure (or theme) and ornament could defuse much of the prevailing superficiality in body adornment. As noted earlier, Rand herself recognized that a shallow beauty or elegance could be used to mask an ugliness or superficiality of spirit, whether in a building, body, or face. Most of Rand's protagonists are "physically" beautiful, but that physicality is metaphorically symbolic of harmony between outer form and inner purpose. As Gail Wynand described Dominique: "You're so beautiful Dominique . . . the one person who matches inside and out" (Rand [1943] 1968, 516).

Thus, third, Rand clearly integrated aesthetics with ethics when she suggested beauty is not possible without "integrity" seeking truth, and "purpose" providing a central theme.[28] Full realization of potentiality, be it in a building or a life, requires integrity, a commitment to truth, to one's purpose. Rand saw such abstract beauty as an aesthetic-moral compass,[29] guiding human actions through a self-chosen purpose marked by a dedication to truth and integrity. In *The Fountainhead*, the physical beauty of Roark and Dominique is a metaphor for the organic relation between human form and purposeful function. Roark's buildings even have aesthetic moral qualities; Dominique describes one of his buildings as being "beautiful, like an anthem" (276).

Fourth, Wright's and Rand's mention of "method" yields insights into their conceptions of beauty. Method, or style, may be characterized as a distinctive manner or mode of expression. Rand believed style reflected a certain manner of cognition or epistemics, and suggested that "method," apart from content, was crucial to the full realization of potentiality. She stated: "The architect [is] . . . the man who had made this possible—the thought in the mind of that man—and not the content of that thought . . . but the method of his thought, the rule of its function" (532). Both Wright and Rand saw the organic role that "method," or style or form, plays in combination with function in realizing great design, whether it be the design of a building or a life. The method by which a mind deals with its content of knowledge will determine the efficiency of its functioning over time, precisely because method and content shape each other through their reciprocal interactions (Rand 1975, 193–94). Method is formal causality integrating the structure and efficiency of functionality in a reciprocal relation, much like the feedback processes inherent in the dynamics of the nonlinear sciences.

Finally, for both Wright and Rand, science and technology are not in conflict with nature, and a dynamic and harmonious organic relation could and should exist between design, technology, nature, purpose, and humans. The beauty of nature also expresses the organicity of the processes and forces of nature in creating the structures of the natural world. Appreciative of such natural beauty, Roark's buildings are always in harmony with the surrounding nature, often as if an extension of nature itself (Rand [1943] 1968, 3, 33, 482, 697). As the culmination of her cultural aesthetics, it is in Roark's buildings that Rand most clearly expresses a Third Wave aesthos in the forms of beautiful strange attractors.

Strange Attractors and the Third Wave Aesthos

But above all chaos is beautiful.

—physicist Ian Stewart

Before examining the Third Wave aesthos as expressed in Roark's buildings, it is necessary to focus greater attention on Rand's theory of concepts. Her epistemology provides not only an original and nonlinear theory of concepts, but unusual insights into the role of aesthetics in human reasoning, showing why humans naturally need and develop aesthetic worldviews to guide their judgments and lives. This explains why a cultural aesthos can be such a powerful motivator across the fields of human endeavor, and suggests deep aesthetic motivations in the clash of Second and Third Wave cultures. Like Roark's buildings, Rand's theory of concepts is also in harmony with the Third Wave.

According to Rand, concepts, or universals, are intrinsic neither to the object nor to the subject. They are identifications of relations among particulars existing objectively in the physical world, or of ideas existing in relation to such particulars. Concepts are relationally objective and have value when they serve purposes related to individual human lives. We are directly aware of the world via the senses, which allow us to apprehend particular "entities" that we distinguish from other entities. To form a concept, we identify relationships among the entities by grasping similarities and differences in their identities. Through a quantitative nonlinear process of measurement-omission, we form a cognitive abstraction of the formal relations, where the specific measurements of the formal relations must be of some quantity, but could be of any quantity. This abstraction represents that which is universal to the given particulars, yet is open-ended, offering variation limited only by context and human purpose (Rand 1990, 83–87). This theory of concepts is essentially aesthetic and nonlinear. Rand's theory seems to be sympathetic to feminist epistemological concerns with regard to linear masculinist deductionism that masquerades as objective "reason." Rand does not reject reason, but she places the processes of reason in a context where objective facts exist in a nonlinear relation with deduction and induction, universality and particularity. Thus, "reason" is freed from the "rationalist" tradition of totalitarian universalism and imposed social order.

For Rand, the world is one of particulars, not of timeless Platonic forms or subjective appearances. These particulars are ontologically represented to our senses as distinctly different entities that exist in complex relations. Against the tapestry of differences, we identify varying proportionalities of similarity and difference in spatiotemporal-conceptual relations revealed in patterns and forms among objects, ideas, and ourselves.[30] Forming concepts means identifying physical, telic, or conceptual proportionalities with referents in the physical world. Concept formation is inherently an aesthetic process as suggested by the very term "concept *formation.*" Concepts are objective in the abstract and universal, subjective in the concrete and particular, and purposeful in context, yet they are not the result of linear processes.

In my judgment, the first level of concept formation described by Rand operates like a beginning nonlinear equation, with the results of the identified varying proportionalities iterated into the original equation. Thus, concept formation and modification resembles a nonlinear process of self-similarity within a wider scope of variation, differentiation, and contrast. The process of concept formation entails identifying purposeful proportionality, or the fitness of the relation between form and function, with the new "result" becoming a new or modified concept. Rand does not use the term "purposeful proportionality," but it is a term that can be used to describe the organic nonlinear formal and temporal relation between form and function, style and substance, or method and content.[31] Induction and deduction are like analogic and nonlinear processes,[32] wherein new particulars are iteratively inserted into the concept-formation equation, often yielding a new concept with new contours and parameters. Nature and reality, the existing physical and social facts, together with human purpose, form the boundary for contextuality and for the feedback processes within which nonlinear causality continually reshapes the formed concept. The cognitive abstraction formed is an "ideal" capable of admitting open-ended variation. Ideal formation is not a priori, or purely an element of linear logic; it is the result of a feedback process of iterative and analogic identification of purposeful proportionality. Through immensely complex reciprocal relations, proportion and purpose (form and function or method and content) simultaneously influence each other, becoming integrated as a conceptual or perceptual unit when properly identified or understood.

Rand's epistemology suggests that the aesthetics of concept formation do not divorce mind from reality, or universals from particulars, or objectivity from subjectivity, or form from function, or style from substance. Embracing universalism and objectivity need not mean uniformity. Embracing subjectivity and particularity need not mean relativism. Embracing form and style need not mean appearances and superficiality. Pursuing beauty and individuality need not mean separating the ideal from the real, or mind from body, or love from sexuality, or lover from lover, in whatever combination. As physio-material needs are more satisfied, individuals will seek more physio-cognitive gratifications, inducing ever more variation-seeking purposes in sexual relations. This kaleidic sexual variation will be simultaneously fueled and satisfied by high social-communications plasticity in the Third Wave. Rand's suggested relational objectivity, as interpreted here, permits universalism and individuality, allowing contextual variation and the subjective individuality sought by Wolf, without either cultural relativism or nihilism. Beauty is culturally contextual yet open-ended—a nonlinear complexity of purposes, forms, and variations.

The aesthetics of concept formation are deeply embedded in our thinking processes, guiding our valuations of the world around us and creating a deep cognitive need to "see" and "feel" such abstractions in varieties of physical forms and experiences. The aesthetics of concept formation give rise not only to the need for art, but also to the need for seeing beauty in nature, culture, and life. Scientific discovery is motivated by the pursuit of beauty, as are our political and cultural visions.[33] While *The Beauty Myth* presents a capitalist industrial aesthetic of imaged humans, self-alienation, and impossible ideals, *The Fountainhead* presents a postindustrial aestheticism that transcends the fading Industrial Age, clearly expressing the spirit of Third Wave scientific and aesthetic dynamics.

Rand presents an aesthos expressed through asymmetric forms that exhibit turbulent processes, fractal self-similarity, chaotic complexity, and kaleidic organicity—all integrating human purpose with nature in beautiful strange attractors. Roark's buildings are extensions of this aesthos. They are designed in harmony with nature while simultaneously improving upon nature. But Rand was not an apologist for all architectural and urban design. While Rand clearly rejected the "moldering ruins" of classical European culture and architecture,[34] she also rejected the dogma of modern architecture and its aesthos of sterile linearity expressed in static, regular, predictable, orderly forms (Rand [1943] 1968, 492). In addition, she was quite appreciative of the beauty and spiritual importance of "an untouched world." This sentiment is expressed in the opening passage of the section of *The Fountainhead* entitled "Howard Roark," where Rand states:

> The leaves streamed down, trembling in the sun. They were not green; only a few, scattered through the torrent, stood out in single drops of a green so bright and pure that it hurt the eyes; the rest were not a color, but a light, the substance of fire on metal, living sparks without edges. And it looked as if the forest

were a spread of light boiling slowly to produce this color, this
green rising in small bubbles, the condensed essence of spring.
The trees met, bending over the road, and spots of sun on the
ground moved with the shifting of branches, like a conscious
caress. The young man hoped he would not have to die.

Not if the earth looked like this, he thought. Not if he could
hear the hope and the promise like a voice, with leaves, tree
trunks and rocks instead of words. But he knew that the earth
looked like this only because he had seen no sign of men for
hours; he was alone, riding his bicycle down a forgotten trail
through the hills of Pennsylvania where he had never been before, where he could feel the fresh wonder of an untouched world.
(527)

Here is a vision of a dynamic nature full of radiant light and colors,
produced through nature's inherent turbulence. There is nothing static
or timeless in this "untouched world"—nature is boiling, leaves are
trembling, trees are bending, branches are shifting, and colors exist in
fiery torrents so bright they do violence to the eyes.

Rand sees the beauty of nature as the outcome of seemingly violent
processes operating in a realm very much like what the nonlinear sciences
would describe as "the edge of order and chaos." She sees nature's forms
exhibiting what could be called a "turbulent harmony." She describes
such a process in a scene depicting Roark working with a gang of men in
a stone quarry:

He stood on the hot stone in the sun. His face was scorched to
bronze. His shirt stuck in long, damp patches to his back. The
quarry rose about him in flat shelves breaking against one another. It was a world without curves, grass or soil, a simplified
world of stone planes, sharp edges and angles. The stone had not
been made by patient centuries welding the sediment of winds
and tides; it had come from a molten mass cooling slowly at an
unknown depth; it had been flung, forced out of the earth, and
still held the shape of violence against the violence of the men
on its ledges. (203)

Roark is working in such conditions because, at this point in the novel,
he has been unable to earn a living by designing his type of visionary

buildings. He leaves New York City to work in a stone quarry, which is the place where he eventually meets Dominique, since her father owns the quarry. It is fitting that they meet in such a naturally violent setting, because throughout the novel they both experience waves of turbulence and seeming chaos, yet these conditions are necessary for both fully to develop themselves. In the following passage, Rand, through the thoughts of Dominique, metaphorically illustrates their existence on waves of turbulence: "She liked to lie with him at the edge of the water; she would lie on her stomach, a few feet away from him, facing the shore, her toes stretched to the waves; she would not touch him, but she would feel the waves coming up behind them, breaking against their bodies, and she would see the backwash running in mingled streams off her body and his" (318).

The waves "breaking against their bodies" are quite symbolic of the turbulent harmonizing that occurs on "the edge of order and chaos," which is exactly where the form of a wave breaks. "Turbulent harmony" is a process that runs throughout Rand's aesthos. And though turbulence might endanger life, it could also lead to higher levels of living and aesthetic experience. Waves of turbulent harmonizing often produce sublime natural beauty and intense sexual eroticism.

Ironically, the "waves" of chaotic turbulence have become key visual and structural metaphors for the dynamics of the emerging postindustrial era, as illustrated by Toffler's Third Wave, Wolf's own Feminist Third Wave, and wave-centric phrases such as "surfing the Web" and "surfing the turbulence." When Rand describes Roark's buildings to convey such ideas, it is as if the philosopher of industrial capitalism is overwhelmed by the intuitive artist of postindustrial aestheticism. This results in a Third Wave aesthos expressed in the buildings of Howard Roark:

STRANGE ATTRACTORS AND THE THIRD WAVE AESTHOS OF ROARK'S BUILDINGS

The Heller House
The house on the cliff had been designed not by Roark, but by the cliff on which it stood. It was as if the cliff had grown and completed itself and proclaimed the purpose for which it had been waiting. The house was broken into many levels, following the ledges of the rock, rising as it rose, in gradual masses, on planes flowing together up into one consummate harmony. The walls, of the same granite as the rock, continued its vertical lines upward; the wide, projecting terraces of concrete, silver as the sea, followed the line of the waves, of the straight horizon. (119)

The Gowan Gas Station

[The gasoline station] was a study in circles; there were no angles and no straight lines; it looked like shapes caught in a flow, held still at the moment of being poured, at the precise moment when they formed a harmony that seemed too perfect to be intentional. It looked like a cluster of bubbles hanging low over the ground, not quite touching it, to be swept aside in an instant of wind speed; it looked gay, with the hard, bracing gaiety of efficiency, like a powerful airplane engine. (156)

Sanborn House

[I]t seemed only that the trees flowed into the house and through it. (166)

The Enright House

He did not grasp it as a building, at first glance, but as a rising mass of rock crystal. There was the same severe, mathematical order, holding together a free, fantastic growth, straight lines and clean angles, space slashed with a knife, yet in a harmony of formation as delicate as the work of a jeweler; an incredible variety of shapes, each separate unit unrepeated, but leading inevitably to the next one and to the whole; so that the future inhabitants were to have, not a square cage out of a pile of square cages, but each a single house held to the other houses like a single crystal to the side of a rock. (238)

Monadnock Valley

He knew that the ledges had not been touched, that no artifice had altered the unplanned beauty of graded steps. Yet some power had known how to build on these ledges in such a way that the houses became inevitable, and one could no longer imagine the hills as beautiful without them—as if the centuries and the series of chances that produced these ledges in the struggle of great blind forces had waited for their final expression, had only been a road to a goal—and the goal was these buildings, part of the hills, shaped by the hills, yet ruling them by giving them meaning.

The buildings were of plain field stone—like the rocks jutting from the green hillsides—and of glass, great sheets of glass used as if the sun were invited to complete the structures, sunlight becoming part of the masonry. There were many houses, they were small, they were cut off from one another, and no two of them alike. But they were like variations on a single theme, like a symphony played by an inexhaustible imagination, and one could still hear the laughter of the force that had been let loose on them, as if that force had run, unrestrained, challenging itself to be spent, but had never reached its end. Music, he thought, the promise the music invoked he had invoked, the sense of it made real—there it was before his eyes—he did not see it—he heard it in chords—he thought there was a common language of thought, sight and sound—was it mathematics?—the discipline of reason—music was

mathematics—architecture was music in stone—he knew he was dizzy because this place below him could not be real. (528–29)

Wynand House

The house was a shape of horizontal rectangles rising toward a slashing vertical projection; a group of diminishing setbacks, each a separate room, its size
and form making the successive steps in a series of interlocking floor lines. It
was as if from the wide living room on the first level a hand had moved slowly,
shaping the next steps by a sustained touch, then had stopped, had continued
in separate movements, each shorter, brusquer, and had ended, torn off, remaining somewhere in the sky. So that it seemed as if the slow rhythm of the
rising fields had been picked up, stressed, accelerated and broken into the
staccato chords of the finale. (610)

Cortlandt Homes

Cortlandt Homes presented six buildings, fifteen stories high, each made in
the shape of an irregular star with arms extending from a central shaft. . . .
The apartments radiated from the center in the form of extended triangles.
. . . The entire plan was a composition in triangles. The buildings, of poured
concrete, were a complex modeling of simple structural features; there was no
ornament; none was needed; the shapes had the beauty of sculpture. (613)

Stoddard Temple to the Human Spirit

Its lines were horizontal, not the lines reaching to heaven, but the lines of
the earth. It seemed to spread over the ground like arms outstretched at shoul-
der-height, palms down, in great, silent acceptance. It did not cling to the
soil and did not crouch under the sky. It seemed to lift the earth, and its few
vertical shafts pulled the sky down. It was scaled to human height in such a
manner that it did not dwarf man, but stood as a setting that made his figure
the only absolute, the gauge of perfection by which all dimensions were to be
judged. . . . There was no ornamentation inside, except the graded projections
of the walls, and the vast windows. The place was not sealed under vaults,
but thrown open to the earth around it, to the trees, the river, the sun—and
the skyline of the city in the distance, the skyscrapers, the shapes of man's
achievement on earth. At the end of the room, facing the entrance, with the
city as the background, stood the figure of a naked human body. (343–44)

Rand's descriptions of Roark's buildings are quite suggestive of the
strange attractors being discovered by chaos theory. In Roark's buildings,
there exist chaotic structure, fractal self-similarity, dynamic flow, relational organicity, all expressed through the asymmetrical forms of strange

attractors existing in reciprocal relations with human purpose and nature. Rand saw structure as "the solved problem of tension, of balance, of security in counterthrusts" (576). Strange attractors result as the product of the chaotic natural tension in the forces and processes of nature, expressed through the structure of Roark's buildings.

In the Heller House, there exists fractal self-similarity within the ledges of the cliff and the many levels and dynamic flow in the rising planes of the building. Organic relations are evident in the integration of the granite cliff and the granite walls rising upward, the concrete terraces flowing outward, following the "line of the waves."

In the Gowan Gas Station, there exists an obvious dynamic flow and organic relation (mixed with an industrial metaphor). The "study in circles" is suggestive of a highly complex form of a smooth circular strange attractor.[35]

In the Sanborn House, there exists a dynamic flow and an organic relation as the house welcomes the surrounding trees.

The chaotic and structural complexity increases in the Enright House and the homes of the Monadnock Valley resort complex. In the Enright House, Rand explicitly presented turbulent harmony in the "space slashed with a knife." Yet, there exists severe structure formed out of the "free growth" of lines and angles, forming a fractal self-similarity in the unrepeated variety of shapes, each determining the next shape and the whole. Thus, there is a reciprocal relation between the variety of shapes and the shape of the whole—"each a single house held to the other houses like single crystal to the sides of a rock." Rand also presents the idea of "free growth," metaphorically recognizing not only the striking and complex pattern of structure, but also the freedom of the creative artist expressed through principles that are similar to natural processes.[36] Terminology similar to "free growth" also appears in descriptions of the processes of chaotic and nonlinear sciences.[37]

Similar principles are developed in Monadnock Valley, beginning with the "unplanned beauty of the graded steps" on the ledges, produced over the centuries through a "series of chances" and a "struggle of blind forces." There is also a fractal self-similarity in the houses, of which no two are alike, yet they reflect "variations on a single theme" to which Rand ascribes the musical metaphor of a "symphony."

The structure of Wynand House also exhibits fractal self-similarity in the "successive steps" of "the interlocking floor lines." Rand expresses again the natural processes of turbulent harmonizing in the "slashing vertical projection," in which the last level appears as if it was "torn off" in the sky by a hand. Organic relations are reflected in the structure that picks up and stresses the "rhythm of the rising fields."

Cortlandt Homes, too, reflects fractal self-similarity and dynamic flow in its asymmetric composition of triangles radiating from the central shafts of the high-rises. Of course, its overall layout suggests organicity in which "the shapes had the beauty of sculpture."

In the Stoddard Temple to the Human Spirit, there exists a deep organicity in the relations of the forms of the temple and the surrounding natural world. This "Temple to the Human Spirit" is not a gargantuan monument to the State, or a gargoylesque monstrosity of the Church. Here the standard is the human form and human potential, symbolized by the single figure of a naked human body—the statue of Dominique. This building generates enormous controversy in the novel because many people cannot comprehend how its unorthodox design relates to "the human spirit." Indeed, throughout the novel, Roark's buildings invite controversy and pejorative descriptions because they are perceived as strange and "disorderly."[38] The Stoddard Temple is the most controversial: it is labeled in the media as "spiritual embezzlement," "an outrageous sacrilege," and "an insolent mockery of all religion" (348–49).[39] The outcry is so great that Roark is sued by Hopton Stoddard for architectural malpractice (350).[40]

Here, the relevance of the trial lies in the testimony of architectural "experts," who claim that Roark's design for the temple is an effrontery to both architecture and religion. In the testimony of Roark's fellow architects, Rand clearly illustrates Roark's break with aesthetic tradition and the inability of his contemporaries to grasp the new asymmetric, nonlinear forms. For example, the "parasitic" architect Peter Keating testifies: "The Stoddard Temple has an improperly balanced plan, which leads to spatial confusion. There is no balance of masses. It lacks a sense of symmetry. Its proportions are inept. . . . It's out of scale. It contradicts the elementary principles of composition. . . . it shows no sense of structure, no instinct for beauty, no creative imagination" (362–63). In addition, famed architect Gordon Prescott testifies: "The correlation of the transcendental to the purely spatial in the building under discussion is entirely screwy. . . . The flowing life which comes from the sense of order in chaos, or, if you prefer, from unity in diversity, as well as vice versa. . . . is here entirely absent" (364). Keating's testimony represents the majority of architects, critics, and members of society who simply cannot

understand or appreciate the spirituality of Roark's buildings. Like Keating, Prescott is testifying against Roark, claiming that "the sense of order
in chaos" is *absent* from the design of the temple. However, precisely
because Prescott is testifying against Roark and is a typical architect,
Rand's point is just the *opposite*—Roark's buildings indeed contain "the
flowing of life which comes from the sense of order in chaos."

Not surprisingly, Rand loves the skyscraper and the New York City
skyline not only because of its symbolism of "egoism" and industrial "capitalism," but also because the skyscraper and the skyline represent her
aesthetic vision of turbulent harmony. In the passage below, Rand describes Dominique's late-night trips on the Staten Island Ferry:

> Once, she took the Staten Island Ferry at two o'clock in the
> morning; she rode to the Island, standing alone at the rail of an
> empty deck. She watched the city moving away from her. In the
> vast emptiness of sky and ocean, the city was only a small, jagged
> solid. It seemed condensed, pressed tight together, not a place of
> streets and separate buildings, but a single sculptured form. A
> form of irregular steps that rose and dropped without ordered
> continuity, long ascensions and sudden drops, like the graph of a
> sudden struggle. But it went on mounting—toward a few points,
> toward the triumphant masts of skyscrapers raised out of the
> struggle. (317)

Here the skyscraper and the skyline exist in reciprocity, where the skyline
of individual skyscrapers becomes a "single sculptured form." This piece
of sculpture is composed of jagged edges and irregular steps that rise in
long ascensions and suddenly drop "without ordered continuity," as some
skyscrapers triumphantly rise out of the struggle of nature's turbulent harmony. For Dominique, the skyscrapers of the New York City skyline form
a sculptured strange attractor.

Conclusion

Ayn Rand is perhaps best known for her passionate and eloquent defense
of science, egoism, and capitalism. However, I have argued that Rand's
cultural aesthetics transcend the fading Industrial Age and suggest an

aesthos for the emerging Third Wave. Neither *The Fountainhead* nor *The Beauty Myth* present complete theories of beauty, yet both present passionate and eloquent aesthetic visions suggesting radically different worldviews. Naomi Wolf is right to call for a "Feminist Third Wave," but it must be a "wave" that is free from outmoded Second Wave structures and ideas. Despite Rand's industrial metaphors, her cultural aesthetics transcend purpose and nature, culture and gender, the Newtonian skyscraper and the Cosmopolitan supermodel, expressing deep intuitive insight into the complex organicity and turbulent harmony of the Third Wave aesthos. Ayn Rand's cultural aesthos is "a strange attractor" feminists may find worth exploring.

Notes

1. Torres and Kamhi 1999 is the first book to analyze Rand's theory of art. While Rand's *Romantic Manifesto* (1971) offers unique and valuable insights into the relationship between philosophy, psychology, and the arts, it does not present a complete philosophy of fine art. It stresses the moral-psychological processes in creating and valuing art, presenting no broad philosophy of beauty or aesthetics in which fine art resides.

2. Hilde Hein (1995, 454–55) suggests these premises must be rejected in any feminist aesthetic. See also Brand and Korsmeyer 1995, 1–114, for a discussion of the relation between feminism and aesthetic tradition.

3. The term "aesthos" is my own and is explained in greater detail in my forthcoming *Chaos at the Edge of Utopia*.

4. In another dialectical vein, Donovan (1993) sees a feminist aesthetic in which there is an integration of beauty and use in craft works to form a "negative critique" of commodity exchange.

5. The term "kaleidic" is used in this article to suggest structure and pattern unfolding temporally through surprising and seemingly chaotic processes, yielding variable tendencies toward formal structures that are not static, uniform, or equilibrating, as in neoclassical economics. Such constant evolution produces ever-changing structures and patterns that are often beautiful to behold, much like the patterns in a kaleidoscope. However, this does *not* mean that reality is unknowable or unpredictable in a general sense, which one might interpret the Austrian economist Ludwig Lachmann (1976) to be saying.

6. One should not underestimate the role of advertising in comparison with "socialist realism." See Schudson 1984, 209–33.

7. Rand, however, was no conservative. She advocated a libertarian separation of state from the realms of ideas, science, sexuality, economics, religion, and so forth.

8. Toffler (1970, 16) estimates the year at "about 1956."

9. The interview was reprinted in Haley 1993. Reportedly, one dozen "Playmates" have stated that Ayn Rand was their favorite author. See *IOS Journal* 6, no. 6 (1997): 5.

10. For a popularized explanation of chaos theory, see Gleick 1987. For a discussion of the science of complexity, see Prigogine and Stengers 1984. The new discoveries of the evolutionary sciences can be found in Kauffman 1995.

11. See Batty and Longley 1994; Lavoie 1989.

12. Friedman (1989) argues that Rand's concerns about anarchism are perhaps unfounded (109–200). Benson (1990) explores how a legal system could emerge and function without a nation-state (349–78).

13. Here Wolf is referring to Betty Friedan's cultural landmark *The Feminine Mystique*, which was reviewed quite favorably in 1963 in Ayn Rand's *Objectivist Newsletter*. See Efron 1963.

14. Here Wolf does not realize that the purpose of the "gold standard" was to maintain for money an "objective" value connected to production, not to subjective government fiat.

15. In a more explicit form, Donovan (1993) presents an aesthetic that integrates feminist and Marxist theory.

16. In Rand [1943] 1968, examples include parasitic architect Peter Keating (17) and the shallow avant-garde actress Eve Layton, described as "Venus rising out of a submarine hatch" (581); and in Rand 1957, Lillian Rearden, the woman of classical beauty and vacuous spirit (33).

17. Hanson (1993) brilliantly illustrates such reactionary criticism from traditional philosophy.

18. For several reasons, pure subjectivist relativism is a non sequitur on a culturewide scale. Across cultures and within cultures, there are *differences* among subjects regarding particular objects of beauty. Is this proof of pure relativism? If so, then how can we explain the widespread *agreements* with regard to objects of beauty across and within cultures? Are we to conclude that there is "nothing" about these "objects" upon which subjects agree, even though such subjects have little in common other than their humanity and the capacity to appreciate objects exhibiting principles or qualities of beauty? Further, aesthetic disagreement still presupposes the existence of objects about which people disagree. Is it possible that subjects can judge different things beautiful for similar reasons? How can we explain things such as the ancient golden ratio and Fibonacci spirals showing up across cultures, and in all kinds of human, organic, and physical phenomena? If beauty is truly "in the eye of the beholder," then are we to presume that the training and efforts of artists around the world to produce their aesthetic objects and experiences have nothing to do with the judgments of the subjects? Further, there is the simple fact that aesthetic experiences happen in the presence of objects and ideas that stimulate such experiences. Ultimately, subjectivist relativism must mean that the mind constitutes the true reality, à la Plato and Kant. Thus, if subjectivist relativism is true, then the blame for the consequences cannot rest with the aesthetic objects in the capitalist media.

19. The relationship of philosophy of beauty to the market and commodities is discussed at length in Vacker and Key 1993.

20. On these points, see Kellert 1993, 7–8.

21. On these points, see Donovan 1993, 55.

22. An example might be the Feigenbaum attractor, in which period-doubling leads from linear order to nonlinear chaos. See Peitgen, Jurgens, and Saupe 1992, 585–93.

23. Rand made it clear she did not think that physical beauty resided in universal physical standards or purely subjective standards but, instead, that the standard was determined by the empirical facts of the cultural context. She states: "In this respect, a good example would be the beauty of different races of people. For instance, the black face, or an Oriental face, is built on a different standard, and therefore what would be beautiful on a white face will not be beautiful for them (or vice-versa), because there is a certain racial standard of features by which you judge which features, which face, in *that* classification is harmonious or distorted" (in Binswanger 1986, 49–50).

24. Some scholars (e.g., Cox [1986]) have maintained that Rand misunderstood Aristotle on the role of the artist.

25. See Butcher 1951, 150–51, 391–92.

26. See also Rand 1997, especially chapter 5, detailing her architectural research and appreciation of Wright's "organic" principles. The spring 1997 issue (no. 21) of *JTF* (*Journal of the Taliesin Fellows*) features a cover story on Wright and Rand, among other articles detailing their relationship.

27. In this regard, see Donovan 1993, 53–54.

28. In a similar vein, French (1993, 76) sees a feminist art that is "useful and beautiful and moral."

29. " 'Don't be astonished if I tell you that I feel as if I'll have to live up to that house' . . . 'I intended that,' said Roark" to Austin Heller. Rand [1943] 1968, 132.

30. This means that there is a relation between the individual subject and object and a relation among the parts of the object, but that these parts are themselves existents, or objects. In identifying beauty, the subject must identify the relations of the existents constituting the "object" and the relations between the object and him- or herself.

31. This term is explained in greater detail in my forthcoming book. See note 3.

32. For a fine description of similar "analinear" processes, see Walter 1994.

33. For example, see Chandrasekhar 1987.

34. Influenced by Wrightian ideas, Rand ([1943] 1968) was very critical of the 1893 Columbian Exposition in Chicago, which glorified the classical architecture of the European traditions. "The Rome of two thousand years ago rose on the shore of Lake Michigan, a Rome improved by the pieces of France, Spain, Athens and every style that followed it. . . . To sanction it was Culture; there were twenty centuries unrolling in moldering ruins" (34–35).

35. This type of strange attractor is known as a Lorenz attractor. See Gleick 1987, 28–29.

36. For example, in describing the Wynand Building, "[Dominique] thought: they say the heart of the earth is made of fire. It is held imprisoned and silent. But at times it breaks through the clay, the iron, the granite, and shoots to freedom. Then it becomes a thing like this" (Rand [1943] 1968, 726).

37. For example, see Turner 1995.

38. Other descriptions include "rebellious," "screamingly funny," "crazy," "queer," "law breaking," "rebellious," "a blot on the profession," and "a wound on the face of the city" (Rand [1943] 1968, 133, 195, 272).

39. "The Stoddard Temple is a brazen denial of our entire past, an insolent 'No' flung in the face of history" (Rand [1943] 1968, 360).

40. Stoddard, on the advice of archvillain Ellsworth Toohey, commissioned Roark to design and build the temple while Stoddard was traveling around the world. Knowing that Stoddard would hate Roark's designs and that there would be an outcry, Toohey hoped to destroy Roark and the ideas reflected in the designs.

References

Banham, Reyner. 1960. *Theory and Design in the First Machine Age.* New York: Praeger.

Batty, Michael, and Paul Longley. 1994. *Fractal Cities.* London: Academic Press.

Benson, Bruce L. 1990. *The Enterprise of Law: Justice Without the State.* San Francisco: Pacific Research Institute for Public Policy.

Binswanger, Harry, ed. 1986. *The Ayn Rand Lexicon: Objectivism from A to Z.* New York: New American Library.

Brand, Peggy Zeglin, and Carolyn Korsmeyer, eds. 1995. *Feminism and Tradition in Aesthetics.* University Park: Pennsylvania State University Press.

Butcher, S. H. 1951. *Aristotle's Theory of Poetry and Fine Art.* New York: Dover.

Chandrasekhar, S. 1987. *Truth and Beauty: Aesthetic Motivations in Science.* Chicago: University of Chicago Press.

Cox, Stephen. 1986. Ayn Rand: Theory vs. creative life. *Journal of Libertarian Studies* 8 (winter): 19–29.

Donovan, Josephine. 1993. Everyday use and moments of being: Toward a nondominative aesthetic. In *Aesthetics in Feminist Perspective,* edited by Hilde Hein and Carolyn Korsmeyer. Bloomington: Indiana University Press.

Efron, Edith. 1963. Review of *The Feminine Mystique*, by Betty Friedan. *The Objectivist Newsletter* 2, no. 7:27. (Reprinted in the *The Objectivist Newsletter* 1–4, 1962–65, 26–27. Palo Alto, Calif.: Palo Alto Book Service.)

French, Marilyn. 1993. Is there a feminist aesthetic? In *Aesthetics in Feminist Perspective*, edited by Hilde Hein and Carolyn Korsmeyer. Bloomington: Indiana University Press.

Friedman, David. 1989. *The Machinery of Freedom*. La Salle, Ill.: Open Court.

Gleick, James. 1987. *Chaos: Making a New Science*. New York: Penguin.

Haley, Alex. 1993. *The Playboy Interviews*. Edited by Murray Fisher. New York: Ballantine.

Hanson, Karen. 1993. Dressing down dressing up: The philosophic fear of fashion. In *Aesthetics in Feminist Perspective*, edited by Hilde Hein and Carolyn Korsmeyer. Bloomington: Indiana University Press.

Haug, W. F. [1971] 1986. *Critique of Commodity Aesthetic*. Minneapolis: University of Minnesota Press.

Hein, Hilde. 1995. Feminist aesthetics in feminist theory. In *Feminism and Tradition in Aesthetics*, edited by Peggy Zeglin Brand and Carolyn Korsmeyer. University Park: Pennsylvania State University Press.

Hein, Hilde, and Carolyn Korsmeyer, eds. 1993. *Aesthetics in Feminist Perspective*. Bloomington: Indiana University Press.

Kauffman, Stuart A. 1993. *The Origins of Order*. Oxford: Oxford University Press.

———. 1995. *At Home in the Universe: The Search for the Laws of Self-Organization and Complexity*. New York: Oxford University Press.

Kellert, Stephen H. 1993. *In the Wake of Chaos*. Chicago: University of Chicago Press.

Lachmann, Ludwig. 1976. From Mises to Shackle: An essay on Austrian economics and the kaleidic society. *Journal of Economic Literature* 14 (March): 54–62.

Lavoie, Don. 1989. Economic chaos or spontaneous order: Implications for political economy of the new view of science. *Cato Journal* 8, no. 3:613–35.

Marcuse, Herbert. 1968. *The Aesthetic Dimension*. Boston: Beacon Press.

Marx, Karl. 1967. *Capital*. New York: International Publishers.

Osborne, Harold. 1970. *Aesthetics and Art Theory*. New York: Dutton.

Peitgen, Heinz-Otto, Hartmut Jurgens, and Dietmar Saupe. 1992. *Chaos and Fractals: New Frontiers of Science*. New York: Springer-Verlag.

Plato. 1956. *Phaedrus*. Translated by W. C. Helmbold and W. G. Rabinowitz. Indianapolis: Bobbs-Merrill.

———. 1974. *The Republic*. Translated by G.M.A. Grube. Indianapolis: Hackett.

———. 1980. *The Laws*. Translated by Thomas L. Pangle. Chicago: University of Chicago Press.

———. 1984. *Sophist: Being of the Beautiful, Part II*. Translated by Seth Benardete. Chicago: University of Chicago Press.

———. 1989. *Symposium*. Translated by Alexander Nehamas and Paul Woodruff. Indianapolis: Hackett.

Poret, Mark. 1980. *The Information Society*. Washington, D.C.: PBS Video.

Prigogine, Ilya, and Isabelle Stengers. 1984. *Order Out of Chaos: Man's New Dialogue with Nature*. Toronto: Bantam.

Rand, Ayn. [1943] 1968. *The Fountainhead*. New York: Bobbs-Merrill.

———. 1957. *Atlas Shrugged*. New York: Random House.

———. 1971. *The Romantic Manifesto: A Philosophy of Literature*. New York: New American Library.

———. 1975. *The New Left: The Anti-Industrial Revolution*. 2d rev. ed. New York: New American Library.

———. 1990. *Introduction to Objectivist Epistemology.* 2d enl. ed. Edited by Harry Binswanger and Leonard Peikoff. New York: New American Library.

———. 1995. *Letters of Ayn Rand.* Edited by Michael S. Berliner. New York: Dutton.

———. 1997. *Journals of Ayn Rand.* Edited by David Harriman. New York: Penguin Dutton.

Schudson, Michael. 1984. *Advertising: The Uneasy Persuasion.* New York: Basic Books.

Sciabarra, Chris Matthew. 1995. *Ayn Rand: The Russian Radical.* University Park: Pennsylvania State University Press.

Toffler, Alvin. 1980. *The Third Wave.* New York: William Morrow.

Torres, Louis, and Michelle Marder Kamhi. 1999. *What Art Is: The Esthetic Theory of Ayn Rand.* Chicago: Open Court.

Turner, Frederick. 1995. *The Culture of Hope.* New York: Free Press.

Vacker, Barry. 1995. Beauty and anarchy. Ph.D. diss., University of Texas, Austin.

Vacker, Barry, and Wayne R. Key. 1993. Beauty and the beholder: The pursuit of beauty through commodities. *Psychology and Marketing* 10, no. 6 (Special issue: *The Pursuit of Beauty*): 471–94.

Walter, Katya. 1994. *The Tao of Chaos: Merging East and West.* Austin: Kairos Center.

Wolf, Naomi. 1991. *The Beauty Myth.* New York: William Morrow.

Wright, Frank Lloyd. 1958. *The Living City.* New York: Meridian.

———. 1960. *Writings and Buildings.* Edited by Edgar Kaufmann and Ben Raeburn. New York: Meridian.

———. 1977. *An Autobiography.* New York: Duell, Sloan & Pearce.

9

Looking Through a Paradigm Darkly

Wendy McElroy

Ayn Rand is arguably one of America's most important women novelists, and her heroines are among the strongest and most independent female characters in American literature. Yet modern feminism tends to dismiss Rand's work contemptuously. Some feminists go so far as Susan Brownmiller and accuse Rand of being "a traitor to her own sex" (1976, 350).[1] Why?

There are several reasons for feminism's general rejection of Rand's work. One is that her championing of capitalism is seen by many contemporary feminists to be absolutely antagonistic to the interests of women.[2] Another more fundamental reason is simply that Rand's worldview does not fit the psychological or political paradigms that most feminists use to analyze society. The difference between Rand and such feminists is particularly pronounced in their analysis of the sex scenes of her two major novels *The Fountainhead* and *Atlas Shrugged*. It is not uncommon to hear feminist critics bluntly describe these sex scenes as depictions of rape.

Consider two typical passages from Rand, the first one from *The Fountainhead*, the second from *Atlas Shrugged*. The first passage describes the initial sexual encounter between Dominique Francon and Howard Roark, who are the major protagonists of *The Fountainhead*. Rand ([1943] 1971, 217) writes that Dominique "tried to tear herself away from him . . . her fists against his shoulders, against his face . . . she tore herself free . . . she let her teeth sink into his hand." During the ensuing struggle, "she fought like an animal . . . she bit his lips" (218).

In *Atlas Shrugged,* the first sexual encounter that the ideal woman, Dagny Taggart, has with the flawed but heroic Hank Rearden, is described in the following terms: "It was like an act of hatred, like the cutting blow of a lash encircling her body: she felt his arms around her, she felt her legs pulled forward against him and her chest bent back under the pressure of his, his mouth on hers" ([1957] 1985, 240).

With these "rough-sex" encounters being so graphically described, it is easy to understand why most feminists, along with many nonfeminists, consider these scenes to be depictions of rape.[3] Indeed, my contention that the scenes have no real connection to actual rape is the hypothesis that requires proof.

It is often considered bad form to analyze a novel as though it were the delivered public opinion of the novelist. Such an approach collapses the difference between fiction and nonfiction, between what is imagined and what is real. But Ayn Rand invites such analysis of her fiction by stating that the ultimate goal of her novels is nonliterary: it is moral. Rand's definition of art explicitly states this theme: "Art is a selective re-creation of reality according to an artist's metaphysical value-judgments. An artist re-creates those aspects of reality which represent his fundamental view of man and of existence" (1975, 99).

In her introduction to the twenty-fifth anniversary edition of *The Fountainhead*, Rand ([1943] 1971) refers to the specific goal she pursues in that work: "This is the motive and purpose of my writing: *the projection of an ideal man*. The portrayal of a moral idea, as my ultimate literary goal, as an end in itself" (vii, emphasis in the original).

Rand's foregoing explanation is likely to antagonize feminists further, for she uses the word "man" to mean "male" and not merely as a generic reference to human being. It is only against her backdrop of the ideal man that Rand proceeds to paint her vision of the ideal woman. This gives the impression that "man" properly precedes "woman" as a subject for consideration.[4] Thus, a "radical" feminist such as Brownmiller is able to conclude that "Roark is Rand's philosophical hero; Dominique is merely an attendant jewel, a prize of prizes" (1976, 350). According to Brownmiller's paradigm of sexuality, this analysis is accurate.

But many feminists often ignore a key aspect of Rand's ideal woman: she is the full intellectual, emotional, moral, and political equal of man. Indeed, Rand's heroine is generally the intellectual and moral superior of every man surrounding her except for that one ultimate man who is the ideal.

In her role as a foil to the ideal man, the heroine's disadvantage is not due to anything that one would normally call inferiority. It derives from what Rand conceives to be the key psychological difference between men and women. The true woman worships the true man. And the purest act of worship for a Randian heroine is when she overcomes her own strength and surrenders on the altar of sex to the appropriate hero. It is this act of worship alone that mitigates an otherwise stable state of equality between the man and the woman.

Before delving into a nonliterary analysis of Rand's fiction, however, it is useful to note certain relevant conditions of her writing. This is not historical relativism. It is giving credit where it is due.

First, Rand's two key novels were written in the '40s and '50s, which were notorious for their repressive sexual attitudes toward women. Yet Rand's characters defy such stereotypes. Consider the three unconventional sexual relationships that Dagny Taggart enjoys in *Atlas Shrugged*: (1) a teenage passion with Francisco d'Anconia in which she is underage; (2) the long-term affair with married man Hank Rearden, which she self-righteously flaunts in his wife's face; and (3) the torrid sex-for-its-own-sake near-rape scene with the ideal man, John Galt, who risks his life to be with her sexually.

Second, Rand chooses to delineate the ideal man in fiction, rather than in nonfiction, for which she is also well known. This choice is a key to understanding the sex scenes. It entirely changes the reader's perspective on whether the scenes truly depict rape, because fiction allows the reader to have a godlike panorama of the psychologies of all the acting characters. We can examine their deepest psychological motives and their most subtle desires. This inestimable advantage is not offered by nonfiction.

In light of this, reconsider Dagny's previously described sexual encounter with Hank Rearden in *Atlas Shrugged*, which appears coercive on its surface. With our godlike perspective, we can eavesdrop on Dagny's psychology as she silently pleads with him, "Yes, Hank, yes—now—. . . Now, like this without words or questions . . . because we want it" ([1957] 1985, 240). Our knowledge of Dagny's unspoken desire for sex with Rearden converts what seems to be an act of rape into one of passionate and mutual consent.

Third, Rand explicitly chooses to write in a Romantic style—Romantic with a capital R. She vehemently rejects the predominant style of contemporary novelists: naturalism. She distinguishes between the two by calling naturalism "concrete-bound, journalistic," whereas "Romanticism is the conceptual school of art. It deals, not with the random trivia of the day, but with the timeless, fundamental, universal problems and values of human existence. It does not record or photograph; it creates and projects. It is concerned—in [Rand's interpretation of] the words of Aristotle—not with things as they are, but with things as they could be and ought to be" (Rand [1943] 1971, v).[5]

Rand is not concerned with chronicling the events of actual relationships: petty tiffs, adulteries, jealousies, and reconciliations. Instead, she selectively re-creates reality so as to present the ideal sexual relationship, which bears no necessary connection to the normal constraints of reality. For example, in the sex scene describing the first encounter between Dominique and Howard Roark, there is a clear presumption that Roark is a man of limited sexual experience.[6] How such a sexual novice possesses the skill and confidence to overpower the sophisticated New York socialite Dominique, in a masterful manner, is never explained. Nor is an explanation required. *The Fountainhead* is not naturalism, it is "Romantic Realism."[7] Rand does not present facts; she selects from among them and sculpts those chosen into a vision of what life should be.[8]

Having established a context for analyzing whether Rand's sex scenes are rape, a key question remains: What constitutes rape?

The word "rape" comes from the Latin *rapere*, which means to "take by force." This is the most uncontroversial and widely accepted definition of rape: nonconsensual sex in the presence of force or the threat of force against the victim or a third party. And it is a definition with which Rand would agree. Although the concept of rape is often expanded to include sex with someone who is so intoxicated or drugged that he or she cannot reasonably render consent, this expansion has no bearing on the discussion of Rand. Her ideal characters never abuse substances. Nor are the women blackmailed or otherwise unduly influenced by anything but their own desires.

The issue of rape, therefore, comes down to a pure question of consent. In every one of Rand's sex scenes, a clear indication of consent is present either in the revealed thoughts of the characters or in their behavior.[9] Consider a previously described scene of sexual "violence" in *Atlas Shrugged*, between Dagny and Rearden: "She found herself, in terror, twisting her body to resist, and, in exultation, twisting her arms around him" (Rand [1957] 1985, 600). Here, Dagny implicitly expresses consent by embracing Rearden's sexual attack. Ironically, the one time that explicit consent occurs between Dagny and Rearden, it is the man who insists upon that point of clarity. Rand writes: "[S]he heard his voice—it was more a statement of contemptuous triumph than a question: 'You want it?' Her answer was more a gasp than a word, her eyes closed, her mouth open: 'Yes'" (241).

Why, then, do most contemporary feminists consider these scenes to constitute rape—to consist of nonconsensual sex? Why are the scenes not considered to be depictions of *rough sex*, in which the "violence" is simply a form of sexual expression that both parties desire?

There are several reasons. First and foremost, in Rand's sex scenes, the woman's consent is often implicit, not explicit, and it is briefly given. On the other hand, the "violence" is extensive and real enough to leave lasting bruises on the heroine's flesh.

Dagny's initial sexual encounter with Francisco d'Anconia in *Atlas Shrugged* is typical of the type of consent the Randian woman renders. "[H]is hand moving over her breasts as if he were learning a proprietor's intimacy with her body, a shocking intimacy that needed no consent from her, no permission. She tried to pull herself away, but she only leaned back against his arms long enough to see his face and his smile, the smile that told her she had given him permission long ago" (107).

If this specific scene is considered in isolation, then the only consent even implied is the smile on *his* face. Only in the context of the novel and of the long-term affair between Dagny and Francisco does it become clear that Dagny has not only consented to sex with him, but she also is eager for it to continue.

In contrast with the almost hidden consent of the woman, the violence of the man is pronounced and often quite graphic. Consider the scene between Dagny and Rearden, in which she tells him of her long-term, though past, love affair with Francisco. "He seized her shoulders, and she felt prepared to accept that he would now kill her or beat her into unconsciousness, and in the moment when she felt certain that he had thought of it, she felt her body thrown against him and his mouth falling on hers, more brutally than the act of a beating would have permitted" (600).

Implied consent in sexual situations is nothing new. Indeed, it is difficult to imagine how a first kiss could develop without some form of implied consent. But the consent offered by Randian heroines can be remarkably subtle. As with Dagny's silent plea for Rearden to ravish her, the consent can be almost invisible. This subtlety lends an aura of rape to these scenes, which are—in fact—depictions of passionate consent and of extreme sexual excitement.

Feminism's discomfort with these depictions may be part of its more general discomfort with the fact that consensual violence (S/M, bondage, mock rape) is a popular way that sex occurs on this planet. Some feminists have been accused of becoming "the new Puritans" of our society, who police the images of graphic sex (e.g., pornography) and the expression of unacceptable sexual choices (e.g., prostitution). Whether or not this accusation is true, much of contemporary feminism definitely draws lines delineating acceptable sexual behavior. And any act with the trappings of violence tends to fall outside those lines.[10]

As the renegade feminist, Camille Paglia (1991, 3) states in her essay "Sex and Violence, or Nature and Art": "Sex is a far darker power than feminism has admitted. . . . Sex is the point of contact between man and nature, where morality and good intentions fall to primitive urges." Although Rand would argue that sex is the point of contact through which morality was expressed and not negated, she would fully embrace Paglia's view of the violent passions aroused by sexuality.

Another aspect of Rand's work that lends a false credibility to the view of her sex scenes as rape is the relative dearth of alternate scenes that express a wider range of sexual response. There are next to no passages depicting tenderness or playfulness in sex. The only gentle display in The Fountainhead, for example, is a later scene between Dominique and Roark. Rand ([1943] 1971, 669) describes the interaction briefly: "[H]e had lifted her in his arms, carried her to a chair and sat down, holding her on his knees; he laughed without sound, as he would have laughed at a child, but the firmness of his hands holding her showed concern and a kind of steadying caution."

Further reasons for the shadow of rape falling across Rand's work are ideological in nature. Feminism, since the 1980s, has tended to expand the definition of "rape" to such an extent that our entire current society has been referred to as "the rape culture," in which all men are "rapists" because they benefit from that culture.[11] For contemporary feminism, the watershed book on rape is *Against Our Will: Men, Women, and Rape*, by Susan Brownmiller. In this work, Brownmiller (1976, 5) insists: "Man's discovery that his genitalia could serve as a weapon to generate fear must rank as one of the most important discoveries of pre-historic time. . . . It is nothing more or less than a conscious process of intimidation by which *all men* keep *all women* in a state of fear" (emphasis in the original).

With such a sweeping and general description of rape, it becomes more difficult to perceive precisely what constitutes consent and what constitutes coercion. Consider the definition of sexual violence that Liz Kelly (1988, 41) offers in her book *Surviving Sexual Violence*: "Sexual violence includes any physical, visual, verbal or sexual act that is experienced by the woman or girl, at the time or later, as a threat, invasion or assault, that has the effect of hurting her or degrading her and/or *takes away her ability to control intimate contact*" (emphasis added).

How do Rand's heroines fit this description? They render consent, either implicitly or explicitly, but they also relinquish at least some control over the intimate contact. Often, they relinquish it all. This is never more apparent than in the classic scene between Dominique and Roark that is their first sexual encounter.[12] To "radical" feminists, this relinquishment may well spell rape. The fact that the Randian sexual acts are often described as acts of ownership and conquest by the man makes matters considerably worse.[13]

A good litmus test by which to determine whether Rand's sex scenes are depictions of rape is probably the initial encounter between Dominique and Roark. In this passage, the heroine is as thoroughly taken, or ravished, as any woman in the Western literary canon. If this encounter can be shown to be merely rough sex between consenting adults, rather than rape, then all the other less violent scenes should be exempted from the charge of rape as well.

Consider the relevant scene from *The Fountainhead*. After being smitten by the sight of Roark working in a quarry, Dominique arranges to have him come to her bedroom to replace a piece of marble in a fireplace she has purposefully defaced. When Roark arrives to do the repairs, he treats her with an insolent arrogance that belies his social station: "She saw the hint of a smile, more insulting than words. He sustained the insolence of looking straight at her, he would not move, he would not grant the concession of turning away—of acknowledging that he had no right to look at her in such manner. He had not merely taken that right, he was saying silently that she had given it to him" (Rand [1943] 1971, 207).

Several nights later, Roark enters her bedroom in the middle of the night through a French window, like a common rapist. Rand describes Roark's subsequent treatment of Dominique: He "took her two wrists, pinned them behind her . . . wrenching her shoulder blades," and "forced her mouth open against his" (217). "He did it as an act of scorn. Not as love, but as defilement" (218). Then, after mutual orgasm, he leaves without a word. Yet as long as a week later, Dominique still thinks of the act in exalted terms: "I've been raped. . . . I've been raped by some redheaded hoodlum from a stone quarry. . . . Through the fierce sense of humiliation, the words gave her the same kind of pleasure she had felt in his arms" (220).

This passage is a clear indication that Dominique not only consented to, but also reveled in, the rather brutal affections of Howard Roark. Indeed, as Rand later explains, it was an act Dominique could have ended at any moment: "She had not given him the one answer that would have saved her: an answer of simple revulsion—she had found joy in her revulsion, in her terror and in his strength. That was the degradation she had wanted" (220).

But Dominique's musings present the reader with a dilemma. She wants the violent sex with Roark and basks in its memory, yet she herself refers to the act as "rape." Clearly, a tension exists between these two reactions. Perhaps the answer lies in the context in which Dominique joyfully repeats to herself, "I've been raped . . . I've been raped." The words come in reaction to a letter from a coworker, Alvah Scarret, who implores her to come back to her job: "It will be like the homecoming of an Empress" (220). Dominique revels in how shocked people who hold her in awe would be to hear the words "I've been raped." Rand describes her fantasizing about throwing the incident in the faces of such people: "She wanted to scream it to the hearing of all" (221). To achieve this contemptuous flaunting, Dominique would be compelled to use hyperbole. After all, saying "I've had rough sex . . . I've had rough sex" would not produce the same reaction.

In *Against Our Will*, Brownmiller (1976, 349) dwells on such musings of Dominique as evidence of "Ayn Rand's philosophy of rape," rather than as evidence of precisely the opposite—Dominique's clear consent to rough sex. Indeed, for Brownmiller, the very fact that the sex was rough seems to negate the possibility of healthy, informed consent on the part of the woman. Dominique's pleasure at being taken automatically converts her from a sexually liberated, consenting woman whose choices should be respected by feminists into what Brownmiller sarcastically calls "a superior woman" with "a masochistic wish . . . for humiliation at the hands of a superior man" (349–50).

Interestingly, Rand (1995, 282) addressed the very issue of Dominique's "rape" in a 5 June 1946 letter to a reader, Waldo Coleman, who "misunderstood" her intentions and who "thought that the lesson to be derived from [the scene] is that a man should force himself on a woman, and that she would like him for that. But the fact is that Roark did not actually rape Dominique; she had asked for it, and he knew that she wanted it. A man who would force himself on a woman against her wishes would be committing a dreadful crime. . . . The lesson in the Roark-Dominique romance is one of spiritual strength and self-confidence, not of physical violence."

Rand amplifies these points in a letter to Paul Smith dated 13 March 1965: "It was not an actual rape, but a symbolic action which Dominique all but invited. . . . Needless to say, an actual rape of an unwilling victim would be a vicious action and a violation of a woman's rights; in moral meaning, it would be the exact opposite of the scene in *The Fountainhead*" (631).

Thus, both Rand and Brownmiller view the same sex act. For one, it is not rape—it is an ecstatic surrender to the ultimate value in life. For the other, it is a symptom of pathology. This difference is the end result of the antagonistic paradigms with which Rand and most contemporary feminists approach sexuality.

But even women who shun the label "feminist" are led to question Rand's sex scenes: Why must sexual ecstasy arise only from angst and struggle? Why not from tenderness and cuddling? The answer lies in the wording of the question. Rand attempts to capture "ecstasy," not merely pleasure. She deals with ultimate expressions, not with common experiences. In *The Romantic Manifesto*, Rand (1975, 153) defends Victor Hugo in terms that could be applied equally to her: "To criticize Hugo for the fact that his novels do not deal with the daily commonplaces of average lives, is like criticizing a surgeon for the fact that he does not spend his time peeling potatoes."

A Randian heroine is simply not the cuddling type whom you kiss upon the cheek. Instead, she seeks and demands the ideal, against which she tests herself. And as Rand comments further: "[T]he higher the values, the harder the struggle" (48). For Rand, greatness requires immense struggle and suffering.

The ideal man is not exempt from this process. Howard Roark—the ideal man of *The Fountainhead*—is forced by his own moral code to destroy the building complex that is his greatest creation, and he is put on trial for that act. John Galt—the ideal man of *Atlas Shrugged*—lives apart from the one woman he must love in secret, in order to create a world that will destroy the railroad that is her passion. In the end, he is literally tortured by those who seek him as salvation. The price of heroism is high.

There is a sense in which the ideal woman and the ideal man are each other's greatest test, as well as their greatest reward. On the battlefield of Randian sex, it is a foregone conclusion that the ideal woman will be overcome by the ideal man. Yet, paradoxically, the woman's surrender resembles nothing so much as a victory: namely, that the ideal man *needs* to conquer her. He needs her to desire him in order to fulfill his destiny as a sexual conqueror. That is why one gesture or expression of disgust from Dominique would have immediately caused Roark to cease ravishing her.

It is in terms of victory in defeat that Rand ([1957] 1985) paints a key love scene between Dagny and Rearden in *Atlas Shrugged*:

> She felt him trembling and she thought that this was the kind of cry she had wanted to tear from him—this surrender through the shreds of his tortured resistance. Yet she knew, at the same time, that the triumph was his, that her laughter was her tribute to him, that her defiance was submission, that the purpose of all of her violent strength was only to make his victory the greater—he was holding her body against his, as if stressing his wish to let her know that she was now only a tool for the satisfaction of his desire—and his victory, she knew, was her wish to let him reduce her to that. (240)

Through scenes of sex that resemble rape, Rand presents us with the culmination of the ideal male/female relationship. For the woman, this apex can be called "enraptured surrender." It is not the breathless, almost passive surrender portrayed by romance novels in which a woman is overwhelmed by a dark mysterious stranger whose kiss bends her backward, both in body and in will. The surrenders of Dominique and of Dagny are a violent, joyful answer to the age-old paradox of what occurs when an immovable object meets an irresistible force. If the immovable object happens to have free will—if she happens to be one of Rand's heroines—then she may choose to move the scant inch it takes to resolve the paradox of which force will prevail.

In *The Fountainhead*, Rand herself provides the perfect metaphor for the emotional sense of what her sex scenes are meant to portray. It occurs in a passage dealing with Steve Mallory's sculpture of Dominique in the nude, which has been commissioned by Roark. Mallory is unable to capture a certain elusive spark that he has tried unsuccessfully to draw from Dominique. Howard Roark enters the room unannounced. Roark is the one man to whom Dominique has surrendered, the one ideal she has not abandoned in a self-destructive plunge through life. She cannot convince Roark to betray his ideals, and, as yet, she cannot embrace them fully herself. She has repeatedly attempted to end her inner conflict by turning away from Roark, only to be driven back each time by her own undeniable need for him. Dominique's sole weapon against Roark is the knowledge that he wants her passionately.

Upon entering Steve Mallory's studio, Roark asks him how the sculpture is proceeding. Dominique's response is to throw off her robe and walk naked to the stand on which she had been posing moments before. In the presence of the man whom she wishes to torment with both the sight of her body and the memory of possessing it, Dominique easily captures the spark. It is a glint of both rebellion and surrender, two of the fundamental emotions Roark inspires in her. Rand ([1943] 1971) describes what Mallory sees: "[N]ow her body was alive, so still that it seemed to tremble, saying what he had wanted to hear: a proud, reverent enraptured surrender to a vision of her own, the right moment, the moment before the figure would sway and break, the moment touched by the reflection of what she saw" (336).

Like Steve Mallory, Rand captures and freezes the peak of her heroines' sexual passion: the instant before they surrender. Sculpting words rather than stone, she creates an ideal woman whose true fulfillment depends on being ravished by an ideal man. Is it any wonder that those feminists who insist upon independent women react with dismay at such raw dependence upon a man?

Ayn Rand's paradigm of sexuality occupies a different cultural and psychological universe than that of "radical" feminists. When they lay their definition of rape, like an ill-fitting grid, over Rand's sex scenes, they miss the point of her writing. This is distinct from disagreeing with the views embodied in Rand's work. It reflects a misunderstanding of the views that, admittedly, fall outside the social norm.[14]

In broad terms, the contemporary culture generally assumes one of two sexual paradigms: First, there is the traditional Madonna/whore complex, which defines women solely by virtue of their sexual behavior. This perspective is often ascribed to those who are conservative, or religious. But even sexual subcultures, such as the prostitute-activist groups like COYOTE (Call Off Your Old Tired Ethics) and PONY (Prostitutes of New York) adopt this paradigm when they proudly define themselves as "sluts" or "whores," and usurp the words as defensive badges of honor.[15] The other currently popular paradigm comes from political correctness, which, in this context, might be called sexual correctness. This paradigm defines women and sexuality in political terms—specifically in terms of gender politics.

Rand presents a third alternative. Her heroines are radical individualists who define their own sexuality, specifically through embracing their gender role vis-à-vis the ideal man. As such, Dagny and Dominique defy the Madonna/whore analysis of women. They revel in carnal pleasures, yet they cannot be sexually approached except by a man who embodies what is sacred. Equally, Dagny and Dominique defy the "politically correct" paradigm. As women, they are role models of strength, intelligence, and independence, yet what is arguably their finest moment lies in the arms of a man. For such a man, Dagny Taggart, who runs the major railroad in America, is even willing to cook and clean in the capacity of housemaid. Consider the psychological surrender embodied in Dagny's reaction to a question posed to her by John Galt. Dagny has just offered to pay for her room and board in his house by becoming his servant. "Is that what you want to do?" he asks. Rand ([1957] 1985, 707) describes Dagny's response: " 'That is what I want to do—' she answered, and stopped before she uttered the rest of the answer in her mind: more than anything else in the world."

The psychological surrender lies in her overeagerness to serve him. Many feminists would consider this surrender to housework to be more egregious than consenting to rough sex. But whatever emotional reaction Rand inspires, her meticulous ideology deserves to be accepted or rejected for what it is and not on the basis of misinterpretation.

On a personal level, I have moments of deep disagreement with—deep emotional reservations with regard to—Rand's paradigm of sexuality. As a woman who has experienced sexual violence, I have an abiding personal ambivalence toward the brutality portrayed in Rand's sex scenes. I became a runaway at the age of sixteen, and for as short a period of time as I could arrange, I lived on the streets. Anyone who has experienced the streets as a home will never be able to walk down a dark alley again with anything akin to a sense of comfort. Equally, any woman who has been battered or raped will probably have difficulty with Rand's harshly graphic sex scenes—and understandably so. Although such women may grasp and enjoy the intellectual values being portrayed, the emotional impact of those values will be lost upon them.

Certainly, it is lost upon me. Rand's ideal of surrender is too violent and too literally bruising for me to embrace willingly. As thoroughly as I appreciate the intellectual values being stylized in the initial sex scene between Dominique and Roark, I cannot get past the fact that—in similar circumstances—I would try to maim any man who caused me that sort of physical pain. Even in the alleged pursuit of ultimate values.

And, yet . . . what heterosexual woman hasn't fantasized about being swept into the strong impetuous arms of Rhett Butler and conveyed up a curving staircase to the satin sheets of ravishment? These gentler, less threatening fantasies of "being taken" seem to survive intact through actual violence, perhaps because they express a natural urge within women (and some men) to relinquish control and be conquered by a mutual passion.

This urge within women is deftly captured by Ayn Rand, and captured in a manner that is typical of both her life and her work: the woman goes to extremes. I am left wondering whether the discomfort caused by her extreme presentations might not be a positive thing. In the final analysis, the main purpose of art might be to shake us all up a bit.

Notes

1. The relevant material from Brownmiller 1976 is reprinted as Chapter 4 in the current volume.

2. In fact, Rand falls within the much neglected tradition of individualist feminism that traces its roots to the nineteenth-century abolitionist movement. See Taylor 1992 and McElroy 1996.

3. See also Harrison 1978 and Gladstein 1978, both reprinted in this volume. These articles express typical feminist reservations about Rand's "rape" scenes.

4. Such an interpretation is reasonable. Rand (1975, 161) states: "My purpose, first cause and prime mover is the portrayal of Howard Roark or John Galt or Hank Rearden or Francisco d'Anconia, *as an end in himself*."

5. See also Cox (1986, 20), who questions the accuracy of Rand's usage of this principle from Aristotle's *Poetics*.

6. Rand repeatedly insisted that one should have sex only with one's highest ideal. As Roark holds extraordinarily high ideals and has never met Dominique before, one is reasonably led to this conclusion. It is reinforced by the fact that Rand cut from the final manuscript of *The Fountainhead* an episode that describes Roark's first sexual encounter with a woman named Vesta Dunning. This scene was posthumously published in Rand 1984. Rand explained that Vesta's character was "superfluous," since "her moral treason was a variant of Wynand's." See Rand 1995, 644. Rand also cut out another character, Heddy Adler, who was to be Roark's mistress. See Rand 1997, 199ff.

7. In her first appearance Dominique is described by Rand ([1943] 1971) with such adjectives as "imperious," "elegant" (111), "cold," "vicious," "contemptuous" (112). She intimidates and contemptuously dismisses all other men. She cuts off an incredibly eligible bachelor with the words: "Don't say that I'm beautiful and exquisite and like no one you've ever met before and that you're very much afraid that you're going to fall in love with me. You'll say it eventually, but let's postpone it" (118).

8. Rand (1975, 168) states: "As far as literary schools are concerned, I would call myself a Romantic Realist." She repeatedly insists that Romantic writers "did not record the choices man had made, but projected the choices man ought to make" (114). She attacks naturalism as "man's new enemy" because it presents a chronicle of events that sweep man along rather than events that are shaped by man's will.

9. As mentioned before: see Rand [1957] 1985, 240.

10. For detailed arguments on this theme, see McElroy 1995, 1996.

11. Susan Griffin (1979) expresses the ideological underpinning of this shift in rape theory. She argues that the true rapist is not the individual man, but the political system of patriarchy.

12. It is not always true that the woman relinquishes control, however. In many of the scenes with Dagny and Rearden, for example, she seems clearly to be in charge, whereas he is a novice.

13. Dominique's words to Roark embody the ideal surrender of "woman" to "man": "Howard . . . willingly, completely, and always . . . without reservation, without fear of anything they can do to you or me . . . in any way you wish as your wife or your mistress, secretly or openly . . . I'll remain what I am, and I'll remain with you—now and ever—in any way you want" (Rand [1943] 1971, 669).

14. Sciabarra (1996, 517) makes a similar observation regarding Rand's political position: "She vehemently opposed the regulatory and welfare state advocated by the liberal and socialist Left. But as an avowed atheist, she rejected the religious views of traditional conservatives, and was unwavering in her support of civil liberties and abortion rights."

15. In an unpublished poem, Norma Jean Almodovar—director of the prostitutes' rights organization COYOTE L.A.—expressed the motive behind this growing trend within the prostitute community. It begins: "I am a woman . . . and if I get out of line, you call me a whore." It ends: "And what if I tell you / I don't care anymore if you call me a whore . . . / What will you call me now?"

References

Brownmiller, Susan. 1976. *Against Our Will: Men, Women, and Rape.* New York: Bantam.
Cox, Stephen. 1986. Ayn Rand: Theory vs. creative life. *Journal of Libertarian Studies* 8, no. 1:19–29.

Gladstein, Mimi Reisel. 1978. Ayn Rand and feminism: An unlikely alliance. *College English* 39, no. 6:680–85.
Griffin, Susan. 1979. *Rape: The Power of Consciousness*. New York: Harper & Row.
Harrison, Barbara Grizzuti. 1978. Psyching out Ayn Rand. *Ms.*, September, 24–34.
Kelly, Liz. 1988. *Surviving Sexual Violence*. Minneapolis: University of Minnesota Press.
McElroy, Wendy. 1995. *XXX: A Woman's Right to Pornography*. New York: St. Martin's Press.
———. 1996. *Sexual Correctness: The Gender-Feminist Attack on Women*. Jefferson, N.C.: McFarland.
Paglia, Camille. 1991. *Sexual Personae: Art and Decadence from Nefertiti to Emily Dickinson*. New York: Vintage Books.
Rand, Ayn. [1943] 1971. *The Fountainhead*. New York: New American Library.
———. [1957] 1985. *Atlas Shrugged*. New York: New American Library.
———. 1975. *The Romantic Manifesto: A Philosophy of Literature*. 2d rev. ed. New York: New American Library.
———. 1984. *The Early Ayn Rand: A Selection from Her Unpublished Fiction*. Edited by Leonard Peikoff. New York: New American Library.
———. 1995. *Letters of Ayn Rand*. Edited by Michael S. Berliner. New York: Dutton.
———. 1997. *Journals of Ayn Rand*. Edited by David Harriman. New York: Penguin Dutton.
Sciabarra, Chris Matthew. 1996. Ayn Rand. In *American Writers: A Collection of Literary Biographies, Supplement IV, Part 2: Susan Howe to Gore Vidal*, edited by A. Walton Litz and Molly Wiegel. New York: Charles Scribner's Sons.
Taylor, Joan Kennedy. 1992. *Reclaiming the Mainstream: Individualist Feminism Rediscovered*. Buffalo, N.Y.: Prometheus Books.

10

The Romances of Ayn Rand

Judith Wilt

The stubborn bestsellerdom of Ayn Rand's novels in America suggests that the immigrant writer had a grip on some key components of the national fantasy life, not least because the novels were her fantasy life too. Alice Rosenbaum had studied history; she aspired to philosophy. But she wrote her long narratives as fiction primarily, she said, to establish the world of her dreams "and then to live in it while I am creating it" (Rand 1992, vi).[1]

To live in it while I am creating it. This is the foundation desire of romance, the shared environment of romance reader and writer within which the preternatural extremes of admiration and humiliation, risk and reward, force and counterforce, are gathered into a sublime equipoise— while I am creating it. This sublime equipoise: if I can no longer live in it after I have created it, it was a romance; if I can live in it after I have created it, it is a philosophy. Deeper than the hunger for love or power is the hunger to be a philosopher, to see the equipoise. More than any other American popular writer, in a manner surprisingly complementary to her older contemporary D. H. Lawrence, Ayn Rand, in her romances, awakes and nourishes that hunger, makes romance feel like philosophy, especially in the young reader.

Eventually the Rand reader, like the reader of Lawrence, comes out of the initial "phase"[2] of questionless shared creating to a critical phase—why does the "new earth" romantically created in these philosophies contain, like the old earth, gendered violence, vengeful apocalypses, scapegoated values (Rand's abhorred "altruism") and races ("the East")? Romance is problematized, philosophy temporarily discredited. But the hunger to be a philosopher remains, no inconsiderable thing for a bestseller to have stirred up, no minor conundrum for the critic, especially now that we have, by way of cautionary tale, several memoirs from the Rand circle published after her death in 1982, which try to trace the alternating nourishment and starvation that her romances were to her and that she and her philosophy were to others.[3]

Like so many Russian Jewish migrants of the first decades of the twentieth century, Alice Rosenbaum came to an America perceived as pure freedom, and went straight to Hollywood, the very frontier of populist creativity. She began writing and working in the movies in 1926 after a fortuitous meeting with and casual sponsorship by Cecil B. DeMille: she was—the comparison is irresistible—Norma Desmond in the poignant flesh, flashing-eyed, imperious, writing and playing her strenuously larger-than-life characters in big-picture style against a world in which the people were getting smaller. From the screenplays and dramas she wrote in the '30s through *We the Living* (1936), *The Fountainhead* (1943), and *Atlas Shrugged* (1957), she enthralled and hectored the opaque and unpredictable American midcentury, middlebrow audience, enlarged by, finally maddened by, those wonderful people out there in the dark.

The phenomenon is fascinating, a gloss on elements in the continuing nostalgia for the American movie decades of the '30s, '40s, and '50s, a sort of pre-postcolonial example of migrant cultural erasure and reconstruction. At the center of the phenomenon is a body of fiction by a woman, an atheist, a Russian Jew, burning with a sort of Messianic pre-post-Holocaust, pre-postfeminist loathing for the behavioral canons of social self-regulation, Dostoyevskian altruism, otherworldliness, and proud victimhood. The mythic core of this work is the construction of the unmoved mover as an ideal, and very Aryan, male, in a recovered Zion.[4] In all of Rand's novels, the lit cigarette figures as the lamp of the smoker's mind, and she steadfastly denied she had contracted the smoker's cancer until she lost a lobe of her lung from it: she couldn't win for losing. Yet amidst all these paradoxes, sad, brilliant, sometimes risible, the novels continue to awake in successive generations of young readers the hunger to be philosophers, to see the equipoise of all the sciences and follow all the big questions in life in from the circumference to an articulable center.

A reader of romances in the 1950s, a feminist teacher of narrative and romance in the 1990s, I felt and feel the hunger to be a philosopher, and see it in the continuing generations of undergraduates who confess a confused and elated impact by this most tendentious and mocked, this most admired and fought-over, of pop culture writers.

The potential danger of Rand's strenuous romances of self-making is easily understood, and already part of the code of American cultural critique. In the 1988 film *Dirty Dancing*, for instance, the young heroine feels empathy for another young woman of a lower class, pregnant and abandoned by an ambitious young Yalie: she asks him to take some responsibility for his action, and the young man treats her to a lecture on the difference between the people who "count" and the people who don't, handing her a copy of *The Fountainhead* for further study of this important principle. Now, Rand's conscious philosophy would in fact damn anyone who disconnects consequence from act, and she is careful to provide in her novels brief examples, from all social classes, of persons with strong, value-creating egos who "count." Yet the formulas of romance require heroes who strive against the world, and heroines who strive against both the hero and the world until their capture by (of) the hero confirms a vitalist counterworld to "the world." And in such formulas the relegation of all but the romantic couple to the secondary status of "world"—brutish, disenergized, mere matter—is likely unless the writer takes the greatest care. Ayn Rand did not take the greatest care: her counterworld of value creators tends to neglect, if it does not formally exclude, all but the heroine and the men among whom, and against whom, she must make her choice, find her equal.

These formulas of classic and popular romance are the subject of much debate in feminist literary and cultural theory, which follows with interest and some vexation the representation of unruly female desire in fictions from *Wuthering Heights* to *Thelma and Louise* on the one hand, and *Pride and Prejudice* to the latest Mary Higgins Clark on the other, wondering what consolations, or lessons, lie in these versions of flight through trials and dangers to a new earth, where (if one lands at all) woman can come home to, or with, a new man. From early speculations by Ellen Moers on the subversive feminist potential of gothic romance to more current arguments by Tania Modlewski, Janice Radway, Diane Elam, and others, the debate starts from the perception that "woman" is in these romances somehow the "natural" disrupter of "the world." An ally and avatar of the "monster" or "villain" even when she is his victim, she scatters the arrangements of "the world" whether she is actively exploring it or simply being pursued through it: indeed, as the fathers and brothers of Ayn Rand's romantic heroines can testify, she is never more dangerous, more likely to be undermining the arrangements of the world, than when she is energetically appearing to conform to them. At the same time, it can fairly be said of romance formulas, so flexible and subtle are they, that the heroine is never more encompassed, contained, than when she is spending her energies in flight or her fury in resistance and subversion. For while desire, as the psychoanalysts say, can only be raised by (for) what we lack, what we lack, once in the trajectory of our flight or our resistance, is not only what we have not yet got, but also what we have left behind. Cast a hopeful eye on the consolations of romance and we can see exploration toward achievement: cast a hermeneutically suspicious eye on this structure, which is large enough to evoke and contain all subversions, and we can see an arrival right back to the point of our departure.[5]

A serious critical treatment of Rand's novels in these contexts is past due, yet may be difficult, so cast in stone are the critical commonplaces about them. I want in this essay to push the critical treatment a few steps farther, in a reading of the novels that attends to their embeddedness in American cultural politics of the twentieth century, beginning with the curious and compelling utopia of "body" that grounds the novels' more conscious philosophy of Reason.

"Single": Body, Gender, Rape

There is no "adolescence" in Ayn Rand's novels: this is surely one secret of her powerful appeal to the young reader. The main characters experience no sudden doubling back of the body upon the will, division of desires, *mise en abime* of lost soul, wail of Brontëan heroine—"I wish I were a girl again. . . . Why am I so changed?" Male and female, they know a unified identity, body-will-work-value, in childhood, and the identity never changes, though it may turn itself inside out to defend itself and the identity may not immediately reach that full self-articulation that is Rand's Reason. The body's drive toward the Reason of self-articulation may express itself in those taxing and sometimes risible anomalies that make Rand's prose "heavy-handed"—conversations between earnestly debating protagonists that roll toward page-long paragraphs, a five-page-long remark by a man at a wedding reception, an eight-page courtroom speech, a sixty-page (!) radio talk. But these speech monoliths truly represent Rand's "single" self textually embodied, the body's mastery of its harmonious powers—to be (in order) to do, to desire to do what leads to being—all validating the most metonymically significant line on the passport of her first fictional heroine, "Kira Alexandrovna Argounova: *single*" (Rand [1936] 1959, 38).[6]

In Rand's moral world, these character monoliths stand over against the death eaters and power mongers, aggressively egoless agents and carriers of nonbeing who, like Lawrence's Hermione or Loerke, represent the seductive call of the river of dissolution. The bodies of the protagonists are taut, a centrifugal geometry of lines "sketched furiously to suggest an unfinished promise" (36), lines "like a stylized drawing" (Rand [1943] 1971, 105). The bodies of the antagonists or those infected by them are loose, husky or pudgy, bloated or stuffed; if they are beautiful, they "shimmer like heavy cream" (Rand 1957, 400).

The body of the protagonist holds tensely to the line that is its own movement (to be to do): watching one such person driving a motorboat, another sees only "three straight lines; its wake, the long shriek of the motor, and the aim of the driver at its wheel" (93). The body of the antagonist slides from that line toward stasis, "two sagging circles, the large one was his stomach, the small one his lower lip" (Rand [1943] 1971, 486). Worse, he communicates this sag to the world, increasingly made nightmarish in Rand's vision by "some horrible kind of softening . . . as if nothing were solid, nothing held any shape at all, and . . . mountains would slither and buildings would switch their shapes like clouds, and that would be the end of the world, not fire and brimstone but goo" (Rand 1957, 890).

For Rand, of course, the apocalypse of goo is the product of twentieth-century thought, Einsteinian, Heisenbergian, Freudian, deracinating de-rationalizing thought dissolving the clean lines and stable constructs of nineteenth-century science, art, industry, and philosophy, which, in her view, restored man's Greek singleness (and singularity) after a long de-tour through "religious" irrationality and otherworldliness. Confronting the goo, character must streamline itself to irreducible essence, pure line/movement always embodied, never fractured, manifested as immovable object.

Stone distinguishes itself from goo, however, only in the presence of irresistible force. Barred by Rand's psychology of singleness from the rich drama of internal division and metamorphosis, characters in her novels must undergo melodramas of ferocious division, violation, reconstitution, at one remove from the single self, *between* bodies, within that small tribe of like-souled "singles," closer than brothers, who can serve as projections of the (forbidden) divisions within the self. These internal melodramas externalized between bodies are classically gendered in the romance of the immovable female and the irresistible male, classically enacted in the plot of rape as self-possession.

Equally classically, however, these romance archetypes of gender can unexpectedly swerve and sag. At one level, Rand's romantic construction of the Ideal (hu)Man relies on the male force and female receptivity-to-form graphed in rape. At a deeper level, her male heroes are created essentially to suffer and state their meanings, curiously immobilized as "demonstrations" of the Real, while the heroines, descendants of the adventuring "argonaut" Argounova, move questing through the world, battering as well as being battered, pursuing, not pursued, detecting and rescuing, having, really, all the fictional fun.

I have space only to sketch this double layering in the key relationships in Rand's three major novels, but first, it seems important to recall the cultural environment in which these romantic triangles, pivoting on sex-ual violence, were conceived, written, and read: world war. "The worst wars are religious wars between sects of the same religion or civil wars between brothers of the same race" ([1943] 1971, 546), says one of the heroes created by this White Russian immigrant of the 1920s. Or rather, the best wars are ideological. Or even, many readers feel her saying, ideo-logical warfare is better than peace, where there is no dominating ideol-ogy, no consolingly totalizing philosophy. Behind the moral and psychic urgency that erupts in sexual and tribal violence between bodies in her fictions lies the apocalyptic glamour of the twentieth century, locked in an ideological strife prolonged from the Russian civil war through two global hot wars and a cold one under a nuclear umbrella.

We the Living, written in the 1930s, recasts the young Alice Rosenbaum's experiences and dreams in the story of the eighteen-year-old Kira Argounova, who wants to build bridges in St. Petersburg and now studies and boils potatoes in Petrograd, while her two lovers, the best men of the Red and the White worlds, self-destruct and slithering profiteers grow fat. The novel sank without a trace in 1936, a partisan polemic, an aspiringly philosophical romance published in a time when studio editors and publishers were calling for "realistic stories about average people" (Branden 1986, 105) like, say, the determinedly unrational protagonists in Of Mice and Men (1937). The Fountainhead appeared to instant popular acclaim in 1943, with its story of a totally nonaligned go-your-own-way architect untrammeled by the repetitive canons of the past or the new compulsions of mass culture and its media and political power brokers, or the perverse world-nausea of the woman he loves.

That moment of high purposefulness was her moment. She wrote Atlas Shrugged over the next fifteen years, vindicated, as she thought, by the development of permanent ideological conflict, the cold war, testifying as a friendly witness for HUAC against a culture still "softening" toward the relativistic goo.[7]

Atlas Shrugged, too, was an instant best-seller in 1957, its word-of-mouth popularity resisting an almost universal critical repudiation. Its apocalyptic fable of a Western industrial system disintegrating despite all that a brilliant female executive can do, because of all that a brilliant male engineer refuses to do, appealed to a postwar Western consciousness still processing its nostalgia for the "good war," just entering a period of "bad wars" with the emerging and "softening" populations of the postcolonial East and South.

But though its romantic triangle implodes over eleven hundred pages in a satisfyingly epic bang, the novel's "demonstration" of the philosophical inevitability of libertarian capitalism and high Western rationalism brought no mass political conversion to Rand. Her philosophy remained unproven in an American culture newly wealthy, hedonistic, pragmatic—and under the cracking crust of its What's-good-for-General-Motors-is-good-for-the-USA mentality still profoundly ambivalent about ideology, even its own. The American reader of Atlas Shrugged might get a genuine thrill out of the demonstration that the love of money, properly viewed as the equal-traded value-added sign of sacred human effort, is the root of all good, especially in a fictional world of wholly owned companies in which the connection between creative effort and money is visible. Rand's transvaluation of "greed" into a "radiant" act of unceasing production, unceasingly rewarded, appealed as a romantic fable, even as a psychological dynamic, but not as a political economy. Flummoxed by a readerly delight that generated no political action, maddened by fiction's eponymous power supremely to Be without (exactly) Doing, Rand gave up on fiction like an enraged husband, though she remained a cantankerous and, to some, a mesmerizing writer and speaker on her philosophical stance, which she called Objectivism, for another quarter century or more.

Her faith in the power of fiction to rebuild culture was high when she wrote her first novel, though. She had, consciously, a universal truth to communicate about the proper philosophical and political connection between self-expression and self-sacrifice, and a less conscious but equally powerful truth to tell about omnivorous female desire.[8] Rand's romantic triangle, here and in her other novels, exists to state this desire. The glamorous, active, intelligent Red hero Andrei, mistakenly allied with the collectivist ego death of the Soviets, is the baseline of the triangle—available to Kira's desire and therefore not the erotic object. The glamorous, intelligent, and despairingly self-castrated aristocrat Leo is unreachable, and therefore is the erotic object, projection of the quenchless "I want to live" of the heroine. Kira will "worship" (Rand [1936] 1959, 193) Leo's emptied shape with a perversely narcissistic passion that turns her heart to stone with the attractive Andrei, for Leo's actual internal "lack" allows her the space to project her omnivorous desire for life upon, and receive it back confirmed from, this virtually speechless Male Muse.[9] Loving the Andrei that "is" would limit the scope of desire; loving "the Leo that could have been" (445) immortalizes it. When, inevitably, an enlightened Andrei removes himself with a soldier's self-execution and the self-destructive Leo walks out on Kira, the female quester simply resituates her desire from person to place, from "the Leo that could have been" to the world outside Soviet culture, outside culture entirely, the world "abroad." "A good soldier" (443) camouflaged for a solitary escape across the border in the snow in the only white garment she can find, her mother's old wedding dress, the young Kira dies from a guard's bullet in a hierogamous nuptial rapture at sunrise, looking, like the speaker of Emily Dickinson's poem 461, for the flag at sunrise, the wifedom at daybreak, the crown of "the living" beyond the borders of life.

The America of the movies, and of the movie decades, *was* the world across the border, she decided, and everything good in it was real. For Rand, as for her heroine, her girlhood in Russia could be the site only of a demonstration of woman's power to *feel* her desire: her adulthood in America would supply her with the world in which that desire need neither be hidden nor postponed for an invisible otherworldly or imaginative fulfillment. The famous Frank Lloyd Wright, she decided, would stand for that fulfillment.[10] The scene would be, not Hollywood (exactly) but New York, another theater of a dominant American public and dramatic, ultimately symbolic, art—architecture. The "war" within which the romantic triangle would violently form would be for control of the media environments, now consciously processing the competing world messages of individual freedom and international or national socialism. The winners in these wars would be, not those who gain control, but those who remain untouched by the temptation of cultural power, not those immune to pain or those who deliver it or those who invite it as an affirmation of existence in or resistance to the world, but those in whom "suffering only goes down to a certain point and then it stops" (Rand [1943] 1971, 354), the point at which the body remembers its own value and expels from that singleness, not pain, but suffering.

Rand's second novel projects Kira's indifference to the spell of the world, along with her desire to build the "new world," onto a male hero, architect Howard Roark. Roark has Leo's look of seamless line, but his look is also his reality, paradoxically because, unlike the stricken aristocrat Leo, Roark has absolutely no past, no history, no place of rift or loss, and only a mild curiosity, at first, about the heat he causes in and takes from the people among whom he will do his work. In a further interesting gender slide, the novel's heroine, Dominique Francon, has Leo's self-castrating world-horror, and it has bred in her, as in him, that quest for self-contempt that for Rand is the sign of a virtually ineradicable self-esteem. There is the usual glimpse of a Brontëan girlhood: Dominique's father remembers her leaping over a hedge, "her body hung in space . . . the flash of a small body in the greatest burst of ecstatic freedom he had ever witnessed" (143). After this flying dream, though, come the discoveries of adulthood, the Joycean nets of culture perceived in the female mode not as opposition but as "support," that is, dependency. In Soviet Russia, the objects of desire were simply not available; in the world of Western freedom, they are available, with conditions: "If I found a job, a project, an idea or a person I wanted—I'd have to depend on the whole world. Everything has strings leading to everything else. We're all so tied together. We're all in a net, the net is waiting, and we're pushed into it by a single desire" (140).

Millions of female readers, programmed in the mixed consumer/Puritan culture of the 1940s and 1950s, identified with this heroine's fierce refusals, her complex desire not to desire, which leaves her free to shock the artistic and media world she works in with brilliantly unpredictable raids in all directions, while it also compels her toward the "single desire" on which she can focus her battle against dependency. In more than one library, the copy of *The Fountainhead* still falls open immediately to the early pages of part 2, where the battle begins with what Rand herself called "rape by engraved invitation" (in Branden 1986, 134).

The scenes are the formulaic stuff of bodice-rippers all right, built in a Lawrentian environment of earth ritual and sacramental violence, with an added ontological touch all Rand's own, a touch still familiar enough to draw appreciative laughs from audiences at 1993's prize-winning play *Angels in America: Perestroika*, where one lover acquires the "visible scars" that legitimize his invisible suffering in an erotic punch-out "like a sex scene in an Ayn Rand novel, huh?" (Kushner 1994, 4.8.112). In the rape event, and only in this event, "the world" that stands over and against the single self finally takes on the lineaments, the embodied line, of another self, another person: "It was strange to be conscious of another person's existence, to feel it as a close, urgent necessity, a necessity without qualifications, neither pleasant nor painful, merely final, like an ultimatum" (Rand [1943] 1971, 219).

At one level, a meeting with the internal other, at another level, the contact with a genuine other, the disturbingly protean rape event is Rand's sublime, fission and fusion, an endless cycle of provocation and satisfaction. Meeting again in tux and gown before an unknowing crowd, the male architect and the female newspaper critic reveal, under cover, their strenuous, and erotic, ethic:

> "Which [way of remaining untouched] is preferable, Miss Francon?"
> "Whichever is hardest."
> "But a desire to choose the hardest might be a confession of weakness in itself."
> "Of course, Mr. Roark. But it's the least offensive form of confession." (265)

The ultimatum figured in antagonism—to dependent desire itself, to her fear of having to solicit the world to keep what she desires in existence—Dominique enters Roark's room that night under a new gender sign, wearing a "high masculine collar" and a hat "like a man," "chaste like a young boy" (278–79). She names her desire as defilement: "I want you like a cat on a fence, or a whore" (279), because that's the way she feels it, and the only way she can feel it. And Roark accepts the name as her first but not final definition of desire. The romantic quest continues for the (mystically required) seven years, through two distance-seeking marriages to Roark's enemies and an ecstatic initiation/collaboration with him in the destruction of a building stolen from Roark's brain, until Dominique can name her desire in Randian form as its own fulfillment, not mortgaged to the world, or even to its object, not, therefore, doomed to crack up the ego in suffering. The Zen equilibrium of this love song looks like an attack, but it constitutes a triumph of will: "If they convict you—if they lock you in jail or put you on a chain gang—if they smear your name in every filthy headline—if they never let you design another building—if they never let me see you again—it will not matter. Not too much. Only down to a certain point" (656).

This principle was, in fact, stated years before to Dominique by the other man who loves her, the "base" figure in the romantic triangle, the man who like Kira's Andrei Taganov understands the foundation value of the ego and its motor, the desire to desire, but who like him takes a mistaken path early, in his decision to ally himself with the ruling power of his world. With Dominique, Gail Wynand reaches the stage she and Roark reached, where the existence of another becomes its own ultimatum, but "when one reaches that stage it's not the object that matters, it's the desire" (522). The particular sense of joyous existence created in the desirer by his or her own desire is the fulfillment of that desire. As in the first novel, interestingly, the man too much enmeshed with "world," the man fundamental to the triangle but not the final object of the heroine's uprisen romantic desire, is the most verbally adept, the person whose presence generates the energies of debate in these novels of ideas.

In Rand's romantic triangles, then, that one desires the worthy object is the equivalent of the philosophical premise "existence exists": desire is fulfillment in a seamless circuit not dependently tied to the need of its potentially endangered or evasive object, not subject to the proverbial green-eyed monster, since the desirer's only true "possession" is her own evoked/confirmed desire. This may not actually work in the uneven structures of "real" life. But Rand can make it so, convincingly so, in the domain of her romances, where, for reasons the opposite of altruistic, one or more of the heroic desiring selves (male) must inevitably lie down, single, with his own confirmed desire, while the (feminine) object evoking that desire reaches into the space of a new world for the (male) apex of all desire, with the solitary "base" male approving/joining that action.[11]

Since all of Rand's key romantic triangles feature a woman and two men, this latter action engages men together in that homosocial desire described by Eve Sedgwick and others as an inevitable accompaniment, perhaps even a hidden goal, of Western romantic form. Her first novel evaded this element of the structure to some extent by emptying the "Leo that is" of all but the heroine's own objectification: Andrei could see Kira's selfhood confirmed by (projected in) her desire for Leo, but he could literally see nothing in Leo himself, form no desire for him. In *The Fountainhead*, though, the structure is complete. So strong is the desire for his beloved's desired to her lover that Gail Wynand gives over his life to Roark, and his final achieved work is the blocking of Roark's enemy with, so to speak, his own body, as he destroys the newspaper that Roark's enemy has just succeeded in capturing to use against him. And so powerful is Roark's homage to this structure that he calls Wynand at the end "the one encounter in my life that can never be repeated" (655).[12]

Also suggestive in this respect is the argument from feminist anthropology, vividly stated in Gail Rubin's 1975 "The Traffic in Women: Notes on the Political Economy of Sex," that the exchange of women in patriarchal societies functioned as sexual expressions of psycho-political alliances, opportunisms, even punishments. In *The Fountainhead*, the agency of the exchange seems emphatically the woman's, the "unrepeatable" homosocial encounter impossible without her: in *Atlas Shrugged*, interestingly, this pattern is duplicated in the way the heroine seems (despite Rand's standard rape imagery) sexually to initiate and "deliver" two men, Francisco d'Anconia and Hank Rearden, to one another and to the alpha (and omega) male in the series, John Galt, before she delivers herself to him.

Single the self may be in a private exchange of value validations between sufficient selves. And double it may become in the struggle signified in the romantic triangle. But the self desires the world as well as the (other) self, projects its worth in work (power) as well as in love (living). And work, as we know even better in this century than Marx did in the last one, is detained in a thousand social systems, a terrestrial social mechanics in which the self is always already enrolled, to submit, to re-form, to rule, or to destroy. Or rather, in the motive (movement) of Rand's apocalyptic plots, first to destroy, then to rule, to reform and, harmoniously, subject. The plot, recapitulating her own adolescence, will (again) be world war.

"Atlantis": Work, World, Theophany

In her last two novels, Rand respatializes her heroine's quest from the "abroad" of America to the beneath (within) image of Atlantis, the world under the waters, the reflected reverse of this one, veiled by a trick of sight, an angle of light, a deceptive show of stasis. In *Atlas Shrugged*, the mythological journey is named; the heroine, in a pursuing plane, follows the "Leo that could have been" through a masking defensive screen that appears to be a sterile valley in Colorado to a Utopian Atlantis of pure action/production. In *The Fountainhead*, this same mythology is implicit in the novel's first paragraph, where the lone Howard Roark, naked on a stone height overlooking a lake, a human form "anchoring" the worlds of "flowing" stone separated by the invisible film of the reflecting and motionless water, travels across that border in a movement simultaneously a dive and a flight.

Importantly, Atlantis is a city, not a garden; a polis, not a tower. To build (in) the city requires a productive relationship with the world and its social mechanic. Second only to the establishment of the single self is Rand's continuing fable of the encounter of the hero with the "motive" of the world, people and principles who/which "run things." Kira wants only to be let alone "to live"; she sees that the wish to "run things" brings only death even to the best, as with Andrei. Dominique's terror of dependency ties her to a quixotic resistance to activity, especially her own, making her a virtual prisoner of the world and its men of power. Howard Roark loathes even the appearance of power: the alternating frustrations and temptations of the world "didn't make me want to rule people. Nor to teach them anything. It made me want to do my own work in my own way and let myself be torn in pieces if necessary" (554). In this curiously passive, even feminized posture, the suffering statement of resistance to power, Roark attracts the obsessive activity of the two men, perhaps the most interesting Rand ever created, who have confronted the world as it "runs," and are, as *The Fountainhead* begins, locked in battle to run the world through its communications media, a kind of power that Rand fears and loathes to the measure of her reluctant desire to possess it.

One of these power brokers is Gail Wynand, tabloid publisher and real-estate lord, who has, like *We the Living*'s Andrei, put his considerable mental and moral energies in the service of his culture's validated philosophy of collectivity, mass man, not, like Andrei, from some vision of a final valuing of each individual working "I," but, like Leo, from contempt of the world that values the mass over the "single." As in the first novel, Rand's questing female hero will sell herself to this apparent enemy, ally herself with "the world" that is set against her taciturn and indifferent Male Muse, in order to test its strength, and his.

In the end, Wynand, like Andrei, will find his way to a true analysis of the purity of his lover's apparent betrayal, and will try to rescue Roark as the country puts him on trial at the end of the novel. But his tabloid empire had been deliberately created as an instrument for the "little" desire of the man in the street: it will not work in the service of a big desire. The best he can do, before separating himself from Dominique and Roark in a kind of proud moral suicide, is to destroy his own newspaper before it falls into the hands of the novel's second power broker and key figure of evil.

Ellsworth Monkton Toohey is Rand's greatest and only true villain, an eerily postmodernist fragmentarian of mythic proportions, a one-man *mise en abime* of "humanitarian compassion" to whose distinctionless, judgmentless, and all-embracing edge the young, the insecure, the divided, come, falter, and, mesmerized, fall. The apocalypse of goo in the flesh, a hypnotic voice dispersing self and hearers in radio waves, Toohey is Rand's bogeyman of Marxian "history" itself, "dissolving" the individual brain in the "irrevocable . . . current" of mass movement (103) and, most interesting of all, "sickened" (664) in some corner of true value by his own success at eroding his culture's belief in the personal ego.

A social critic and commentator, a terrifyingly acute student of human nature, Toohey seems to be everywhere and know everyone in Rand's democratized and media-ruled New York. He attracts the insecure to him because he projects, and actually harbors, the "selflessness" his culture claims to admire. So, selfless, egoless, he acts only at a distance, through invisible "influence," but each of his disciples and readers functions like a small mine he can aim and explode at the time it can most forward his agenda, which is, ultimately, to bring the whole world to the kind of impasse of pure negativity, degraded inertial activity, that he detects as its hidden desire. A brilliant diagnostician, he is what Dominique calls him, "a monolith . . . a testing stone for people," a revealer of essences (120). As such, he vibrates all through the novel with Rand's own passionate loathing for the average, the common, the manipulable "matter" of mass man. Like all successful "monsters" in romance, he has something of his creator in him: readers unerringly, if confusedly, identify with this biting, overshadowing analyst at least as much as they do with the man of action whom he opposes.

While he is insistently "busy," Toohey is not a man of action: unceasingly inventive, he is not "creative." A Scholastic in her way, Rand sees a unified cosmos in which evil has no power but what it borrows from the perversion of the good. Toohey is fundamentally inert, but he can rock the world nevertheless, for his collaboration with the world's inertial desire, its death wish, puts him at the point where he can transform what for Rand is the source of power—Reason—into what for her is its opposite—Magic, or "mysticism." Unseeable, unanalyzable, uncriticizable Mysteries, whether "god," "the Aryan race," or "the people," are now in the ascendant, feminized as "instinct" and "emotion." Feminized too is the person who enters into and owns these things, once nicknamed "Elsie" Toohey, until he chose his own, still darker nickname, "Monk" Toohey, and became their priest. For Rand, this pantheon of mysticisms has replaced the true entity at the heart of the Real, the individual. She would not, of course, accept the postmodern contention that "the individual" is also a mystic construction. For she is *its* priest.

Though he is not himself a builder, then, the feminized monkish Ellsworth Monkton Toohey must always be on the lookout for one whose creations he can make his own. He has seen Roark's buildings and Dominique's resistance to Roark, and knows the meaning of both. American to the core, he delights to destroy Roark publicly through the court system, a jury of common men passing judgment on an uncommon one. Both of the trials in *The Fountainhead* are about buildings that came, "complete" and Atlantean, from Roark's brain, but that in the construction are "mongrelized" into expressions of mass man. Toohey destroys one building and forces Roark to destroy another, in a scene that evokes the idea-Atlantis under the apocalyptic sublime: "In the flash when walls rose outward and a building opened like a sunburst . . . she saw the city

enveloped in light" (644). But the jury of "the world," in a startling
about-face that reflects Rand's own fantasy of instant mass assent for a
lengthily asserted libertarian ideal, frees the destroyer-architect to build
again. In the final paragraph, Roark stands atop the Wynand Building,
the unmoved mover. The active figure is once again the female protagonist, a flying figure riding up a construction elevator in a Pilgrim's Progress through the rushing vistas of the Atlantean city, "the pinnacles of
bank buildings . . . the crowns of courtyards and the spires of churches,"
to the sacred apex of desire, where "there was only the ocean and the sky
and the figure of Howard Roark" (695).

Rand's well-wishers, both the romantics and the rationalists, rather
regret *The Fountainhead*'s theophanic finale, regret even more the literally
over-the-top theophany that concludes *Atlas Shrugged:* "On the highest
accessible ledge of a mountain. . . . He raised his hand and over the
desolate earth he traced the sign of the dollar" (Rand 1957, 1168). Rand
was unrepentant, though paradoxical. She was both damned and praised
for slipping religious mysticism through the back door of her rationalist
romances via a steadily deployed rhetoric of sacred words and images that
she condemned in her prose essays and introductions. But she still fought
for the "man worship" she believed was the origin and end of ethics.[13]
She passionately rejected what she saw as the "murky" traditions of Russian mysticism and altruism, and sought a transvaluation of values apart
from twentieth-century tribalisms of nation and race, evoking, like Lawrence, a new postpersonal "humanity." Yet her language and plot structures hew closely to the Fraserian synthesis of Western myth: at the
center of them is the body of the god, the suffering body of the god, and
the new earth he, emphatically he, fructifies. The source and producer of
energy, Rand's man-god is, in *Atlas Shrugged,* not only silent but invisible,
yet everywhere immanent to desire, known portentously by his absence.
This god is not dead, but—a capitalist to the core—on strike.

The romantic triangle assumes some interesting intermediate confor-
mations in the eleven hundred pages of *Atlas Shrugged* not least because,
for the first time, the rising figure is a woman who "runs things." Dagny
Taggart is the granddaughter of the founder of an American transcontinental railroad and is now its vice-president of operations: she keeps
trains running like arterial blood through the body of the nation (17), an
America on the downward slope of the twentieth century, mired in the
apocalypse of goo. The "men of the mind" gather toward each other and

toward the woman, as always only a single woman,[14] in a twilight moment of arterial shrinking that is only partially to be explained by the anticompetitive spirit of altruism that a looting and taxing government policy is now enforcing to flatten and disperse all inventive and industrial activity. The rest of the explanation is contained in the mysterious phrase of bitter fatalism (and secret glee) that starts the novel, at once every loafer's excuse for his ignorance and ennui and every responsible person's defiant phrase of resistance, the equivalent of "oh, what the hell" (or, later, "Catch-22")—"Who is John Galt?"

He is, of course, the figure at the top of the tower, the Atlas under the earth. The mystery of the novel holds him at bay for two-thirds of its eleven hundred pages while the romance engages its questing woman, its female detective, in an exploration of a world not being "run" but rather "running down" despite, and because of, the creative persons at work in it.

Two of these men are Dagny's lovers, in a familiar constellation. One, the copper magnate turned playboy Francisco d'Anconia, apparently repeats the pattern of a Leo or a Gail Wynand, a supremely intelligent and active man who has surrendered to "the world" in his hatred of it. The other, the steel maker Henry (Hank) Rearden, actually plays Dominique's part to Dagny's Roark; in their romance she must teach him that his sexual desire for the railroad executive he admires is not a betrayal of his mind by his body or a chaining of his will to his flesh, but rather a sign of the "singleness" of all truly personal desire.

Throughout these romances, with Francisco in her teens before he "changed," in her mid-thirties with Rearden while he learns, Dagny maintains the emotional connection between her love of work and her love of the workers who are her equals, dimly recognizing, however, that neither lover quite matches, provides full erotic complementarity for, her love of her work and that self-esteem that expresses itself in work. This is reserved for a phantasmic and theophanic figure from her childhood imagination, the man beyond the horizon who holds the rails in his hand, the final form of the Leo that could have been (220). As the world of Atlas Shrugged "runs down" and the creative workers in the economy who are her equals (all dramatized as men) disappear one by one after speaking with a mysteriously knowledgeable person moving behind the scenes, Dagny sees that figure again, though, since he stands between her and the work she equates with her self-love, she must call him the destroyer.

Thinking of him rouses a rage tied to erotic desire: "I would have shot him, afterwards, if I had discovered his role. . . . I would have shot him, but not before . . ." (779).

The engineer and inventor John Galt exists to fulfill Dagny's erotic desire, but not before . . . not before he destroys her work. The man she meets pursuing "the destroyer" to a hidden valley in Colorado is in fact coordinating the new apocalypse: "I have pulled every girder from under Taggart Transcontinental and, if you choose to go back, I will see it collapse upon your head" (780). All this violence stems safely (from Rand's philosophical point of view) from a morality not of attack but withdrawal, a morality that values the self-love/work equation too much to let it into the world at all.

For it is not just the psychic burden of the false dichotomy between body and will, "low" and "high" desire, that the Atlases of Rand's novels must "shrug," it is, as the title figure suggests, the whole burden of the (visible) world and its organization of work that must be set down, abandoned, exploded. Rand maintains a fine line between suffering as ego-discovering and suffering as a subtle form of egoism: finer still is the line she draws between work as world-creating and work when it maintains an evil system that is in fact world-destroying. The new project of *Atlas Shrugged* is to give up (power in) the world without renouncing the self, withhold the work that is all that stands between the world and destruction, to take one's finger out of the dike in full responsibility for the resulting drownings. To shrug. This appalls Dagny; she loathes irresponsibility, victimhood, the whole psychic paraphernalia of renunciation in man, and especially in woman. What Rand's narrative would have her learn is that the exercise of her very virtues—the compulsion to create, the power of action and decision, the refusal to abandon what has been made, the sense of herself as inexhaustible energy—all these are retarding the necessary breakup of the old world and the creation of the new. She is keeping the trains moving, in the service of the enemy. *She* is the destroyer.

As a young reader of romances, I was almost as exhilarated by this voluptuous call for the cleansing apocalypse as I was by the dangerous glamour of hierogamous rape–as–self-possession. As a middle-aged middle-management female intellectual in a striving but decidedly imperfect network of educational corporations, I am amazed to find myself still often responding (in fantasy at least) to this paradoxical, and, in today's world, arguably feminist, call to take possession of my sometimes undervalued work by refusing to work. "The strike" is essentially a way of making visible the invisible, pointing to that which has become the norm. And feminist theorists from Mary Wollstonecraft and Virginia Woolf to Mary Daly and Adrienne Rich have argued that women's unpaid maternal and cultural labor (reproduction, volunteer work, psychological "caretaking" of all sorts) is the original type of invisible work, while contemporary historians and sociologists have told the tale of the routing of women to the lower strata of paid work, of the relative stagnation of wages in some "feminized" branches of professions—general medicine in Soviet Russia, English teaching in America.[15]

In the first part of the novel, Rand's protagonists maintain the naive confidence that they will achieve their goals because they work harder, they know what's right, they're able to act with foresight, whereas the dull and inept, the irresponsible shirkers and the petty timeservers and timid turf protectors, don't know how to act. But Rand's narrative responds with the still prickling truths of political entropy in a world whose economy privileges consumption, whose ethic criminalizes pleasure and respects guilt and suffering, whose ontology prizes the fragment and the particle and scoffs at the notion of the universal, the absolute, the "complete."

Well. We are all trying to write our way around that one. Rand's way is a ferociously universalist and absolutist narrative reminiscent of the "root-and-branch" extirpation prophecies of some Western theologies. The first two-thirds of the novel generates considerable moral power around the logic of "the strike," but the last third of the novel licenses with disturbing gusto an extraordinary pageant of "righteous" violence ranging from a thinly disguised nuclear catastrophe[16] to a disturbing moment of personal initiation for the finally enlightened Dagny, who signals she is ready to "give up" her railroad and the world for Atlantis beyond the horizon by shooting a man to death.

This initiation of the heroine interestingly links the endings of The Fountainhead and Atlas Shrugged, and confirms, I would argue, a further link between the violence of romantic rape and that of the relationship of hero and heroine to "the world." At the climax of the earlier novel, Dominique agrees to join Roark in the act that will explode the housing project that was built according to Toohey's scheme to "mongrelize" Roark's original design. Dominique's part is to perform a female act of mercy, to lure the project's guard out of danger and send him on an errand to get gas for her deliberately stalled car. But the unspoken meaning of his plot and her acceptance is that she has joined Roark in the world apart from "the world," the romance world of pure energy as against "the world" of matter. And in the maelstrom that characterizes that counterworld, it matters little whether one unleashes the force of the explosion, as Roark does, or receives it, as Dominique does.

In this sense, as in others, romance wants to make the lovers and their genders simply two undistinguishable poles generating the current; something in romance wants to dislodge gender entirely. But the maelstrom here, as in the rape that first united them, is in fact structured by extreme male violence and the flowering of female capacity, body and spirit, to receive and withstand and return it. In *Atlas Shrugged,* the male and female poles initially generate a similar current realized in a long postponed sexual encounter in an underground railroad tunnel that in its climax mixes elements of a gendered rape and a kind of genderless train crash. The main gender difference is less in the violence offered, in this case "viciously" from each body to each body, than in the "enlighten-ment" that comes to the woman: this new "shock of pleasure" enables her to "know her most complex values by direct [sensual] perception" (956), whereas the man already "knows" that. In the earlier novel, Roark's destructive social violence is only the prelude to his more serious project, to stand his trial on the principle of his possession of his intellec-tual property and let "the world" tear him to pieces if it wishes to, and Dominique's role is to join him in that complex and arrogant submission, take, so to speak, the "feminine" charge of it. In the later novel, John Galt moves to do the same, offering his naked body to his torturers as a demonstration that they can do nothing without the loan of his energy, even successfully torture him.

In this curious submission, he resembles the Christian man-god whom Rand consistently fights in her novels. At the climax of the novel, strapped to the machine that delivers electric jolts to a body described as "the statue of man as a god" (1141), Galt suffers at the hysterical insis-tence of men desiring but incapable of exercising real "motive power," men exercising inertially the regime of Power without motive enough even to save their own lives by keeping alive the only intellect that can arrest the destruction of their economy and their world. In a Randian version of "turn the other cheek," Galt, "the living generator" (1146), even instructs his torturers how to fix the machine when it breaks down.

The rescue scene at the end, when Dagny discovers where Galt is being held and directs Galt's friends where to find him, is deliberately contrived so that none of the male heroes need kill anyone. Throughout the several pages of violence, the men wound or bind or intimidate the dozens of guards they face, without needing to kill in order to rescue Galt. But the female hero, in a spotlighted scene with a hapless young guard paralyzed by indecision, must make this visible and shocking break with "the world" that tied her ownership of her own work to a moral code that, in Rand's view, consistently substitutes others for the self, consistently substitutes rote rules of conduct for the strenuous and self-creating moment-to-moment activity of moral choice. So, the young guard who cannot choose becomes the occasion for the female hero's final entry into the circle of Reason, world of Atlantis, Rand's version of modernist Impersonality. So, "calmly and impersonally, she, who would have hesitated to fire at an animal, pulled the trigger and fired straight at the heart of a man who had wanted to exist without the responsibility of consciousness" (1148). The man-god ready to die, the female hero licensed to kill, now form the completed demonstration of the new humanity in its elliptical agency, its ambiguous morality.

Overdetermined romances of agency, Rand's novels represent the furious exasperation of the precocious girl denied access to the world of doers and makers. They represent, in a more covert way, the angry envy of the "border" mind at its distance from the (tainted) goods and (corrupted) opportunities of the West, at the way Western capitalism has flubbed its Atlantean promise. Strenuously rationalist, her narratives deny "class" in their presentation of Aristotelian man, of American individual man, carefully picking out here a Minnesota farmer, there a New York construction worker, who see the world in Randian terms, as an aristocracy of wealth creators allied with the working deserving poor against the idle middle classes of bureaucrats, managers, and manipulators of mass culture. At the same time, the narratives consistently display a naive and contemptuous Victorian class equation of virtue with success: "I can run a good railroad. I can't run it across a continent of sharecroppers who're not good enough to grow turnips successfully" (84).

Strenuously meritocratic, the narratives also appear to ignore race, yet in them a classic Orientalist judgment (in Edward Said's terminology)[17] makes everything Northern and Western attract, everything Eastern and Southern repel. The northern industrial town that supported the Twentieth Century Motor Company adopts, when that company leaves, a Southern bartering-sharecropping economy. The ideal of the evildoers is the imagined life of an Indian rajah running jewels through his fingers while he steals his slave's last grains of rice (948). Western industrial production is "a value not to be questioned" (948), while Eastern contemplation is the source of horror. The evil heirs of the Twentieth Century Motor Company have rejected their Western heritage and regressed Eastward philosophically and politically: "I am through with the world of machines, manufactures and money, the world enslaved by matter. I am learning the emancipation of the spirit as revealed in the great secrets of India" (323). John Galt may affect to speak metaphorically, but it is clear what quarter of the globe is endangered by what other quarter of the globe in the regression he fears and excoriates: "you—who leap like a savage out of the jungle of your feelings into the Fifth Avenue of *our* New York and proclaim that you want to keep the electric lights, but to destroy the generators" (1038).

In a demonstration of the relationship between the lights and the generators, between the world and the single self-authorized soul, the city of New York collapses in blind war at the end of *Atlas Shrugged*, while Dagny and Galt escape to Colorado. The bureaucrats throttle each other over control of the last power stations, and the decent people panic and flee—a scene burned on the brain of twentieth-century readers by decades of war photography. Those in the planes above the stricken city have dropped no bombs to cause this, have instead simply withdrawn their fire, but it doesn't help morally that their satisfaction as "the lights of New York go out" in violence is not manic but "austere" (1158–59).

Generators in the dark, the single-purposed protagonists of Rand's novels would be ludicrous without a world to *turn* on—and to turn *on*. Contending against one world, lighting up another, the protagonist of romance always has a perplexing relationship with the "world." In the last words of the novel, Galt and Dagny signal their readiness to "go back to the world," while the rest of the refuseniks in Galt's Gulch rewrite the American Constitution—though it is unclear how they will generate the New Atlantis without falling into the inevitable corruption that accompanies "running things."

The reader of Rand's novels, noting their narrow class and race reference, their delight in scenes of destruction, their scarcely concealed contempt for the bewildered and the doubting, and their scarcely concealed horror at the impingement of the "unchosen" and "undeserving" of family and community lives upon the single self, may well feel that the novels amount simply to the dictum that a few choice spirits deserve to run the *Reich* for the next thousand years.[18] But a closer look at the novels reveals also those hallmark qualities of the philosophical romance that continue to engage the young reader and tease the mature one: the exalted love of one's own life, an erotics of admiration and a politics of joy, a utopian economy of rational values where the moral is the practical, the body faithfully reports the spirit, competitive activity is always only productive, where "made" meaning is also shared meaning and two persons who love a third person will also love each other. Rand's ego proved in some respects resistant to the better strokes in the pattern of her ideology; this undertow can be seen too in the novels. Her poignant faith in the principle of rational noncontradiction became increasingly an irrational refusal to brook contradiction; her rebarbative womanhood turned into curious channels of "man worship"; her longing for "purity" and horror of mongrelization yet echo the most terrible excesses of the twentieth-century ideologies she most passionately despised. These are familiar paradoxes of our century, part of the reason, perhaps, why the novels of Ayn Rand make a persistent subcurricular hum in the reading culture we live in. A stricter hearing is in order.

Notes

1. This is from Rand's journal on the writing of Atlas Shrugged, portions published as part of the introduction to Rand 1992. Expanded journal entries can be found in Rand 1997, particularly part 4. Rand wrote a fair amount about her personal theories of and experience with artistic creation, available especially in the essays from her Objectivist Newsletter and The Objectivist from the 1960s, the most important of which were collected in The Romantic Manifesto (1971).

2. High-achieving women from Billie Jean King to Hillary Clinton have testified to their Ayn Rand "phase": Boston writer Gail Caldwell (1994) remembered one passionate summer spent reading all Rand's words "in a grain silo," though she does not necessarily recommend that venue.

3. See especially the full-length books by Nathaniel Branden (1989) and Barbara Branden (1986), which tell a bittersweet story of passionate intellectual and emotional engagement with Rand's ideas, a genuine admiration transformed over the years into a will to believe, a denial of the idol's flaws, a destructive love triangle intellectualized on all sides until the inevitable fall from grace of the Brandens and savage repudiation by the idol. See also Barbara Branden's essay in the current volume.

4. I can find no treatment of Rand's novels in the context of Jewish American writing (a categorization she would certainly have abhorred, along with all categorizations not specified by herself), but her proximity to (and distance from) contemporaries like Anzia Yezierska and Edna Ferber, especially as they treat the struggle with (and for) autonomy, secularism, commercial capitalism, the "promised land" of American security and mobility, would be well worth analysis. Merrill (1991) suggests that Rand may be using Judaic symbolism especially in Atlas Shrugged (61–62). And King (1992) suggests that "Rand's whole shtik was a gargantuan displacement of her never-admitted fear of anti-Semitism" (127).

5. For the feminist debate on romance, see Moers 1976, especially the chapters "Gothic Heroinism" and "Travelling Heroinism." Radway 1984 and Modlewski 1982 offer a good spectrum of celebration and vexation; Elam 1992 and Langbauer 1990 place a more contemporary spin on the debate. Perhaps the most dense and fascinating treatment of the complex role of popular romances in collaborating with, evading, and also critiquing patriarchal culture is to be found, actually, in a superbly nuanced 1991 novel by Mary Gaitskill, *Two Girls, Fat and Thin*, about two passionate readers of Ayn Rand's novels. Melissa Jane Hardie deals with the Gaitskill-Rand connection in her essay in the current volume.

6. In her foreword to *We the Living*, Rand ([1936] 1959, ix) calls the novel "as close to an autobiography as I will ever write."

7. Rand 1997 features her HUAC testimony and other unpublished material dealing with American Communism. See chap. 10.

8. Resisting the religious premises of a Hugo or a Dostoyevsky, Rand yet worked in the robust nineteenth-century tradition of epic fiction as a call to return to original Values. Chris Matthew Sciabarra (1995), in a comprehensive study of the Russian sources of Ayn Rand's philosophy and aesthetics, has proposed an additional source for the faith that art can effect radical change—the poet philosophers of the Russian Symbolist school: "While Rand would have opposed the explicitly Dionysian ideal of Russian Symbolism, she appears to have fully absorbed its impulse to transform culture through art" (208). Sciabarra's chapter 8, "Art, Philosophy, and Efficacy," also treats the complex interaction between the conscious and subconscious powers that Rand believed to lie at the heart of artistic production.

9. Rand's "man worship," as developed both in her fiction and her gender theories, has affinities, perhaps, with the Male Muse–projection/reception strategy of the great woman writers of the nineteenth century, a strategy described compellingly by Gilbert and Gubar 1979 and elaborated by Tayler 1990. For these critics, one method by which a woman artist in a patriarchal culture may legitimize her unruly creative desire is to imagine it given, even forced upon her in a species of rape, by a divine male, a method developed in opposite gender order by the "ancient" Western epic poets and then refined, Christianized, and further eroticized in the enabling writing myth of Milton's *Paradise Lost*.

10. Like Rand's hero-architect, Wright was a builder who believed that architecture should embody the values of an ideal humanity, though Wright's ideals were emphatically communitarian, if not collectivist, whereas Rand's were individualist, if not solipsist. According to Secrest's biography (1992), neither Rand nor Wright really understood the other (496–97). Rand 1995 features revealing correspondence with Wright (108–19). Her architectural research for *The Fountainhead*, which drew from Wright's autobiography among other sources, is featured in chapter 5 of Rand 1997.

11. Sedgwick 1985 gathers several strands of contemporary psychological and gender-study thought in its analysis of the "folk-perception" of the erotic triangle, strands that emphasize the centrality of male rival (or ally) relationships in the triangle. Rand's triangles fit this analysis: for Gail Wynand as much as for Dominique, for Hank Rearden as much as for Dagny Taggart, the "man-gods" Howard Roark and John Galt are the final shape of desire.

12. Since, as I would argue, female desire, redoubling in tensed opposition to itself, is at the bottom of all Rand's constructions of desire, there would be no room for male-male desire in her characterizations except as reflections of this structure. Rand, conscious here, as in her rape scenes, that she was figuring the unmentionable, is believed by Nathaniel Branden to have included a tart reference to this "foolishness," later cut, in an early draft of the novel, where Wynand tells Roark: "I love you—in every sense except the one a fool would think of first" (reported in Sciabarra 1995, 421 n. 68).

13. In the twenty-fifth anniversary edition of *The Fountainhead*, Rand ([1943] 1971, x–xi) discussed her difficulty: "Religion's monopoly in the field of ethics" has preempted the language ("worship," "reverence," "sacred") for communicating supreme emotional engagement with a philosophy

of life, so that she can be easily "misinterpreted" for her use of these words. Feminist post-theological discourse ponders this same issue, addressing it in, for instance, the punning Anglo-Saxon neologisms of Mary Daly and the Franco-Greek neologisms of Helene Cixous and Julia Kristeva.

14. Siblings, like most family figures, thwart the individual in Rand's fiction; there is a thwarting sister in We the Living, and a decidedly evil brother in Atlas Shrugged. Atlas Shrugged also contains Rand's first and only soul sister, a working-class young woman who marries Dagny's evil brother, James, thinking her achievements are his. She challenges the supposed bitch-sister, saying, "I'm the woman in this family now," to which Dagny replies, "That's quite all right, I'm the man" (Rand 1957, 396). In the end, Cherryl Taggart cannot bear the revelation of James's evil, even with Dagny's sisterly help, and commits suicide.

15. See, for example, the first section of Woolf 1938 and the introduction to the section "Invisible Work: Unacknowledged Contributions" in Kahn-Hut, Daniels, and Colvard 1982, 137–43.

16. Rand met J. Robert Oppenheimer in the late 1940s through producer Hal Wallis, who suggested she write a screenplay about the development of the atom bomb. Letters of Ayn Rand (1995) contains correspondence with Esther Stone (15 February 1945) revealing that "after much research, including interviews with Robert Oppenheimer and Gen. Leslie Groves, AR did a complete treatment and seventy pages of script for a movie tentatively titled 'Top Secret' " but nothing came of it (221). Rand's "Analysis of the Proper Approach to a Picture on the Atomic Bomb," notes of her interviews with Oppenheimer and others, and the general outline of her screenplay are featured in chapter 9 of Rand 1997. Some of Oppenheimer's personal mannerisms, and his bitter intelligence about the anti-intellectualism of American culture, became part of her portrait of the developer of "Project X."

17. Said (1978) argues that eighteenth- and nineteenth-century linguists, historians, travelers, and philosophers "constructed" a middle and far East "in need" of Western discovery and shaping, while establishing norms of Western identity based on its capacity to fulfill this imagined need. See also Said 1993 for literature's representations of, and complicity in, this process.

18. More than one postwar American utopian/dystopian fiction proposed that the only cure for a humanity seemingly bent on self-destruction was the imposition of order by a being from beyond the horizon: I think here of the benign order of the film The Day the Earth Stood Still, the malign order of The Invasion of the Body Snatchers, and the ambiguous order of Arthur C. Clarke's still engrossing novel Childhood's End (1953). Hunt (1984) makes other connections between Rand's dystopia and the pulp science fiction of her learning period, the American 1930s, and of our reading period, the period of best-selling thrillers about planetwide conspiracies.

References

Branden, Barbara. 1986. The Passion of Ayn Rand. Garden City, N.Y.: Doubleday.

Branden, Nathaniel. 1989. Judgment Day: My Years with Ayn Rand. Boston: Houghton Mifflin.

Caldwell, Gail. 1994. Summer reading places. Boston Globe, 19 June, sec. B, p. 26.

Clarke, Arthur. 1953. Childhood's End. New York: Harcourt, Brace, World.

Elam, Diane. 1992. Romancing the Postmodern. New York: Routledge.

Gaitskill, Mary. 1991. Two Girls, Fat and Thin. New York: Poseidon.

Gilbert, Sandra M., and Susan Gubar. 1979. The Madwoman in the Attic: The Woman Writer and the Nineteenth-Century Literary Imagination. New Haven: Yale University Press.

Hunt, Robert. 1984. Science fiction for the age of inflation: Reading Atlas Shrugged in the

1980s. In *Coordinates: Placing Science Fiction and Fantasy*, edited by George E. Slusser, Eric S. Rabkin, and Robert Scholes. Carbondale: Southern Illinois University Press.

Kahn-Hut, Rachel, Arlene Kaplan Daniels, and Richard Colvard. 1982. *Women and Work: Problems and Perspectives*. New York: Oxford University Press.

King, Florence. 1992. *With Charity Toward None: A Fond Look at Misanthropy*. New York: St. Martin's Press.

Kushner, Tony. 1994. *Angels in America: A Gay Fantasy on National Themes*. Pt. 2, *Perestroika*. New York: Theatre Communications Group.

Langbauer, Laurie. 1990. *Women and Romance: The Consolations of Gender*. Ithaca, N.Y.: Cornell University Press.

Merrill, Ronald E. 1991. *The Ideas of Ayn Rand*. La Salle, Ill.: Open Court.

Modleski, Tania. 1982. *Loving with a Vengeance: Mass-Produced Fantasies for Women*. Hamden, Conn.: Archon Books.

Moers, Ellen. 1976. *Literary Women*. Garden City, N.Y.: Doubleday.

Radway, Janice. 1984. *Reading the Romance: Women, Patriarchy, and Popular Literature*. Chapel Hill: University of North Carolina Press.

Rand, Ayn. [1936] 1959. *We the Living*. New York: New American Library.

———. [1943] 1971. *The Fountainhead*. 25th anniversary ed. New York: Bobbs-Merrill.

———. 1957. *Atlas Shrugged*. New York: Random House.

———. 1971. *The Romantic Manifesto: A Philosophy of Literature*. New York: New American Library.

———. 1992. *Atlas Shrugged*. 35th anniversary ed. Introduction by Leonard Peikoff. New York: Penguin.

———. 1995. *Letters of Ayn Rand*. Edited by Michael S. Berliner. New York: Penguin Dutton.

———. 1997. *Journals of Ayn Rand*. Edited by David Harriman. New York: Penguin Dutton.

Rubin, Gail. 1975. The traffic in women: Notes on the political economy of sex. In *Toward an Anthropology of Women*, edited by Rayna Reiter. New York: Monthly Review Press.

Said, Edward. 1978. *Orientalism*. New York: Pantheon Books.

———. 1993. *Culture and Imperialism*. New York: Random House.

Sciabarra, Chris Matthew. 1995. *Ayn Rand: The Russian Radical*. University Park: Pennsylvania State University Press.

Secrest, Meryle. 1992. *Frank Lloyd Wright*. New York: Alfred A. Knopf.

Sedgwick, Eve Kosofsky. 1985. *Between Men: English Literature and Male Homosocial Desire*. New York: Columbia University Press.

Tayler, Irene. 1990. *Holy Ghosts: The Male Muses of Emily and Charlotte Brontë*. New York: Columbia University Press.

Woolf, Virginia. 1938. *Three Guineas*. New York: Harcourt, Brace, World.

11

Who Is Dagny Taggart? The Epic Hero/ine in Disguise

Karen Michalson

In the beginning, all heroines were fictional and all heroines were real. That is why there were no heroines.

The "feminine" dallied in the shady realm of near-history in the form of snake goddesses and fertility figures and flower-bedecked priestesses and semihistorical Cretan queens.

And despite the material evidence for queens and high priestesses and goddesses, there were no hierarchies. And men (there were men too, although of a different sort than we have today) lived in peaceful partnership with women, and there was no competition, and nobody excelled or made more money than anybody else, so nobody had to feel bad about themselves. Besides, there were rigid bureaucracies to collect taxes and force everybody into the joyful equality that all right-thinking members

200 Feminist Rereadings of Rand's Fiction

of these societies advocated anyway. And women (and maybe men too) made great discoveries in metallurgy (but only for ornamentation and not for destructive weapons) and collectively invented agriculture. And as an added bonus everyone had indoor plumbing and there was plenty of leisure time to carve pregnant women in stone.

And then, around 4200 B.C.E. or 2000 B.C.E. or something-thousand B.C.E., Eastern invaders with male gods and bronze weapons destroyed the goddess cultures and instituted warrior cultures of male dominance, competition, and conquest.

And hence Western civilization.

Which is why Western culture never developed a paradigm for heroic women, and why heroes in the Western literary tradition are all men.

This is not my myth. It is only my retelling of a myth handed down by Riane Eisler, Merlin Stone, and other feminist writers.[1] I am not interested in whether this story is archaeologically or historically valid. I am interested in fiction making, in the uses of this story qua story, and in appropriating it for writing about Ayn Rand's supremely heroic creation, Dagny Taggart, the protagonist of *Atlas Shrugged*.

I find this feminist creation myth a useful starting place for writing about what, for many feminists, is a troubling disconnect in the character of Dagny Taggart, a disconnect that appears sharply to focus an apparent misogynic strain in Rand's writings by demonstrating Rand's seeming inability to recognize even the strongest women as self-sufficient individuals.

Dagny Taggart is arguably one of the strongest heroes in Western literature. She is one of the very few female characters, perhaps the only female character, in important, influential Western literature who possesses all of the traits of the traditional epic hero. These traits include, of course, the familiar catalogue of being a figure of national or cultural importance, of embodying the culture's highest values, of having adventures in a worldwide setting, of performing and achieving superhuman feats, and of performing actions and undergoing experiences that the gods take an active interest in.[2]

Dagny is an epic hero in an archetypal simplicity that is as stunning as the functional simplicity of her unadorned physical appearance and her uncluttered apartment. She is a figure of national importance, both because she is a nationally known vice-president of a transcontinental railroad and because the fate of the nation depends on her ability to get essential goods transported to vital areas as the country's infrastructure breaks down. She embodies and lives by the highest values in the world of Rand's novel: individualism, purpose, self-actualization. Her adventures take place in a setting of epic proportion, the United States. In fact, since Rand envisions a United States that is undergoing a period of severe economic and social decline, Dagny's actions also occur against a setting of mythic and apocalyptic proportions, that of a great civilization in its death throes. Her actions and achievements are superhuman in the sense that most of her colleagues are in awe—or a little afraid—of her ability to keep a railroad running despite shortages of supplies and manpower that cripple other large businesses. The gods take an active part in her actions in the sense that many of the other heroes of this world, the producers whose achievements make the difference between worldwide savagery and civilization, whose minds produce the seeming miracles of creating new metals and designing new bridges to move tons of supplies through arcs of empty space, work for and against her success.

However, Dagny seems more than willing to assume traditional subservient female roles in relation to the three heroic male characters who become her lovers: Francisco d'Anconia, Henry (Hank) Rearden, and John Galt. To please Galt, Dagny, the brilliant independent mind that runs a transcontinental railroad, cooks and cleans house like any Harriet-style 1950s housewife. Why did Rand endow her glorious female hero with weak knees for stronger men? Does this character trait, this seeming disconnect, compromise Dagny's status as a hero?

If the above description of the epic hero sounds simplistic and familiar, that is precisely the point of this essay. When Rand created Dagny, she was consciously drawing on the epic-hero archetype, in all of its historical simplicity. She was writing *Atlas Shrugged* in the 1950s, when archetypal and comparative studies of Western epic-heroic literature were current. I am not implying that Rand consciously or deliberately drew from those academic studies. She might have, but she didn't need to. There is plenty of biographical and literary evidence that her heroic characters were influenced by the creations of Victor Hugo and Fyodor Dostoyevsky, and that she held a lifelong fascination with Hollywood motion pictures that often depicted heroic characters.[3] I am stating that at the time Rand wrote *Atlas Shrugged*, the traditional literary definition of heroism was essentially simplistic and unproblematic. Everyone from professional intellectuals to eager schoolkids lining up for Saturday matinees knew a

heroic character on seeing one, and few publicly questioned or challenged or attempted to deconstruct the "politics of meaning" embedded
in the archetype.

Except, perhaps, Rand herself, which is why, I would argue, she has
been so misunderstood by feminists. But more on that later.

Here's my myth.

In the beginning, all heroines were fictional and all heroines were real.
That is why there were no heroines.

The Great Mother Herself does not mean. She is. There is a dark
swollen presence existing at the fringes of history in faceless stone carvings of female figures. The Great Mother is a name we give to this "feminine" presence, but it is our name, not Hers. She is a presence, not a
persona.

The Great Mother was life and death, and so did not differentiate
between them, for the intimacy Her cultures had with death meant that
birth and fertility were valued beyond all things. The Great Mother was
nature in all Her chthonic violence, the worship of exploding fecundity
being a violent response to the violence of sudden, inexplicable, nonexistence. As Camille Paglia ([1990] 1991, 43) reminds us: "The goddess'
animal fecundity was cruelly dramatized in ritual. Her devotees practiced
castration, breast-amputation, self-flagellation or slashing, and dismemberment of beasts." Mother Earth was womb and tomb. Life and death
are one in ritual. The Mother was All.

That is why, in the beginning, the Great Mother had no stories and no
adventures and committed no heroic deeds. There were no differentiated
character aspects of Herself for poets to make tales about. None that
survived into the Western literary tradition, anyway. We can and do
make tales at a distance out of silent artifacts, but they are only our
Western way of invading and colonizing the prehistoric material for our
own uses. Literature is an act of invasion, an immortal weapon of the
invader cultures. The oldest written epic, Gilgamesh, is essentially about
the separation of life and death, for Gilgamesh, the male hero, is out to
conquer death by gaining eternal life. He can't. The unknown poets who
wrote and compiled the known versions of the world's first literary epic
created a fictional world in which immortality is unobtainable, although
for Gilgamesh, the world's first literary hero, a lifelong youth, that is, a
life undifferentiated by age and change, is still an option, albeit a fading
one. Gilgamesh learns of this possibility from Utnapishtim, an immortal
human who lives in a region separated from the rest of the world and

who clearly belongs to a past age in which birth and death are undifferentiated. The Flood that destroyed humanity was the same Goddess womb from which Utnapishtim was born into immortality, living forever in a realm outside the world that the hero, Gilgamesh, must cross a river of death to find.

The dirty joke is that a serpent, the Mother Goddess's oldest form, carries away the plant that would have granted the hero undifferentiated youth. The snake as undifferentiated Mother Goddess, symbol of eternity, sheds Her skin, devours Herself, and disappears from literature just as literature is born, leaving tension and plot and the futile attempts of male heroes to fight and conquer death reverberating through the next forty centuries of literature. Life and death are no longer one, they are now in eternal tension. When the serpent reemerges centuries later in *Genesis* or centuries after that in *Paradise Lost,* it will usually be associated with only one division of divinity, Satan, the fallen part of a once unified host of angels in eternal war with God. It will bear such little resemblance to the first serpent that the Virgin Mary, pale medieval echo of the Mother Goddess, will usually be depicted in Church statuary as crushing a serpent with her heel. The serpent also leaves behind her the earliest literary example of differentiated aspects of the Mother Goddess in the form of individual characters: the Sumerian goddesses Ishtar and Ninsun and the temple priestesses who manifest the Mother Goddess as individual women.

Heroes are always orphaned, born of the Great Mother as She leaves. One of the definable characteristics of the Western hero is that if he is not a true orphan, he is usually raised by someone other than his biological parents, as are Oedipus and King Arthur. Having an excess of parents often serves to obscure the hero's ties to his biological parents, granting him a certain freedom to stand alone without the burdens and obligations of family ties. One can't save the village or the nation from destruction while concentrating on the more local concerns of a family. As Hank Rearden realizes early in *Atlas Shrugged,* he can't devote himself to creating a revolutionary metal with the potential of benefiting the world while squandering his time on pleasing the whims of his wife, mother, and brother.

It was the poets of the invader cultures that first endowed the primal Mother Goddess with distant daughters who had definable personalities and a penchant for action: Athena of Athens, who founded a city; Artemis of Ephesus, who changed Actaeon into a stag; Aphrodite of Cyprus, who helped Paris win Helen. In the minds of Homer and Virgil and Ovid, the Goddess is verbally dismembered into literary immortality.

My point is that literature is not of the Great Mother. Without differentiation, there is no tension. Without tension, without the acknowledgment of differences and opposites, there is no plot line and character, there is no literature. Art is always being born of violence, immortal art of immortal violence. Every word imprisons the blankness of the page; every slash of paint assaults the canvas; every chord rapes silence into shudders of sound waves. Our primary evidence of the Mother's presence is stone carvings, silent, immobile, and undifferentiated in their facelessness.

Dagny is a hero, that is, a character created in the tradition of epic heroes. She also happens to be female.

The problem with Dagny, for many feminist readers who see feminism as inextricably entwined with a collectivist political agenda, is that she thwarts those readers' preference for female "heroes" who are snake goddesses, who represent the utopian "partnership society" that Riane Eisler postulates as having once existed. However, the Western canon has developed and defined a hero archetype that is essentially a character who thrives in what Eisler calls a "dominator society." Goddess help any heroine who smacks of the "dominator," because what's at stake here, from a collectivist perspective, is not her femininity but the crime of excelling beyond her sisters. Collectivist feminists might want Dagny to run the railroad, but only perhaps if she makes it a cooperative venture with other women and disenfranchised men, and doesn't make others feel they can't measure up to her implacable talents. And preferably, it isn't really a railroad that Dagny runs, because there is something vaguely discomforting about the phallus imagery of the trains, no doubt an invention of "male" science and engineering. Collectivist feminists eschew heroines that must be looked up to; they're too hierarchical and "male." But in the Western literary canon, an equal isn't a hero.

And in the mythology of collectivist feminism, a "hero" is more likely to be less-than-equal, oppressed, ignored. Collectivist feminist "heroes" are not figures of national importance; they are oppressed nameless Others who have never "been given a voice" by an oppressive society. They do not represent the highest values of their culture. They spend their time "clarifying and developing new values." They do not traverse physical settings of epic proportion; they "go into themselves." They do not create new worlds or save old ones; "they share insights" and "new ways of defining who we are." They are fictional and they are real because, alternatively, feminist heroes don't exist in the sense of fitting comfortably within a largely male-defined Western hero archetype that defines itself on individual achievement. From a collectivist perspective, every achievement must be redefined as a collective achievement or denigrated as worthless. Every tension, every difference, is smoothed into the nonexistence of the oceanic womb of primal ooze. "We are all One in the Goddess," goes the cry of contemporary women's spirituality groups. The gods and goddesses do not take an active interest in the actions of feminist heroes, for they are Goddesses. Actionless and whole.[4]

Which is, I suspect, one reason collectivist feminist literary critics have written almost nothing on Rand's work and why Rand's novels are conspicuously absent from most women's studies departments and English-department reading lists. Dagny is, above all, a creature of action and accomplishment. She makes the trains run on time.

The other problem is that Rand herself creates a tension, a verbal dismemberment between her ideal of the "feminine" in her philosophy and in her fictional creations. How does one reconcile Rand's statement that a "woman should not be President of the United States" with Rand's own narratorial comment when describing Dagny's childhood determination one day to run Taggart Transcontinental: "She was twelve years old when she told Eddie Willers that she would run the railroad when they grew up. She was fifteen when it occurred to her for the first time that women did not run railroads and that people might object. To hell with that, she thought—and never worried about it again" (Rand [1957] 1985, 55). Or how does one reconcile Rand's pronouncement that a "feminine woman . . . never loses the awareness of her own sexual identity and [men's] . . . a properly feminine woman does not treat men as if she were their pal, sister, mother—or leader" (Rand 1968, 1), with Dagny, who is introduced to the reader as "unfeminine, as if she were unconscious of her own body and that it was a woman's body" (Rand [1957] 1985, 20), and whose first action in the novel is to assume leadership over a group of male railroad workers who are afraid to take responsibility for moving a train that is stopped on the wrong siding. In fact, when a male passenger and the male engineer both sarcastically address her as "lady," and tell her she doesn't know anything about trains and railroad procedures, the scene becomes heavily charged with sexism, but Dagny calmly rises above their prejudices through her competent leadership. After she solves the crisis, the brakeman asks the engineer who Dagny is. " 'That's who runs

Taggart Transcontinental,' said the engineer; the respect in his voice was genuine. 'That's the Vice-President in Charge of Operation' " (24).

The issue with Dagny that a lot of feminist readers miss is that she is always in charge, even in her relationships with the male heroes of the novel. And I would like to suggest that Rand's philosophical statements about the essence of femininity really come down to that: being in charge. Of course a properly feminine woman does not treat men as if she were their pal, sister, mother—or leader. In the real world, where men have enjoyed centuries of political and economic power over women, "pal, sister, mother, or leader" are all roles that are defined in relation to men.

Perhaps a properly feminine woman has no need to define herself as anyone's pal, sister, mother, or leader (which implies followers). A properly feminine woman is a hero in her own right. She is self-actualized and self-defined without reference to anyone else. Dagny is nobody's pal. In fact, in her youth, potential "pals" constantly tell her she's "unbearably conceited" (55) because she is so work-driven she has no time for social niceties. She is James Taggart's sister, but resists this relationship throughout most of the novel, preferring to be defined by her accomplishments rather than by the accident of her birth. She is nobody's mother, for she is free of children. She is not a leader, because she does not conceive of the social-political hierarchy this implies. Dagny seeks no followers. To the contrary, she views all of the incompetent men and women in the novel with utter indifference unless they are preventing her from accomplishing her work.

In fact, it is striking that in Galt's Gulch, Rand's utopia, there are no leaders and there is no government. There is certainly no president. The gulch is a friendly anarchy of free traders who offer each other the highest respect in terms of trading labor for each other's labor.[5] As John Galt, for whom the gulch is named, explains to Dagny, "we have no laws in this valley, no rules, no formal organization of any kind" (664).

A properly feminine woman is a woman who is strong enough not to have her essential nature defined by anyone else. Dagny defines the meaning of her own actions. The traditional, socially ascribed meaning of her actions does not define her.

For the sake of space, I shall confine myself to three examples of how Dagny defines herself in ways that violate both traditional feminist and traditional antifeminist expectations. These examples concern Dagny's three lovers, and while they appear to exemplify the apparent disconnect

in Dagny's character that might elicit discomfort in many feminist readers, a close reading shows that they actually demonstrate that Dagny is as
radically *sui generis* as an epic hero ought to be.

The first action occurs when Francisco d'Anconia slaps Dagny because
she half-seriously threatens to lower her standards and become less of an
achiever in return for social popularity. The incident is worth quoting at
length:

> "Well, I've always been unpopular in school and it didn't
> bother me, but now I've discovered the reason. It's an impossible
> kind of reason. They dislike me, not because I do things badly,
> but because I do them well. They dislike me because I've always
> had the best grades in the class. I don't even have to study. I
> always get A's. Do you suppose I should try to get D's for a change
> and become the most popular girl in school?"
>
> Francisco stopped, looked at her and slapped her face.
>
> What she felt was contained in a single instant, while the
> ground rocked under her feet, in a single blast of emotion within
> her. She knew that she would have killed any other person who
> struck her; she felt the violent fury which would have given her
> the strength for it—and as violent a pleasure that Francisco had
> done it. . . . *She felt pleasure in what she suddenly grasped about him,
> about herself and about his motive.*
>
> She braced her feet to stop the dizziness, she held her head
> straight and stood facing him in the consciousness of a new
> power, feeling herself his equal for the first time, looking at him
> with a mocking smile of triumph.
>
> "Did I hurt you as much as that?" she asked.
>
> He looked astonished; the question and the smile were not
> those of a child. He answered, "Yes—if it pleases you."
>
> "It does."
>
> "Don't ever do that again. Don't crack jokes of that kind. . . .
> When you grow up you'll understand what sort of unspeakable
> thing you said.". . .
>
> He looked at her for a long moment. . . . "Dagny, you're won-
> derful."
>
> "I always thought you thought so," she answered, her voice
> insolently casual. (100, emphasis added)

When Dagny returns home, she lies to her mother about the source of her bruise. "She did not do it to protect Francisco; she did it because she felt, for some reason which she could not define, that the incident was a secret too precious to share" (100).

Is the future vice-president of Taggart Transcontinental, Rand's strong epic hero/ine, an oppressed woman reveling in her own abuse? Is this scene meant to be read as a justification for strong men beating strong women, and therefore as evidence of some latent misogyny in Rand's writing? I would argue no, but I would also argue that, in this scene, Rand is subverting the traditional, classic dynamic that often exists in abusive relationships in order to satirize them. To begin with, Dagny, the most brilliant, gifted student in her class, is threatening to destroy her own brilliance in exchange for popularity, something "nice girls" in the 1950s were often socially pressured into doing. Young women in school were often advised to "play dumb" and "hide their intelligence" if they expected to attract young men. Women who haven't been willing to hide their learning and intelligence have been saddled with pejorative terms like "bluestocking" and "witch" for centuries. When Dagny threatens to abuse herself by forgoing her gifts, to "get D's instead of A's," Francisco looks at her in hurt astonishment and slaps her. Note that physical abuse and, in some cases, torture have been methods used traditionally to keep women from excelling, from enjoying too much liberty, from being too uppity. Francisco slaps Dagny for all the opposite reasons—he is hurt that she would even joke about becoming less than what she really is. He is serious about her not compromising her gifts. It is supremely important to him that Dagny be the hero she is, and her threat not to be is as much a slap to him as his physical response is to her.

Maybe even more so, because Dagny, far from feeling broken, smiles in triumph because she understands that Francisco's reaction is a tacit admission of the value he places on her achievement. She takes the slap, *in this context,* coming from Francisco, the only other person Dagny knows at this point in her life who shares with her the realization that "the code of competence is the only system of morality that's on a gold standard" (100) as a personal validation of her worth. Note that Dagny is not masochistic; in fact, she would have "killed any other person who struck her." But coming from any other person (note the neutral word "person," meaning any other man or woman who would have struck her), the slap would have been a punishment for excelling beyond her place, not a response to her refusal to excel. Dagny understands how hard this action would be to explain to anyone else because physical abuse is generally understood as a way to punish women for excelling. She also knows how hard it is for people to recognize her as an aspiring railroad engineer because she is a woman. For these reasons she must keep this incident, precisely because it is a validation the rest of the world would pervert through condemnation, a "secret too precious to share."

I believe that Dagny is the only important female hero in Western literature who is physically struck for refusing to excel at a nontraditional pursuit. Try to imagine Lancelot roughing up Guinevere for refusing to don armor and lead men into battle, or Casaubon roughing up Dorothea for refusing to write better books and to become a more important scholar than he intends to be. It's hard to do, because there is no literary tradition of men valuing women's achievements to the point of exerting violence to defend them, or women hurting men by refusing to excel at traditionally male pursuits.

That is what makes Rand's feminism in her fiction so radical and hard to read. It functions very much like the archetypal epic hero in disguise, the wandering king who appears as a poor peasant, or, in this case, the epic hero figure who appears, for the first time, as a woman.

Another scene that seems to point to a disconnect in Dagny's character involves her second lover, Hank Rearden, but again the context of this scene is crucial. Rearden earns Dagny's love and admiration through his achievements, not simply through his status as a successful male entrepreneur. She admires Rearden's plans for the bridge for her Rio Norte line as much as she admires him, maybe more. My point is that she loves Rearden because he creates bridges and new metals. She doesn't love the bridges and metals merely for his sake. The difference is that between a traditional woman trapped in dependency and a self-sufficient hero who is strong enough to admire the achievements of another hero. This difference is shown most clearly when Dagny bargains for a bracelet, the first object manufactured with the first heat of the first order of Rearden's new metal, from Rearden's wife, Lillian.

Lillian, the traditional wife, makes a thin, intentionally transparent pretense about admiring this bracelet when Rearden first gives it to her. She does so only because it is from him and she's supposed to do the socially expected thing and say something gracious. Lillian, however, makes sure that her contempt for the gift is conveyed through her sarcastically formulaic appreciation, "Henry, it's perfectly wonderful! What originality! I shall be the sensation of New York, wearing jewelry made of the same stuff as bridge girders, truck motors, kitchen stoves, typewriters, and—what was it you were saying about it the other day, darling?—soup kettles?" (42). A little later, after receiving encouragement from Rearden's mother and brother, who have commented at length on how his intense commitment to work is only selfishness, Lillian holds up the bracelet and comments, "What would happen to Henry's vanity if he didn't have us to throw alms to? . . . A chain. . . . Appropriate isn't it? It's the chain by which he holds us all in bondage" (48).

Lillian's comment is resonant with the way she later perceives Dagny when Dagny enters Lillian's anniversary party. Lillian, who has previously only seen Dagny in business suits, is astonished to see her in a revealing dress, because "one never thought of Dagny Taggart's body. . . . the diamond band on the wrist of her naked arm gave her the most feminine of all aspects: the look of being chained" (133). I feel it necessary to point out the obvious here, that this is not Rand's assessment of femininity but Lillian's, one of Rand's least sympathetic fictional creations. Lillian can only conceive of herself (and, by extension, all women) as essentially dependent and reduced to manipulating and whining for attention. She is threatened by Dagny, whom she later refers to as "perfectly sexless" and "an adding machine in tailored suits" (219), because Dagny violates all the social conventions Lillian has ever known by being a self-sufficient, competent businesswoman. The only way Lillian knows how to make sense of what she perceives as uncharacteristic "femininity" in her rival is a metaphor of bondage, for Lillian only understands femininity as being chained.

Later at the party, Lillian complains to two smartly groomed women about her own bracelet, "Why, no it's not from a hardware store, it's a very special gift from my husband. Oh yes of course it's hideous. . . . I'd exchange it for a common diamond bracelet any time, but somehow nobody will offer me one for it" (151).

Dagny challenges Lillian to make good her offer and extends to her the diamond bracelet she is wearing, which a shocked Lillian accepts in exchange for the metal one. In this exchange, Dagny symbolically makes mincemeat out of the "woman in chains" metaphor because she wears the metal bracelet, not as a chain, but in appreciation of what its metal means to her railroad, her work, and her career. As Dagny clasps the metal bracelet on her wrist, she offers a radical new definition of femininity ironically disguised in the language of tradition: "Inexplicably, she felt a touch of feminine vanity, the kind she had never experienced before:

the desire to be seen wearing this particular ornament" (152). This is a rebuke to Lillian's perception, because "particular ornament" implies that it is the metal, not the generic concept of bracelet or chain, that Dagny's "feminine vanity" arises from. It is an ornament of achievement, cast from the very same metal out of which she will build her new railroad line. Dagny's newfound feminine vanity is a result of pride in her achievements as much as, maybe even more than, it is a result of wearing something Rearden made. It's the metal first, and by extension the man who made it.

Dagny's attitude toward the bracelet is a rational one based on values. The metal represents her own work and achievement as much as it represents Rearden's. Lillian's attitude is based on her unquestioning acceptance of the socially defined meanings of material objects. No one ever told her to think of the metal used in bridge girders as romantic, so she doesn't, even though it is just those products of industry that make it possible for her to throw romantic parties in heated rooms with exotic hothouse flowers in the middle of a winter storm. The diamonds have no personal resonance for Lillian. She admires them as a traditional symbol of love, used in rings to symbolize a yoking or a binding, and as a visible sign of wealth. But for her, diamonds represent love and wealth merely because "everyone says" they do, not because she has learned to think for herself and define the terms of her own life. It's social status first, and by extension the diamonds.

When Dagny is alone in her office, thinking about her love for the rails, she articulates the clearest expression of what love and sexual desire mean to a woman who is not oppressed by either: "There was some unbreakable link between her love for her work and the desire of her body; as if one gave her the right to the other, the right and the meaning; as if one were the completion of the other—and the desire would never be satisfied, except by a being of equal greatness" (210).

Context is crucial to the scene in which Dagny and Hank Rearden become lovers, because throughout this scene, which many readers have likened to a rape, it is clear that Dagny is the partner who is consciously and rationally in control, not Rearden. Rearden, whose only experience with women has been with clinging dependents like his wife and mother, for a long time has trouble thinking of Dagny as female. Rand makes it clear that this is Rearden's confusion, brought on by a world that has perverted and denigrated what a woman should be and by the difference between Dagny and every other woman he's known. When Dagny tells him she's going to live on the railway site they're building out in Colorado, he worries about her safety, and she laughs, startled. "Why, Hank, it's the first time you've ever thought I wasn't a man" (196). This comment sends Rearden into a troubled internal monologue about his inability to reconcile how society has taught him to regard women and how he regards Dagny: "You trusted me, didn't you? To recognize your greatness? To think of you as you deserved—as if you were a man? . . . Don't you suppose I know how much I've betrayed? The only bright encounter in my life—the only person I respected—the best businessman I know—my ally—my partner in a desperate battle. . . . The lowest of all desires—as my answer to the highest I've met" (196, all ellipses in the original). Rearden has been taught to believe that his sexual desires are low, something to be ashamed of, and he can't reconcile his sexual desire for Dagny with the genuine admiration and respect he has for her. In fact, in another reversal of traditional gender roles, it is Dagny who teaches a confused Rearden about sex. After their first sexual encounter, Rearden vents his confusion and self-loathing in language that, at times, sounds very much like that used for centuries by young women voicing morning-after regrets concerning their loss of honor: "I've given in to a desire which I despise. . . . It's depravity—and I accept it as such. . . . now if you wish to slap my face, go ahead" (243).

In response to Rearden's self-loathing, Dagny laughs, and says without embarrassment the sort of thing that one hears from roguish men in fiction but not women: "That is all I want, Hank. I want you in my bed—and you are free of me for all the rest of your time. . . . I do not want your mind, your will, your being or your soul, so long as it's to me that you will come for that lowest one of your desires. . . . You think this is a threat to your achievement but not to mine. . . . You hold it as your guilt and I—as my pride" (244). It is Dagny who feels no confusion or shame concerning the fulfillment of her desires, which she refers to as her "proudest attainment" (244), and Rearden who comes across like a "fallen woman," riddled with guilt, who nevertheless knows he will fall again, who agonizes over the oath he made to his spouse and his loss of virtue. Rearden does not have the "being-of-equal-greatness" model in his head as Dagny does; he can only understand his experience as a fall from the grace of his own values, and so he suffers the tension of being unable to reconcile the pure desire he feels for Dagny as the embodiment of his own highest values, with the social training that says he's immoral if he prefers a woman who is his equal in the workplace to a wife who despises and denigrates his life's work. Dagny and Rearden are more in the tradition of male buddies who share work activities, and engage "shoulder to shoulder" in traditionally masculine pursuits together, than that of the more familiar Romeo and Juliet kind of lovers one finds in Western literature.

The fact that they each comment on their own feelings, pleasure or shame, in their sexual encounter without seeming to acknowledge the other's feelings is not callousness so much as an implicit recognition that each of them embodies the other's highest values, that they see themselves in each other and have therefore earned the right to be together, as "equal beings of greatness." But it is Dagny who, in the course of the novel, leads Rearden to accept this way of thinking. It is Dagny who leads this particular partnership of equals.

It is also useful to look at Dagny's willingness to become John Galt's housekeeper during her first stay in Galt's Gulch, because at first glance her decision does come across like another potential disconnect. House-keeping and cooking are traditional, low-value "female occupations" that epic heroes avoid in favor of doing more interesting things like winning battles and saving countries. Why does an important railroad magnate like Dagny volunteer to be a housekeeper and describe herself in self-deprecating terms like "servant" (707)? Context is crucial here, and it is not the context of the real world, where such activities are held as de-meaning woman's work, but the context of Galt's Gulch, Rand's utopia and vision of the ideal society of heroes.

Dagny is a trespasser in the gulch. She has unwittingly crashed the gate in her plane and entered utopia without asking for the consent of the inhabitants. As John Galt explains, that gives him the right to hold her there for one month, the same time frame during which the other inhabitants honor a voluntary agreement not to leave the gulch. Further-more, an account has been established in her name at Mulligan's Bank with money that the philosopher-turned-pirate Ragnar Danneskjöld has taken from state-sponsored looters, a sum that amounts to a refund of what Dagny has paid in income taxes over the years. Galt wishes to charge her fifty cents per day while she is recuperating from her plane crash in his house, a bill she can pay from her account. Dagny, however, refuses to claim her money, because she can't bear the thought of Dan-neskjöld, a man she considers so beautiful that she can't endure the

thought of him being "subjected to the shocks, the strains, the scars reserved for any man who loved his work" (701), risking his life for her
money.

Since Dagny is physically incapacitated and housebound but mobile,
there really is little else she can offer as compensation for room and
board, and when she proposes to earn her keep as a cook and housemaid,
"her voice had the shrewd, confident, deliberating slowness of a trader"
(707), not the plaintive wheedling of a would-be dependent. Galt certainly does not expect this offer. Her proposal shocks and surprises him,
and he asks her first if that's what she really wants to do before he accepts
it. It is also important to note that in strictly economic terms Dagny will
make a profit as a housekeeper, because Galt will pay her room and board
and $10.00 per month.

A more telling argument, though, is Dagny's own view of housekeeping, which is consciously at odds with everything she's known in the
outside world:

> There is reason, she thought, why a woman should wish to cook
> for a man . . . oh, not as a duty, not as a chronic career, only as a
> rare and special rite in symbol of . . . but what have they made of
> it, the preachers of woman's duty? . . . The castrated performance
> of a sickening drudgery was held to be a woman's proper virtue—
> while that which gave it meaning and sanction was held as a
> shameful sin. . . . [previous ellipses in text, following ellipses
> mine]. . . . She leaped abruptly to her feet. She did not want to
> think of the outer world or of its moral code. (720–21)

There's a context that surrounds Dagny's domestic endeavors that many
feminists miss, just as Lillian misses the true meaning of the metal bracelet. There's a difference between a woman cooking dinner for a man as a
"castrated performance" (interesting word choice), that is, as a dependent housewife who has no other option in life and whose talents and
gifts are reduced to kitchen drudgery, and a hero cooking dinner as a
rational conscious choice because she wants to offer some kind of pay-
ment for room and board and avoid dependency. When Dagny keeps
house for John, it is in this sense a heroic act, motivated by her desire
not to enter complicity with Ragnar in his having risked his life. She
takes pleasure in watching John eat, but it is her own pleasure that concerns her, not his. In a very real sense, in the context of Galt's Gulch,

Dagny first has to be a hero herself to be truly capable of keeping house for Galt; that is, she has to have an exceptionally strong sense of self-sufficiency.

When Dagny keeps house for John Galt, it is a heroic act, but that is not the same as saying that *all* domestic work for *all* (or even most) women is heroic. A "rare and special rite" that exists temporarily between Galt and Dagny should never be a "duty" or a "chronic career" as it unfortunately is for most women outside of Galt's Gulch, where the meaning of housekeeping has been corrupted by "second-handers" who feel it is every man's right to have a housekeeper and every woman's duty to be one. This is the attitude that feminists rebel against, but in utopia, the gulch, even "sickening drudgery" is imbued with heroic meaning. In the best of worlds, under the best of circumstances, Rand shows us what traditional female occupations ought to look like—temporary jobs, not "chronic careers," anticipating by several years the feminist stand that women should be paid for housework. It's important to stress that this occupation is temporary—Dagny engages in it for one month. On her return to the gulch at the end of the novel, as the world crashes to an end, we learn that Dagny is going to run the first railroad between New York and Philadelphia, her proper career. It is also worth noting that the residents of the gulch engage in all kinds of occupations, including un-skilled manual labor to which the outside world would not generally ac-cord high status. In utopia, the point is to do one's job well, whatever it is.

Just as male heroes throughout the Western canon by tradition have temporarily given up their pursuits for one special lady whom they love—I'm thinking of countless chivalrous speeches where men swear to be-come their lady's slave and do her bidding just for her favor—Dagny, like a knight errant to his lady, becomes a servant to demonstrate strength, self-sufficiency, competence, and to win favor. But the point is that it's her choice and strength that motivates her to do so.

So why are there so few women in Galt's Gulch, and why didn't Rand create more strong women in *Atlas Shrugged*? Is Dagny to be read as inher-ently better or different in kind from all other women, a special case that no other woman can aspire to as a role model? Or is she, as I am arguing, Rand's model of what a strong woman looks like, a rebuke to a world that puts more burdens and restrictions on heroic women than on heroic men?

Cherryl Brooks, Dagny's sister-in-law, offers a possible answer to these questions. Cherryl is a poor shopgirl. Unlike Dagny, she did not inherit a large business to run, and she did not grow up with access to education or training. She is, however, in all respects, like Dagny in terms of her motivation, energy, and drive to succeed. When James Taggart asks her about her life, Cherryl answers:

> "My old man's never been any good, and Ma didn't care whether he was or not, and I got sick of it always turning out that I was the only one of the seven of us that kept a job, and the rest of them always being out of luck, one way or another. I thought if I didn't get out it would get me—I'd rot all the way through, like the rest of them. So I bought a railroad ticket one day and left. . . . Oh, I don't know, but . . . [ellipses in text] but people do things in the world. I saw pictures of New York and I thought . . . somebody built those buildings—he didn't just sit and whine that the kitchen was filthy and the roof leaking and the plumbing clogged and it's a goddamned world and . . . we were stinking poor and not giving a damn about it. That's what I couldn't take—that they didn't really give a damn." (249, all ellipses mine except where noted)

If Cherryl had had Dagny's birth and circumstances, one could easily imagine her running a major business. They are so similar that Dagny tells Cherryl they are sisters "through their own choice" (824), not through Cherryl's marriage to Dagny's brother, James. Unfortunately, Cherryl is young, poorly educated, and naive enough to believe that James Taggart is the true force and brains behind Taggart Transcontinental, and so she worships him as a hero. "Worship" is a word that James Taggart himself uses. "Why do you worry so much about the great men? . . . What are you, a hero worshipper of some kind?" Her quiet response is, "Mr. Taggart, what else is there to look up to?" (248). "Worship" and "look up to" imply hierarchy, not equality. This is why James Taggart is attracted to her. Cherryl knows greatness as something to aspire to, but does not see herself as having reached it. Taggart is flattered by her unearned admiration and eventually marries her, and Cherryl believes for a time that her status as his worshipful wife is higher than anything she might have achieved through her own efforts.

However, when Cherryl learns that James is a complete incompetent who has been taking credit for Dagny's accomplishments, she confronts a devastating insight:

"Those girls that you used to buy for the price of a meal, they would have been glad to let their real selves become a gutter, they would have taken your alms and never tried to rise, but you would not marry one of them. You married me, because you knew that I would not accept the gutter, inside or out, that I was struggling to rise and would go on struggling—didn't you?"

"Yes!" he cried. (839)

Cherryl realizes what many feminists would later realize about the institution of traditional marriage, that marriage is a way to control and break a strong woman's spirit, to ensure that she never rises beyond the domestic sphere to become a hero in the (male) world of action. Cherryl runs away in horror of her condition. Her status as the grateful, dutiful wife, in the traditional sort of marriage women have been expected to aspire to for centuries, a marriage that is even likened to a Cinderella fairy tale, is the tool that crushes her spirit. The questions in her head are her response to her oppression: "Why are you doing it to me—she cried soundlessly to the darkness around her. Because you're good—some enormous laughter seemed to be answering from the roof tops and from the sewers" (840). Cherryl chooses death rather than life in a world in which her innate greatness will be used to oppress her, reminiscent of a hero falling on his sword to avoid dishonor.

The fact that a woman like Dagny can and does exist is Rand's rebuke to a world in which female heroes are, in a sense, disguised, unrecognizable. There are fewer female heroes in *Atlas Shrugged*, not because most women are inferior to Dagny, but because most women are in situations like Cherryl's. Rand has created a female epic hero, perhaps the first, and the problem some readers have had in recognizing her is that there's really no difference between her and her male counterparts. Like Rearden, many readers in the 1950s were conditioned to view Dagny's attributes as "male" and so could not reconcile her heroic acts with her gender. Some feminists have the same problem, to the extent that some major strains of feminism posit themselves against individual achievement and traditional ideas of heroism, which are defined as "male."

But then, when the Mother Goddess was first written out of Her undifferentiated stone carvings and into Her action-oriented individualized literary manifestations, She too went disguised when she walked among men. Athena always hides herself in armor.

Notes

1. Versions of this myth can be found in Eisler 1988 and Stone 1976. See also Neumann 1955 and Briffault 1927. This myth has also been appropriated for the uses of fiction making by many popular novelists, including Bradley (1982) and Renault (1958).

2. Literary critics have commented on these familiar characteristics of epic heroes so often it almost seems unnecessary to mention them. For five notable classic discussions of epic literature, see Bowra 1945; Campbell 1949, [1952] 1966; Tillyard [1954] 1966; Frye 1957, 315–26.

3. For discussions of Rand's literary influences, see Sciabarra 1995; Gladstein 1984, 76–78. For discussions of Rand's relationship with the motion-picture industry, see Branden 1986, 73–118 and 184–251.

4. This faceless, undifferentiated, nameless, collectivist feminist non-"hero" does not exist in *literature*, although she does exist in many women's groups as a semifictional construction out of real life. "All heroines are fictional and all heroines are real." I'm primarily thinking of my experiences in many women's groups in which "hero" is a word that is usually reserved to describe an anonymous victim of a horrible crime who now "speaks for all women" because "all women" are defined as undifferentiated, interchangeable victims of patriarchal aggression. These "heroes" never have names, although they sometimes have "names," as in "Jane," who relates what it's like to experience domestic abuse, or "Susan," who relates her experience with incest. None of these figures are ever individually recognizable enough to be fictional characters or real women, but are an undifferentiated amalgam of both. All is One in the Goddess.

Let me add that I am in no way criticizing the ambiguous anonymity of crime victims relating heartbreaking experiences. I am merely pointing out that these semifictional figures are often redefined and co-opted as "heroes" by collectivist feminists, and that this definition of "hero" has nothing in common with the *literary* definition of the traditional epic hero discussed above.

Some readers might find the following anecdote of passing interest in terms of the incompatibility of the Western *literary* canon with collectivist feminist aesthetics. A colleague once wrote a short piece that was intended to be an example of "socialist feminist writing." There were no characters, only abstractions like "the girl," who spent most of her time "frying fish" for "the mothers of the village, of which there were many." None of these abstract noncharacters had any inner life or conflict or an individual name or anything one usually encounters in a literary character. There was no plot. There was no particular setting, except for the abstraction of "the village." This was a deliberate experiment in writing without using any of the traditional Western elements of fiction, in producing something that wasn't "literature" (that patriarchal violent ordering of language to privilege a few males) but rather what the author called a "radical discourse" and a "new way of seeing ourselves." The piece's genre was interesting in terms of this discussion, too, because the piece wasn't differentiated enough to have one. The author said it wasn't fiction and it wasn't nonfiction; it was an undifferentiated blend of both.

5. Rand, of course, often denied that she was an anarchist. There is an interesting contradiction between Rand the political philosopher and Rand the novelist here, but since I am exclusively interested in Rand the novelist, this contradiction lies outside the scope of this essay.

References

Bowra, C. M. 1945. *From Virgil to Milton*. London: Macmillan.
Bradley, Marion Zimmer. 1982. *The Mists of Avalon*. New York: Ballantine.
Branden, Barbara. 1986. *The Passion of Ayn Rand*. Garden City, N.Y.: Doubleday.

Briffault, Robert. 1927. *The Mothers: A Study of Sentiments and Institutions*. 3 vols. New York: Macmillan.
Campbell, Joseph. 1949. *Hero with a Thousand Faces*. Bollingen Series 17. Princeton, N.J.: Princeton University Press.
———. [1952] 1966. *Heroic Poetry*. New York: St. Martin's Press.
Eisler, Riane. 1988. *The Chalice and the Blade: Our History, Our Future*. San Francisco: HarperCollins.
Frye, Northrop. 1957. *Anatomy of Criticism*. Princeton, N.J.: Princeton University Press.
Gladstein, Mimi Reisel. 1984. *The Ayn Rand Companion*. Westport, Conn.: Greenwood Press.
Neumann, Erich. 1955. *The Great Mother: An Analysis of the Archetype*. Translated by Ralph Manheim. Princeton, N.J.: Princeton University Press.
Paglia, Camille. [1990] 1991. *Sexual Personae: Art and Decadence from Nefertiti to Emily Dickinson*. New York: Vintage Books.
Rand, Ayn. [1957] 1985. *Atlas Shrugged*. New York: New American Library.
———. 1968. An answer to readers (about a woman president). *Objectivist*, December, 1–3.
———. 1989. *The Voice of Reason: Essays in Objectivist Thought*. Edited by Leonard Peikoff. New York: New American Library.
Renault, Mary. 1958. *The King Must Die*. New York: Pantheon.
Sciabarra, Chris Matthew. 1995. *Ayn Rand: The Russian Radical*. University Park: Pennsylvania State University Press.
Stone, Merlin. 1976. *When God Was a Woman*. San Diego: Harcourt Brace Jovanovich.
Tillyard, E.M.W. [1954] 1966. *The English Epic and Its Background*. New York: Barnes & Noble.

Part Three

Toward a Randian Feminism?

12

Was Ayn Rand a Feminist?

Nathaniel Branden

When I am asked about Ayn Rand and feminism, I often find myself thinking of two incidents in *Atlas Shrugged* involving Dagny Taggart, the heroine of the novel.

Here is the first. "She was twelve years old when she told Eddie Willers that she would run the railroad when they grew up. She was fifteen when it occurred to her for the first time that women did not run railroads and that people might object. To hell with that, she thought and never worried about it again" (Rand 1957, 51).

In the second incident, Dagny is an adult. "Lillian moved forward to meet her, studying her with curiosity. . . . [S]he found it strange to see Dagny Taggart in an evening gown. It was a black dress with a bodice that fell as a cape over one arm and shoulder, leaving the other bare; the naked shoulder was the gown's only ornament. Seeing her in the suits she wore, one never thought of Dagny Taggart's body. The black dress seemed excessively revealing—because it was astonishing to discover that the lines of her shoulder were fragile and beautiful, and the diamond band on the wrist of her naked arm gave her the most feminine of all aspects: the look of being chained" (136).

Taken together, these two passages illustrate the complexity, and perhaps the ambiguity, of Ayn Rand's view of women.

She was always pleased when someone told her she "thought like a man." And yet, when asked if she would have preferred to be born a man, she invariably answered, "God no! Because then I'd have to be in love with a woman!"

I never thought this was funny, and she always insisted it was not her intention to be funny. But if she was serious, what were the implications of what she was saying? If she was putting down women, she was putting down herself—this inference was unavoidable.

On more than one occasion, I remarked to her that while there were several heroic male characters in *Atlas Shrugged*, there was only one truly outstanding woman. Why were there not more variants of the heroic woman in the story? I asked. I recall her once chuckling and answering, "That didn't interest me. And, after all, this is *my* fantasy!"

Ayn Rand was a ferociously intellectual, proudly self-assertive power-house of independence who described herself as a "man-worshiper." To anyone who might imagine that this entailed a contradiction, she would say, "Check your premises."

The heroines in her novels are indifferent to convention, deeply self-confident, guiltlessly sexual, and, in the case of Kira Argounova in *We the Living* and Dagny in *Atlas*, the equal of any man in energy and ambition. None of them are mothers, and there is nothing discernibly maternal in their characterizations. Motherhood (and fatherhood) hardly exist in the universe of the novels. Rand herself never considered having children. (She told me that when she was a very young girl, she wrote a story about a woman who had to choose between saving the life of her husband or that of her child, and chose to save her husband, with Rand's clear approval.) In her novels, her heroines' intense femininity is grounded in their reverence for *man*. Their attitude is almost primordial, for all their intellectuality, and this is not said as a criticism: it is one of the factors that make Rand's women so interesting.

Rand often spoke enthusiastically about the legend of Brunhilde, a warrior-woman able to defeat any man in combat, who swore she would give herself only to the man who could prevail against her—which Sieg-fried, overcoming every obstacle, alone was able to do. Kira, Dominique Francon (*The Fountainhead*), and Dagny are *spiritual* warriors, unim-pressed by most of the men they meet, and lonely for their Siegfried, the one man strong enough to "conquer" them—strong enough, let it be emphasized, not in muscles or wealth but in intellect, self-esteem, and character. And by "conquer," Rand meant "inspire them to sexual/ro-mantic surrender."

Once, when asked why she used such a word as "surrender," Rand answered that one should look at human anatomy and the nature of sexual intercourse. She no doubt would have agreed with Camille Paglia's observation that man is contoured for invasion, woman for receptivity. Happy, even aggressive receptivity is still a different experience from male thrusting. In the context in which Rand used it, "surrender" was emphatically not a negative word but a positive one. It was associated with admiration and trust.

As far as her view of women and of human rights is concerned, Rand's work is entirely compatible with the dominant direction of nineteenth-century feminism. Historically, feminism was born as a demand, not for special entitlements provided by means of political coercion, but for equal treatment with men before the law. These feminists did not view *men* as the enemy, or capitalism, but *government*. Their battle was with the state—and with the traditional, religious idea of woman as man's subordinate. These women were individualists who fought to be treated as such: treated as *persons*. Rand's philosophy, Objectivism, holds that sexism, like racism, is a form of biological collectivism, and therefore Objectivism would have entirely supported the demand of nineteenth-century feminists for equal rights before the law, such as the right to vote, or to own property in one's own name, or to have legally unimpeded access to the marketplace.[1] In addition, women historically have been taught that self-sacrifice is their noblest duty. Objectivism opposes the entire notion of human sacrifice, whether the sacrifice of self to others or others to self. It insists that human beings be treated as ends in them-selves, not as means to the ends of others. In upholding an ethics of rational or enlightened self-interest, Objectivism champions a woman's right to live as a free, independent entity. Finally, Rand's novels offer powerful role models of autonomous, self-assured, and self-assertive fe-males who have been sources of inspiration to countless numbers of

women. Looked at from the perspective of nineteenth-century individualist feminism, there is much in Rand to embrace and be enthused about.

Further, it is worth remembering that in almost every part of the world
and throughout virtually all the centuries behind us, women have been
regarded, and have been taught to regard themselves, as the inferior of
men. Some version of woman-as-inferior is part of the "cultural unconscious" of just about every society we know of—and part of the "cultural
conscious" as well. Women's second-class status is a pronounced aspect of
every brand of religious fundamentalism—be it Jewish, Christian, Islamic, or Hindu. It is at its most virulent in societies dominated by religious fundamentalism, such as modern Iran. Rand's writings could not
possibly be more antithetical to this perspective in every conceivable
respect. It is no accident that the most frenzied attacks on her books have
come from religionists. A rejection of the religious vision of life is present
on every page, implicitly when not explicitly. Her books are a celebration
of life on earth and of the glories possible to humans *in this world*. And her
women are no less unconventional than her men, in outlook, personal
authority, and self-esteem. Paraphrasing a line from *The Fountainhead*,
her books are a defiant *No* flung in the face of many of our traditions. So
here, too, we can see in what way her work would support the aspirations
of individualist feminism.

However, when we consider some of the strains of feminism that have
emerged in the last two decades, the story is entirely different. Rand was
a champion of reason, individualism, self-responsibility, independence,
and—capitalism. The left-wing, or "radical," feminism of the nineties
sees reason, logic, and science as a "male conspiracy" to oppress women.
Indeed, its most extreme exponents have virtually declared war on Western civilization, which they characterize as a product of "dead white
males." All the basic premises of "radical" feminism entail collectivism
and statism. It sees man—and capitalism—as the enemy, and the government as its agent, ally, and protector (when officials support its social
agendas; otherwise, they are just another group of blind or oppressive
males). It seeks not freedom but, in many contexts, *escape from freedom*—
evidenced by the fact that it often looks to political coercion as the
means to advance its aims, whether through affirmative action or tax-
supported day-care centers or every kind of regulation of business activity
imaginable, including regulation of speech. Its basic portrait of woman is
of woman-as-victim, not as strong and self-responsible. Its basic portrait
of man is of man-as-oppressor. The act of sex, even between people who

are married and in love, is sometimes described as rape (see, e.g., Andrea Dworkin). These are ideas with which more and more young college women are being indoctrinated.[2]

Granted that this type of feminist has never represented more than a small minority. More moderate varieties of feminism do exist, which do not set themselves against man or Western civilization. Even among today's more mainstream feminists, however, there is a strong tendency to look to the state as women's rescuer, thereby implying that women cannot flourish in a condition of freedom but are children requiring special protection. And unfortunately, it is the more extreme antimale, anticapitalism, anti–Western civilization, anti-reason-logic-and-science version that has achieved dominance in our educational centers and in the media. This is made clear in appalling detail in Christina Hoff Sommers's superb study *Who Stole Feminism?* The new form of Marxist class warfare is gender warfare—this is the social contribution of "radical" feminism.

There is nothing in the philosophy of such feminism that Rand would not despise. It is the antithesis of nineteenth-century individualist feminism. As to the extreme wing of these modern feminists, it would be quite in character for them to declare that "Ayn Rand was not a woman" or, at any rate, that she was "a traitor to her sex," to quote Susan Brownmiller's indictment in *Against Our Will: Men, Women, and Rape.*[3]

I want to pick up two themes alluded to earlier, and relate them to Rand's view of women: her description of herself as a "man-worshiper," and her line in *Atlas* about "the most feminine of all aspects: the look of being chained."

To begin with, there were two different senses in which she used the expression "man-worshiper." The first is explained in her introduction to the twenty-fifth anniversary edition of *The Fountainhead*, where she writes of man worship as reverence for man at his highest potential. Here, she clearly means "man" in the generic sense that includes woman.

However, in other contexts it is clear that she identifies femininity with man worship understood as hero worship of the man—assuming the particular man is worthy of it. It is easy to misunderstand her on this point because she never fully articulated what she meant and because, in her novels, her heroes treat the women they love with unreserved respect, admiration, adoration, and "worship." There is no hint of inequality in their view of one another, no suggestion of the man's "looking down." Her concept of romantic love entails passionate *mutual* admiration at the center of the relationship. It is hard to think of another novelist in whose work this vision is dramatized so powerfully.

I recall a conversation I had with her in the early years of our relationship, when she was expounding on her idea of feminine hero worship. I was in my twenties at the time. I asked her: "Don't men worship women? I mean, the women they love?"

"Oh, I suppose so, but that's not how I would think of it. By 'worship,' I mean our highest capacity for admiration, reverence, looking up. I see man as superior to woman, and—"

"Oh, Ayn," I protested. "You don't. You're joking!"

"I am not joking," she answered seriously.

"Superior in what? Intelligence? Creativity? Moral worth?"

"No, of course not. In spiritual or intellectual matters the sexes are equal. But man is bigger, stronger, faster—better able to cope with nature."

"You mean, at a purely physical level?"

"The physical is not unimportant." Later, I often heard her reiterate this point.

I would return to this issue more than once, because I did not feel fully comfortable with her point of view. I did not like the language of "inferior" and "superior" applied in any way to men and women as such. Yet I was intrigued to discover, and thought it important, that many of the most independent, strong-minded women I met shared Ayn's perspective.

Ayn would smile good-naturedly at my evident bafflement over this issue. I understood, of course, that she was not talking about men in general but man at his highest, man the abstraction—the masculine principle. Once she said to me, as if to make the issue clear once and for all, "Don't you understand that a truly strong woman *wants* to see man as stronger? Certainly *her* man." When I asked why, she answered, "For the pleasure of surrendering."

I persisted, even though I felt a lightbulb going on. "So in a way the issue is sexual?"

"Of course." Then she added, "And beyond that, the pleasure of being helpless at times, of laying down the burden of strength. In a way, that also is sexual. A woman can't do this with a man she doesn't look up to. Be honest. You understand me perfectly. This is exactly how you expect a woman to feel about you."

"Maybe so," I conceded reluctantly, "but I wouldn't try to defend my position philosophically."

"I would," she said brightly.

What was abundantly clear was that, at least in romantic contexts, Ayn *liked* the idea of man—*her* man—as "superior," if only in a very abstract sense.

I once asked her if she imagined that Galt or Francisco or Rearden, the three men in love with Dagny, ever thought of her as "inferior." "*Of course not,*" Ayn answered instantly. "It would not be proper for a man to think in such terms." But this did not alter her basic position.

Both as a lecturer and as a writer, Ayn Rand loved to shock, and I do not doubt that some element of that motivation was operating when she wrote the line about "the most feminine of all aspects." As a metaphor, as poetry, she enjoyed the idea of woman being "ravished"—not by *any* man, to be sure, but by a hero. We know from Nancy Friday's *My Secret Garden* that millions of women are turned on by fantasies of being "ravished" or "overcome" by a dominant male figure. We know it also from the best-selling "romance" novels, the most commercially successful genre in publishing history. It is psychologically naive to pathologize all such fantasies, as many modern feminists so stridently do.[4] The fantasy is transcultural. It would be absurd to insist that it tells us nothing about the female psyche. I am emphatically not speaking of rape, which is a despicable crime and has been so regarded by ethical men and women everywhere.[5] I am speaking of the desire to surrender to, or be overcome by, a strong male in what is experienced as a romantic context. All women may not share this feeling; but we know that many women do, Ayn Rand among them. Neither Ayn Rand nor Brunhilde was weak, dependent, or a clinging vine, and what would a Siegfried want with a weak, dependent, clinging vine, anyway? Strength longs for the challenge of strength.

Describing the first sexual encounter between Dagny and Hank Rearden in *Atlas*, Rand (1957, 251) writes: "[S]he knew . . . that her defiance was submission, that the purpose of all of her violent strength was only to make his victory the greater." No strong woman can experience herself fully—in the romantic sense—with a man she perceives as weaker than herself. No strong man can experience himself fully—in the romantic sense—with a woman he perceives as low in independence, personal authority, and self-assertiveness. If Aristotle was right in declaring that a friend is another self, how much more applicable is that idea to romantic love, to the relationship between a man and a woman? This is why you will not see a passionate love affair between a person of high self-esteem and one of low self-esteem; a difference of that kind has no erotic charge. The image of a woman "chained," in the passage quoted, is a metaphor intended to isolate woman in her sexual aspect only and her desire to be "owned" by the man she loves. To take this image literally is to confess an extraordinary ignorance of man-woman relationships and the psychology of their intimate interactions.

Where did Ayn Rand stand with respect to feminism (a term she never liked)? A feminism that sees woman at her best, as a heroic figure, will find support and validation in Rand's writings. A feminism that defines woman as victim and man as her evil oppressor will see Rand as the enemy—because Rand sees woman not as weak but as strong, and because Rand sees romantic love between woman and man as an expression and celebration of their esteem for each other as well as their esteem for themselves.

Notes

1. Rand did not discuss "sexism" explicitly, but her position is logically implied by her discussion of racism in Rand 1964, 172–85. This essay was originally published in the September 1963 issue of the *Objectivist Newsletter*, which she and I co-edited and co-published.

2. For example, see Sommers 1994 and Bernstein 1994.

3. See Chapter 4 of the current volume.

4. I will add that such contemporary individualist feminists as Joan Kennedy Taylor and Wendy McElroy do *not* pathologize these daydreams.

5. I once heard Rand tell someone at a lecture, "If you think the 'rape scene' in *The Fountainhead* is an actual rape scene, I suggest you read the passage again. If it is rape, it is rape by engraved invitation. No hero of mine would ever permit himself an actual rape, which would be contemptible."

References

Bernstein, Richard. 1994. *Dictatorship of Virtue*. New York: Alfred A. Knopf.
Rand, Ayn. 1957. *Atlas Shrugged*. New York: Random House.
———. 1964. *The Virtue of Selfishness*. New York: New American Library.
Sommers, Christina Hoff. 1994. *Who Stole Feminism?* New York: Simon & Schuster.

13

Ayn Rand and the Concept of Feminism: A Reclamation

Joan Kennedy Taylor

In looking at Ayn Rand's life, one would expect her to have been a feminist, or at least to have been sympathetic to feminists, because theirs were the voices in the United States that championed the kind of life she intended to have: a life in which her right to pursue work and love was independent of marriage. Think of how unusual it was in her era for a woman to be totally dedicated to her work and even to enter a field (philosophy) where women rarely ventured. She didn't use her husband's name. She created heroines who had passionate and unconventional love affairs without guilt, and were not punished for that fact. These were hallmarks of the early Greenwich Village Feminists, and had she been a few years older and come to the United States a few years sooner, one could see her staying up all night with some of the women who, up to and during World War I, devoted themselves, not just to the suffrage movement, but to claiming the right to be individuals. Nancy Cott (1987), who has documented this period, tells us that those in the 1910s who called themselves "Feminists" were primarily devoted to the freedom to choose one's work and "assigned more liberatory meaning and value to passionate heterosexual attachment than did any women's rights advocates before them" (45).

But Ayn Rand did not discuss *feminism* as such, and it is unlikely that she had positive associations with the term, given her negative discussion of "Women's Lib" in her essay "The Age of Envy" (1971). In fact, philosopher David Kelley, who founded the Institute for Objectivist Studies and is one of the leading authorities on the philosophy of Objectivism, has raised an intriguing possibility in a private conversation—that Rand had considered *feminism* to be an invalid concept, even though she never directly addressed the subject in those terms. I decided to make this idea the subject of this paper. I examined what evidence there is in her writings, including not only her *Introduction to Objectivist Epistemology* but various articles that discuss concepts, valid and invalid concept-formation, and "Women's Lib." And, in order to make the best possible case for the invalidity of the concept in Objectivist terms, I interviewed David Kelley on this subject on the afternoon of Wednesday, 20 November 1996, in his office at the Institute for Objectivist Studies in Poughkeepsie, New York.

Applying Ayn Rand's Definitions

"A *concept*," wrote Rand (1990, 15), "is a mental integration of two or more units which are isolated according to a specific characteristic and united by a specific definition." Later in the same work, she wrote: "There are such things as invalid concepts, i.e. words that represent attempts to integrate errors, contradictions or false propositions . . . or words without specific definitions, without referents, which can mean anything to anyone, such as modern 'anti-concepts'" (47). In "'Extremism,' or the Art of Smearing," Rand (1967, 176) describes an "anti-concept" as "an artificial, unnecessary, and (rationally) unusable term, designed to replace and obliterate some legitimate concepts—a term which sounds like a concept, but stands for a 'package-deal' of disparate, incongruous, contradictory elements taken out of any logical conceptual order or context, a 'package-deal' whose (approximately) defining characteristic is always a non-essential. This last is the essence of the trick." There certainly is a smear word "feminism," often used by conservative men to designate *any view of the role of women that I disagree with, if promulgated by women I neither like nor find attractive.* But clearly, feminism as espoused by feminists is not designed by its advocates to smear themselves, so it is not an "anti-concept" in that specific sense, and does not fall within the limits of our inquiry at the moment.

But might it be an invalid concept? Not by one peripheral test. Invalid concepts, wrote Rand (1990, 47), "are usually—though not necessarily—short-lived, since they lead to cognitive dead-ends." As a word with a history (since at least the turn of the twentieth century, and applied to ideas and actions of well over a hundred years earlier), "feminism" is certainly here to stay.

David Kelley took the argument further. "The problem has always been," he said, "that the 'ism' part of 'feminism' suggests a doctrine, a belief, an outlook, an ideology. And so the question is, what is the content? If that's the genus, then the concept would have to identify a class of people on the basis of certain beliefs that they share in common, and those beliefs should be ones that make them essentially alike, at least within that domain—the political domain." When I asked him to sum up why he thought Ayn Rand would see *feminism* as an invalid concept despite her support of individual rights for women and the right to abortion, he argued: "Because it brings together and tries to unite under a single label, a single concept, people and ideas that are too different to be classified together. They share only an accidental feature: that the issues they are most concerned with have to do with women. But what their *position* on those issues is, is as far apart as individualism and collectivism,[1] or pro-reason and anti-reason."

What Feminism Is

Let me say right away that I think this is a serious charge that feminists must respond to, even if one thinks (as I do) that feminism is essentially what might be called a psychosocial doctrine rather than a narrowly political one. It is certainly true that any overview of feminism (e.g., Barbara Sinclair Deckard's *Women's Movement*, Nancy Cott's *Grounding of Modern Feminism*, or Alice S. Rossi's 1973 anthology of writings dating back to 1771, *The Feminist Papers*) begins by dividing feminists into subgroups with differences of opinion on solutions to the problems on which they may agree. This is particularly true of the political allegiances of feminists. In the late sixties, young women in Students for a Democratic Society became aware of the extent to which the male students with whom they worked were refusing to accept them as intellectuals, and rebelled to form their own feminist groups with a New Left slant. Marxist women added *patriarchy* to *capitalism* as a force that had oppressed them. Although, numerically, the core of the new feminist movement overwhelmingly called itself liberal, this was still the era of New Deal liberalism that saw no necessary limits to government power or the reach of benevolent programs. So politically, this new feminism seemed in many respects a far cry from the classical liberal movement in the nineteenth century that only wanted men to "take their feet off our necks and permit us to stand upright," in the words of Sarah Grimké (1838).

The main result in the sixties and seventies was a "women's movement" that tried to concentrate on political action, social action, and individual transformation all at once. "Diversity" was the slogan of the day, what present-day Republicans call "the Big Tent." But what this meant was that Betty Friedan, and radical refugees from SDS, and Marxist feminists, and antiwar nuns, and lesbian activists, and scholars who were reprinting John Stuart Mill and Elizabeth Cady Stanton were all coming together to march down Fifth Avenue on the fiftieth anniversary of woman suffrage in 1970, and there were endless behind-the-scenes conflicts and jockeyings for control.

What did these people have in common? Most of them thought that it was the idea expressed in the second issue of *Ms.* magazine: "If you asked us our philosophy for ourselves and for the magazine, each of us would give an individual answer. But we agree on one thing. We want a world in which no one is born into a subordinate role because of visible difference, whether that difference is of race or sex. That's an assumption we make personally and editorially, with all the social change it implies. After that, we cherish our differences" ("A Personal Report from *Ms.*," 7; cited in Taylor 1977, 16). This is hardly a definition of feminism.

However, let us look at some definitions and see where they agree. A recent British paperback, *Introducing Feminism*, starts by saying: "What is feminism? *Women demanding their full rights as human beings!*" (Watkins, Rueda, and Rodriguez 1994, 3, emphasis in the original). *Webster's New Collegiate Dictionary* (1980, s.v. "feminism") gives two definitions: "1: the theory of the political, economic, and social equality of the sexes; 2: organized activity on behalf of women's rights and interests." Another definition that I have found useful is that of Janet Radcliffe Richards, author of *The Sceptical Feminist,* who says "that there are excellent reasons for thinking that *women suffer from systematic social injustice because of their sex.* . . . Feminism has come to be associated with particular theories about what kind of thing is wrong and whose fault it is; how it came about and what should be done to put matters right" ([1980] 1982, 1–2, emphasis in the original; cited in Taylor 1992, 126).

These definitions emphasize action. But is feminism, as David Kelley's statement implies, most essentially a political movement? Although both social analysis and action seem to be necessary parts of a definition of feminism, I would claim that the action need not necessarily be political. Today, feminism remains a strong social force even though contemporary feminist political groups like NOW are finding it difficult to identify specifically feminist political goals. Such political action seems to have degenerated into a joining with other people's protests (as the *Ms.* quote above unwittingly implies): civil rights, gay marriage, multicultural concerns. The exception to this is that some groups have targeted single-purpose goals (but even these are not exclusively feminist) like reproductive freedom and anticensorship.

There have been (and undoubtedly will be again) periods in which feminist political action devolves out of the clash between the ideas of feminism and the laws that society has instituted based on contemporary ideas of women's "place." Issues such as suffrage, married women's right to form contracts and own property, and, in our more recent past, the failed ERA fight (which feminists can remember as a successful fight against protective labor legislation) have sparked long political campaigns. But feminism, in my view, is wider than a political movement. It is an ethical-sociopolitical *theory,* going back to a firm insistence on individual rights before the law for women as well as men, but also carrying on a running and very important battle with societally determined sex roles. Sometimes the theory necessitates political action and sometimes not; often individual change and choices bring much more profound social change.

Indeed, when I broached to David Kelley the idea of this feminist overview of society as being more important than specific political movements, he was receptive:

> Here, I certainly recognize—Ayn Rand certainly recognized—the social pressure of a set of mores or expectations regarding a woman's role that were inimical to women pursuing their individual interests as rational beings and realizing their potential. And it's a good thing that those have changed. And the group of people who call themselves feminists I think had a lot to do with it. So in that sense I would be more inclined to say (I have no idea about Ayn Rand), "Well, maybe there is some validity to this." That maybe in psychological terms—personal, social terms—male/female relationships and issues and differences *are* fundamental enough in human life, and the values surrounding them important enough, that a certain concern with and position about that is something we *do* need to designate with a concept.

But he added that a concept that would try to unite this view with views "favoring egalitarianism, and attacking rationality and individualism," was "still very questionable."

The Objectivist Ethics and the Friedan Revolution

Indeed, we can characterize feminism as an ethical-sociopolitical view in Objectivist terms in the following way: Even though Ayn Rand consistently used the word "man" to mean "human being" in her writings, feminism is the view that the Objectivist ethics apply to women as well as to men. Consider: Rand (1964, 25) says that the three cardinal values ("that which you act to gain and/or keep") are *reason, purpose,* and *self-esteem,* the three basic corresponding virtues ("act[s] by which one gains and/or keeps [them]") are *rationality, productiveness,* and *pride.* The standard for choosing these values and virtues, says Rand, in the essay "The Objectivist Ethics," is "that which is proper to man—in order to achieve, maintain, fulfill and enjoy that ultimate value, that end in itself, which is his own life." The essay distinguishes this standard from those of both hedonist and altruist systems of ethics.

The book that started the contemporary wave of feminism in this country (as distinguished historically from the nineteenth-century Woman Movement and the turn-of-the-century Feminist movement of sexual liberation and artistic fulfillment) was Betty Friedan's *Feminine Mystique*. This book details the extent to which a Freudian view of woman's nature had promulgated the idea that women were primarily sexual beings who damaged their sexual capacity by overuse of their intellects and by pursuing productive careers. The effect of this was that by the late fifties (the book was published in 1963) the proportion of women in college populations had markedly decreased (47 percent in 1929; 35 percent in 1958) and 60 percent of women college students were leaving before graduation in order to marry. The average age of women when they married was twenty, and was dropping into the teens. The result? Widespread misery. Wrote Friedan: "It is my thesis that the core of the problem for women today is . . . a problem of identity—a stunting or evasion of growth that is perpetuated by the feminine mystique," and a resulting failure to develop "the firm core of self or 'I' without which a human being is not truly alive." The only way to counteract this, she wrote, was for women to choose productive goals and purposeful activity and to return to school to train themselves for meaningful careers.

In Rand's terms, we could say that Friedan's book described the result of the acceptance by millions of women of the philosophy of altruism, of their defining themselves as somebody's wife or somebody's mother, instead of living by the Objectivist ethics.

This fact was not overlooked at the time. *The Feminine Mystique* was hailed in a review as "one of the most illuminating psychosocial studies ever to be published about the United States" and "a brilliant, informative, and culturally explosive book" that "should be read by every woman—and by every man—in America." That review was written by Edith Efron, and appeared in the July 1963 issue of the *Objectivist Newsletter*. A footnote announced that the book was available from NBI Book Service. Since Ayn Rand was an extremely careful editor of everything published in the *Newsletter* and saw to it that only books worthy of being sold by the book service were reviewed, it seems clear that she herself admired and agreed with Friedan's main points.

These were: Freudianism had influenced psychology, sociology, and anthropology, resulting in a number of influential books on sex roles

238 Toward a Randian Feminism?

and the differing psychologies of men and women. These, in turn, had influenced educators to focus on preparing girls for marriage, at the expense of the intellectual content of higher education for women. As a result of this social pressure, young women expected nothing more from life than marriage.

These trends, which were carefully documented by Friedan, had shunted women into marriage and away from education and jobs that would have been less available anyway, due to the effects of legislation favoring returning World War II veterans. The G.I. Bill of Rights flooded colleges and universities with veterans, and consequently there was less room for women (many institutions of higher learning established quotas for them). At the same time, there was a mass disestablishment of women from their wartime jobs because the law required that veterans get back the jobs from which they had been drafted. Cultural (and legal) forces had combined, in ways that even Friedan didn't know (or at least didn't mention) at the time, to pressure women back into the home.

When attention was called to this situation by *The Feminine Mystique*, what was the result? It varied. Most of the suburban housewives about whom Friedan was writing did not become the extreme "Women's Libbers" that Ayn Rand later wrote about, because they were concentrating on their own lives rather than on social change in general. Many of them were supported by their husbands in returning to school or looking for jobs; many became feminists looking for support from other women as they changed their lives. Some younger unmarried women became radicalized and activist, as did some urban married intellectuals.

Thus began a social revolution in which women left the safety of their homes to seek jobs or to return to school for further education, radically changing American demographics. Political groups were formed. Betty Friedan herself was one of the founders of several of them, including the National Abortion Rights Action League (NARAL) and the National Organization for Women (NOW), which brought together into small consciousness-raising groups approximately a hundred thousand women seeking to become aware of the effects that the feminine mystique had had on their assumptions of what was possible for them and on their past choices. Women scholars began researching and reprinting the works of nineteenth-century feminists, and brought the history of the movement for women's rights back to academic attention.

As in the nineteenth century, the roots of this twentieth-century movement were individualist. And, as in the nineteenth century, the individualism gradually combined with collectivist ideals. In the nineteenth century, populism modified laissez-faire ideals in many political circles, including what was then known as the Woman Movement. In the twentieth century, a mix of radical and New Left women sprang up to vie for media attention with those just seeking to improve their lives.

Smearing Feminism

At the end of her review in the *Objectivist Newsletter*, Edith Efron wrote in 1963 about Friedan's suggestion of a "G.I. Bill of Rights" for women:

> Mrs. Friedan may have made this proposal because she does not understand the Statist implications of the phenomenon she is combatting. In an early chapter of her book, she equates the "feminine mystique" with *Kinder, Kuche, Kirche*, the slogan with which the Nazis reduced women to breeding animals; and she asks why the Nazi view of woman received such unanimous support from the "thinkers" of America—why it was so readily integrated into the modern American culture. It is an excellent question, but Mrs. Friedan ends her book without answering it. The answer is this: Doctrines which deny mind, independence and individuality are magnetically attractive to Statist "intellectuals" in all societies; the feminine mystique was totally harmonious with the anti-reason, anti-individualism of modern American liberals. (27)

Compare this with the following passage written by Ayn Rand several years later, in her 1971 essay "The Age of Envy":

> As a group, American women are the most privileged females on earth: they control the wealth of the United States—through inheritance from fathers and husbands who work themselves into an early grave, struggling to provide every comfort and luxury for the bridge-playing, cocktail-party-chasing cohorts, who give them very little in return. Women's Lib proclaims that they should give still less, and exhorts its members to refuse to cook their husbands' meals—with its placards commanding: "Starve a

rat today!" (Where would the cat's food come from, after the rat is starved? Blank out.)

The notion that a woman's place is in the home—the *Kinder-Kuche-Kirche* axis, is an ancient, primitive evil, supported and perpetuated by women as much as, or more than, men. The aggressive, embittered, self-righteous and envious housewife is the greatest enemy of the career woman. Women's Lib pounces upon this aggressiveness, bitterness, self-righteousness, envy—and directs it toward men. (It gives the lie, however, to one masculine prejudice: women are thought to be catty, but no cat and very few men could experience the degree of malicious hostility that these women are now displaying.) (Rand 1975, 173–74)

As we can see, different concretes are stressed in the two passages, making the two overall evaluations of "women's place" and their attempts to change it strikingly different. Friedan (as well as Efron) was concentrating on the millions of women who had been persuaded to forgo careers and for whom career training had dried up. Ayn Rand later saw the resulting housewives as envious of careers and displacing that envy toward men. Even the Nazi slogan that is invoked to describe the situation is treated differently—Efron attributes it correctly to the Nazis, whereas Rand seems to attribute it, at least in part, to the housewives themselves. In fact, the discussion of Women's Lib by Rand fits her definition of an anticonceptual smear: feminists are not defined by their diversity in addressing women's problems, or by their concern with the treatment of women by social forces, but as man-haters—who constituted a very tiny part of the feminist movement in the early seventies. I complained about this to David Kelley, saying that Rand's description by no means represented either the historical sweep of feminism or even a definition of what was going on at any one time nationwide. He agreed with me.

> Objectivism has had a bad habit of picking on the worst, the most vicious examples of other cultural movements and saying, "That's what it's all about," reading these examples into the motives of everyone participating in that other movement. Sometimes people who practice this defend it by saying, "Well, even if ordinary people don't realize it, this is the real meaning of what they're defending."

But I think it is generally fallacious, even if that is the objective implication of the position, to assume that therefore that's relevant to the actual motives and ideas of all the people. I think it's obvious, if you look at feminism or environmentalism—to take two of the leading widespread cases—that the vast majority of the people who are participating in those movements have a mix of ideas, and many of them fine.

So that has been a problem with Objectivism. And Ayn Rand set the pattern for it. She did this herself; she jumped to conclusions. On the other hand, I think that people who participate in such movements have a responsibility to look at whom they are making alliances with, and, in particular, who is speaking in their name. Most Americans tend not to be very ideological; they get involved in things on the basis of fairly concrete concerns—if you want to fix it, let's work together. They act from a combination of concrete-boundness and a kind of innocence. And it has allowed some very, very bad people to become powerful spokesmen.

The Big Tent

There's another reason that Ayn Rand's attitude may have changed between 1964 and 1971.

The key to what happened may be found in Ayn Rand's essay "Anatomy of Compromise," where she sets forth three rules about principles and how they work:

1. In any *conflict* between two men (or two groups) who hold the *same* basic principles, it is the more consistent one who wins.
2. In any *collaboration* between two men (or two groups) who hold *different* basic principles, it is the more evil or irrational one who wins.
3. When opposite basic principles are clearly and openly defined, it works to the advantage of the rational side; when they are *not* clearly defined, but are hidden or evaded, it works to the advantage of the irrational side. (Rand 1967, 145)

Since the 1960s, there have been two political objectives that an overwhelming number of people calling themselves feminists have agreed on—reproductive freedom (including both birth control and abortion) and the Equal Rights Amendment. In these two political goals for which contemporary feminism has fought, we can see that Rand's rules have worked.

First, the fight for reproductive freedom. Betty Friedan tells us in her 1976 book, *It Changed My Life*, that at the 1969 meeting that organized the National Association for Repeal of Abortion Laws (NARAL), she insisted on a preamble to the charter that read, "Asserting the right of a woman to control her own body and reproductive process [is] her inalienable, human, civil right, not to be denied or abridged by the state, or any man," because, as she put it, the proposed charter had "not one single mention of the right of the woman to decide and choose in her own childbearing. It was all about the right of the doctor to perform an abortion without going to jail" (122). As a result of this clear statement of principle, no one who disagreed with a woman's right joined NARAL. Nor did NARAL attract people who felt that population control was rightly a government concern, but that in the contemporary United States abortion was a preferred option. Nor is it home today for those who feel that the right to abortion does not entail a corresponding right to bear a child. Not only did NARAL influence a Supreme Court decision legalizing abortion, but it is still a consistent, respected organization that attracts the support of many libertarians as it continues to fight against state restrictions on that right.

The ERA, on the other hand, failed. When feminists demanded in 1971 that the House and Senate Judiciary Committees consider an equal rights amendment, they surprised the politicians by refusing to care that the amendment would invalidate the complex network of protective labor legislation for women that had been carefully assembled since 1908. They wanted equality before the law rather than government protection for women in the labor market, and battled other advocates for women who supported the gross distortion of the labor market through limiting the hours, wages, working conditions, and legal occupations of women. This was the issue that had caused the ERA to be opposed by liberals and that had led Eleanor Roosevelt to oppose an equal rights amendment. And, as Betty Friedan pointed out, this issue had also caused NOW, when it first supported the ERA, to lose the mailing privileges it had previously obtained from the United Auto Workers of America (Friedan 1976). But on this issue, the feminists won. In the first wave of support for equal rights in the seventies, enough equal rights amendments were passed on the state level to kill protective labor legislation forever.

However, the broad coalition of feminists with widely divergent political agendas had people in it who hoped that the federal amendment could ultimately change society for women's benefit in unspecified ways. Instead of reiterating that only governments were affected by the amendment, they began talking about the pay disparity between men and women. So the political touchstone for supporting the amendment became "equality," not "rights"—even leading some feminists to the position that no matter what restrictions governments might impose, the crucial question was that they should be imposed equally on men and women. Thus, if men were being drafted, it was only fair for women to be drafted too. And some feminists who opposed laws favoring "maternity leave" as a discriminatory singling out of women in the labor force (which could be expected to be contrary to their economic interests, as was protective labor legislation) were placated into support by the naming of the Family Leave Act—even though everyone knows which sex is most likely to avail itself of such leave.

Finally, the amendment that everyone agreed in the beginning would never restrict private action, only state and federal discriminatory action against women, went down in flames under a consistent conservative attack that seemed more and more plausible because of the actions of ERA supporters.

Similarly, the individualist civil libertarians in the feminist community made no public objection to allowing feminists with whom they disagreed under the umbrella of the Big Tent. Now we have only ourselves to blame for the fact that antipornography feminists (who seem also to consider men and their sexuality *per se* dangerous to women) have persuaded much of the media that they are the "real" feminists and that the feminist message entails censorship of any materials deemed sexually explicit.

Semantic Issues

But such collaborations have taken place within the liberal camp. Still, Ayn Rand didn't denounce all "liberals"; she said she was speaking to "the nontotalitarian liberals." Again, we have to ask, why the difference?

First, we have to look at the historical relationship between the terms "liberalism" and "feminism." In the nineteenth century, liberalism, worded as it was in terms of *men*, was also applied only to men. It was "men" who had rights—in English-speaking countries, women had the common law. In the United States, a movement to support the rights of women grew up parallel with the movement to abolish slavery—because the civil status of married women was in many ways the same as that of slaves. Married women couldn't own property (including the wages that they earned). They couldn't enter into contracts or sue in court. If accused of committing a crime in the presence of the master (husband), a woman was not held accountable, because it was presumed she was only obeying him. Women certainly could not vote or serve on juries. So the first feminist actions and writings were classical liberal in nature, asking for no special treatment but for equal rights and social and educational parity.

It shouldn't surprise people too much that when liberalism was modified by progressivism in the late nineteenth century, feminism was modified too. The Enlightenment belief that government's role was solely to increase liberty by protecting the rights to life, liberty, and property gradually changed to include visions of improving society through expanded laws and regulations.

What was then called the Woman Movement became concerned with the duties of women toward society because of their supposedly higher nature. Women were exhorted to make society purer and to uplift the poor—again, through laws and regulations, especially against prostitution and alcohol. At the turn of the century, there was a move to reclaim the individualist roots of this movement by calling it "feminism"—to reemphasize rights rather than duties. Men couldn't join the Woman Movement, but they could be feminists, and support their sisters (and wives) in their proper claims.

But as the liberal emphasis on rights and individual liberty was diluted with issues requiring an expansion of government power—in order to bestow benefits on its citizens in the name of "freedom from want" or "the right to shelter" in the twentieth century—feminism was not exempt from this dilution. In terms of its strictly political content, feminism was a subset of liberalism. The two movements, though, never entirely gave up their emphasis on the individual: for the liberal, the individual's civil liberties; for the feminist, the individual woman's right to the pursuit of happiness. And for feminism especially, cyclical rediscoveries of the issue meant a rediscovery of the arguments of classical liberal feminist writers such as Mary Wollstonecraft, Elizabeth Cady Stanton, Margaret Fuller, and John Stuart Mill.

So let us ask, given this history, why did Ayn Rand not abandon the term "liberalism"? I asked David Kelley, and his answer points the way, I think, to resolving the questions that Ayn Rand's definitions pose with respect to feminism.

> You have to distinguish conceptual from semantic issues. Concepts as cognitive tools are a means of understanding reality. And a given concept's content is determined by what things in reality it integrates, in accordance with what omissions and what measurements, according to Ayn Rand's technical theory. And it's valid or invalid depending on whether, first of all, the integration is consistent (if it embodies contradictions, it's invalid) but also whether or not it's integrating in terms of essentials. But once you have a concept, it has to be expressed in a word, and it has to be a common word in a common language, to serve the purposes of communication. And words accumulate connotations, and the meaning is one that has to be reasonably widely shared in order to be usable in communication.
>
> She never really developed a philosophy of language, building on the theory of concepts, that would give us a set of policies for deciding the kind of issues we've been talking about, about words like "liberalism." Sometimes concepts have a popular meaning that you can't subscribe to, but you want to keep the concept and alter the meaning or the connotation. Sometimes the concept is too corrupted and you throw it away. Now, "liberalism" is the name for a political ideology that presents a global position. In the nineteenth century, it was the proper term for what we now call "libertarianism." If people had simply hijacked the term, in the way that the Stalinists tried to use the word "democrats" to describe themselves, it might easily be reclaimed. But there has been just enough of a continuity from the classical to the twentieth-century liberals to allow it to be plausibly redefined to include welfare rights. I don't think [Ayn Rand] ever fought to reclaim it.[2]

After our interview, David Kelley wrote me a letter in which he summarized our discussion of the terms "feminism" and "liberalism" as concepts:

> When we discussed this analogy, the thought uppermost in my mind was that "liberalism" as a concept is a clear case of integrating by fundamentals—the advocacy of liberty being the most fundamental issue in political philosophy—and is thus undeniably valid. The only question then is a semantic one: would it be worth the effort, and the possible confusion, to try to reclaim the term from welfare state liberalism? In the case of "feminism," however, I have doubts about its validity as a concept, before we even get to the semantic issues, because I don't think it isolates a political outlook in terms of fundamentals.[3]

In turn, I would like to summarize my disagreements with Kelley. I think he is probably right in his view of what Ayn Rand would think of the issue: that *feminism* is an invalid concept because the differences between men and women have little or no political significance. I think she would hold this because it was never an area that particularly interested her. In addition, the idea that *feminism* is concerned essentially with differences can seem plausible.

However, I think her theory of concepts requires an opposite conclusion. On the level of abstraction in which liberalism can be termed the political advocacy of liberty, feminism is the advocacy of equal liberty for women. This has been an issue of extreme political significance in history, and is politically significant today in many parts of the world, particularly Third World countries. Politically, as I have said, feminism may be viewed as a subset of liberalism. But it requires a separate term because it advocates changes in society as well as in the law. In this sense, it is a concept that overlaps liberalism, advocating liberty in both the political and the social universes. Liberalism has no official view on how social institutions such as religions should treat their members and differentiate between them; feminism does. Liberalism has no official view on whether women should be educated; feminism does. Liberalism postulates a society in which social problems are solved by people joining in organizations rather than by government, but it issues no official call for cooperation; feminism calls for women to communicate with and to support each other in their pursuit of social justice.

Not all liberals are or should be feminists. Many find the sex roles called for by traditional religions important to them. Many are uncomfortable with emphasizing gender. But not to *like* the content of a concept is no reason to deny its validity.

The final area in which I would disagree with David Kelley is the relevance of semantic issues to the point in question. Since I see feminism as a valid concept that is not in its entirety a subset of liberalism, I think these issues are the key to reclaiming it. Here, feminists themselves must take the lead. We rightly want liberty to be universally applicable to all women, but that does not mean that every view of what serves women should be welcome, anymore than Stalinists should be welcome within the liberal tent.

There is certainly legitimate disagreement on tactics within the feminist movement. But when some people claim a totally contradictory meaning for feminism—for instance, that it is not based on individualism, or that women should not adopt the "masculine" values of logic and reason, or that women are always the victims of male sexuality and therefore governments (made up, after all, primarily of men) need expanded powers to protect us from the "assault" of sexually explicit material—then we should state clearly that this is not our vision of feminism.

Since the individualist thread in feminism has never been denied, even by those collectivists that Kelley calls the Left, it is my opinion that *feminism* as a concept is worth reclaiming by the many individualists who are working in its name today. And, if necessary, we should use the qualification "individualist," as Ayn Rand qualified her audience of "nontotalitarian" liberals.[4] We will have to do this to make clear our opposition to the tactic of expanding government programs and regulations, which seems appropriate both to many contemporary feminists and to many contemporary liberals.

Unless, of course, we decide to fight to reclaim the concept *liberal*, too.

Meanwhile, despite Ayn Rand's condemnation of "Women's Lib," and the insistence of some of her followers that she would issue a blanket condemnation of all feminism, her novels will continue to nourish young women and lead many of them toward feminism. Why? Because the young woman with individualist impulses needs, above all, to find believable and inspiring examples of what is possible for women to make of their lives. We are fed by images of women achieving successful and emotionally rewarding lives, and these are not easy to find. To quote Nathaniel Branden (1994, 288–89):

In almost every part of the world, and throughout virtually all the centuries behind us, women have been regarded, and been taught to regard themselves, as the inferior of men. Some version of woman-as-inferior is part of the "cultural unconscious" of just about every society we know of—and in the cultural *conscious* as well. Woman's second-class status is a pronounced aspect of every brand of religious fundamentalism—be it Jewish, Christian, Islamic, or Hindu. . . . Woman-as-inferior is not an idea that supports female self-esteem. Can anyone doubt that it has had a tragic effect on most women's view of themselves?

These assumptions are in our culture and in our art, and it is rare for an Ayn Rand to come along and provide us with a view of an alternate universe. For that, we feminists are in her debt.

Notes

1. Throughout this essay, the terms "individualism" and "collectivism" refer to a metaphysical emphasis on the primacy of the individual or the group, respectively, in social action (and in deciding what social actions are morally proper), and not to any specific set of political beliefs. I understood Kelley to be referring to an emphasis on individual rights versus a belief that rights derive from the group and can therefore be modified by consensus. By this definition, people who call themselves "conservatives" or "liberals" might belong to either group. So might people who call themselves "feminists." My own conviction is to prefer the individualist assumption in all thought about politics.

2. On the issue of reclaiming concepts from their "corrupted" meanings, David Kelley and I had spent some time discussing Ayn Rand's use of the word "selfishness" to denote a virtue, despite its negative connotations.

3. However, Kelley may have given more credence to my arguments than is apparent in this letter. In a speech he gave on 4 October 1997, at a conference entitled "Atlas and the World," held at the Renaissance Hotel in Washington, D.C., to celebrate the fortieth anniversary of the publication of *Atlas Shrugged*, he allowed himself to invoke the concept of feminism that I am discussing here, by referring to Ayn Rand as "the first feminist."

4. David Kelley mistrusts such qualifications, however. He states: "You have to keep adding qualifications, like *individualist* feminism, or *pro*-reason, or *pro*-liberty, so it becomes like stone soup. You call it stone soup, but all the flavor comes from the other ingredients you're putting into it, and the stone is doing no work."

References

Branden, Nathaniel. 1994. *The Six Pillars of Self-Esteem*. New York: Bantam.
Cott, Nancy F. 1987. *The Grounding of Modern Feminism*. New Haven: Yale University Press.

Efron, Edith. 1963. Review of *The Feminine Mystique*, by Betty Friedan. *Objectivist Newsletter* 2, no. 7:27.

Friedan, Betty. 1976. *It Changed My Life: Writings on the Women's Movement*. New York: Random House.

Grimké, Sarah. 1838. *Letters on the Equality of the Sexes and the Condition of Women*. Boston: Isaac Knapp.

Rand, Ayn. 1964. *The Virtue of Selfishness: A New Concept of Egoism*. New York: New American Library.

———. 1967. *Capitalism: The Unknown Ideal*. New York: New American Library.

———. [1971] 1975. The age of envy. In *The New Left: The Anti-Industrial Revolution*, 2d rev. ed. New York: New American Library. Originally published in *The Objectivist*, July–August 1971.

———. 1975. *The New Left: The Anti-Industrial Revolution*. 2d rev. ed. New York: New American Library.

———. 1990. *Introduction to Objectivist Epistemology*. 2d enl. ed. Edited by Harry Binswanger and Leonard Peikoff. New York: New American Library.

Richards, Janet Radcliffe. [1980] 1982. *The Sceptical Feminist: A Philosophical Enquiry*. Boston: Routledge & Kegan Paul.

Taylor, Joan Kennedy. 1977. The second American revolution may be here. *Libertarian Review*, July, 16.

———. 1992. *Reclaiming the Mainstream: Individualist Feminism Rediscovered*. Buffalo, N.Y.: Prometheus Books.

Watkins, Susan Alice, Marisa Rueda, and Marta Rodriguez. 1994. *Introducing Feminism*. Cambridge, Mass.: Icon Books.

14

Ayn Rand's Philosophy of Individualism: A Feminist Psychologist's Perspective

Sharon Presley

"Ayn Rand," write philosophers Douglas Den Uyl and Douglas Rasmussen, "is among the most controversial figures of our time. The sense of vehemence emanating from the pens and mouths of her critics is matched only by the devotion of her admirers" (1984, ix). A major reason for both the vehemence and the devotion is Rand's fierce adherence to a philosophy of ethical individualism. Extolling the "virtue of selfishness," her philosophy of Objectivism maintains that the individual is the paramount unit of society and that no person should live for the sake of another. There are many critics of this "selfish" philosophy (e.g., O'Neill [1971]; Kohn [1990]), and indeed of all individualistic philosophies, who see strict individualism as morally reprehensible and contrary to the common good (e.g., Sampson [1977]; Hogan [1975]; Lasch [1978]). Among these critics are many feminist writers (e.g., Fox-Genovese [1991]; Eisenstein [1981]) who espouse what psychologist Carol Gilligan (1982) calls a "morality of responsibility and caring," as opposed to a "morality of rights." They would perceive Rand's "selfish" philosophy as antithetical to the notion of a feminist ethic. Yet at the same time, Rand's admirers, feminists among them, interpret her philosophy as benign and socially positive. These latter feminists (e.g., Taylor [1992]; McElroy [1982]) would argue that there is no necessary contradiction between Rand's views on individualism and feminist ethics in general.

Is there in fact a contradiction between Rand's philosophy of individualism and feminist ethics? Is her philosophy socially benign or harmful to society? In order to answer these questions, a series of issues needs to be addressed: What does Rand's philosophy actually espouse? How does it fit in with ethical individualism? What aspects of Rand's individualism are particularly problematic for feminist theory? Is a reconciliation possible, and if so, what benefits can be derived from such an integration of Rand and feminism?

To deal fully with all aspects of these questions is beyond the scope of this paper. What this discussion can contribute, however, is a perspective not commonly heard in the philosophical and political debates about individualism—a social psychologist's analysis. One shortcoming in previous discussions has been the lack of attention to the behavioral research relevant to a consideration of the place of individualism within feminist theory. Philosophical analysis alone cannot answer the questions raised about the consequences of individualism. Whether the application of a particular philosophy is socially beneficial or socially destructive is not just a theoretical issue; it is also a behavioral issue that feminists need to examine. Does social psychology have research evidence to offer that will throw some light on these questions? I think so. This essay, therefore, is an attempt to explore Rand's philosophy of individualism from a feminist-psychological perspective.

Ethical and Psychological Individualism

In his authoritative book *The Psychology of Individualism* (1984), psychologist Alan Waterman, a professor at Trenton State College, compares ethical and psychological individualism, pointing to a large body of psychological literature addressing many of the same issues as philosophers of individualism. Drawing upon the writings of Aristotle, Locke, Mill, Thoreau, Nietzsche, and others, he describes the three themes of ethical individualism as eudaimonism, personal responsibility, and ethical universality. Eudaimonism, or the effort to recognize and live in accordance with the "true self," is, in his view, central to a sense of personal identity as described by psychologists such as Erik Erikson, and central to the notion of self-actualization (ongoing realization of potentials, capabilities, and talents) as postulated by Abraham Maslow. The idea of personal responsibility is also reflected in the work of Julian Rotter on the internal locus of control. Rotter's research examines the degree to which individuals see their behavior as controlled by luck, chance, fate, or powerful others (external locus of control) or by their own efforts or abilities (internal locus of control). Thus the dimension of internal-external locus of control is a construct reflecting the degree to which individuals accept personal responsibility for their actions. The idea of ethical universality has many points of correspondence with the work of psychologist Lawrence Kohlberg (1969) on principled moral reasoning, including the ideas of absolute moral values and human rights, principles that apply equally to all people, a notion of justice, a requirement to treat all others with respect for their integrity as human beings, and a sense of personal commitment to one's ideals.

The virtues attributed to individualism, says Waterman, are self-realization, self-interest, self-care, self-respect, personal responsibility, self-reliance, originality, creativity, rationality, respect for the integrity of all persons, and tolerance for free expression. These virtues have a long intellectual history that can be traced from philosophers like Mill and Locke through contemporary psychologists such as Carl Rogers, Abraham Maslow, and Rollo May.

Rand and Ethical Individualism

Ayn Rand sees these individualist traits as virtues. Rationality and self-interest are the basis of her ethical system. Self-respect corresponds to her idea of self-esteem and her concept of pride (by which she means the "pleasure one takes in one's own efficacy") (Rand 1964, 38). Personal responsibility, or the capacity for choice and for bearing the consequences of choice, is reflected in Rand's advocacy of the responsibility to choose to think. The virtue of creativity is reflected in her concept of productivity: "[P]roductive work is the road of man's highest achievement and calls upon the highest attributes of his character: his creative ability" (26).

Respect for the integrity of all persons is reflected in Rand's concept of the universality of rights. In Rand's view, people are legally free to take any action they please so long as they do not violate the rights of others. "When one speaks of man's right to exist for his own sake, for his rational self-interest, most people assume automatically that this means his rights to sacrifice others. . . . The Objectivist ethics holds that human good does not require human sacrifice and cannot be achieved by the sacrifice of anyone to anyone" (30–31). Seeing the principle of free and voluntary trade as the most rational principle for human relationships, Rand argues that a trader does not treat men as masters or slaves, but as independent equals (31). Tolerance for free expression is reflected in her adamant opposition to censorship.

Individualism and Feminism

The themes of personal responsibility, personal autonomy, self-discovery, self-sovereignty, and demand for equal rights found in the individualist feminist tradition illustrate the ethical individualism that Waterman describes.[1]

Both advocates and critics of individualism agree that American feminism is a product of the individualist perspective.[2] The relationship between individualism and feminism is not only a long-standing one, as feminist writer Joan Kennedy Taylor explains, but a healthy one. Taylor tells us that from the nineteenth-century women's movement to modern writers like Betty Friedan, the individual woman's rights and happiness have played a prominent role in feminist rhetoric.

However, the Anglo-American tradition of individualist feminism has come under attack in recent years. Elizabeth Fox-Genovese, for example, argues that individual rights derive from the community rather than being prior to it. While agreeing with Taylor that feminism is essentially individualistic in character, she laments the relationship. Feminism in all its guises, states Fox-Genovese (1991), is itself the daughter of that (male) individualism to which so many feminists are opposed. Individualism, she argues, is detrimental to a sense of community and to social justice. Other critics even go so far as to deny that the human individual is capable of self-determination or free will, arguing that individuals are "socially constituted" (e.g., Jagger [1983]; Scheman [1983]; MacKinnon [1989]).[3]

Individualism Under Attack

The vices attributed to individualism by its critics, says Waterman, are self-absorption, narcissism, unscrupulous competition, alienation, atomism, privatism, deviance, rationalization, worship of objectivity, relativism, and nihilism (Waterman 1984, 71). Psychologist Edward Sampson, for example, has written extensive criticisms of psychological individualism and its allegedly destructive effects on society. In his view, the self-contained person is one who does not desire or require others for completion in life. Sampson (1977) views self-containment as the extreme of independence: wanting or needing no one. He hints at an even darker side—not just that people won't cooperate but that in pursuit of their own interests they will actively work against others in unscrupulous ways.

Christopher Lasch, in his book *The Culture of Narcissism* (1978), writes of a competitive individualism that, in its logic and decadence, is carried to the extreme of a Hobbesian war of all against all. Narcissists are impulse-driven, consumed by the desire for immediate gratification. They have a deep disturbance in their self-esteem; without meaningful values, they are incapable of forming commitments and loyalties. Though he recognizes that the old rugged individualism is not the same as the new, he still decries the "evils of untrammeled individualism" (9). Lasch doesn't just equate narcissism with mere selfishness; he ascribes to it nearly every one of the vices that have been attributed to individualism.

Another liberal critic, Alfie Kohn, author of *The Brighter Side of Human Nature* (1990), not only attacks individualism, but ethical egoism as well. "Sometimes ethical egoism stares out at us from the covers of vulgar self-help groups and sometimes it takes a subtler guise. . . . Ethical egoism in short begets psychological egoism—that is, the common belief that we *should* restrict ourselves to self-interest, however that belief manifests itself, will ultimately incline us to see this exclusive devotion to the self as a fact of life" (196).

The critics of individualist feminism share Lasch's, Kohn's, and Sampson's concerns about the consequences of "unbridled" individualism. Lasch's attacks on "competitive individualism" complement the criticisms launched by Elizabeth Fox-Genovese (1991), Zillah Eisenstein (1981), and Sylvia Ann Hewlett (1986). Such authors attack not only the philosophical basis of individualist feminism but what they see as the implied economic one also (i.e., capitalism). The criticism of the alleged extreme self-containment of ethical individualism that both Sampson and Lasch decry is reflected too in what some feminists (e.g., Hewlett [1986]; Fox-Genovese [1991]; Frazer and Lacey [1993]) consider individualism's lack of attention to communitarian concerns. In her attack on individualist feminism, Fox-Genovese (1991, 7) argues that her book "offers a critique of feminism's complicity in and acceptance of individualism—or rather of its contemporary atomized version that replaces the early and glorious recognition of the claims of the individuals against the state with the celebration of egotism and the denial or indefensible reduction of the just claims of the community."

The critics also oppose what they see as the concept of the "abstract individual" that comes out of the individualist tradition. In *The Politics of Individualism*, L. Susan Brown cites, as an example of this, Zillah Eisenstein's criticism of John Stuart Mill. Eisenstein asserts that Mill "posits the individual isolated and disconnected from social relations" (in Brown 1993, 17). Support for this assertion—that individualist feminism is constituted by notions of abstract individuals isolated from social context— can also be found in the writings of Jagger (1983), MacKinnon (1989), and Scheman (1983).

In contrast to the liberal views of Sampson, Lasch, and Kohn, psychologist Robert Hogan (1975) takes a conservative approach, asserting that individualism undermines traditional societal structures that are vital to the effective functioning of the community. With his colleague Emler, Hogan even attacks psychology's emphasis on internal locus of control as desirable, arguing that such a position is often unrealistic and will lead people to frustration and guilt (Hogan and Emler 1978). These authors are also deeply critical of Kohlberg's stage theory of moral reasoning; they view it as too individualistic and without regard to societal norms and social tradition. The autonomy in moral decision making characteristic of Kohlberg's sixth and highest stage of moral development, a stage at

which the individual makes judgments on the basis of universal principles, is also attacked by Wallach and Wallach in their book *Psychology's
Sanction for Selfishness* (1983). "It is difficult to see how the general good,"
they write, "will be furthered by one's always giving one's own principles
precedence over the laws and agreements of one's group" (261).

Though hardly a conservative, feminist psychologist Carol Gilligan's
criticisms of Kohlberg's theory complement these contentions. She argues, as we will soon see, that Kohlberg's theory does not reflect an "ethics of care and responsibility"; it concentrates only on an "ethic of rights"
that posits an abstract individual divorced from concern for the welfare
of others or for the community (Gilligan 1982).

In summary, the proponents of ethical individualism conceive of it as
promoting both self-interest and the interests of the community. The
critics view such individualism as socially destructive and personally
alienating.

Is individualism detrimental to a sense of community, as Fox-Genovese and other critics claim? Does it lead to rampant egoism? The philosophical, ethical, and political battles over these questions will no doubt
continue for many years to come both within and without the feminist
community. What has been little discussed and indeed virtually ignored,
however, is actual behavioral research. What does the psychological research literature actually say about individualism? Philosophy and ethics
can be debated, but behavior can be tested.

In considering these questions, I will speak to the issue of Rand's philosophy: Is it as meretricious as her critics claim? Does it suggest a portrayal of human nature that is realistic and consistent with a
psychologically healthy society? Or would it lead to the kind of "dog-eat-
dog" society that Rand is often accused of promoting? If individualism is
socially harmful, as its critics claim, any reconciliation with feminist ethics would not be possible. If, on the other hand, it is beneficial, then
individualism—Rand's individualism—may offer feminism a way to
champion both a better society and the individual women whom feminists see as oppressed by existing mores.

The Psychology of Individualism: Research Evidence

In *The Psychology of Individualism*, which provides an extensive examination of the literature relevant to the psychological correlates of individu-

alism, Waterman argues that the research evidence supports the claim that individualist characteristics are socially healthy and beneficial. Waterman identifies four individualist characteristics that have been extensively researched: sense of personal identity, self-actualization, internal locus of control, and principled moral reasoning. Using a number of hypotheses, he statistically examined the interrelationship of these individualistic qualities and optimal psychological functioning.

Waterman found confirmation for almost all of his hypotheses. He found strong support for the hypothesis that individualists are less likely to have debilitating affective states, including anxiety, depression, and alienation, and support for a relationship between self-acceptance/self-esteem and qualities of personal identity and internal locus of control. In regard to the latter results, Waterman (1984, 154) comments, "Given the direction and strength of the observed findings, it would seem implausible to maintain that individualist personal qualities are psychologically damaging."

The hypothesis that individualists would have more sophisticated and efficient cognitive functioning received moderate support, with the relationship most evident for moral reasoning and sense of personal identity. "These results pose a problem for the critics of individualism," says Waterman. "Cognitive skills involved in IQ tests, formal operational thought, creativity, etc. are generally considered desirable, yet it is among people with the individualist qualities of a sense of personal identity, self-action, and principled moral reasoning that they are most likely to be found" (155).

There was also strong support for a relationship between tolerant social attitudes and nonmanipulative acceptance of others on the one hand and a sense of personal identity on the other. "The results obtained for this hypothesis run directly counter to the expressed concern of the critics that the individualistic qualities would contribute to mistrust, manipulation of others, and unscrupulous competition," asserts Waterman. "The observed findings are consistent with the theory that persons characterized by the four individualist qualities, having higher self-esteem and less defensiveness, will thereby have less tendency to perceive persons with differing viewpoints as a threat who must be rejected" (156).

Strong support was also found for a relationship between cooperation and helping behavior and the four individualist characteristics. If individualists possessed the qualities attributed to them by critics—atomistic self-containment, narcissism, alienation—"they would be most unlikely to engage in cooperative behavior," Waterman writes. "Yet it is just those persons with individualist qualities who are the ones willing to participate in mutually rewarding activities and be willing to help others" (156–57).

Though critics such as Lasch (1978) have lamented individualists' supposed lack of meaningful commitments, Waterman found strong support for the idea that they have closer, more mutually rewarding social relationships than the average. There is no apparent contradiction between self-realization and achievement of friendship and love relationships. In fact, the two appear closely interconnected in individualists. "Individualists," writes Waterman (1984, 157), "appear more capable of sharing their personal feelings, of being emotionally supportive, and of committing themselves to the people for whom they form relationships."

In summary, Waterman argues persuasively that research has demonstrated the "adaptive advantages of the individualistic qualities, both personally in the form of emotional well-being and competence, and for others in the form of social interdependence" (158–59). How then, asks Waterman, could the critics of individualism have arrived at a conclusion so at variance with the empirical research? Why are the critics so off base?

The error, Waterman suggests, may stem from the mistaken belief that the values implicit in our psychological theories are the same as those embodied in our social institutions. Since our society nominally espouses individualism, it is perhaps understandable that those values would be held accountable for contemporary problems. But, asserts Waterman, the qualities described by critics are far different from the personal qualities advocated on the basis of ethical individualism. Indeed, one of the ironies of the controversy over individualism is that proponents and critics voice the same outrage over the same types of human functioning. Why then do the critics lay the responsibility at the doorstep of individualism?

For Waterman, the critics take societal advocacy at face value and assume that individualistic values are those people are actually trying to implement. In contrast, the proponents of ethical individualism, including Rand, attribute the malaise not to the practical consequences of implementing individualistic values, but to the utter disregard of those values in everyday life. "For far too many people," writes Waterman, "the high sounding appeal to individual values is no more than a rationalization for actions that are in diametric opposition to the actual content of those values" (77). It is also clear from their writings that the critics—

whether liberal, in the case of Sampson (1977), Lasch (1978), and Kohn (1990), conservative, in the case of Hogan (1975), or socialist feminist, in the case of Fox-Genovese (1991) and Eisenstein (1981)—are politically and ideologically opposed to individualism and its implicit libertarian political content. A strong ideological stance sometimes engenders demonizing of the opposed position; it is arguably the case here.

"What the critics of individualism appear not to have perceived," Waterman argues, "is that the proponents of ethical individualism are not advocates of the societal status quo." Waterman (1984, 166) contrasts the values of ethical individualism with actual social practices:

> Ethical individualism places a value on self-realization through submitting to the rigorous demands necessary for the full development and utilization of one's talents. In contrast, the message in our media is one of short-run hedonism, of happiness through material consumption, of success without hard work. Ethical individualism involves the values of personal freedom and personal responsibility expressed through individual decision-making and accountability. In contrast, our society has established a network of social service bureaucracies that . . . actually limit both freedom and responsibility. . . . Ethical individualism implies the universal value that each person is an end in himself or herself . . . a value that constrains manipulative and coercive social relationships. In contrast . . . the practices of our political system foster special interests. . . . Given these discrepancies, it is not surprising that our society is creating not individualists but narcissists.

Rand's View of Morality

Rand would have little to disagree with in Waterman's analysis of the critics of individualism. She states in many of her essays that our society does not implement individualistic values. Her concept of individualism is not one based on "short-run hedonism" or "success without hard work"; quite the contrary—she did not advocate the kind of narcissism Lasch (1978) bemoans. In a statement that belies the idea that the hedo-

nistic greediness of Lasch's narcissists is comparable to Rand's philosophy, she states:

> If you achieve that which is the good by a rational standard of
> value, it will necessarily make you happy; but that which makes
> you happy, by some undefined emotional standard is not neces-
> sarily the good. . . . This is the fallacy of hedonism—happiness
> can be properly the purpose of ethics but not the standard. . . .
> The philosophers who attempted to devise an allegedly rational
> code of ethics gave mankind nothing but a choice of whims: the
> "selfish" pursuit of whims (Nietzsche)—or "selfless" service to
> others . . . such as the ethics of Bentham, Mill, Comte and all
> social hedonists. (Rand 1964, 29–30)

Rand's Objectivism also opposes the idea of coercing, manipulating,
or harming others to get what one wants. In contrast with the claim, for
example, that individualists "will actively work against others in unscrupulous ways," Rand asserts, "The moral cannibalism of all hedonist and
altruist doctrines lies in the premise that the happiness of one man necessitates the injury of another" (30). "The two most prominent features of
Rand's moral view," writes philosopher Eric Mack (1984, 123), "are her
defense of rational selfishness and her insistence on the existence of and
respect for human rights." Rand contrasts these doctrines with all varieties of self-negating ethics, that is, with all versions of the view that
individuals should sacrifice themselves or should be sacrificed by others
to further the interests of some significant others, for example, god, society, the race, the noble, or the wretched.

Rand's view has many points of correspondence to the influential theory of moral judgment offered by psychologist Lawrence Kohlberg (1969).
His developmental theory postulates that people go through increasingly
more cognitively and morally sophisticated stages of moral decision making. He assumed that the core of morality and moral development was a
matter of rights and duties as prescriptions, with an emphasis on the idea
of justice and reasoning as the essence of morality (Kohlberg, Levine, and
Hewer 1983). In the most widely circulated version of Kohlberg's theory
(though not in his final formulation), the highest stage is Stage 6, the
stage of universal ethical principles. The few who attain this admittedly
rarefied stage are those who are following self-chosen ethical principles
as opposed to accepting what one's family or the law says is right. The

highest principled stages represent ideas of social contract and justice that enable a person to make independent moral judgments. Stage 6 entails the belief as a rational person in the validity of universal moral principles and a sense of personal commitment to them, the belief that persons are ends in themselves and must be treated as such. It entails respect for the individual and for equality of human rights (Kohlberg 1969; Kohlberg, Levine, and Hewer 1983).

Rand's moral theory is also characterized by universal moral principles that apply to all, with an emphasis on reasoning, justice, and individual rights (Rand 1964). Even the idea that one's own values—if rationally derived on the basis of universal moral principles—are above the law of a particular country is clearly portrayed in her novel *Atlas Shrugged* (1957). In this novel, the protagonists go "on strike" against a government that no longer protects individual rights and a society that no longer cares. They are willing to operate outside the laws of this government.

Rand and Gilligan's "Ethics of Care"

Kohlberg's theory of morality (and thus, by implication, any view characterized by the same features, such as Rand's theory) has been criticized by feminist psychologist Carol Gilligan in her book *In a Different Voice* (1982). She argues that men and women differ in their approach to moral decision making and that Kohlberg's theory of moral decision making is sexist and biased against women because it represents only "male" thinking about morality. She postulates two frameworks of moral decision making: a morality of rights (preferred by males) versus a morality of responsibility (preferred by females). The morality of rights, she says, differs from the morality of responsibility in its emphasis on separation rather than connection, in its consideration of the individual rather than the relationship as primary. The rights, or justice, perspective is characterized by an emphasis on the consequences of others' actions on the individual and on the doctrine of fairness (to treat all the same). By contrast, the responsibility, or care, perspective emphasizes the consequences of one's action on others (do no harm) and the doctrine of equity (balancing the difference between self and others). "The ethic of care and responsibility," argues Gilligan, "is at least as valid and mature as the ethic of rights and justice" (19).[4]

Gilligan's ideas have understandably won many adherents in the feminist community. There is good reason to criticize psychology and some of its major theorists for being biased against women and their experiences. Freud's theories, which viewed women as morally inferior to men, were unquestionably phallocentric and sexist, as were those of Erik Erikson, an influential developmental psychologist and theorist. The history of psychology is replete with examples of biased research, attempts to use research to denigrate women as inferior, and wholesale neglect of women's experiences.

Though Gilligan herself believes that the ethics of rights and the ethics of caring have equal moral weight, many of her adherents have not been so prudent. In their rush to embrace this newly discovered support for women's virtues, they have let the pendulum swing too far to the opposite extreme, from women as morally inferior to women as morally superior. In their eagerness to unseat the idea of women as inferior, they have reinvented the sex-role stereotypes of nurturing, caring women, and cold-hearted, linear men. Katha Pollitt, feminist writer and associate editor of the *Nation*, in her incisive analysis of "difference" feminists versus "equality" feminists, calls Gilligan's relational, nurturing woman a contemporary version "of the separate-spheres ideology of the Victorians" (1995, 55).

Other feminist writers have expressed concern over the implications of Gilligan's theory. Frazer and Lacey (1993, 63) call her research "problematic in that it takes gender division as given and monolithic" and lends itself to a biological interpretation that few feminists would find acceptable. Even Fox-Genovese (1991, 235) makes an indirect criticism of the adverse influence of Gilligan when she writes, "Some feminists have been tempted to assume that women, 'naturally' more nurturing than men, can draw from their experience newly generous models of morality and justice." This is a position that Fox-Genovese views as weak and exclusionary. Ayn Rand, too, whose morality is so clearly an example of the ethic of rights and justice, would have disagreed with Gilligan's idea that men and women use different frameworks to think about morality.

The psychological research supports the critics of Gilligan. Despite the popularity of Gilligan's theory, the evidence that men and women think differently about moral decisions is rarely supported by research evidence (Tavris 1992). In virtually every study that has looked for differences between men and women in their moral frameworks, no significant differ-

264   Toward a Randian Feminism?

ences have been found. This has led psychologists Anne Colby and William Damon (1987), among others, to conclude that there is little scientific support for gender differences in moral judgment. "In study after study," writes feminist psychologist Carol Tavris (1992, 85), "men and women use both care-based (such as 'which outcome will cause the least hurt for all of the people involved') and justice-based reasoning (such as 'whether there is a moral code to which all individuals should adhere')."

In discussing the enthusiastic feminist response to Gilligan's theory, Tavris sounds an important warning to those who "intuitively" respond favorably to it. She writes: "[A]ccepting ideas on the basis of their intuitive application to oneself has its risk" (82). She cites the warning of two psychologists who state: "Many women readers find that the comments by women quoted in Gilligan's book resonate so thoroughly with their own experience that they do not need any further demonstration of the truth of what is being said . . . *intuitively* we feel that Gilligan must be right . . . [but, a warning]: Women have been trapped for generations by people's willingness to accept their own intuitions about the truth of gender stereotypes" (82–83, emphasis in the original).

Tavris also cites noted psychologist Martha Mednick, who comments that the belief that women speak in a different moral voice "has been widely and enthusiastically accepted by many feminist scholars in numerous disciplines . . . for reasons that are quite independent of its scientific merit" (83). In ending her discussion of Gilligan, Tavris concludes: "As long as people think in opposites, they will be prevented from envisioning a future that will combine, for example, 'male' access to power and 'female' values and skills. They will continue to define problems in a narrow way, instead of expanding the possibilities. . . . That is why the woman-is-better school is ultimately as self-defeating as the woman-is-deficient school it hopes to replace" (92).

Current thinkers in feminist ethics show a variety of attitudes toward the notions of an ethic of care and an ethic of rights and justice, according to the editors of *Explorations in Feminist Ethics* (Cole and McQuin-Coultrap 1992). Some reject the rights perspective; others recognize the equal worth of both. Still others argue the importance of integrating the two perspectives for a fuller moral outlook. Echoing other feminist critics who are concerned that the exclusive endorsement of an ethics of care merely reinvents gender-role stereotypes, the editors suggest several notes of caution. First, they state that traditional activities of caregiving have often been defined as a response to the needs of patriarchal male institutions. Second, the notions of caregiving enshrine the very image of what patriarchal males desire to see in women, a "male moral fantasy." Third, an ethics of care may not be easily applicable to the public arena of decision making. The editors also provide reasons for not rejecting an ethics of rights, pointing out that the rights perspective provides a moral minimum for interpersonal behavior and has been influential as a rallying cry to improve the lot of the oppressed.

Rand's Concept of Selfishness

If an ethics of care is to be an element of contemporary feminist ethics, as many feminists suggest, then how might Rand's concepts of "selfishness" and "altruism" exclude her from the fold of feminist theory? Proclaiming the "virtue of selfishness," she decries "altruism" as evil, a view that has generated much criticism of Rand from other quarters (e.g., O'Neill 1971; Kohn 1990). On the surface, "selfishness" is certainly not an idea that lends itself to easy integration with any ethics that celebrates the concept of "caring."

Rand, however, uses the two terms in an almost perversely idiosyncratic way that does not correspond to either common or academic usage, though she denies the idiosyncrasy. "The definition ascribed to selfishness is wrong, an intellectual 'package-deal' responsible for the arrested moral development of mankind," she asserts in *The Virtue of Selfishness* (1964, vii). "The exact meaning and dictionary definition of the word 'selfishness' is: *concern with one's own interests . . . concern with his own interests* is the essence of a moral existence, and that man must be the *beneficiary of his own moral activities."*

The *Oxford English Dictionary* (1979), however, defines "selfishness" as "regard for one's own interest or happiness to the *disregard* of the well-being of others" and "selfish" as "devoted to or concerned with one's own advantage or welfare to the *exclusion* of regard for others" (emphasis added). What Rand insists on defining as selfishness is actually closer to what is meant by "egoism," as, for example, in the OED definition of "egoism" as "the theory which regards self-interest as the foundation of morality."

Her idiosyncratic use of the term "selfish" has left Rand open to charges that she advocates a destructive social Darwinism. Believing that egoism implies a split between what is good and what is good *for me*, critic Alfie Kohn (1990, 195), for example, launches a not untypical attack against Rand: "[N]evertheless, versions of ethical egoism continue to soothe economists with an invisible hand, to reassure needy seekers of themselves who live by the tenets of the human potential movement, to excite new generations of adolescents captivated by the meretricious screeds of Ayn Rand." With a deft sleight of hand, Kohn then changes the well-established definition of egoism from merely "concern with one's self-interest" to "exclusive concern," illegitimately equating egoism with selfishness, thus enabling him to argue that egoism is bad.

Few advocates of ethical or psychological egoism, including Rand, do in fact rule out concern for others. Rand never argues that we should simply disregard the well-being of others. In *The Virtue of Selfishness*, for example, she asserts that "concern for the welfare of those one loves is a rational part of one's selfish interests" (Rand 1964, 44). Nor does she condone hurting others or disregarding their rights in order to pursue one's own ends. We do not have a right to abrogate the rights of others, she believes, nor do the rights of individuals conflict.[5]

Are advocates of Rand's philosophy self-centered, egotistic, and unconcerned with others, as the critics would have us believe? Waterman's research suggests that individualists are cooperative, willing to help others, and concerned with the rights and welfare of others, but is this research relevant to Rand's advocates? Rand's critics would probably hasten to say no. In the absence of any direct research evidence to back up their claims, the attacks of critics such as Kohn remain speculative and partisan.

While I would not argue that Objectivists would necessarily rank high on measures of charitable behavior, some indirect evidence suggests that they may not be the moral monsters the critics imagine. In my research on political resisters to authority, several subsamples included many libertarians significantly influenced by Rand. These libertarians, as well as the other resisters, were characterized by high levels of moral judgment that placed them at the level of universal ethical principles as measured by a Kohlberg-influenced scale called the Defining Issues Test (Presley 1982, 1985). Another measure of the willingness to use or control others gave no indication of high levels of manipulative or exploitative behavior in this sample. The narcissistic "individualists" pictured by the critics of individualism would be characterized by Preconventional Level, Stage-2 thinking—the stage Kohlberg (1969) describes as a primitive "I'll scratch your back if you'll scratch mine," "what's in it for me" way of thinking, in contrast to the Postconventional Level, Stages 5 and 6, that emphasizes the idea of universally applicable individual rights. While this indirect finding is hardly conclusive evidence, it does provide an actual sample of the Randian group in question, which is more than what the critics have to offer.

Rand's View of Altruism

Rand's view of altruism as "evil" is another area that causes consternation among her critics and suggests an area of concern to those who see a place for an ethics of care. Again, however, we see that her definition is highly idiosyncratic. Rand views altruism as synonymous with self-sacrifice, with the "idea that man should place others above self as the fundamental rule of life" (Peikoff 1991, 240). In her view, "Altruism declares that any action taken for the benefit of others is good, and any action taken for one's own benefit is evil" (Rand 1964, viii). Thus, she believes that altruism, as she defines it, leads not to benevolence but to social destructiveness and the absence of justice. "It means that altruism permits no view of men except as sacrificial animals and profiteers-on-sacrifice, as victims and parasites—that it permits no concept of a benevolent coexistence among men—that it permits no concept of *justice*" (ix).

Rand's definition of altruism does not correspond with either everyday or standard psychological usage. In common usage, altruism is often used as a synonym for "benevolence" and helping others. The OED reflects this common usage in its definition of altruism as "devotion to the welfare of others, regard for others, as a principle of action," and "altruistic" as "benevolent." This definition actually corresponds more closely to what psychologists call "prosocial behavior." Prosocial behavior refers to actions undertaken voluntarily and intentionally to benefit someone else (Kohn 1990; Lippa 1990). This confusion between the terms "prosocial" and "altruistic" is common. In *The Heart of Altruism* (1996), Kristen Monroe writes that the literature on altruism reveals a remarkable lack of agreement over what is meant by the term, with the term often being used interchangeably with giving, sharing, cooperating, helping, and other forms of prosocial behavior.

It is likely that the confusion and interchangeability of these words in

common usage have led some critics to believe that Rand is against helping others. Rand, however, has no necessary objection to benevolence or
to helping others.[6] She simply believes that self-sacrifice is not the way
to do it. Helping others in an emergency situation, when they are temporarily helpless, for example, seems reasonable to her as long as one can
afford it. Though she believes that we should feel respect and goodwill
toward others because of our shared humanity, it should also be noted
that her idea of when benevolence is appropriate is more restricted than
what even many libertarians would feel comfortable with. She says, for
example, "It is only in emergency situations that one should volunteer to
help strangers" (Rand 1964, 48). Since many small acts of kindness and
charity to strangers do not necessarily involve emergencies, but hardly
represent sacrifices as she defines them, we can only speculate how literally she meant this statement.

Relational Feminism and Feminist Ethics

Gilligan's emphasis on women's special contributions, such as nurturing
and caregiving, is not new to feminism. Karen Offen (1988) argues, in
her essay on defining feminism, that historically there have always been
two distinct traditions within feminist thought—the "relational" and the
"individualist." "Viewed historically," she writes in Signs, "arguments in
the relational feminist tradition proposed a gender-based but egalitarian
vision of social organization. They featured the primacy of a companion-
ate, nonhierarchical, male-female couple as the basic unit of society,
whereas individualist arguments posited the individual, irrespective of sex
or gender, as the basic unit" (136). Relational feminism, she goes on to
say, emphasized women's rights as women (defined principally by their
childbearing and/or nurturing capacities) in relation to men. In contrast,
the individualist feminist tradition emphasized more abstract concepts of
individual rights and celebrated the quest for personal independence in
all aspects of life, while downplaying socially defined roles and sex-linked
qualities.

Offen argues that both the relational and individualist traditions of
feminism are important to feminism. "As we plot a future path, we must
draw on the most valuable features of both historical traditions. What
feminists today must do—and are now beginning to do—is to reappro-

priate the relational path . . . to reclaim it for its concern for broad social goals, and to reweave it again with the appeal to the principle of human freedom that underlies the individualist tradition" (156). This line of thinking is consistent with the advice proffered by Tavris (1992, 92): "The Doctrine of the Beautiful Soul [referring to woman as nurturing and caring] is comforting, but if it simply allows women to feel better about themselves without doing anything that might . . . require real change, it is not enough. . . . We can continue to reclaim the psychological qualities long associated with female deficiency by celebrating them not as glories of female nature but as potentials in human nature." Rather than see the two feminist traditions as opposites, Offen suggests that both lines of reasoning have a place in feminism. Unlike the most extreme followers of Gilligan (who insist on polarizing the ethics of care and the ethics of rights as "women's" and "men's" moralities) and the socialist critics of individualist feminism (who wish to discard individualism altogether), Offen, Tavris, and the editors of *Explorations in Feminist Ethics* suggest, each in their own way, that a balance needs to be struck between relational and individualist perspectives.

Rand, Individualism, and Feminist Ethics: A Reconciliation

Rand has been a consistent critic of false polarizations and false dualisms. She sees much traditional thinking as characteristically falling into two opposing camps, each of which is partly correct. But the "either-or" oppositional view that both camps accept is, in her view, incorrect. Chris Matthew Sciabarra (1995, 403 n. 5) writes: "Rand rejected nearly every imaginable dichotomy: mind vs. body; idealism vs. materialism; rationalism vs. empiricism; internalism vs. externalism; intrinsicism vs. subjectivism; concepts vs. percepts; reason vs. emotion; the conscious vs. the subconscious . . . conventional egoism vs. traditional altruism; love vs. sex; anarchism vs. statism; atomistic individualism vs. organic collectivism."

The false dichotomies of "conventional egoism vs. traditional altruism" and "atomistic individualism vs. organic collectivism" that Rand draws to our attention speak to the issue of balance that Offen and other feminists seek. Nothing in Rand's philosophy requires giving up caring about others in order to be an individualist. Explicitly rejecting the idea of sacrificing others to obtain one's ends, she calls for egoism, not egotism. The idea of the atomistic individual who cares for no one and runs roughshod over others is a far cry from Rand's advocacy of universal principles of justice that require respect for the rights of all.

Behavioral research also supports Rand's contention that the dichotomy between egoism and altruism is a false one. Psychological individualists are neither atomistic egotists who care nothing about others nor socially destructive amoral monsters. They are instead characterized by cooperativeness, high levels of moral reasoning, good social relationships, and concern for others.

Rand's warning against false philosophical alternatives is also consistent with the feminist rejection of the "women-as-morally-superior" position (Offen 1988; Pollitt 1995; Tavris 1992). As Tavris (1992, 92) explains: "[T]hinking of the sexes as opposites implies . . . an underlying antagonism or conflict, the pitting of one side against the other, one way (which is right and healthy) versus the other's way (which is wrong and unhealthy)."

To promote such a moral dichotomy is dangerous for women. Uncritical endorsement of the idea that women are morally superior and that the ethics of care is better than the ethics of rights not only leads to a reinvention of sex-role stereotypes—it is a recipe for continued oppression. The age-old belief that women should sacrifice themselves to the needs of others—family, child, husband—has kept women oppressed over the centuries. An insistence on an ethics of care without the balance of an ethics of rights could all too easily lead back to oppressive justifications for continued self-sacrifice, renunciation of the self, and rejection of individual autonomy. Without a balance of both responsibility and rights, concern for others and concern for self, women run the risk of becoming merely "Beautiful Souls," with no power or freedom, with no inviolable self apart from their relationships with family and others.

What Rand can contribute to feminist ethics is a moral justification for preserving the integrity of the self, for maintaining individual autonomy. Her philosophy of individualism can remind us about the dangers of self-sacrifice and provide a warning against rejecting individualism in the name of caring. It can help us recognize social interdependence without self-sacrifice or rejection of individualism.

Individualist feminists recognize that the idea of egoism versus altruism, individualism versus community, is a false dichotomy. As Joan Kennedy Taylor (1992, 12) writes:

When the group being referred to is a free association of people with a common goal uniting to achieve that goal, the group acts as an extension of its individual members and is no contradiction to individualism. A group formed by individual choices nourishes the individualism—in fact, human nature is such that many life-serving goals can only be reached by people willing to act in concert. So the accusation that individualism means rampant and fragmented egoism is a misunderstanding of what individualism entails.

Understood in this sense, such a group of individuals cooperating together for mutual benefit does not negate the value of group action. Instead, it leads naturally to a sense of community. As psychiatrist Peter Breggin stresses in *Beyond Conflict* (1992), both "love" (caring, nurturance, sharing, cooperation) and "liberty" (voluntary exchanges, rejection of coercion, personal autonomy) are necessary ingredients for a loving community that is both nonoppressive and workable.

Caring, community, and relationships are not contradictions to Rand's individualism. Her philosophy, if properly implemented, could lead to a flowering of the full potential of individual women and to an optimal setting for development and expression of love and caring between free, equal, and autonomous individuals who neither oppress others nor let themselves be oppressed.

Notes

1. See, for instance, Mill and Mill 1970; Friedan 1974; Offen 1988; McElroy 1982; Taylor 1992; Brown 1993.

2. See, for instance, Offen 1988; Fox-Genovese 1991; Taylor 1992; Brown 1993.

3. Critics of the critics of individualism are concerned with what they consider to be an attitude reflecting a "politics of domination." "Like many other collectivists," writes L. Susan Brown (1993, 23), "Scheman's rejection of all forms of individualism betrays a deep uneasiness with the idea of human freedom."

4. In the last revision of his theory, Kohlberg expanded it to include more of the "ethics-of-care" perspective. Kohlberg admits that the principle of altruism, care, or responsible love has not

been adequately represented in his work. But he argues that there are not two different moral orientations. Justice is rational, and it implies empathy (Kohlberg, Levine, and Hewer 1983).

5. Rand's use of the terms "selfish" and "altruistic" is by no means uniformly attacked by philosophers. Noted philosopher Antony Flew (1984, 187), for example, has written: "The characteristics that Rand wants to promote as selfish or to diminish as sacrificial are . . . by no means the same as those the vulgar depreciate as the one or commend as the other."

6. On the virtue of benevolence and its consistency with Rand's ethics, see Kelley 1996.

References

Breggin, Peter R. 1992. *Beyond Conflict: From Self-Help and Psychotherapy to Peacemaking.* New York: St. Martin's Press.
Brown, L. Susan. 1993. *The Politics of Individualism.* Montreal: Black Rose Books.
Colby, Anne, and William Damon. 1987. Listening to a different voice: A review of Gilligan's *In a Different Voice.* In *The Psychology of Women: Ongoing Debates,* edited by M. R. Walsh. New Haven: Yale University Press.
Cole, Eve Browning, and Susan McQuin-Coultrap, eds. 1992. *Explorations in Feminist Ethics: Theory and Practice.* Bloomington: Indiana University Press.
Den Uyl, Douglas J., and Douglas B. Rasmussen, eds. 1984. *The Philosophic Thought of Ayn Rand.* Urbana: University of Illinois Press.
Eisenstein, Zillah. 1981. *The Radical Future of Liberal Feminism.* New York: Longman.
Flew, Antony. 1984. Selfishness and the unintended consequences of intended action. In *The Philosophic Thought of Ayn Rand,* edited by Douglas J. Den Uyl and Douglas B. Rasmussen. Urbana: University of Illinois Press.
Fox-Genovese, Elizabeth. 1991. *Feminism Without Illusions: A Critique of Individualism.* Chapel Hill: University of North Carolina Press.
Frazer, Elizabeth, and Nicola Lacey. 1993. *The Politics of Community: A Feminist Critique of the Liberal-Communitarian Debate.* Toronto: University of Toronto Press.
Friedan, Betty. 1974. *The Feminine Mystique.* New York: Dell.
Gilligan, Carol. 1982. *In a Different Voice: Psychological Theory and Women's Development.* Cambridge, Mass.: Harvard University Press.
Haan, Norma, Eliane Aerts, and Bruce Cooper. 1985. *On Moral Grounds: The Search for Practical Morality.* New York: New York University Press.
Hewlett, Sylvia Ann. 1986. *A Lesser Life: The Myth of Women's Liberation in America.* New York: William Morrow.
Hogan, Robert. 1975. Theoretical egocentrism and the problem of compliance. *American Psychologist* 30:533–40.
Hogan, Robert, and N. P. Emler. 1978. The biases in contemporary social psychology. *Social Research* 45:478–34.
Jagger, Alison. 1983. *Feminist Politics and Human Nature.* Brighton, East Sussex: Harvester Press.
Kelley, David. 1996. *Unrugged Individualism: The Selfish Basis of Benevolence.* Poughkeepsie, N.Y.: Institute for Objectivist Studies.
Kohlberg, Lawrence. 1969. Stage and sequence: The cognitive-developmental approach. In *Handbook of Socialization Research and Theory,* edited by D. A. Goslin. Chicago: Rand McNally.
Kohlberg, Lawrence, C. Levine, and A. Hewer. 1983. *Moral Stages: A Current Formulation and a Response to Critics.* Basel, N.Y.: Karger.

Kohn, Alfie. 1990. *The Brighter Side of Human Nature: Altruism and Empathy in Everyday Life.* New York: Basic Books.

Lasch, Christopher. 1978. *The Culture of Narcissism: American Life in an Age of Diminishing Expectations.* New York: W. W. Norton.

Lippa, Richard. 1990. *Introduction to Social Psychology.* Belmont, Calif.: Wadsworth Publishing.

Mack, Eric. 1984. The fundamental moral elements of Rand's theory of rights. In *The Philosophic Thought of Ayn Rand,* edited by Douglas J. Den Uyl and Douglas B. Rasmussen. Urbana: University of Illinois Press.

MacKinnon, Catherine A. 1989. *Toward a Feminist View of the State.* Cambridge, Mass.: Harvard University Press.

McElroy, Wendy. 1982. The roots of individualist feminism in nineteenth-century America. In *Freedom, Feminism, and the State: An Overview of Individualist Feminism,* edited by Wendy McElroy. Washington, D.C.: Cato Institute.

Mill, John Stuart, and Harriet Taylor Mill. 1970. *Essays on Sex Equality.* Chicago: University of Chicago Press.

Monroe, Kristen R. 1996. *The Heart of Altruism: Perceptions of a Common Humanity.* Princeton, N.J.: Princeton University Press.

Offen, Karen. 1988. Defining feminism: A comparative historical approach. *Signs: A Journal of Woman in Culture and Society* 14, no. 11:119–57.

O'Neill, William F. 1971. *With Charity Toward None: An Analysis of Ayn Rand's Philosophy.* Totowa, N.J.: Littlefield, Adams.

Peikoff, Leonard. 1991. *Objectivism: The Philosophy of Ayn Rand.* New York: Dutton.

Pollitt, Katha. 1995. Marooned on Gilligan's island: Are women morally superior to men? In *Reasonable Creatures: Essays on Women and Feminism.* New York: Vintage Books.

Presley, Sharon Lee. 1982. Values and attitudes of political resisters to authority. Ph.D. diss., City University of New York Graduate Center.

———. 1985. Moral judgment and attitudes toward authority of political resisters. *Journal of Research in Personality* 19:135–51.

Rand, Ayn. 1957. *Atlas Shrugged.* New York: Random House.

———. 1964. *The Virtue of Selfishness: A New Concept of Egoism.* New York: New American Library.

———. 1982. Selfishness without a self. In *Philosophy: Who Needs It.* Indianapolis: Bobbs-Merrill.

———. 1988. *The Voice of Reason: Essays in Objectivist Thought.* Edited by Leonard Peikoff. New York: New American Library.

Sampson, Edward E. 1977. Psychology and the American ideal. *Journal of Personality and Social Psychology* 35:767–82.

Scheman, Naomi. 1983. Individualism and the objects of psychology. In *Discovering Reality,* edited by Sandra Harding and Merrill B. Hintikka. Dordrecht: Reidel.

Sciabarra, Chris Matthew. 1995. *Ayn Rand: The Russian Radical.* University Park: Pennsylvania State University Press.

Tavris, Carol. 1992. *The Mismeasure of Woman: Why Women are not the Better Sex, the Inferior Sex, or the Opposite Sex.* New York: Simon & Schuster.

Taylor, Joan Kennedy. 1992. *Reclaiming the Mainstream: Individualist Feminism Rediscovered.* Buffalo, N.Y.: Prometheus Books.

Wallach, M. A., and L. Wallach. 1983. *Psychology's Sanction for Selfishness: The Error of Egoism in Theory and Therapy.* San Francisco: W. H. Freeman.

Waterman, Alan. 1984. *The Psychology of Individualism.* New York: Praeger.

15

Ayn Rand: The Woman Who Would Not Be President

Susan Love Brown

I would not want to be president and would not vote for a woman president. A woman cannot reasonably want to be a commander-in-chief.

For a woman to seek or desire the presidency is, in fact, so terrible a prospect of spiritual self-immolation that the woman who would seek it is psychologically unworthy of the job.

—Ayn Rand, "About a Woman President"

Ayn Rand has long been known as a champion of individual liberty and of moral values derived from an objective view of reality. It is hard to find in contemporary times a voice more clear and unswerving on the subject of individual self-interest and its implications for all aspects of human life. Yet, we can also acknowledge that Rand has been neglected by feminist and women's studies scholars. Although Rand's expressed attitudes support the equality of women, the undercurrents of her fiction and her explicit statements, such as those above, often belie this position, suggesting a contradiction within Rand's own thinking. This contradiction results in mixed messages about the nature and role of women in relation to men.

This paper explores the origin and nature of that contradiction, the source of which is the conflict between the principles of individualism and Rand's definition of femininity as hero worship. I will show that Rand's concept of hero worship is an attempt to resolve the great cognitive dissonance within Rand herself—a dissonance created by an underlying and largely unconscious cultural model of gender that dichotomizes human characteristics in such a way as to cause people to choose between their sexual identity and their human identity.

Rand's great intellect and devotion to reason placed her femininity in jeopardy. Adopting hero worship as a principle helped Rand to secure her femininity by creating a symbolic subordination to men according to gender-role stereotype. Unlike some women, Rand does not sacrifice her own intellect in the real world in order to conform to gender-role stereotypes. Like many artists, she resolves her cognitive and emotional dilemmas in the world of imagination. However, Rand's thinking itself is compromised when the topic turns to women and the presidency.

Rand's position on women and the presidency is a generalization applied to all women, and one that Rand attempts to justify through rational argument. Since Rand expressed all her views publicly as an integral part of her philosophical outlook, they must be taken seriously and examined and interpreted in a scholarly fashion. In this paper, I place Rand and her ideas within a cultural and psychological context. That is, I expose the underlying gender-role assumptions at the root of her thinking—assumptions that she herself may have accepted without question. Using her own words and those of her close associates, I demonstrate how Rand's solution to her personal problem of gender identity affects the way in which others may read her work.

Rand and the Highest Authority

In "About a Woman President," Rand explicitly states that women are not inferior to men either in their general abilities, their intelligence, or their use of reason, yet she singles out the office of the presidency as the one to which a rational woman would never aspire. Rand dispenses with all the usual reasons why one might object to a female president (inability to do the job, emotionalism, marriage versus career), denying that any of them pertain. "Women may properly rise as high as their ability and ambition will carry them; in politics, they may reach the ranks of congresswomen, senators, judges, or any similar rank they choose" (1989, 268).

But the presidency is the single exception, according to Rand. "It is not a matter of ability, but of her *values*," Rand tells us. The key question for Rand is, *"What would it do to her?"* This might be restated as "What would it do to her femininity?"

Rand argues that "woman *qua* woman" would have a "fundamental view of life" in which "the essence of femininity is hero worship," which she defines as "the desire to look up to man." Denying that "worship" means "dependence, obedience, or anything implying inferiority," she states that it is "an intense admiration." Rand is careful to state that "the object of worship is specifically his *masculinity*, not any human virtue she might lack."

Rand tells us that a woman would not feel this way about every man— only about the man who is the object of her attentions, although it "colors her attitude toward all men." This means that a woman is always aware of her own sexual identity and that of men. "It means that a properly feminine woman does not treat men as if she were their pal, sister, mother—or *leader*" (268).

Because the office of the presidency represents the "highest authority"—a position in which a person has no "equals," only "inferiors"—a rational woman would find the position "unbearable." She does not speak of this as a personal opinion or as a question of personal values. In fact, Rand states in the strongest possible language: "By the nature of her duties and daily activities, she would become the most unfeminine, sexless, metaphysically inappropriate, and rationally revolting figure of all: a *matriarch* " (269).

What is wrong with this argument?

First of all, Rand is being disingenuous when she tells us, in reference to the hero worship that she says defines femininity, " 'To look up' does not mean dependence, obedience, or anything implying inferiority. It means an intense kind of admiration." Rand is trying to have it both ways: denying that hero worship is about inferiority and telling us that the reason a woman would not want the presidency is because she would have only inferiors. Implicit in Rand's argument about the presidency is the assumption of the superior-inferior, leader-follower, and dominant-submissive relationship of the president to everyone else. If "worship" meant only intense admiration, then the presidency would be irrelevant to a romantic relationship, whether held by a woman or a man. Only if the "superiority" of the office is granted does Rand's argument make sense.

One can admire inferiors, equals, and superiors, but one can only "look up to" one who is above oneself. Rand assumes that the relationship between masculinity and femininity is one of dominance and subordination. Because Rand's subordination of women occurs at such high levels of abstraction, it is easy to think that it does not occur at all. However, her reserving the presidency as the sole exception is symbolic of Rand's ultimate inability to see women and men as equals, her protests to the contrary notwithstanding.

Since Rand wrote "About a Woman President," we have acquired more knowledge of the historical and cultural role of gender stereotypes and the way in which they influence our thinking and actions. We have seen women take positions as heads of state all over the world—Golda Meir in Israel, Indira Gandhi in India, Margaret Thatcher in England, Benazar Bhutto in Pakistan, Corazon Aquino in the Philippines. These women were all inducted into office in normal circumstances. The presence of women in the highest political positions all over the world reminds us that objective reality does not support Rand's contention about the female psyche; therefore, we must look for the source of contradiction within Rand herself.

The next part of this paper explores the source of the conflict between the equality of women and men that Rand espouses and her definition of femininity as hero worship. Because Rand does not question the way in which gender roles dichotomize human traits, she falls prey to this cultural dichotomy in her own thinking.

Culture, Psychology, and the Origins of Hero Worship

Human beings are cultural animals. We thrive in all earth's environments because we are able to project symbols outside ourselves and, in so doing, pass on to the next generation the knowledge we have acquired (Hallowell 1955, 2–13). The shared understandings that accumulate over time among a group of people constitute culture. Culture is a repository of all the wisdom of a people, but it is also the repository of error.

Gender is one of the most pervasive forms of culture. As Londa Schiebinger (1993, 4) notes, "gender was to become one potent principle organizing eighteenth-century revolutions in views of nature, a matter of consequence in an age that looked to nature as the guiding light for social reform."[1] Notions of gender are often deeply embedded in our thinking. Our cultural models of gender, and the gender-role stereotypes that arise from them, assert notions of femininity and masculinity that conflict with the realities of human nature generally and with the realities of individuals particularly.

Core gender identities are generally in place by the time we are two or three years old (Stoller 1985, 11). As Robert Stoller states:

> The term *gender identity* . . . refers to the mix of masculinity and femininity in an individual, implying that both masculinity and femininity are found in everyone, but in differing forms and to differing degrees. It is not the same as maleness and femaleness, which connote biology; gender identity implies psychologically motivated behavior. Though masculinity fits well with maleness and femininity goes with femaleness, sex and gender are not necessarily directly related. Many biologically intact men have to try to avoid having what they feel are feminine impulses and behavior; the converse is true for women. There can even be rather complete gender reversal, as in the case of biologically normal males and females who live as members of the opposite sex.
>
> But these designations do not serve us well unless we are also clear what is meant by masculinity and femininity. Masculinity or femininity is defined here as any quality that is felt by its possessor to be masculine or feminine. In other words, masculinity or femininity is a belief—more precisely, a dense mass of beliefs, an algebraic sum of ifs, buts, and ands—not incontrovertible fact. In addition to biologic anlagen, one gets such beliefs from parental attitudes, especially in childhood, these attitudes being more or less those held by society at large, filtered through the idiosyncratic personalities of parents. Therefore, such convictions are not eternal truths; they shift when societies change. An American Indian warrior wore his hair long and felt masculine; a Prussian represented his claim to manliness with very short hair. Masculinity is not measured by hair length but by a person's conviction that long or short hair is masculine. (11)

Much of our understanding of what is masculine and feminine has been acquired unconsciously and uncritically before we even have a command of language, and continues to be enhanced as we grow.

Glynis M. Breakwell, in a table based on findings of I. K. Broverman and colleagues (1972), notes that characteristics attributed to women and men tend to cluster into two groups—those describing competency and those describing warmth-expressiveness—and tend to be opposites. Thus, in the competency cluster, women are not aggressive, not independent, not competitive, not ambitious, very submissive, very passive, and they have difficulty making decisions; men are aggressive, independent, competitive, ambitious, dominant, active, and they make decisions easily. On the other hand, when we look at the warmth-expressive cluster, men are blunt, loud, and unaware of the feelings of others; they have no need for security and do not express tender feelings easily. Women are tactful, quiet, and aware of others' feelings; they have a strong need for security and express tender feelings easily (Breakwell 1990, 213).

These oppositional characteristics, dichotomizing the sexes and defining femininity and masculinity, are "one-dimensional." They define women as possessing "emotionality and spontaneity without rational calculation in the pursuit of self-interest," while they define men as " 'instrumental' in orientation: strength, aggression, and relationships are used as a means to other ends" (213). Breakwell elaborates:

> Few people, male or female, would recognize themselves in these archetypical portraits. Indeed all the evidence about differences between the sexes supports cynicism with regard to the dominant social beliefs. Psychologists have found no consistent evidence of the proposed differences between the sexes in relation to levels of competitiveness, dominance, nurturance, suggestibility, sociability, activity, or desire for achievement. . . . They have found no reliable differences in anxiety levels, cognitive or analytic abilities, or amounts of self-esteem. . . . There are small differences in average levels of aggression: men are on average more aggressive but there is tremendous overlap of scores, with many women just as aggressive as men . . . the sex of a person will not predict their individual abilities.[2] (213–14)

Nancy Chodorow (1989, 23) reaches a similar conclusion: "Cross-cultural research suggests that there are no absolute personality differences between men and women, that many of the characteristics we normally classify as masculine and feminine tend to differentiate both the males and females in one culture from those in another, and in still other cultures to be the reverse of our expectations."[3]

Evidence from Russian culture shows the same tendency to dichotomize human characteristics by gender, though Russian culture has its own distinct take on this dichotomy. First of all, traditional Russian peasant culture saw the land and, consequently, the nation itself as Mother. Joanna Hubbs, in *Mother Russia* (1988, 230–31), tells us:

> The persona of woman as priestess and redeemer, the chief repository of virtue in the form of agape, is central to Russian literature of the nineteenth and twentieth centuries, a literature which served as the principal outlet for the political, social, and religious aspirations of the educated classes. The desire for a woman savior is expressed in a constant adulation of the ethical strengths of the good woman and the refusal to consider the virtues of male heroism. Male identity is perceived as precarious, contingent, existing only in the ethereal world of ideas rather than rooted in the "real" world. Woman, on the other hand, is regarded as the essence of stability, of life, of growth, of *lichnost'* (individuality) itself. She is "whole" (*tsel'naia*), while man is neurotic, torn.

The Russian way in which human characteristics are divided up between male and female is similar to those of Europe and the United States. Russian autocracy and patriarchy and the equation of Russian land with the Mother translated very easily into an image that fit comfortably with the division of human traits into masculine and feminine. As Sciabarra (1995, 66–95) points out, Russia was not isolated from the cultural currents of the rest of the world in its Silver Age—the age during which Ayn Rand grew up. The Russian middle class had always had an affinity for Western ideas and shared many of its predispositions toward dichotomizing sex roles.[4]

According to Lynne Attwood, concepts of masculinity and femininity in the Soviet Union held by professionals were pretty traditional. Attwood (1985, 66–67) describes the pedagogical beliefs about differences between boys and girls:

> Girls are more emotional and subjective than boys. They are more shy and modest. They are more sensitive, taking praise and

censure more to heart. They are less brave than boys. . . . They
are less inclined towards investigative and inventive behaviour.
. . . They are, none the less, more impulsive. They are better than
boys at understanding simple and commonplace ideas, but worse
regarding more specialised concepts. . . . It is easier to get girls to
follow instructions. Different school subjects attract girls and
boys. Girls tend towards arts subjects such as history and literature, especially poetry, and dislike physics, biology and maths;
while boys are more interested in handcrafts and sport.

I do not view Rand's gender problem as unique—in fact, it is quite
common among intelligent women who feel they must choose between
their identities as women and the reality of their existence as people with
sizable intellects. However, women choose to solve this problem in a
variety of ways.

"Whatever form it takes, a myth of primary femininity always lends
credence to the social conventions that define the positions—whether
sexual or social—of domination and submission as respectively masculine
and feminine," warns Louise J. Kaplan in *Female Perversions* (1991, 193).
"The way I see it, the myth of primary femininity is itself a disguise for the
forbidden and frightening masculine ambitions and strivings that 'nice'
women are not supposed to entertain" (200).

What is very clear in Rand's work is that she learned to value the
masculine over the feminine within the Russian cultural context and
later in that of the United States. "The human qualities she cared about
were, she believed, specifically masculine attributes; above all, purposefulness and strength. . . . Man, she would say, is defined by his relationship
to reality; woman—by her relationship to man" (Branden 1986, 18).

A key factor that strongly influenced Rand's thinking with regard to
gender, and placed her in conflict with her cultural environment and her
self, was being praised primarily for her intellectual abilities. This, in
combination with the particular relationships she had with her parents
(distant with her father and full of conflict with her mother) and the
trauma experienced by having her world disrupted by war and revolution,
led Rand to resolve her gender conflicts in particular ways.[5]

The sources of conflict with which Rand dealt her whole life began in
her childhood, as conflicts usually do, and no matter how great a thinker

Rand became in her mature years, as a child she was vulnerable to the events around her like any child, and she set out to cope with them as best she could.

Rand, speaking of the mother she disliked, says, "She disapproved of me in every respect except one: she was proud of my intelligence and proud to show me off to the rest of the family" (quoted in Branden 1986, 5). According to Barbara Branden, "Implicit in Alice's reminiscences about her childhood is the fact that, from her parents and from the other adults she encountered, love and admiration were purchased by the qualities of her mind. . . . she placed on intelligence what can only be termed a moral value; intelligence and virtue were to become inextricably linked in her mind" (1986, 7).

This intelligence was not only general but specific: Rand was very good at mathematics and logic, and she was even encouraged to become a mathematician by her teacher. "I felt that it was too abstract, it had nothing to do with actual life. I loved it, but I didn't intend to be an engineer or to go into any applied profession, and to study mathematics as such seemed too ivory tower, too purposeless—and I would say so today" (Rand quoted in Branden 1986, 35). The enthusiasm over Rand's mathematical abilities reinforced the emphasis on her mind and its most abstract abilities. Rand identified with her mind to such a degree that its image almost became identical with Rand herself.

Why, then, did she feel the need to invent hero worship (or man worship)?

I hypothesize that hero worship served at least three purposes: (1) it allowed Rand to claim her femininity in the face of an intellect that clearly fell into the "masculine" side of the dichotomy; (2) it provided her with a way to have in fantasy the love denied her in reality by her father and Leo, the object of her first love and heartbreak; (3) it allowed Rand surreptitiously to admire those "masculine" qualities that she also possessed but did not find in the men around her.

Barbara Branden makes a very convincing argument that Rand came from a family of strong women and acknowledged the power of her mother, Anna Rosenbaum, within the family:

> It was Anna who was the dominant figure in the Rosenbaum household, as Ayn, despite her lack of warm feeling for Anna, always acknowledged. . . . It was Anna who determined the direc-

tion her family's lives should take. It was Anna who decided, after the Communist revolution, that the family must seek safety in the Crimea; it was Anna who found the way to get them there. It was Anna who supported the family when they returned to Petrograd, despite Fronz's disapproval of her working for the Communists. It was Anna who decided that Ayn should be allowed to emigrate to America, despite Fronz's fears for her safety. It was Anna who took responsibility for handling the complicated process of securing Ayn's passport and making the necessary arrangements. In the life of his family, Fronz was a dim, passive figure; Anna was the power.[6] (1986, 90)

This suggests an inspiration for the drive and ambition that Rand herself demonstrated in her own life—never doubting that she should be doing the things she did. But Rand was up against two powerful motivations for augmenting her own sense of femininity: (1) by exhibiting such a powerful mind, she contradicted the long-held and pervasive attitude of Western thought that reason was the province of the masculine mind (with "intuition" being the province of the feminine mind), and (2) the very ambition and drive that she possessed—those characteristics that she shared with her mother—threw her sense of her own femininity out of balance because they too were considered to belong to the masculine side of the dichotomy (see Breakwell's list above).

Leon Festinger, in his theory of cognitive dissonance, hypothesizes that the presence of "inconsistencies," or dissonance, "will motivate the person to try to reduce the dissonance and achieve consonance" and that "the person will actively avoid situations and information which would likely increase the dissonance" (1957, 3).

Rand learned early in life to quell the dissonance within herself through fantasies about the ideal man. But in constructing her notion of the ideal man, Rand adopted deeply ingrained features of masculine gender-role stereotypes. Hero worship was designed to meet Rand's personal needs as a woman, rather than solely to discover the heroic in *all* humans.

Rand's works certainly demonstrate that she placed value on independent, intelligent women. But she also struggled with the problem of femininity and masculinity. In her early works—short stories and her first published novel—Rand placed women at the center, and this created problems for Rand herself and most often led to tragedy for the women.

Solving a Problem: Women and Hero Worship in the Early Works

From *The Early Ayn Rand* to *We the Living,* Rand's initial impulse was to place women at the center of her works as key actors. They nevertheless stood out as man-worshipers. As Leonard Peikoff points out: "When a woman with this kind of character sees her deepest values actualized and embodied in a specific man, man-worship becomes (other things being equal) romantic love. Thus the special quality of the Ayn Rand romantic love: it is the union of the abstract and the concrete, of ideal and reality, of mind and body, of uplifted spirituality and violent passion, of reverence and sexuality" (in Rand 1984, 4).

Although the patterns present in the later novels are also present in nascent form in her early fiction, Rand struggled, before those patterns became full blown, with their concomitant gender side effects.

In "The Husband I Bought" (6–31), a short story written in 1926, Rand presents the dilemma of Irene Wilmer, a rich woman so in love with Henry Stafford that she uses her fortune to get him out of debt in exchange for marriage. Irene's love for Henry seems more of an infatuation, and his for her questionable. What is significant about this story is the length to which Irene goes to maintain her marriage. Irene embodies stereotypic "feminine" characteristics: she does housework without being noticed and seemingly without effort, she is always a willing lover, she is always beautiful to look at, and she and Henry do not talk to each other.

Yet, the nature of love remains unexplored, and because of this, Henry's shift of affection from Irene to a more glamorous woman seems frivolous. Because Henry is honorable, however, he will not leave Irene voluntarily after she has spent her fortune to get him out of debt. So Irene, loving Henry and wanting him to be happy, stages her own infidelity to force him to break with her. In the end, Irene indulges in what seems like a good deal of subterfuge and self-sacrifice: she sacrifices her fortune, her reputation, her love, and her life for Henry.

Rand, no doubt, would deny that this is self-sacrifice, because Henry is Irene's highest value. But, if so, questions still remain about this peculiar psychology. Why is Henry held as Irene's highest value? He hardly seems worth it. Why cannot Irene simply confront Henry with the truth—tell him that she does not want him to suffer in a marriage to her and is, therefore, granting him a divorce? Why does Irene not value her own life highly enough even as a secondary value to at least get on with it once Henry is lost to her?

"The Husband I Bought" is a sterling example of masochism in which normal feelings of heartbreak become exalted values. It is as though plunging to the depths of despair validates the heights of love that Irene once knew. Rather than allow Irene to feel her pain and mourn her loss and then recover, Rand condemns her to an early death from indifference to life. Rand's denial of sacrifice when a high value is involved is an equivocation, for in a hierarchy of values another value is always waiting to be exercised. Irene essentially sits down and dies, deprived of a man whom she loves but who does not love her. Irene has no work, something that Rand will later declare more important than even one's friends and family. In fact, Rand considers a person who puts friends and family first as "immoral" (1964, 7).[7] Yet, this is exactly what Irene does.

It is clear that Irene also does not value her own life and that Rand has not yet learned, in this early story, how to reconcile violent feelings of grief over the end of a love affair with her instinct toward self-interest. The denial of pain appears repeatedly in Rand's work as attitudes expressed by her heroes and heroines. This denial is a root cause of the distortion of values, especially when it comes to romantic relationships. "The Husband I Bought" seems to be an early purging of feeling, as well as a solid expression of man worship. It illustrates one of the key problems with man worship—that it can be lopsided and seems to provide no way out for the person on the giving end. Thus, highest values are perverted to self-sacrifice.[8]

Kira Argounova of We the Living is the only one of Rand's major heroines who is a prime mover, perhaps because she is the character with whom Rand's real life is most closely associated. Kira sees the situation in Russia very clearly, and she figures things out for herself. She is the intellectual equal, if not superior, of Andrei and Leo because she alone has figured out the inconsistencies in the lives they lead and attempts to remedy the problem through her own actions. It is telling that the name "Kira" is a Russian form of "Cyrus," the hero of a children's story that Rand read when she was small and who became her first object of hero worship (Branden 1986, 13).

Rand positions Kira between two men, Leo and Andrei. Although Rand clearly views Leo as the romantic object, Andrei is the character with more integrity and a genuine love for Kira. Kira is attracted to Leo by his looks: "He was tall; his collar was raised; a cap was pulled over his eyes. His mouth, calm, severe, contemptuous, was that of an ancient chieftain who could order men to die, and his eyes were such as could watch it" (Rand [1936] 1959, 43).

Kira's attraction to Leo's brutality is a further illustration of the tendency of Rand's heroines toward masochism. And the way in which Rand interprets man worship in this context clearly demonstrates that it invokes female subordination, as in the passage in which she describes Leo as "not a lover, but a slave owner" (312).

Kira's only husband in *We the Living* turns out to be death itself. As she walks toward the border in her white wedding gown, she is felled by a border guard. Her gown is stained by her own red blood as if a deflowering ritual had taken place. Ironically, Rand captures something of the Russian cultural view of women when she describes Kira's gown as the "medieval gown of a priestess" (432).

Kira is independent and a motive force in her own life, but the price of independence is too high. After this novel, the feminine centrality gives way in Rand's work to a masculine centrality to which the feminine is subordinate. Although her women are not static, neither are they any longer the prime movers. They become the students of men. Granted, they must be extraordinary enough to warrant the heroes they long for, but they are never allowed to equal them in action or understanding.

The Apotheosis of Man and Reason

As we look through Rand's fiction, it becomes apparent that after her early fiction, including *We the Living* (and certainly hinted at there), only woman *qua* woman exists. There is no woman *qua* human being, for she is subsumed once and for all by the generic "man" that pervades Rand's speech and writing. Thereafter, women are only defined by their relationships to men.

It is with *Anthem* that Rand establishes the superiority of the male principle, fully accepting the gender-role stereotype and its consequential dichotomizing of human beings. *Anthem* is a prolegomenon to the two major novels that follow, and its exquisite simplicity reveals the imbalance between male and female in Rand's vision. Here, the exaltation of masculinity and reason come together powerfully for the first time.

Anthem is the story of Equality 7–2521 (later called the Unconquered or

Prometheus), who lives in a futuristic society so collectivized that the term "I" has disappeared. Rand wrote the novel in the first-person plural, so that the main character speaks of himself as "we." In the course of the novel, Equality 7–2521, who tries to be good, in spite of an intelligence that makes him wish for what he cannot have, rediscovers electricity and ultimately the existence of the individual. In the course of doing so, he sees and is attracted to Liberty 5–3000, whom he calls the Golden One, and she follows him into the wilderness, proving her worthiness to be his consort.

In *Anthem*, the masculine principle laid bare completely subdues the feminine. It is clear that Rand equates the discovery of self and reason with masculinity, keeping femininity in its culturally prescribed role of love object, passivity, and motherhood. For example, Liberty 5–3000 does not even pick her own name—Prometheus picks it for her. She becomes Gaea, "the mother of the earth and of all gods" (Rand [1946] 1969, 99). Although he does say, "I shall call to me all the men and the women whose spirit has not been killed within them and who suffer under the yoke of their brothers" (101), Prometheus, when he later discovers a house in the mountains and lays his plans for the future, does not include Gaea. "Here, on this mountain, I and my sons and my chosen friends shall build our new land and our fort," Prometheus writes toward the end of *Anthem* (104). He says nothing about Gaea or possible daughters assisting in this effort. The principle of androcentricity is full blown here, and the feminine is subsumed under it.

In the two novels that made Rand's name and launched her philosophical views into the world at large, *The Fountainhead* and *Atlas Shrugged*, the full intellectual and structural subordination of women to men is realized as men are elevated to the rank of heroes and gods. The subordination that occurs is structural, and it is a direct consequence of Rand's putting into place the full thrust of her concept of hero (or man) worship. That is, in the attempt to create heroes for herself, Ayn Rand makes men the key actors and the intellectual prime movers of her novels.

In Rand's most celebrated novels, it is men who are the purveyors of reason, and men who are the teachers of women. This is not readily apparent, because both Dominique Francon and Dagny Taggart are women ahead of their times in the amount of freedom and independence they exercise. But while both Dominique and Dagny are willing to risk their lives for the men they love, they do not originate thought. In fact, Dominique and her relationship with Howard Roark represent a casebook in sadomasochism and a warning about the pathology that can follow the perversion of the feminine-masculine dichotomy in the service of hero worship.

In *The Fountainhead*, Rand hits her stride. The novel is divided into four parts, each named after a male character: Peter Keating, Ellsworth M. Toohey, Gail Wynand, and Howard Roark. Dominique Francon, the heroine, who is the love interest of Keating, Wynand, and Roark, does not actually appear in the novel for one hundred pages. When she does appear, she is petulant and disliked by her own father. Independently wealthy and college educated, Dominique is rudderless and ruthless.

Dominique is the least admirable of all of Rand's heroines because she has no purpose and furthermore believes that if she did, she would be a slave to it:

> If I found a job, a project, an idea or a person I wanted—I'd have to depend on the whole world. Everything has strings leading to everything else. We're all so tied together. We're all in a net, the net is waiting, and we're pushed into it by one single desire. You want a thing and it's precious to you. Do you know who is standing ready to tear it out of your hands? You can't know, it may be so involved and so far away, but someone is ready, and you're afraid of them all. And you cringe and you crawl and you beg and you accept them—just so they'll let you keep it. And look at whom you accept. (Rand [1943] 1993, 143)

Dominique fears wanting anything too much, except her freedom. "To ask nothing. To expect nothing. To depend on nothing" (144). She attempts to destroy whatever would have such a hold over her, and this includes the man she loves, Howard Roark.

The lesson that Dominique has to learn is that it is possible to have something that no one can take away, and the person to teach it to her is Howard Roark. She meets Roark in the quarry owned by her father, and they exchange frank, sexual glances and stares. Once again, Rand presents the initiation of sex and love as an act of sadomasochism and of feminine subordination and passivity: "One gesture of tenderness from him—and she would have remained cold, untouched by the thing done to her body. But the act of a master taking shameful, contemptuous possession of her was the kind of rapture she had wanted" (217).

For Roark's part: "They had been united in an understanding beyond the violence, beyond the deliberate obscenity of his action; had she meant less to him, he would not have taken her as he did; had he meant less to her, she would not have fought so desperately. The unrepeatable exaltation was in knowing that they both understood this" (218).

With this controversial scene, Rand betrays the inequality but complementarity in her view of gender roles. That a man must conquer a woman, and that the willingness and tenderness of both partners in this initial act would be devalued, not only rounds out our view of Rand's concept of man worship as slavery and torture, but illustrates once again how conventional a view of gender roles and sexuality Rand actually possesses. This sort of scene is played out dozens of times in Hollywood movies and in gothic romance novels. Rand merely uses her intellectual brilliance to justify it in a way more eloquent than usual.

Speaking of gothic heroines and the propensity toward masochism in that genre, Michelle A. Masse (1992, 3) says, "[T]he intertwining of love and pain is not natural and does not originate in the self: women are taught masochism through fiction and culture, and masochism's causes are external and real." She continues: "Masochism is the end of a long and varyingly successful cultural training. This training leaves its traces upon individual characters and upon the Gothic itself, which broods upon its originating trauma, the denial of autonomy or separation for women, throughout the centuries. Women's schooling in masochism, the turning inward of active drives, seems to naturalize that denial and makes it appear to spring from within rather than without."

Although *The Fountainhead* is not a gothic novel, the behavior of its heroine seems to fit like a gothic glove. "The ideology of romance insists that there never was any pain or renunciation, that the suffering they experience is really the love and recognition for which they long or at least its prelude," says Masse (3–4). Dominique equates her surrender to Roark with the loss of freedom, and for this reason she does not want to know his name—in a kind of ironic twist on the gothic heroine's sensibilities. But she both loves and hates him; she wants to destroy him. "I have hurt you today. I'll do it again. I'll come to you whenever I have beaten you—whenever I know that I have hurt you—and I'll let you own me. I want to be owned, not by a lover, but by an adversary who will destroy my victory over him, not with honorable blows, but with the touch of his body on mine" (Rand [1943] 1993, 273). Dominique wants to destroy what she most admires and, in doing so, suffers complete debasement of herself and her values.

It is not Rand's personal taste or belief in love and sex at issue here, so much as the symbolic consequences of that belief system couched in the underlying masculine-feminine dichotomy of Western culture. For the aggressive-passive relationship—the dominance-submission, the conquering-conquered, the sadomasochistic symbolism of the sex act and self-torture of the love relationship that Rand proposes—becomes generalized beyond the sexual domain itself to relationships generally between women and men.

It is Howard Roark who gives direction to Dominique Francon and meaning to her life. But it is architecture that gives meaning to Roark's own life. No matter how much Dominique wounds herself or Roark—shifting commissions away from him to less talented architects, lying about his talent to the world (or pretending to), showing complicity in the very kinds of attitudes she claims to disdain—she can never elevate herself to his status, or lower him to hers. She can only attach herself to him in the end and look up to him like a god—a god who is her salvation. In fact, in her notebooks, Rand spoke of Dominique as "the perfect priestess."[9] The psychology behind Dominique's character is a pathological outcome of feminine-masculine relations as conceived by Rand.

Fortunately, Rand manages to curb these sadomasochistic tendencies in her masterpiece, *Atlas Shrugged*. In this work, she presents a female character unparalleled in any of her other work. Dagny Taggart is Rand's most complete woman.[10] Dagny has all the markings of Rand's ideal woman: she is wealthy, beautiful, educated, excels in a masculine profession (engineering), and she runs a railroad. She is independent of thought and action, and she is deeply in touch with her own sexuality. *Atlas Shrugged* was first published in 1957—a time in the United States when undercurrents of female discontent were just beginning to rise to the surface. In this respect, Dagny Taggart was well ahead of her time as a career woman with her own moral standards.

Although Dagny is an active heroine, her role in relation to Galt—the most ideal of the ideal men in *Atlas Shrugged*—represents the reconstitution of feminine subordination to masculine principle. Although Dagny enters a typically male profession, she is subordinated for gender purposes through her positioning as the practical vice-president versus the creator (or even destroyer) represented by John Galt. Thus, Rand reestablishes the superior position of the masculine over the feminine. *Atlas Shrugged*, in one respect, is the story of how John Galt teaches Dagny that her approach to life is wrong—that there are overriding principles involved that he knows and must teach her. But there is nothing that Dagny can teach John Galt. Dagny is a marvelous female character, but she is part of a pattern that privileges men and masculinity. One might say that she hits a metaphysical glass ceiling due to her femininity.

As Virginia Woolf (1979, 65) noted: "To cast out and incorporate in a person of the opposite sex all that we miss in ourselves and desire in the universe and detest in humanity is a deep and universal instinct on the part both of men and of women. But though it affords relief, it does not lead to understanding."

To the question, "Who is John Galt?" we can then answer, "Ayn Rand."

In her quest to create men she could admire, Rand denies to her female characters the depth and breadth of thought and creativity that she allows her male characters. Roark creates skyscrapers, Rearden invents a miracle metal, and Galt stops the motor of the world. Although Dagny Taggart comes close, no female character in Rand's novels can measure up to this kind of creativity and productivity.

Rand, Feminism, and the Legacy of Female Subordination

The struggle of women and men to free themselves from the entanglements of cultural models of gender does not rest only on the clarification of rights. Beyond the defining of individual rights, we must also take into account the accuracy with which our cultural models convey reality to us. In other words, it is not enough to establish the rights of women in order to eliminate inequities in society. It is the unconscious and unchanging status of our cultural models of gender that threatens to recreate systems of female subordination even in cases in which rights are clearly defined.

There is a tendency for those who sympathize with Rand's philosophical positions to let her off too easily when it comes to questions of gender. They fail to acknowledge how great a contradiction there was between her professed stance and her actual behavior and conclusions. Rand—as she herself often declared—was not a feminist, not because she did not believe in the equality of women, but because she did not value women as people and because she did not understand how her own contradictions compromised them.[11] Any human being is capable of purpose, action, and creativity, but Rand reserves these characteristics for men. Her women are born wealthy and beautiful—their occupations handed to them through their family connections. While Roark and Galt have had to earn their way, fight for what they wanted, prove their worthiness, Rand's heroines merely exist.

Nathaniel Branden once said that any conflict between reason and emotion was a conflict between two ideas (1969, 68). In Rand's case, the ideas in conflict were (1) women as men's intellectual equals and (2) reason as the province of masculinity. Rand never resolved the conflict, because she never allowed it to become conscious. Her repression of feeling made this contradiction forever inaccessible to her conscious mind. Consequently, the conflict influenced her ability to reason effectively wherever gender issues were concerned.

Rand was known proudly to proclaim that she was not a feminist. She did not see feminism as a movement to establish rights or to acknowledge women as full human beings—a move that might have solved her dilemma. Rather than the consequence of an independent mind, Rand's conception of gender constitutes her integration of her personal psychological needs and culturally acceptable role models. Because this is the case, Rand's gender assumptions, arising from emotional needs that she did not acknowledge, are in conflict with her rational view of women as individuals and the equals of men.

In her position on a woman president, Rand attempts to justify with reason what is essentially an irrational but deeply held emotional conviction: that in order to be feminine, a woman must have a man to look up to. Although many of us might take the position that women and men can be equals, friends, and lovers without compromising any of those positions, such a position is impossible for Rand because she has internalized contradictory sets of assumptions.

Her only way out of these contradictions—the only way she can make all of the assumptions work—is to subordinate women to men in a single aspect of their lives. Since this allows Rand to have everything of importance that she wants, the sacrifice seems insignificant. However, it is larger than she thinks, for in her most significant works, reason is equated with men, and women are subordinated generally. Thus, the relative positioning of women to men, as becomes apparent in Rand's argument about a woman president, is unconsciously replicated in all of her fictional works from *Anthem* on. The ultimate cost of Rand's gender struggle is the structural inequality of women.

However, there is an even greater irony here from which Rand could never escape: that it was a woman who created the ideal men and infused them with her own reason. The fact that Rand found it necessary to create such men, like Pygmalion created Galatea, breathing reason into them from her own great mind, calls attention to the facts: (1) that at least one woman existed who had such a mind; (2) that in her lifetime, Rand never in fact found a man who, to her satisfaction, was her intellectual equal.

Western models of masculinity and femininity are elaborate but inadequate representations of sexual reality. Thus, they are in conflict with real men and women. The dissonance generated by the conflict between one's inclinations and cultural expectations is a difficult burden to bear. Human beings are ingenious, and they can use their minds and imaginations to fashion solutions that quell the dissonance and create some comfort, however temporary. But there is often slippage between the real and the imagined—a slippage that impels us toward the rationalization of our own defenses of weakness.

Rand rejected the masculine fields of engineering and mathematics, which she was, in fact, urged to pursue by those who knew her talents. She also rejected philosophy proper, at first, in spite of her talent as a logician, in favor of the more approved (for women) field of novel writing, in which she could indulge her fantasies and have a field in which to play out her conflicts. She rejected an academic or business environment for the glamour and sparkle of Hollywood. She wrote not for the purpose of developing her own important ideas, but to create her ideal man. Indeed, Rand never had children but formed around her a "family" of which she was, in fact, the dreaded matriarch who ended her life having driven away most of its members (Branden 1986, 386–404).

Rand's life and work, then, can be seen in terms of a total strategy that emerged from the attempt to accomplish two opposing ends: to exercise her powerful intellect and to claim the very "femininity" it suborned. Rejection of the highest office in the land was a symbolic emotional act, not a rational one—a sacrifice necessary to make the strategy work. And that is why Ayn Rand was a woman who would *not* be president.

Notes

1. Schiebinger (1993) traces the historical route through which cultural models of gender were inculcated into science itself. See also Schiebinger 1989.

2. Breakwell cites the following to support her conclusions: Archer and Lloyd 1982; Broverman et al. 1972; Deaux 1985; Eichler 1980; Fransella and Frost 1977; Glennon 1979; Maccoby and Jacklin 1974; Williams and Giles 1978. See also Tavris 1992. These are primarily psychological studies.

3. Some of the cross-cultural studies cited by Chodorow include D'Andrade 1966; Whiting 1963; Whiting and Child 1953; Whiting and Whiting 1975. For specifically anthropological—that is, cross-cultural—approaches to gender, see Sanday 1981; Brettell and Sargent 1997.

4. Biographical details about Rand's life are scarce. The major source used here is Branden 1986. The facts about Rand's early life discussed in Branden's book are based on interviews with Rand herself. Other sources include Sciabarra 1995; Rand 1995, 1997. For a discussion of the Silver Age and its influence on Rand, see Sciabarra 1995, 31–35. Sciabarra discusses at length the Russian Symbolists, their inculcation of Nietzschean ideas, and their emphasis on an androgynous ideal (34). Rand seems to have picked up on the Nietzschean ideas in their work but not that of androgyny. As I show, for Rand the exercise of certain male prerogatives (like running a railroad) is more of a novelty than a statement of androgyny. In her own thinking, she makes a clear distinction between metaphysical masculinity and femininity. In any event, the concept of androgyny itself is problematic in many cases where it is advanced, because it leaves in place the fundamental assumptions of basic difference (as opposed to biological difference) that it is determined to remedy.

5. Barbara Branden (1986) points out that Rand's childhood was largely an unhappy one. "Her father's seeming indifference to her and her mother's disapproval had to be sources of anguish to the child" (5). Rand told Branden that it was not until she was fourteen that she felt close to her father; it was then that they began discussing ideas (4). Rand's struggles with her parents have all of the markings of a classic Oedipal adventure in which a young girl sees her mother as a rival and her father as an ideal man, and may very well be the source of Rand's need to have her femininity affirmed.

6. "Fronz" may have been a nickname Rand used for her father, whose name was Zinovy Zakharovich Rosenbaum. Rand's mother was Anna Borisovna Rosenbaum. Rand's real name was Alissa Zinovievna Rosenbaum. Regarding this matter, see Sciabarra 1995, 389 n. 1. Branden (1986) refers to the young Rand as "Alice."

7. Rand (1964, 7) explicitly states: "If they place such things as friendship and family ties above their own productive work, yes, then they are immoral. Friendship, family life, and human relationships are not primary in a man's life." She also states, "I believe that women are human beings. What is proper for a man is proper for a woman. The basic principles are the same." She further states, "There is no particular work which is specifically feminine. Women can choose their work according to their own purpose and premises in the same manner as men do."

8. Indeed, Rand's emphasis on "highest" values creates a genuine dilemma for human beings generally. What happens when the person deemed our highest value does not hold us as a highest value in return? This is a problem that is present in all of Rand's novels and that she never directly addresses.

9. Quoted from Rand's journal, cited in Peikoff 1993, 696. Also in Rand 1997, 89.

10. Indeed, it is Dagny Taggart people usually think of when they see feminist tendencies in Rand's work. For example, see Gladstein 1978, reprinted in this volume.

11. A feminist, as defined here, is someone who thinks not only that women should have equal rights with men but that women have equal metaphysical status. Although I have no doubt that Rand believed women to have equal rights, I think that she equivocates about their humanity when she speaks of man's "metaphysical" superiority. For example, in a letter to a high school teacher dated 2 May 1964, Rand responds to Thomas A. Bond with regard to a "Rand Temple," designed by one of his students, in which figures of John Galt and Dagny Taggart appear: "Speaking Symbolically, if the figures are dubbed 'John and Dagny,' their positions should be reversed, because an ideal woman is a man-worshipper, and an ideal man is the highest symbol of mankind" (1995, 623). In

her essay "The Age of Envy," Rand makes a distinction between "equality before the law" and "metaphysical equality" (1975, 164). She assumes that metaphysical equality is a matter of individual variations, in which case human beings cannot be equal (164–65). Therefore she, like many classical liberal thinkers, makes the mistake of equating egalitarianism with a desire to erase real human differences. I would argue that this is an erroneous approach. By "metaphysical equality," Rand is really talking about "identity." Human beings are not identical; therefore, they are not "equal" in the sense of being the same. However, from an anthropological and biological viewpoint, all human beings are equally human in that they all possess the qualities that define human beings as a species, and therefore possess a common human nature in spite of the variations that exist among them. Also, men as individuals are as different from one another as they are from women; therefore, as individuals and collectively, women and men deserve equal metaphysical status. In fact, individual rights have their basis in an assumption of human equality—a point often overlooked but that serves as the real moral basis of human life. Because of her overemphasis on the individual, Rand overlooks this fundamental assumption common to almost all classical liberal theoreticians. Beyond this, Rand clearly lacks sympathy for women generally, which must at least make us suspicious of some of her views. For example, in her harangue against Women's Lib in the same essay, Rand states: "As a group, American women are the most privileged females on earth: they control the wealth of the United States—through inheritance from fathers and husbands who work themselves into an early grave, struggling to provide every comfort and luxury for the bridge-playing, cocktail-party-chasing cohorts, who give them very little in return" (173).

This characterization of American women is as much of a caricature as the movement Rand derides here. It assumes "privilege" rather than the possibility that women have contributed anything to their own well-being in the form of both wage labor and unremunerated work. Rand here also defends a system that, at the time this essay was written, did in fact have laws still denying women equal rights with men in terms of freedom to work, property rights, and rights over their own bodies. And like many other commentators, Rand viewed feminism as a monolithic social movement. Feminism is a broad-based philosophical approach that has many different ideological and theoretical strains. See Tong 1989.

References

Archer, John, and Barbara Lloyd. 1982. *Sex and Gender*. Harmondsworth, Middlesex: Penguin.

Attwood, Lynne. 1985. The new Soviet man and woman: Soviet views on psychological sex differences. In *Soviet Sisterhood*, edited by Barbara Holland. Bloomington: Indiana University Press.

Branden, Barbara. 1986. *The Passion of Ayn Rand*. Garden City, N.Y.: Doubleday.

Branden, Nathaniel. 1969. *The Psychology of Self-Esteem: A New Concept of Man's Psychological Nature*. Los Angeles: Nash Publishing.

Breakwell, Glynis M. 1990. Social beliefs about gender differences. In *The Social Psychological Study of Widespread Beliefs*, edited by Colin Fraser and George Gaskell. Oxford: Clarendon Press.

Brettell, Caroline B., and Carolyn F. Sargent, eds. 1997. *Gender in Cross-Cultural Perspective*. 2d ed. Upper Saddle River, N.J.: Prentice Hall.

Broverman, I. K., D. M. Broverman, F. E. Clarkson, P. S. Rosenkrantz, and S. R. Vogel. 1972. Sex-role stereotypes: A current appraisal. *Journal of Social Issues* 28:59–78.

Chodorow, Nancy J. 1989. *Feminism and Psychoanalytic Theory*. New Haven: Yale University Press.

D'Andrade, Roy. 1966. Sex differences and cultural institutions. In *The Development of Sex Differences*, edited by Eleanor Maccoby. Stanford: Stanford University Press.

Deaux, Kay. 1985. Sex and gender. *Annual Review of Psychology* 36:49–81.

Eichler, M. 1980. *The Double Standard: A Feminist Critique of Feminist Social Science*. London: Croom Helm.

Festinger, Leon. 1957. *A Theory of Cognitive Dissonance*. Stanford: Stanford University Press.

Fransella, F., and K. Frost. 1977. *On Being a Woman*. London: Tavistock.

Gladstein, Mimi Reisel. 1978. Ayn Rand and feminism: An unlikely alliance. *College English* 39, no. 6:680–85.

Glennon, Lynda M. 1979. *Women and Dualism: A Sociology of Knowledge Analysis*. New York: Longman.

Hallowell, A. Irving. 1955. *Culture and Experience*. New York: Schocken.

Hubbs, Joanna. 1988. *Mother Russia: The Feminine Myth in Russian Culture*. Bloomington: Indiana University Press.

Kaplan, Louise J. 1991. *Female Perversions*. Garden City, N.Y.: Doubleday Anchor.

Maccoby, Eleanor E., and Carol N. Jacklin. 1974. *The Psychology of Sex Differences*. Stanford: Stanford University Press.

Masse, Michelle A. 1992. *In the Name of Love: Women, Masochism, and the Gothic*. Ithaca, N.Y.: Cornell University Press.

Peikoff, Leonard. 1984. Introduction to *The Early Ayn Rand: A Selection from Her Unpublished Fiction*, edited by Leonard Peikoff. New York: New American Library.

———. 1993. Afterword to the 50th anniversary ed. of *The Fountainhead*. New York: New American Library.

Rand, Ayn. [1936] 1959. *We the Living*. New York: Random House.

———. [1943] 1993. *The Fountainhead*. 50th anniversary ed. New York: New American Library.

———. [1946] 1969. *Anthem*. Caldwell, Idaho: Caxton Printers.

———. 1957. *Atlas Shrugged*. New York: Random House.

———. 1964. *Playboy* interview: Ayn Rand. Alvin Toffler, interviewer. *Playboy*, March, 35–43.

———. 1975. *The New Left: The Anti-Industrial Revolution*. 2nd rev. ed. New York: New American Library.

———. 1984. *The Early Ayn Rand: A Selection from Her Unpublished Fiction*. Edited by Leonard Peikoff. New York: New American Library.

———. 1989. *The Voice of Reason: Essays in Objectivist Thought*. Edited by Leonard Peikoff. New York: New American Library.

———. 1995. *Letters of Ayn Rand*. Edited by Michael S. Berliner. New York: Dutton.

———. 1997. *Journals of Ayn Rand*. Edited by David Harriman. New York: Dutton.

Sanday, Peggy Reeves. 1981. *Female Power and Male Dominance: On the Origins of Sexual Inequality*. Cambridge: Cambridge University Press.

Schiebinger, Londa. 1989. *The Mind Has No Sex? Women in the Origins of Modern Science*. Cambridge, Mass.: Harvard University Press.

———. 1993. *Nature's Body: Gender in the Making of Modern Science*. Boston: Beacon Press.

Sciabarra, Chris Matthew. 1995. *Ayn Rand: The Russian Radical*. University Park: Pennsylvania State University Press.

Stoller, Robert J. 1985. *Presentations of Gender*. New Haven: Yale University Press.

Tavris, Carol. 1992. *The Mismeasure of Woman: Why Women are not the Better Sex, the Inferior Sex, or the Opposite Sex*. New York: Simon & Schuster.

Tong, Rosemarie. 1989. *Feminist Thought: A Comprehensive Introduction*. Boulder: West-view Press.

Whiting, Beatrice B., ed. 1963. *Six Cultures: Studies in Child Rearing*. New York: John Wiley & Sons.

Whiting, Beatrice B., and John W. M. Whiting. 1975. *Children of Six Cultures: A Psycho-Cultural Analysis*. Cambridge, Mass.: Harvard University Press.

Whiting, John W. M., and Irvin L. Child. 1953. *Child Training and Personality*. New Haven: Yale University Press.

Williams, J. A., and H. Giles. 1978. The changing status of women in society: An inter-group perspective. In *Differentiation Between Social Groups*, edited by H. Tajfel. London: Academic Press.

Woolf, Virginia. 1979. *Women and Writing*. New York: Harcourt Brace Jovanovich.

16

Rereading Rand on Gender in the Light of Paglia

Robert Sheaffer

Ayn Rand's attitudes toward feminist issues represent a serious problem for many of her contemporary followers. Especially problematic are her views on the desirability of male dominance in heterosexual relationships, and her descriptions of erotic encounters that appear to some to be rape. Writing during the early years of modern feminism, Rand rejected feminist demands *in toto* with a sense of disgust exceeding even that which she evinced toward collectivism. The idea of "woman as victim" struck her as even more absurd than that of "the poor as victim": "Every other pressure group has some semi-plausible complaint or pretense at a complaint, as an excuse for existing. Women's Lib has none" (Rand [1971] 1975, 175). Consequently, most feminists have either ignored Rand or treated her with contempt. However, a careful reading of the

Randian canon suggests that it contains much valuable material that has too long been overlooked.

A peculiar paradox of Rand is that while Randian heroines such as Dagny Taggart or Dominique Francon doggedly pursue excellence in their own careers, they nonetheless explicitly seek out men who will outshine them. When they are so fortunate as to find one, they worshipfully bask in the glow of his more brilliant male light. Some might dismiss the pronouncements of fictional characters as not necessarily representing Rand's own views. However, in Rand's philosophical novels, the protagonists invariably state Rand's own views quite distinctly, just as the antagonists can be counted on to enunciate whatever views she despises.[1] Even when a protagonist displays a weakness or flaw, it would seem to be a flaw that Rand recognized in herself. Rand's nonfiction works clearly confirm her fictional characters' beliefs that male dominance in a relationship is healthy, normal, and, indeed, desirable: "[F]or a woman *qua* woman, the essence of femininity is hero worship—the desire to look up to man" (Rand [1968] 1989, 268).

This attitude, of course, is difficult to understand from the perspective of mainstream contemporary feminism. Where could Rand possibly have gotten such ideas, especially since her female protagonists are otherwise so strong and independent, and reject the role of homemaker and mother? Many contemporary Randians have gone to considerable lengths to distance themselves from Rand's views on sex roles and feminism, as well as to cast her apparently misguided views in the best possible light. This is especially true of Randian sympathizers outside the official Objectivist camp. "If ever there was a woman whose life and thought should have brought her into the feminist movement, Ayn Rand was that woman," writes Joan Kennedy Taylor (1992, 24). "And yet, paradoxically, she considered herself an enemy of feminism and often wrote and spoke of feminists in pejorative terms." Taylor clearly thinks that Rand was mistaken on this issue. However, the context of Rand's critiques clearly indicates that they are directed toward feminists who endlessly proclaim women to be "victims." Rand was certainly not against the liberation of women as individuals.

Where did Rand get her ideas on the positive aspects of male dominance? Was she indoctrinated by her society, and by her time, to conform to the socially accepted view of a woman's role? This would seem, from what we know of Rand, unlikely: Any attempt to argue that Rand was coerced by intense social pressure in favor of traditional sex roles would look feeble given the ease with which she withstood the even more intense pressure within her social milieu to acquiesce in socialism, which at that time was as powerful in intellectual circles as feminism is today. Furthermore, Rand did rebel in large part against the view of a woman's role that prevailed during the period 1930–65, when most of her works were written. What could have inspired a major woman writer to advocate and depict strongly nontraditional roles for her female characters, yet still insist on the validity of traditional heterosexual relationships? Are there any recent developments or insights within contemporary feminism that can help us to understand Rand's thinking on this subject?

A new insight into the source of Rand's ideas on heterosexual relationships might be found in the writings of Camille Paglia, a maverick feminist and one of the leading literary critics of our age. As was Rand, Paglia is a woman of Herculean accomplishment and almost inexhaustible energy. Like Rand, Paglia promotes the idea that a woman can, and often should, take on traditionally male roles. Also like Rand, Paglia understands the fundamental ambivalence of the woman of accomplishment toward domination by men: it can have some good aspects, along with the bad. Paglia argues that those who proclaim male dominance and female submission to be arbitrary social constructs do so primarily from ideological fervor, not solid evidence. She shows (for example, in Paglia 1992, 240–45) how much of the widely accepted contemporary feminist position is based upon abysmally unsound scholarship. "Despite my deviant and rebellious beginnings," she writes, "I have been led by my studies to reaffirm the most archaic myths about male and female. I aim to recover the truth in sexual stereotypes" (108).

Both Nathaniel Branden and Leonard Peikoff, as Chris Matthew Sciabarra (1995, 199) notes, now uphold the position that "there are culturally related differences in how men and women deal with their emotions. In this culture, women are encouraged to exercise their emotions, whereas men are encouraged to intellectualize them. . . . In this regard, both Branden and Peikoff agree, surprisingly, with modern feminist methodology." In saying this, Branden and Peikoff are echoing the prevailing feminist teaching that observed differences between male and female behavior are the effects of arbitrary social conditioning, making such differences accidental, not essential.

Significantly, none of the latter-day Randians who proclaim sex roles to be culturally determined identifies any other culture where this difference between the sexes is absent, let alone reversed. Widespread claims of "gender-reversed" societies supposedly chronicled by Margaret Mead were denied by Mead herself. Even Simone de Beauvoir, one of the Founding Mothers of contemporary feminism, concurs that "[s]ociety has always been male; political power has always been in the hands of men" (1974, 79). Steven Goldberg (1993) suggests that, contrary to claims that are widespread in women's studies classes and texts, all human societies, without exception, display male dominance of social hierarchies, expect dominance by the male in dyadic relationships, and associate whatever achievements are most highly valued by that society with the male sex. All claimed exceptions are found to be unsupported by primary anthropological sources, that is, ethnologies of the society in question. Goldberg examines every claimed exception to the universality of patriarchy that has (to his knowledge) thus far been presented. In every case, upon consulting a formal ethnography describing that society (sometimes even written by the person later claiming an exception!), the supposed exception is found to be invalid. Often a considerable degree of ingenuity has been expended to manufacture an "exception" where none exists. Anyone wishing to maintain that sex roles are arbitrary social constructs must explain why every human society that has ever existed has come up with the same supposedly arbitrary construct. Goldberg considers, and rejects, nonbiological explanations for this remarkable human universal.

Ayn Rand's marriage to Frank O'Connor clearly represented an example of inverted sex roles. While the early writings of the Rand circle attempt to portray O'Connor as a Galt-like hero (e.g., Branden and Branden 1962), it is now indisputable that, though he was a very generous and decent man, Frank O'Connor was no John Galt. Barbara Branden notes that Rand made all the major decisions in their marriage, such as where to live (Branden 1986). Rand was invariably the one who initiated sex. O'Connor would play the role of peacemaker, trying to smooth ruffled feathers after every philosophical or personal conflict. This means, of course, that Ayn took on the traditionally male role of dyadic dominance, while Frank played the traditionally female role of conciliator and helpmate. Nathaniel Branden described Frank O'Connor as "a very, very passive man . . . not intellectually inclined . . . not motivated by powerful purposes in any sense" (in Gladstein 1984, 9). That makes him the precise opposite of John Galt. Given that Rand glorified the concept of man-as-hero, it would seem that no matter how much genuine affection she felt for her husband, she cannot have failed to be profoundly disappointed by his lack of heroism and dominance. This supposition would explain why her major novels were fundamentally a woman's quest for a hero, and perhaps why she began her affair with Nathaniel Branden.

Undoubtedly, the greatest stumbling block to Rand's contemporary feminist followers is the scene in *The Fountainhead* where Howard Roark enters Dominique's bedroom uninvited, throws her down on the bed, and ravishes her. Dominique, we are told, simultaneously craves domination by Roark and also fears it and powerfully fights against it. But when Roark perseveres and has his way with her, she surrenders, and experiences the highest ecstasies of passion. We learn that "the act of a master taking contemptuous possession of her was the kind of rapture she had wanted" (Rand 1943, 231), a sentiment that, to contemporary feminists, sounds utterly blasphemous. It is also a strange position to be espoused by a writer who keeps reminding us that "A is A." How can Dominique "want" to be taken by Roark, yet at the same time "not want" it and struggle against it? This comes dangerously close to maintaining "A and not-A." Indeed, the logical dichotomy between Dominique's sexual desires and her mental desire to retain control should have alerted Rand that sexual attraction is not simply "the physical expression of a tribute to personal values" (Rand 1957, 491), as she would have Francisco d'Anconia later state. If it were, talented men would be sexually excited by female academics and artists of any age and bodily shape, instead of young cheerleaders and centerfolds. Does Rand seriously expect us to believe that the female body is, or at least should be, irrelevant to male sexual response? In real life, sexuality is often, at bottom, highly irrational, despite Rand's insistence that it ought not to be.

Seen from the perspective of Paglia, those who denounce the so-called rape scene in *The Fountainhead* are taking an excessively narrow perspective. Those of us who have been trained in the modern feminist tradition are hypersensitive to any situation that might look like rape. However, Paglia would argue that the controversial scene in *The Fountainhead* is by no means an unambiguous rape. Paglia (1994) has explained how, because of the female's natural ambivalence and indecision concerning sexuality and her habitual use of indirect and often ambiguous stratagems, the mating game must sometimes result in actions that look like rape. She notes, "Sex is inherently problematic" (32). She observes that "aggression and eroticism are deeply intertwined," and describes courtship as "a dangerous game in which the signals are not verbal but subliminal"

(1992, 51–52).[2] Therefore, to call the bedroom scene in *The Fountainhead* a "rape" is to misunderstand the subtleties of sex, a misunderstanding that some contemporary feminists seem to encourage.

In the novel, Rand sets forth very clearly the cat-and-mouse game that Dominique had been playing with Roark, one that clearly indicated to him her sexual interest. Upon seeing him working in the quarry, she senses his strength and masterfulness. They exchange long and amorous glances. She conceives a passion for him, and keeps coming back to watch him work. There is no other reason for her to do so except her infatuation with him, since there is no business need for her to stand watching over the quarry. She deliberately breaks a stone in the fireplace in her bedroom, then takes great pains to invite Roark—and only Roark—to come in to take measurements for a new stone. Her demeanor and conversation while in the bedroom indicate clearly that the purpose of the visit is not strictly business. When the new stone arrives, she sends again for Roark to install it. However, sensing the game she is playing, Roark sends instead an older, unattractive little man, presumably to discover Dominique's reaction. Afterward, she seeks Roark out to convey to him her anger, at his thwarting of her game plan, by asking, "Why didn't you come to set the marble?" To seek him out to ask such a question is tantamount to a direct admission of sexual interest; if all she cared about was the marble in her bedroom, rather than the man who might insert it, such a question would make no sense. At this point, Roark decides that the time for the endgame has arrived, and that night he creeps into her bedroom to do what he believes she has been signaling that she wants.

Because Rand once remarked that Dominique Francon represented Rand in a bad mood, some have argued that the "rape" scene in *The Fountainhead* is an aberration, and not representative of Rand's thinking on the erotic. It is interesting, however, that in detailing the relationship of Howard Roark and Dominique Francon in her journals, Rand generalizes the principle: "*Like most women*, and to a greater degree than most, [Dominique] *is a masochist* and she wishes for the happiness of suffering at Roark's hands. Sexually, Roark has a great deal of the sadist, and he finds pleasure in breaking her will and her defiance" (Rand 1997, 231, emphasis added).

This model guides Rand in many instances throughout her fiction. A similar quasi-rape, or ravishment, exists in Rand's play, *Night of January 16th* (Rand [1933] 1971, act II, p. 82). Karen Andre is a young stenographer who is on the first day of her first job, working for the wealthy Bjorn Faulkner. She later says, "He seemed to take a delight in giving me orders. He acted as if he were cracking a whip over an animal he wanted to break." Not only does Miss Andre seem not to mind such dominating behavior, but her subsequent attachment to him suggests that she relishes it greatly. At the end of the first workday, Bjorn asks her whether she has ever "belonged to any man." She replies that she has not. "He said he'd give me a thousand kroner if I would go to the inner office and take my skirt off. I said I wouldn't. He said if I didn't, he'd take me. I said, try it. He did" (83). This sex scene is much briefer than the one in *The Fountainhead*, offering us correspondingly less opportunity to discern the nuances of the situation. However, it is significant that when Bjorn threatens to "take" Karen, she, instead of running for the door, screaming for help, replies "try it." This indicates at least some degree of consent, however ambiguous. Karen remains with Bjorn that night, obviously very taken with him, and subsequently lives with him for ten years. Since Bjorn begins by offering Karen money in exchange for sex, some might object that the incident represents, not a rough seduction, but prostitution. However, Karen declines the proffered sum and in effect challenges Bjorn to come try and conquer what he had attempted to buy, suggesting that her sexual interest in him is genuine.

In *Atlas Shrugged* (1957, 956), Dagny Taggart has her first sexual encounter with the mysterious John Galt, whom she previously met in the hidden paradise of Galt's Gulch, while she is inspecting one of her company's railroad tunnels under Manhattan. Working incognito as a manual laborer, he follows her into a deserted corner of a tunnel. Without speaking a word, he begins undressing her, and her passion swells into total ecstasy. Only afterward does he speak to her. In *We the Living*, the second sexual encounter between Kira Argounova and Leo Kovalensky also takes place in total silence: "[W]ithout a word, he unbuttoned her dress; she stood still and let him undress her" (Rand [1936] 1959, 111). (In their first sexual encounter, on a boat, Leo simply orders Kira to take her clothes off; she, of course, complies.) Such "rough seductions" are too numerous in the Randian canon to be dismissed as mere aberrations or "bad moods."

Today, of course, some jurisdictions have criminalized such silent sexual encounters. These games may well be dangerous ones to play, but Rand's scenes do not depict "rape," except in the expanded sense suggested by some contemporary feminists. Millions of women, reading

Rand's stories, have found them and continue to find them to be wonderfully romantic. The possibility of miscommunication when playing such games is indeed considerable, with serious or even fatal consequences for the man should he miscalculate. However, for centuries this kind of game has been the only game in town—you either play it this way or don't play at all. Ambiguous and indirect stratagems have been used by some women from time immemorial to entice attractive men, and any critic of these so-called rape scenes who fails to recognize that fact would seem to be largely ignorant of world literature and history.

Furthermore, a comparison of the much-reviled scene in *The Fountainhead* to the standard fare of contemporary romance novels, which sell many millions of copies each year and are read almost exclusively by women, indicates that Rand clearly sensed the pulse of the often-unexpressed, secret desires inside the hearts of millions of modern women. These romance novels, which are usually considered to be delightfully sensual and exciting, typically tell the story of a heroine who, being ravished by the right kind of attractive rogue, falls madly in love with him. Should it be so surprising that certain mainstays of female mass-market romance novels might turn up in the writings of a celebrated female Romantic novelist? The irony is that, while Rand denounced writings that offered sensual titillation to the masses, her own novels contained many of these very same elements.

But even the radical feminist Catherine A. Mackinnon views heterosexual relations as implying male dominance, which to her is the ultimate obscenity. Mackinnon, who claims to discern no difference between heterosexual intercourse and rape, admits that, for many women, "dominance is eroticized" (1989, 177). This constitutes her explanation of why most women not only submit to being raped (i.e., having intercourse), but even seem to enjoy it. That the eroticization of dominance might contain elements that are healthy and normal is apparently not a hypothesis worthy of consideration.

A woman's ambivalence toward sexuality, and her tendency to fall in love with a man who takes possession of her, are well established in world literature. As an unwavering booster of Victor Hugo, Rand must surely have been familiar with his novel *Le roi s'amuse*, which was adapted into the libretto for Verdi's opera *Rigoletto*. In it, the king, who wanders about incognito, toys with a young maiden's affections. He crudely ravishes her, humiliates her, then abandons her. Yet later, when he finds himself in a perilous situation, the maiden gives her life to save his.

Elsewhere in the world of Romantic opera, a paradigm of sexuality may be found in Bizet's wildly popular *Carmen*, whose title character is perhaps the supreme archetype of the *femme fatale* in all the world's opera; she celebrates the ineffability, even perversity, of love in her deathless phrases:

> L'amour est enfant de Bohème
> Il n'a jamais, jamais connu de loi
> Si tu ne m'aimes pas, je t'aime
> Si je t'aime, prends garde a toi!

> Love is a Gypsy child
> It has never, never known any law
> If you don't love me, I love you
> If I love you, watch out!

Paglia (1991b, 13) writes that "feminism dismisses the femme fatale as a cartoon and libel. If she ever existed, she was simply a victim of society, resorting to destructive womanly wiles because of her lack of access to political power. The femme fatale was a career woman *manquée*, her energies neurotically diverted into the boudoir. By such techniques of demystification, feminism has painted itself into a corner." Given the way that Carmen's phrases have resonated in the world's psyche for the last century, I submit that they have vastly greater authenticity than any latter-day reduction of human sexuality to a set of slogans, rational values, or political prescriptions. Even Simone de Beauvoir acknowledges the impossibility of ever understanding sexual desire, let alone controlling it, or reducing it to a set of principles: "The fact is that eroticism implies a claim of the instant against time, of the individual against the group; it affirms separation against communication; it is rebellion against all regulation; it contains a principle hostile to society" (1974, 212). I am convinced that de Beauvoir's characterization is quite correct.

Paglia, who acknowledges her debt to de Beauvoir, writes: "The permanence of the femme fatale as a sexual persona is part of the weary weight of eroticism, beneath which both ethics and religion flounder. Eroticism is society's soft point, through which it is invaded by chthonian nature" (1991b, 15). The undefinable, uncontrollable, and even perverse operation of human sexuality makes eroticism the soft underbelly of every ordered society. It is a naturally occurring erosive force like wind and tide, whose operation tends to break down all structures intended to be permanent: dynasties, alliances, corporations, and most especially families. The extreme puritanism that has long been recognized as a trait of Protestant and other strongly achievement-oriented societies is probably a recognition of the threat posed by erotic impulse to all deliberate, long-range plans.

Paglia (1991a) discusses quite explicitly her own conflict between sexual desire and the desire to retain control. She explains that her own sex life "has been an absolute disaster, because I've never been able to connect with someone. On the one hand, I'm attracted to men, but cannot give up my independent power as a woman to them—I cannot submit." Before the bedroom scene, Dominique Francon might have said exactly the same thing. Like Rand, Paglia expects that a fully satisfactory heterosexual relationship requires a man who is willing and able to be dominant, and a woman who is willing and able to submit. For women as powerfully intimidating as Paglia or Rand, such opportunities must be rare indeed. Paglia (1991b, 80) observes that while the Judeo-Christian tradition depicts female chastity as "devout self-sacrifice, . . . the Greeks saw chastity as an armed goddess of brazen ego," apparently reflecting their notion of the kind of woman who could successfully fend off male advances. Seen in the light of the modern world, the Greek model appears better to match reality.

Perhaps the best insight into Rand's thinking on the issue of male dominance can be gained from her essay "About a Woman President," in which she explains why she "would not vote for a woman president," and why "a woman cannot reasonably want to be a commander-in-chief" (Rand [1968] 1989, 267). She rejected the idea not on the grounds that no woman could do the job—Rand conceded that some probably could. She dismissed as "nonsense" the idea that women are inherently inferior, or too emotional to do the job. Rather, the problem that Rand foresaw is that "for a woman *qua* woman, the essence of femininity is hero worship—the desire to look up to man" (268). The president being "commander-in-chief," the very pinnacle of authority, any woman occupying such a position could find no man to look up to.

Hence, according to Rand, the problem with having a woman president lies not in a woman's ability, but rather in *what it would do to her*: "The issue is primarily psychological. It involves a woman's fundamental view of life, of herself and of her basic values" (268). The very act of a woman's becoming the supreme leader would render her, in Rand's view, no longer a woman. Another Randian irony is that practically nobody actually views the American president as the kind of supreme leader deserving of total submission, but Randian thinking appears to require that at least some people be imagined to deserve obedience, whether or not they actually do. Rand appears to be writing about the presidency not as it actually is, but rather as an abstract idea representing the pinnacle of successful striving for leadership and accomplishment. She is apparently viewing "the presidency" as the concrete representation of "the most difficult job to conquer," and she despairs for the femininity of any woman who might conquer what every man could not.

The leadership difficulty as construed would apply only to a heterosexual woman. It presumably would not rule out the possibility of a woman president who was a lesbian, and hence able to look downward into the hierarchy for a submissive feminine partner. It would also not pertain to a woman who was uninterested in sex and hence in need of no partner at all. However, Rand dismisses such choices as "metaphysically inappropriate." While she does not specifically mention lesbianism, she maintains her own paradigm of the heterosexual/romantic/man-worshiper to be the only "rational" choice for a woman, adding that "if she is *not* rational, she is unfit for the presidency or for any important position, anyway" (269).

This extremely vital essay is maddeningly short, making one wish Rand had dealt with some obvious implications of her theory, and also with complicating factors (but then Rand seldom worried a great deal about "complicating factors"). One factor she did not consider is the issue of parallel hierarchies. For example, a woman who was president might nonetheless look up to a man who was the greatest living artist, or the greatest scientist. History might well judge a great scientist or artist to be of greater significance than an undistinguished head of state.

But let us suppose that an unambiguous rank ordering of all achievers' accomplishments were possible, and that a woman ends up at the top. She obviously has no man to look up to, which, according to Rand, is for a "woman *qua* woman" a "metaphysically inappropriate" situation. Now suppose that a woman finds herself in the number two position: presumably, vice-president. Rand saw a difficulty *only* when a woman is at the absolute top. Yet, realistically, how different would the situation be for a woman who is second in command? The woman vice-president faces exactly the same dilemma as the woman president *unless* the hero she worships happens to be her running mate, the president himself.

Now let us move slowly downward from the very pinnacle, and observe how slowly the picture changes. Consider the case of a woman who finds herself at the 99.8 percentile on the hierarchy, say, a very important business executive. Rand foresaw no problem for her: "Even though she is the highest authority within that concern, she deals constantly with men who are not under her orders" (269). (Note how Rand considers a man's taking "orders" from a woman to render him *ipso facto* unworthy of her romantic affection. Given Rand's position of dominance within her own marriage, it seems highly unlikely that she could have hero-worshiped her husband, Frank O'Connor, although she obviously tried to convince others and perhaps herself that she did.)

If only one man in five hundred ranks above a certain unattached female executive, then for her 99.8 percent of all men are automatically ruled out as unworthy of hero worship. Undoubtedly nearly all of the remaining men are "taken," since there is an enormous demand for unattached men near the top. (There is, however, a correspondingly great surplus of unattached men in Salvation Army soup kitchens, since the demand for such unsuccessful men as romantic partners is virtually nil.) A man in a correspondingly high position can potentially choose a mate from among the 99.8 percent of women below him in the hierarchy, many of whom will be highly flattered by his advances, although Rand would insist that he must pursue and win the "most difficult" one, who presumably lies just below him in the hierarchy. The equally successful woman, however, must immediately *rule out* all but 0.2 percent of the men. This implies that while career advancement enhances a man's romantic prospects, for a woman it severely restricts them. I think that Rand fingered an extremely important issue here: female heterosexuality and female achievement seem to be inherently antithetical, even though Rand did not seem to understand the implications of her argument. The more you have of one, the less you can have of the other. Take either to an extreme, and you exclude the other completely, as in the case of the woman president.

Although it is not logically impossible for Dagny Taggart to find her John Galt, the odds are certainly stacked against her. Today's world contains a considerable number of Dagny Taggarts gazing far above themselves, looking for an infinitesimally small number of available John Galts. The real-life Ayn Rand never found hers. Where are all these heroic, manly, uncompromising, unattached men supposed to come from? Had Rand asked herself such a question, "Blank out" would have necessarily been the reply. Apparently it never occurred to Rand that, in promoting such ideals, she might be setting up her female followers for years of disappointment comparable to her own. Given such realities, only the congenital optimism of the hopeless romantic prevents her from either (*a*) lowering her standards, (*b*) reconciling herself to celibacy, or (*c*) embracing lesbianism. Rand's own example is telling, since no doubt her failure to find her own John Galt must have gnawed at her innards for decades. Romantic heterosexual hero worship may well be a viable option for the average woman, but it becomes increasingly difficult the higher the woman moves up the scale of heroism herself. It is indeed nearly impossible for the woman who herself sits very high up on the scale. Rand's novels may be read as a kind of epic quest by an unusually intelligent and accomplished woman seeking the Holy Grail of an unattached heroic dominant manly man. Such a man must necessarily be painted larger than life, to make him seem worthy of the hero worship of a heroine.

Nowhere does Rand seem to have considered those consequences to her female protagonists' prospects for future hero worship that result from their own pursuit of professional success. If a woman attains the position of a low-level executive, she forces her man to attain a higher-level one in order to keep her affection. If she becomes an assistant professor, he must attain at least the level of full professor. If she is elected to the House of Representatives, he must become at least a Senator. As soon as he fails to outshine her, he becomes unworthy of hero worship. There is the additional problem that, although he may outshine her while she is young, her loving admiration for him may slowly turn to contempt if during the ensuing years her accolades should grow faster than his. Thus the man married to a fast-rising career woman is placed under sustained, unrelenting career pressure, not for money's sake, but for love's.

Paglia (1994) bemoans the desexualization that seems to be the norm at the highest levels of female achievement. It is a problem, she suggests, that is at its worst in the Anglo-American world: "Unfortunately, when women achieve high positions in Britain and America, it seems to be at the price of their sexuality . . . at the executive level of the industrialized world, we may be cutting ourselves off at the neck. Our battle is not just with the male establishment but with ourselves: how do we keep mind and body together?" (180). Paglia, who professes lesbianism, seems to have dealt with the problem by doing without men entirely, a choice that she admits has carried for her a high cost. Paglia maintains that "[w]omen who want to achieve are at war with nature, as shown by the hormonally disordering effects of career stress or extreme athletic training" (41).[3] Nonetheless, Paglia encourages anyone who is so inclined to battle heroically the tyranny of nature, so long as he or she is aware of the potential risks.

Some may argue that this whole line of reasoning is invalid, and that hero worship has nothing to do with romantic love. However, Rand's entire concept of Romanticism is based upon hero worship. Furthermore, it is not difficult to show that the model above does indeed match the choices made by the great majority of women in real life. While it has been common for many decades for male doctors to marry female nurses, there is absolutely no hint of any trend suggesting that female doctors and male nurses, both nontraditional and presumably nonsexist, are linking up. Women, feminists included, try to marry men above them on the socioeconomic ladder, holding out as long as necessary (indeed, sometimes forever) to find such men. So long as women largely refuse to choose their mates in accordance with feminism's professed indifference to hierarchies, it remains a losing strategy for a man to act in accordance with new rules that even feminists themselves may violate.

Paglia has written at length on the interplay of sexual dominance and submission in literature. She notes that "flattery *is* sexual subordination. Hierarchy is conceptualized eroticism, which is why, as homely Henry Kissinger said, power is the ultimate aphrodisiac" (1991b, 144). Paglia approvingly quotes Richard Tristman's observation that "[a]ll sexuality entails some degree of theater. All sexual relations involve relations of dominance. The desire for equality in women is probably an attenuated expression of the desire to dominate" (243).

Paglia is keenly aware of the necessary interplay of hierarchal and sadomasochistic themes in the dance of the sexes: "Sex is not the pleasure principle but the Dionysian bondage of pleasure-pain. So much is a matter of *overcoming resistance*, in the body or the beloved, that rape will always be a present danger" (27). Rand, likewise, is certainly not innocent of this knowledge. Dominique Francon is told that Roark may have been in jail: "She hoped he had. She wondered whether they whipped convicts nowadays. She hoped they did" (1943, 219). Apparently, for Dominique, the contemplation of the whipping of the man for whom she lusts is a source of erotic pleasure. Not long afterward, Roark describes to Francon the exquisite pains he suffers in his sore muscles every night, a description that clearly arouses her. Their bedroom "rape" scene occurring soon thereafter is filled not with the sweet light of Apollo, but rather with Dionysus's intense pleasure-pain.

When John Galt and Dagny Taggart finally couple in the subterranean darkness, they do not smile and cogitate; rather, she sinks her teeth into the flesh of his arm. Soon she feels his mouth "seizing her lips with a pressure more viciously painful than hers" (Rand 1957, 957). The Marquis de Sade would have understood. Karen Andre falls madly for Bjorn Faulkner, who "acted as if he were cracking a whip over an animal he wanted to break" (Rand [1933] 1971, act II, p. 82). When John Galt is tortured by the evil moochers, they hold him naked, strapped to a mattress. He still nonetheless looks like "a statue of ancient Greece" (Rand 1957, 1141), which, to Paglia (1991b, chap. 4), is one of the most enduring of all "sexual personae."

The specter of Nietzsche has long hovered uninvited over the Randian canon, and from time to time an exorcism is attempted. However, the Nietzsche-Rand connection is much too powerful to deny. Rand claimed to have been a true disciple of the great and logical Aristotle. However, Aristotle as depicted in the works of Rand is quite unlike that philosopher known to scholars. For example, Aristotle unabashedly defends slavery and the total inferiority of women in his *Politics* (bk. 1, chap. 5). Rand leaves her readers largely unaware that such major problems exist in the works of the Greatest Thinker Who Ever Lived. Indeed, the very pitch and tone of Rand's writings are as *un*-Aristotelian as they can be. Whereas Aristotle is known for his excess of verbiage, his long and rambling philosophical "explanations," Rand is notorious for her shrill polemics, for her sweeping generalizations, for rapidly dispensing with even seemingly intractable problems, and for her almost uniquely bitter tone. Nietzsche is the one philosopher whose style and tone almost perfectly match Rand's. Both bitterly denounce altruism, pity, and Christianity. Both ceaselessly emphasize self-reliance, and express scorn for those who fail to meet their high standards. And both are unrestrained in their attacks on Plato and Kant. More than seventy-five years before Rand shocked a generation by proclaiming selfishness to be a virtue, Nietzsche's Zarathustra praised "blessed selfishness, the wholesome, healthy selfishness, that springeth from the powerful soul" (*Thus Spake Zarathustra*, bk. III, chap. 54).

Ayn Rand's journals reveal that Rand considered prefacing *each part* of *The Fountainhead* with quotations from Nietzsche (1997, 219). Indeed, Nietzsche even poses the question "Who is Zarathustra?" (bk. IV, sec.

11) in virtually the same manner as does Rand in *Atlas Shrugged:* "Who is John Galt?" He is the Overman, the son of Zarathustra.[4]

But if we are to be brutally honest, as is Paglia, we must acknowledge that the ghost of the Marquis de Sade hovers over the Randian canon as well. Yet it would be unfair to hold this against Rand. Paglia (1991b, 260) explains that "[d]ecadence is inherent in Romanticism. Sadomasochism . . . is already present in Romantic eroticism from its first formulation by Rousseau." Paglia reminds us that even sweet little Emily Dickinson, America's favorite Romantic poet, writes of severed heads, plucked eyes, amputation, impalement, and necrophilia (chap. 24).

In *Atlas Shrugged*, published in 1957, Francisco d'Anconia enunciates a theory of love as a *rational* value, indeed, the highest of rational values: "They think that your body creates a desire and makes a choice for you. . . . Show me the woman [a man] sleeps with and I will show you his valuation of himself. . . . The man who is proudly certain of his own value, will want the highest type of woman he can find, the woman he admires, the strongest, the hardest to conquer—because only the possession of the heroine will give him the sense of an achievement" (489–90). Why a hero must expend valuable energy in wooing the woman who is "the hardest to conquer" is not explained, but merely asserted. Feminists resent the depiction of women as trophies to be "conquered." Supposedly this is to bolster the hero's "sense of achievement," as if building an industrial empire, or inventing a radically new type of motor, were not achievement enough. Were heroes to be satisfied with women who are relatively easy to "conquer," the number of dragons slain and inventions invented would rise dramatically.

That this formula may represent a self-interested statement on the part of a female novelist unhappy in her own marriage, a "come get me" statement, seems not to have been previously considered. That a man may prefer not to live a life of constant mettle testing and jockeying for position seems likewise not to have occurred to Objectivists. Indeed, the honest desire for an uncomplicated life and the longer life span that a lower blood pressure makes possible would seem to constitute a perfectly legitimate reason for a heroic man's choosing a "woman *qua* woman" instead of "the hardest [woman] to conquer," especially since the latter may well be pursuing women herself. Indeed, Rand's refusal formally to consider issues concerning homosexuality leaves many interesting questions unresolved: if a heroine is a butch lesbian, what metaphysical wrongs has she committed if she seeks out not the "hardest-to-conquer" woman, but instead a very female *femme?* Would this not be just as deplorable as a heroic man's choosing a woman who is not difficult to woo? The view of love as springing from the cerebellum, enunciated in *Atlas Shrugged*, seems to be a repudiation of Rand's earlier position of love as a fundamental conflict between a woman's desire to remain in control and her desire to hero-worship a man. I view this later position as a rationalization (literally) of love, attempting to rescue it from the dark irrational realm that Nietzsche calls "the Dionysian," which Paglia refines further into "the chthonian." In the mature Randian philosophy, such realms are inhabited only by demons. Nothing good can possibly come from "the irrational." So unless Rand was willing to forswear love entirely, it must be proclaimed to be "rational." Attempting to deny and/or repress the Dionysian, Rand sought to attribute love and sex to Apollo alone. This was a great mistake. If Dominique Francon had understood love to be the highest of rational values, she would have felt no ambivalence about her desire for a man who seemed to meet all her criteria. It would not have been necessary for her to devise a cat-and-mouse game to lure him into her bedroom: she could simply have conversed with him about philosophy, and after discovering that they held compatible philosophical premises, they could merrily have hopped into bed. It would not even have been necessary to contemplate him being whipped, or to dwell upon his muscles' torment, or for Dagny to sink her teeth into anyone else's flesh. However, in the real world, the contradictory and irrational feelings experienced by Dominique and Dagny, and the ambiguous stratagems employed by the former, ring much truer than Rand's attempted formulation of love as algebra.

Seen in the context of Paglia's reevaluation from a position of greater sophistication and sounder scholarship on issues of sex roles, the definition of rape, and the inherent ambiguities of courtship, Rand's writings on gender become both more understandable and easier to justify. While orthodox Randians still insist on the correctness of Rand's views on sex roles, as well as everything else, many contemporary neo-Randians appear to have uncritically accepted simplistic and unsound victim-feminist positions, which depict male dominance in entirely negative terms. They therefore feel obligated to repudiate Rand's views on heterosexual relationships in the strongest possible terms. However, reinterpreted in the light of what we have learned from Paglia, Rand's views on the positive aspects of male dominance deserve to be given as much respect as her writings on other subjects.

Notes

1. For a scorecard to tell you which players are on which team, see Gladstein 1984, chap. 3.
2. Paglia (1992) provides a detailed critique of contemporary feminist theories of rape.
3. This warning is not an idle one: For a discussion of the medical consequences confronting women who zealously pursue the feminist lifestyle, see Silverstein and Perlick 1995.
4. For more about Nietzsche's influence on Rand, see Sciabarra 1995, 100–112.

References

Aristotle. 1984. *The Complete Works of Aristotle*. Vol. 2. Rev. Oxford trans. Edited by Jonathan Barnes. Princeton, N.J.: Princeton University Press.
Branden, Barbara. 1986. *The Passion of Ayn Rand*. Garden City, N.Y.: Doubleday.
Branden, Nathaniel, and Barbara Branden. 1962. *Who Is Ayn Rand? An Analysis of the Novels of Ayn Rand*. New York: Paperback Library.
de Beauvoir, Simone. 1974. *The Second Sex*. Translated by H. M. Parshley. New York: Vintage Books.
Gladstein, Mimi Reisel. 1978. Ayn Rand and feminism: An unlikely alliance. *College English* 39, no. 6:680–85.
———. 1984. *The Ayn Rand Companion*. Westport, Conn.: Greenwood Press.
Goldberg, Steven. 1993. *Why Men Rule*. Chicago: Open Court.
Mackinnon, Catherine A. 1989. *Toward a Feminist Theory of the State*. Cambridge, Mass.: Harvard University Press.
Nietzsche, Friedrich. 1905. *Thus Spake Zarathustra*. New York: Random House.
Paglia, Camille. 1991a. Interview. *San Francisco Examiner*, 7 July.
———. 1991b. *Sexual Personae: Art and Decadence from Nefertiti to Emily Dickinson*. New York: Vintage Books.
———. 1992. *Sex, Art, and American Culture*. New York: Vintage Books.
———. 1994. *Vamps and Tramps*. New York: Vintage Books.
Rand, Ayn. [1933] 1971. *Night of January 16th*. New York: New American Library.
———. [1936] 1959. *We The Living*. New York: New American Library.
———. 1943. *The Fountainhead*. Indianapolis: Bobbs-Merrill.
———. 1957. *Atlas Shrugged*. New York: Random House.
———. [1968] 1989. About a woman president. In *The Voice of Reason: Essays in Objectivist Thought*, edited by Leonard Peikoff. New York: New American Library. Originally published in *The Objectivist*, December 1968.
———. [1971] 1975. The age of envy. In *The New Left: The Anti-Industrial Revolution*, 2d rev. ed. New York: New American Library. Originally published in *The Objectivist*, July–August 1971.
———. 1993. *The Fountainhead*. 50th anniversary ed. New York: New American Library.
———. 1997. *Journals of Ayn Rand*. Edited by David Harriman. Foreword by Leonard Peikoff. New York: Penguin Dutton.
Sciabarra, Chris Matthew. 1995. *Ayn Rand: The Russian Radical*. University Park: Pennsylvania State University Press.

Silverstein, Brett, and Deborah Perlick. 1995. *The Cost of Competence: Why Inequality Causes Depression, Eating Disorders, and Illness in Women*. New York: Oxford University Press.
Taylor, Joan Kennedy. 1992. *Reclaiming the Mainstream: Individualist Feminism Rediscovered*. Buffalo, N.Y.: Prometheus Books.

17

Sex and Gender Through an Egoist Lens: Masculinity and Femininity in the Philosophy of Ayn Rand

Diana Mertz Brickell

Feminist writer Susan Brownmiller once called Ayn Rand "a traitor to her own sex" (1975, 315).[1] In a certain respect, Brownmiller is correct; Rand described herself as a "male chauvinist" (in Merrill 1991, 70). She argued, in one of her only writings on women, that a rational, properly feminine woman would not desire to be president of a nation (Rand 1988, 267). In her ethical writings, Rand used "the rational man" as the exemplar for all humans; in fact, women are rarely even present in examples, except as the wives or lovers of men.[2]

Nevertheless, such a misogynistic image of Ayn Rand is incomplete and misleading; much of Rand's fiction and nonfiction writing, as well as her own life, exemplify important and radical feminist ideals. The heroines of her novels display an intelligence, independence, and emotional strength—coupled with a genuine femininity and sexuality—that is rarely exhibited by female fictional characters. In a 1968 essay, Rand clearly rejected the idea that the intellects or abilities of women are inferior to those of men, arguing that "women need and should have careers, for the same reasons as men" (268). Ayn Rand herself, as a prominent, controversial, and uncompromising woman of ideas, also serves as an inspiration to younger women. In my own case, the fact that the author of *The Fountainhead* was a woman was nearly as revolutionary as the ideas contained within the novel.

Rand's writings on explicitly feminist issues, however, constitute only a fraction of what her philosophical thought has to offer feminism. In particular, her Objectivist philosophy can give rise to a unique and valuable perspective on gender, one that is flexible regarding the particular qualities of individuals without lapsing into relativism. Using Ayn Rand's ethical egoism and individualism, and the writings of former Rand associate Nathaniel Branden on sexual identity, we can greatly expand our understanding of the ways in which ideals of masculinity and femininity can and ought to function in our lives. Additionally, Dagny Taggart, the heroine of *Atlas Shrugged*, serves as an exemplar for the qualities of independence and authenticity integral to a normative account of gender.

Feminists have always taken an interest in the subject of gender—the ways in which individuals experience and express their biological sex— and for good reason. Conceptions of masculinity and femininity naturally shape an individual's sense of self and interactions with others. How a woman evaluates her physical appearance, the different ways spouses and lovers relate, and the disparate expectations of sons and daughters all rely upon ideals of masculinity and femininity (in addition to moral concepts such as empathy and justice). Moreover, as feminists have successfully argued, implicit notions of behavior appropriate to each sex, retained from childhood, often result in artificial, harmful limitations in men's and women's lives.

However, while feminist writers from the Enlightenment to Betty Friedan generally focused on the influence of gender roles in the lives of individuals, more recent feminist writings on gender tend to devote their attention to the origins and effects of gender roles at a cultural and institutional level. In *Sexual Politics*, for example, Kate Millett (1970) engages in a substantial discussion of the relationship between sex and gender only to conclude that sexual politics is grounded in "the 'socialization' of both sexes to basic patriarchical politics with regard to temperament, role, and status" (26). In the 1995 edition of *Women: A Feminist Perspective*, although two substantial articles discuss sex roles (Lips 1995, 128–48; Henley and Freeman 1995, 79–91), there is only a single paragraph directly addressing how we *ought* to think of ourselves as men and women.

These two feminist commentaries, like so many others, overlook the necessity of offering individuals alternative, nontraditional visions of masculinity and femininity that can be incorporated into everyday life. By regarding the personal as political, these writers inevitably overlook those innumerable aspects of gender that reflect an individual's inner sense of self as a man or a woman—and are therefore profoundly personal. At the root of this feminist social perspective on gender is a form of collectivism, one that regards the groups "male" and "female" as more metaphysically fundamental and ethically important than the individuals constituting that group (Peikoff 1982, 17). As a result, collectivist feminists frequently offer little in the way of guidance toward greater awareness and self-direction in personal ideals of masculinity and femininity.

The collectivist approach to gender is not, in fact, justified by the ways in which ideals of masculinity and femininity are experienced, expressed, or transmitted. It is only individuals who feel joy and confidence in an authentic sense of masculinity or femininity or who endure the pain and alienation of conforming to norms that conflict with their inner characters. Only individual men and women are capable of critically examining and deciding to change the attitudes and behaviors related to their sex. Broad social changes, as in the case of the feminist movement of the seventies, stem from such changes within a multitude of individuals. Finally, masculinity and femininity, even as norms broadly accepted in a particular society, are only conveyed by particular individuals to other individuals. And so the fact that many elements of our gender ideals are learned from others only requires us to be attentive to the impact of an individual's personal relationships, not to adopt a macro, collectivist perspective on the subject itself.

In contrast to collectivist feminism, Rand's own philosophy is perfectly consonant with the individualist perspective required by the nature of sex and gender. For Rand, any properly grounded science of the humanities has to begin with the study of individual humans, "not any loose aggregate known as a 'community'" (1967, 15). In the case of gender theory, Rand's individualism necessitates an understanding of the relationship between individual men and women and their ideals of masculinity and femininity before any investigation of the broad social impact of those ideals is undertaken. Additionally, Rand's emphasis on the life and well-being of the individual leads us to a positive account of how men and women ought to think about masculinity and femininity in their own lives.

Before an Objectivist account of gender can be developed, however, we must clarify a distinction largely overlooked by Rand in her comments on femininity—the distinction between the biological concept "sex" and the cultural and psychological concept "gender." "Sex" subsumes the broad physiological variations between males and females, such as the differences in genitalia. "Gender" refers to the acquired (often culturally based) characteristics and ideals through which an individual experiences and expresses his or her sex, such as varying perceptions of sexual intercourse and distinct styles of clothing. As such, these two concepts distinguish an individual's biological sexual identity from the psychological experience and expression of that sexual identity (Branden 1980, 90).

This distinction between sex and gender does not require attributing all differences between men and women (except the obvious anatomical ones) to socialization. Certain feminists, including Gloria Steinem, have adopted this position, which regards sex differences as "artificial and insignificant" and "dismisses all suggestions of genuine, irreducible sex differences as 'sexist,'" on the basis of the belief that "the acceptance of natural sex difference is dangerous" to women (Midgley 1988, 33, 37). Nevertheless, the scientific evidence on biologically based sex differences, such as disparities between male and female brains, points to the opposite conclusion: there may well be significant innate differences between males and females (even if only diverging tendencies) that impact behavior (Gibbons 1995, 119–22).

Nonetheless, proving such differences to be biological is a difficult task, requiring far more than mere widespread asymmetries between the sexes. The distinction between sex and gender demonstrates that the existence of nearly universal differences between men and women within a culture (or even between cultures) could still be the result of upbringing rather than biology. As such, the distinction primarily serves to undermine many traditional arguments for restrictive gender roles, in which a certain set of behaviors, attitudes, and responsibilities are deemed proper to each sex on the basis of pseudo-scientific arguments about the different "natures" of men and women. In 1792, Mary Wollstonecraft attacked Rousseau, in *Vindication of the Rights of Woman*, for precisely this type of traditionalism. She argued that Rousseau "proceeds to prove that woman ought to be weak and passive, because she has less bodily strength than man; and hence infers that she was formed to please and to be subject to him, and that it is her duty to render herself agreeable to her master" ([1792] 1983, 173).

In more recent years, sociobiologists have argued for traditional sex roles on similar grounds. These arguments attempt to move from general patterns of difference between men and women to normative prescriptions by regarding deviation from those general patterns as a violation of the innate natures of men and women. A clear conceptual distinction between sex and gender shows that these types of arguments require more proof than is (and perhaps can be) offered.

Rand's own failure clearly to distinguish between sex and gender is a contributing factor to her more traditional, rigid views of femininity and masculinity. Both her opposition to a woman president and her advocacy of male dominance and female submission in sexual intercourse can be traced to the portions of her ideals of masculinity and femininity that depend upon fallacious appeals to the nature of men and women.

In her essay "About a Woman President," Rand (1988) argued that a properly feminine woman would not *desire* to be president, not because women lack the necessary intelligence or emotional strength for the job, but due to the psychological requirements of femininity (267–68). In Rand's view, "the essence of femininity is hero worship—the desire to look up to man." This act of looking up "does not mean dependence, obedience, or anything implying inferiority," but rather "an intense kind of admiration" possible only to an independent woman (268). A woman would undermine her capacity to look up to men—and thus her femininity—if she became the president of a nation, for the position would require her "to act as the superior, the leader, virtually the *ruler* of all men she deals with, [which] would be an excruciating psychological torture" (269).

Although Rand never wrote about her corresponding view of masculinity, clearly it is not the mirror image of femininity, that is, "heroine worship." If that were the case, then for a man to be president of a nation, to be the leader of all the women he interacts with, would be similarly excruciating. Barbara Branden confirms that Rand's perspective on gender was indeed lopsided; she writes, "[M]an, [Rand] would say, is defined by his relationship to reality; woman—by her relationship to man" (1986, 18). Because Rand never justified these conceptions of masculinity and femininity by grounding them in the actual biological differences between men and women, her account resembles traditional appeals to an innate psychology of the sexes.

Rand's views on sexual intercourse—in which psychologically healthy sex entails male domination and female submission—follow a similar pattern. The sex scenes in Rand's novels all involve dominance and submission, often in conjunction with a certain violence and brutality found within them. In the first moments of a meeting between Leo and Kira in *We the Living* (1959, 108), "his arms crushed her with the violence of hatred, as if he wanted to grind their coats into shreds against each other." In the "rape" scene from *The Fountainhead* ([1943] 1971, 210), it is precisely because Roark's actions are "an act of scorn . . . not love, but defilement," that Dominique does, for the first time, "lie still and submit." In the first love scene between Dagny Taggart and John Galt in *Atlas Shrugged* ([1957] 1985, 888), Dagny "felt her teeth sinking into the flesh of his arm, she felt the sweep of his elbow knocking her head aside and his mouth seizing her lips with a pressure more viciously painful than hers."

This theme of male sexual domination over the female in Rand's novels is not merely a reflection of her personal preferences; the same views are formalized in Nathaniel Branden's *Psychology of Self-Esteem*, published shortly after the end of his almost twenty-year association with Rand. In that work, Branden ([1969] 1971, 208) argues that because "man is the bigger and stronger of the sexes" and because "it is [the man] who penetrates and the woman who is penetrated, . . . man experiences the essence of his masculinity in the act of romantic dominance; woman experiences the essence of her femininity in the act of romantic surrender."

The biological facts cited by Branden do not sufficiently validate his connection of masculinity to dominance and femininity to surrender. In fact, Branden's more recent comments on sex and gender have retreated from such strong claims in order to discuss healthy masculinity and femininity in terms of self-acceptance and affirmation of one's sexual nature (1996, 1; 1980, 91). As one might expect, this more recent conception of sexuality is coupled with a clear distinction between sex and gender (or "sexual identity"). In *The Psychology of Romantic Love*, Branden (1980, 90) writes, "while our sexual identity, our masculinity or femininity, is rooted in the facts of our biological nature, it does not consist of our being physically male or female; it consists of the way we psychologically *experience* our maleness or femaleness."

Nathaniel Branden's discussion of masculinity and femininity in *The Psychology of Romantic Love* does, in fact, provide a solidly Objectivist account of one aspect of gender: the internal *experience* of masculinity or femininity. In short, he describes masculinity and femininity as an individual's relationship to his or her sexual nature, where the proper relationship is one of acceptance and celebration.[3] Although Branden does not touch upon the innumerable ways in which individuals *express* that gender to others in their outward behavior, his analysis is significant in its own right and helps account for the function of gender in social interaction.

According to Branden, our sense of masculinity or femininity is "the product and reflection of the manner in which we respond to our nature as a sexual being" (90). A woman's implicit evaluation of the male body, or a man's level of confidence in an intimate encounter with a woman, for example, contributes to that individual's basic sense of self as a woman or a man. And because "we do not experience ourselves merely as human beings, but always as a male or a female," and because "sexuality is an inherent part of our human nature," an individual's "psychosexual identity" is inherently important to his or her life (90–91).

Branden goes on to give a normative account of masculinity and femininity in terms of "an affirmative response to our sexual nature" (91). This, he writes, "entails a strong enthusiastic awareness of our own sexuality; a positive (fearless and guiltless) response to the phenomenon of sex; a disposition to experience sex as an *expression* of the self, rather than as something alien, darkly incomprehensible, sinful, or 'dirty'; a positive and self-valuing response to one's own body; an enthusiastic appreciation of the body of the opposite sex; a capacity for freedom, spontaneity, and delight in the sexual encounter" (91–92).

Branden then informally defines masculinity as "the expression of a man's belief that the creation of woman was nature's most brilliant idea" and femininity as "the expression of a woman's belief that the creation of man was nature's most brilliant idea" (92).

There is an additional element central to the internal experience of masculinity and femininity that Branden does not directly discuss, namely, an appreciation for what one has to offer the opposite sex as a man or a woman. Within the context of a romantic relationship, the "polarity" between a man and a woman allows a greater awareness of and appreciation for the unique qualities of the sexual self that each individual brings to a relationship (93). These qualities in the other, such as empathy, emotional strength, and openness, can bring a man and a woman a heightened sense of their own masculinity and femininity.

Notably, Branden's account of the internal experience of gender does not prescribe that men ought to have a particular set of qualities and women another. Although differences between the sexes arising from physiology and culture will result in substantial similarities between personal ideals of masculinity and femininity, the genuine normative principles of gender are limited to acceptance and celebration of the sexual self. There is neither need nor justification for sets of masculine and feminine standards of behavior, but rather, as Branden commented in a 1996 interview, a need for greater focus on honest acceptance of our "natural inclinations" with respect to masculinity and femininity, "without concern about cultural stereotypes of what [is] 'appropriate' " (1).

On the one hand, the connection between biology and the internal experience of masculinity and femininity is relatively simple; on the other hand, the ties between biological sex and the outward expressions of masculinity and femininity often seem arbitrary or illusory. How can certain levels of emotional responsiveness, codes of dress, styles of communication, and even colors rightly be considered the province of one sex or the other? What justifies, if anything, the particular connection of certain behaviors, responsibilities, and physical appearances to male or female domains?

One feminist has described the connection between these cultural expressions of gender and biological sex as "a complex web of increasingly tenuous metaphorical association" (Nelson 1992, 147). But "symbolic association" is perhaps a better description; within a culture, certain behaviors take on symbolic meaning and convey information about an individual's sexual self to others. Just as actions such as shaking hands and waving are meaningful by virtue of established social conventions of greeting, so too the way a woman touches a man in casual conversation or the way a man attends to his physical appearance is meaningful by virtue of established conventions or norms of gender. Because these symbolic behaviors convey information, they serve as a window to the characters and personalities of individual men and women, thereby allowing us to make more accurate and quicker judgments about the types of relationships we wish to pursue with them.

Variations in the meanings attributed to these culturally symbolic actions do not just exist between cultures; even within a culture, individuals will interpret identical behaviors differently, as a result of their particular values and beliefs. For example, some men enjoy the forthrightness of an assertive woman, while others feel threatened by it; some women appreciate a man's emotional sensitivity, even though others see it as weakness. And clothing that by some is considered sexy will often be considered by others to be either tame or whorish. The numerous meanings attributed to behaviors greatly diminish the possibility of any significant social ostracism, thus allowing men and women a greater flexibility in their expression of gender. Individuals can feel freer to express natural tendencies, in styles of clothing or ways of relating to others, for example, because they will, in all likelihood, find others who seek out those qualities.

The cultural flexibility of meanings attributed to expressions of gender does not imply that individuals ought to be relativistic in their own judgments of gender norms. On the contrary, the range of meanings requires individual men and women to make countless choices about how to express their masculinity or femininity, thereby necessitating a clear, rational standard by which to judge gender norms. Tradition is certainly no reliable guide to the rationality of gender norms, given the history of destructive, harmful practices—from footbinding and corseting for women to drafting men to go to war (Rand 1988, 119). On the other hand, Ayn Rand's egoism—in which human life is the ultimate standard of value, and the highest ethical purpose of humans is their own life and happiness—equips individuals with a method by which to judge norms of gender (Rand 1964, 25, 27). By that standard, individuals ought to make choices on the basis of whether the symbolic behaviors that express gender further their life and happiness or diminish it. Unlike altruistic and collectivistic ethical standards, Rand's egoism frees individuals from the most common underlying argument for restrictive gender roles—that individual men and women ought to sacrifice themselves for the sake of a higher social good.

Although Rand's standard of value is simple in the abstract, the application of that standard to particular cultural ideals of masculinity or femininity is a difficult process. Because our ideals of gender are deeply integrated into our lives and because there is often a myriad of costs and benefits to gender norms, how to separate the beneficial elements from the harmful is frequently less than obvious. Fortunately, the analyses provided by Susan Brownmiller in *Femininity* and by Warren Farrell in *The Myth of Male Power* are, largely, concrete applications of an ethical standard founded on the individual's life and well-being. Throughout these works, both writers focus on the particular ways in which gender ideals frustrate or further the pursuit of important goals in the lives of individuals.

Based upon Brownmiller's analysis, a woman might ask, for example: Do the requirements of a feminine physical appearance, such as high heels, restrict my movement or cause pain or medical problems? Do they focus my attention on inconsequential details of life, such as the state of my nails? Do they try to impose an unrealistic shape on my body? Do traditional female methods of relating with others prevent me from being taken seriously at work? Do they make it hard for me to refuse requests for favors?

Based upon Farrell's analysis, a man might ask: Do traditional fathering roles leave me less involved with my children than I'd like to be? Does the structure of male friendship inhibit the give and take of emotional support? Do ideals of male bravery that serve to protect women and children result in my taking unreasonable risks? Does the role of material provider of the family push me into a dangerous or unfulfilling job?

Although one might question the universal applicability of Brownmiller's and Farrell's analyses, they are predominantly compatible with the egoistic standard of value found in Rand's ethics. As such, they provide concrete guidance to individual men and women in using that standard to make rational decisions about how to express masculinity or femininity to others.

Because Rand's ethical standard allows for considerable, legitimate variation between individuals, based on their unique qualities and capacities, authenticity in expression of the sexual self is perhaps the most important element of normative gender. Authenticity is the disposition faithfully and openly to present one's inner person to others. As such, it is a species of the virtue of integrity, which Rand (1964, 46) defined as "loyalty to one's convictions and values [and] the policy of acting in accordance with one's values, of expressing, upholding, and translating them into practical reality," a loyalty in which the values in question constitute one's inner self. With respect to gender, authenticity is a natural outgrowth of self-acceptance in the internal experience of masculinity or femininity; if we are honest with ourselves about our sexual nature, then we are likely to be honest about it with others.

In practice, authenticity often requires a great deal of independence and courage, for the social pressure to conform to particular norms of gender can be substantial.[4] As difficult as authenticity may be, individuals can gain greater control over their own lives—when a couple decides that the husband ought to stay at home with the children, when a man asks for emotional support from a friend, or when a woman defends her right not to provide her parents with grandchildren. As such, authenticity in expression of our sexual selves is the way in which an individual honors that part of his or her existence, by refusing to fake it to please others.

In *Atlas Shrugged*, Rand illustrates the necessity of authenticity and independence in femininity through the contrast between the characters of Dagny Taggart and Lillian Rearden. Dagny Taggart, the heroine of the novel, never attempts to hide her unusual position as a skilled and highly intelligent railroad executive; she is open and up-front about her beliefs and intentions. For example, in a press conference announcing the opening of a new line, Dagny responds to protests to her lack of altruistic concern for the public welfare by saying, "Miss Taggart says—quote—I expect to make a pile of money on the John Galt Line. I will have earned it. Close quote" ([1957] 1985, 224). This authenticity is coupled with an independence from social ideals of femininity; Rand writes that Dagny "was twelve years old when she told Eddie Willers that she would run the railroad when they grew up. She was fifteen when it occurred to her for the first time that women did not run railroads and that people might object. To hell with that, she thought—and never worried about it again" (55).

On the other hand, Lillian Rearden, one of the antiheroines, is outwardly submissive to others while simultaneously resorting to underhanded tactics in order to control them. At a party, Lillian comments to Dagny, "I am quite resigned to taking second place in the shadow of my husband. I am humbly aware that the wife of a great man has to be contented with reflected glory" (134). Yet Lillian uses her knowledge of an affair between her husband, Hank Rearden, and Dagny in order to manipulate her husband into signing over his most precious possession— the formula and rights to Rearden Metal—to the government.

The sharpest contrast between Lillian and Dagny appears in Lillian's subsequent attempt to force Dagny into appearing on a radio program to praise the government's totalitarian policies. Lillian informs Dagny of how she manipulated Hank into giving up Rearden Metal, saying, "[H]e would have gladly died to defend it, rather than surrender it to the men he despised. . . . I believe that you hold a philosophy which disapproves of sacrifice—but in this case, you are most certainly a woman, so I'm sure that you will feel gratification at the magnitude of the sacrifice a man has made for the privilege of using your body" (788). Lillian then threatens to make the affair public unless Dagny appears on the radio program. Lillian's manipulations, because they depend upon a desire to hide the inner character from public view, are ineffective in light of Dagny's authenticity and independence. Feeling pride, rather than shame, in her affair with Hank Rearden, Dagny exposes the affair herself while on the radio program, in order to show the unjust means used to obtain Rearden Metal (791–93). The true irony of the contrast between Lillian and Dagny is that while Dagny is widely regarded by the society of *Atlas Shrugged* to be wholly unfeminine, Lillian is that society's perfect image of femininity.

Ayn Rand's Objectivism, then, despite some antifeminist tendencies, has substantial philosophical insights to offer feminism. Her ethics provides a fertile ground on which to develop an account of gender sensitive to the unique qualities and dispositions of individual men and women, as well as to the sanctity of the life and happiness of those individuals. As such, it is one of the few philosophies capable of liberating men and women from the harmful and destructive gender roles that have existed throughout most of human history. And so, whatever Ayn Rand's sins, being "a traitor to her own sex" cannot fairly be counted among them.

Notes

1. The relevant material from Brownmiller 1975 is reprinted in the current volume.

2. See, for example, "The Ethics of Emergencies" in Rand 1964, 43–49.

3. As Branden notes (1980, 94), his comments on gender in *The Psychology of Romantic Love* are made within the context of man-woman relationships, "even though much of what is said clearly applies to homosexual love relationships." The discussion here follows that same pattern, not due to any bias against homosexuality, but rather because I suspect that the concepts of masculinity and femininity function somewhat differently in heterosexual and homosexual relationships. Thus, I would neither wish to presume uniformity between heterosexual and homosexual relationships nor attempt a separate discussion of gender in homosexual relationships (a subject of which I have too little knowledge).

4. For men and women who live in an environment, whether a nation or a household, in which violence is inflicted upon those who stray from gender roles, authenticity is obviously impossible and ought not be considered a moral imperative. As Rand said ([1957] 1985, 949), "morality ends where a gun begins."

References

Branden, Barbara. 1986. *The Passion of Ayn Rand.* Garden City, N.Y.: Doubleday.
Branden, Nathaniel. [1969] 1971. *The Psychology of Self-Esteem: A New Concept of Man's Psychological Nature.* New York: Bantam.
———. 1980. *The Psychology of Romantic Love.* New York: Bantam.
———. 1996. Interview by Karen Reedstrom. *Full Context,* October.
Brownmiller, Susan. 1975. *Against Our Will: Men, Women, and Rape.* New York: Simon & Schuster.
———. 1984. *Femininity.* New York: Linden Press.
Farrell, Warren. 1993. *The Myth of Male Power.* New York: Simon & Schuster.
Freeman, Jo, ed. 1995. *Women: A Feminist Perspective.* 5th ed. Mountain View, Calif.: Mayfield.
Gibbons, Ann. 1995. The brain as "sexual organ." In *Readings in the Biological Bases of Human Behavior,* edited by Paul Garber, 2d ed. Needham Heights, Mass.: Simon & Schuster.
Henley, Nancy, and Jo Freeman. 1995. The sexual politics of interpersonal behavior. In *Women: A Feminist Perspective,* edited by Jo Freeman, 5th ed. Mountain View, Calif.: Mayfield.
Lips, Hilary. 1995. Gender role socialization. In *Women: A Feminist Perspective,* edited by Jo Freeman, 5th ed. Mountain View, Calif.: Mayfield.
Merrill, Ronald E. 1991. *The Ideas of Ayn Rand.* La Salle, Ill.: Open Court.
Midgley, Mary. 1988. Natural sex differences. In *Feminist Perspectives in Philosophy,* edited by Morwenna Griffiths and Margaret Whitford. Bloomington: Indiana University Press.
Millett, Kate. 1970. *Sexual Politics.* New York: Avon.
Nelson, Julie. 1992. Thinking about gender. *Hypatia* 7, no. 3:139–54.
Peikoff, Leonard. 1982. *The Ominous Parallels.* New York: Mentor.
Rand, Ayn. [1943] 1971. *The Fountainhead.* New York: New American Library.
———. [1957] 1985. *Atlas Shrugged.* New York: New American Library.
———. 1959. *We the Living.* 2d ed. New York: New American Library.
———. 1964. *The Virtue of Selfishness.* New York: New American Library.
———. 1967. *Capitalism: The Unknown Ideal.* New York: New American Library.
———. 1988. *The Voice of Reason.* New York: New American Library.
Wollstonecraft, Mary. [1792] 1983. *Vindication of the Rights of Woman.* New York: Penguin Books.

18

The Female Hero: A Randian-Feminist Synthesis

Thomas Gramstad

My philosophy, in essence, is the concept of man as a heroic being, with his own happiness as the moral purpose of his life, with productive achievement as his noblest activity, and reason as his only absolute.
> —Ayn Rand, appendix to *Atlas Shrugged*

Heroism is the *only* alternative.
> —Phyllis Chesler, *Patriarchy: Notes of an Expert Witness*

Ayn Rand formulated and presented a new vision of human being. She achieved a wide-ranging integration of mind and body, a unified conception of love, sex, self, and relationships. She viewed love as a response to values, and romantic love as a unity of reason and emotion, virtue and desire, admiration and passion, human pride and animal lust. Sex, for Rand, is an expression of self-esteem—a celebration of oneself and of existence. A relationship provides a trade of spiritual values, offering psychological visibility (and thereby spiritual growth) through the perception of oneself as an external reflection in another self.

And yet, despite this achievement, Rand made a mistake—a mistake that limits the range of her achievement and undercuts the scope of her integration, a mistake that preserved elements of Platonism and collec-

334 Toward a Randian Feminism?

tivism in her integration of love and sex. Rand maintained a Platonic view of gender, which translates into gender-role collectivism. The goal of this article is to identify these elements and their effects, to establish how and at what levels they contradict more fundamental ideas in Rand's philosophy, and, finally, to suggest an extended Randian position that incorporates gender individualism and feminist insights, thus providing the foundation for a Randian-feminist synthesis.[1] I hope to unleash a hidden potential in Rand's thought, from which a conceptual foundation for the Female Hero can be established.

Ayn Rand's View of Gender

What exactly was Rand's view of gender? A careful analysis of the Randian canon reveals that Rand had a view that remained unchanged—one is tempted to say unchallenged—throughout her entire life. This view permeated the fabric of her thinking, surfacing at irregular intervals both in her fiction and nonfiction.

For example, there is this description of Dagny Taggart, the powerful heroine in *Atlas Shrugged* (1957, 136): "[I]t was astonishing to discover that the lines of her shoulder were fragile and beautiful, and that the diamond band on the wrist of her naked arm gave her the most feminine of all aspects: the look of being chained." For Rand, a person's physical appearance expresses his or her gender, and Rand operates with distinct and separate bipolar gender roles (masculinity and femininity) linked to the person's biological sex (maleness and femaleness, respectively). Hence, the look of being chained is associated with femininity, and femininity is seen by Rand as the psychological expression of biological femaleness.

There is also this description of Dominique Francon, the heroine of *The Fountainhead* ([1943] 1986, 262): "She stood leaning back, as if the air was a support—solid enough for her thin, naked shoulder blades. . . . She seemed too fragile to exist; and that very fragility spoke of some frightening strength which held her anchored to existence with a body insufficient for reality." One finds that all of Rand's heroines are of very slender—or fragile—build. This includes Kira in *We the Living*, Karen Andre in *Night of January 16th*, and the various heroines in *The Early Ayn Rand*.

The sex in Rand's novels is always described as a combat of wills, and sometimes as a physical combat, such as the notorious "rape" scene in *The Fountainhead*[2] and Bjorn Faulkner's "rape" of Karen Andre in *Night of January 16th* (Rand 1968, 82–83). To a lesser degree, this also applies to Dagny Taggart's sex scenes in *Atlas Shrugged*, especially the one with John Galt (1957, 956–57). This is not a combat of equals, and the woman is never the aggressor. The man is always superior in both mental and physical strength.[3]

Here is another description of Dagny Taggart that illustrates this ideal: "She stood as she always did, straight and taut, her head lifted impatiently. It was the unfeminine pose of an executive. But her naked shoulder betrayed the fragility of the body under the black dress, and the pose made her most truly a woman. The proud strength became a challenge to someone's superior strength, and the fragility a reminder that the challenge could be broken" (154).

Several other examples of male dominance may be found in the pieces of fiction compiled in *The Early Ayn Rand*, for example, "Kira's Viking" and "Vesta Dunning."[4] Interestingly, the editor of this collection, Leonard Peikoff, identifies a development in Rand's writing whereby the early fiction, with dominating heroines, rather quickly turns into the male domination typical of Rand's mature fiction (in Rand 1984, 4). Peikoff, in further describing the Randian heroine's feelings for her hero, calls her "the opposite of a feminist" (34). And in yet another instance, he offers this description: "The hero, who now has primacy over the heroine, is a completely recognizable Ayn Rand type" (259).[5]

A discussion of the nature of sex in *Atlas Shrugged*, aimed at explaining the integration of mind and body, love and sex, evaluation and desire, and often repeated in Rand's nonfiction (Rand [1961] 1968; Binswanger 1986), also carries with it strong gender role implications:

A man's sexual choice is the result and the sum of his fundamental convictions. Tell me what a man finds sexually attractive, and I will tell you his entire philosophy of life. Show me the woman he sleeps with, and I will tell you his valuation of himself. . . . He will always be attracted to the woman who reflects his deepest vision of himself, the woman whose surrender permits him to experience—or to fake—a sense of self-esteem. The man who is proudly certain of his own value, will want the highest type of woman he can find, the woman he admires, the strongest, the hardest to conquer—because only the possession of a heroine will give him the sense of an achievement, not the possession of a brainless slut. (Rand 1957, 489–90)

Just as Rand's heroines are slender/fragile and feminine, her female villains are often athletic or large, and unfeminine or masculine, such as Eve Layton in *The Fountainhead*[6] or Comrade Sonia in *We the Living*.[7] There seems to be a pattern in which heroes are masculine, heroines are feminine, female villains are unfeminine or masculine, and male villains are unmasculine or feminine. Rand seems to engage in the gendering of evil, in that characters whose gender identities and/or gender expressions are considered inappropriate to their biological sex are portrayed as evil. This tendency is apparent in Rand's fiction and nonfiction.

Gender in Rand's Nonfiction

According to Rand: "[M]en are metaphysically the dominant sex" (Rand 1975a, 175). What exactly does it mean to be a "metaphysically dominant sex"? The answer may be found in an article in *The Objectivist* written by psychologist Nathaniel Branden (1968), Rand's close associate for eighteen years and the founder and former leader of the first Objectivist movement:

> The difference in the male and female sexual roles proceeds from differences in man's and woman's respective anatomy and physiology. Physically, man is the bigger and stronger of the two sexes; his system produces and uses more energy; and he tends (for physiological reasons) to be physically more active. Sexually, his is the more active and dominant role; he has the greater measure of control over his own pleasure and that of his partner; it is he who penetrates and the woman who is penetrated (with everything this entails, physically and psychologically). . . . [M]an experiences the essence of his masculinity in the act of romantic dominance; woman experiences the essence of her femininity in the act of romantic surrender.[8]

Here, Branden describes man as the romantic initiator and aggressor, and woman as the challenger and responder to the man.[9] Throughout the Randian canon, this formulation is not merely a preference, but a natural law. It is fair to say that this is a part of Rand's philosophy, even though "sexual psychology" is not strictly a part of any of the five major philosophical disciplines.[10] But the errors that Rand makes concerning gender are philosophical in that they contradict or entail philosophical principles and positions. Moreover, Rand's gender credo is a part of Objectivist culture. But the credo itself is unsupported by scientific knowledge and logically incompatible with the larger context of Objectivism as a philosophical system. Furthermore, it is both anti-individualist and antifeminist.

Since the substance of Rand's claims are addressed throughout this article, it is worth quoting at length from her important essay "About a Woman President":

> For a woman *qua* woman, the essence of femininity is hero worship—the desire to look up to man. "To look up" does not mean dependence, obedience, or anything implying inferiority. It means an intense kind of admiration; and admiration is an emotion that can be experienced only by a person of strong character and independent value judgments. . . . Hero worship is a demanding virtue: a woman has to be worthy of it and of the hero she worships. Intellectually and morally, i.e., as a human being, she has to be his equal; then the object of her worship is specifically his *masculinity*, not any human virtue she might lack. . . . Her worship is an abstract emotion for the *metaphysical* concept of masculinity as such. . . . It means that a properly feminine woman does not treat men as if she were their pal, sister, mother—or *leader*. . . . To act as the superior, the leader, virtually the *ruler* of all the men she deals with, would be an excruciating psychological torture. It would require a total depersonalization, an utter selflessness, and an incommunicable loneliness; she would have to suppress (or repress) every personal aspect of her own character and attitude; she could not be herself, i.e., a woman; . . . she would become the most unfeminine, sexless, metaphysically inappropriate, and rationally revolting figure of all: a *matriarch*. This would apply to the reigning queen of an absolute monarchy,

but it would not apply to a woman in any field of endeavor other than politics.[11] (Rand [1968] 1988, 267–69)

Rand mentions Joan of Arc as the most heroic woman—and the most tragic symbol—in history, not primarily because she was burned at the stake, but because she had to assume the role of leader in order to revive the fighting spirit of the soldiers.[12] It is interesting to compare Rand's view of Joan of Arc with her penchant for gendering characters. Rand's view seems to be that the heroism of Joan of Arc is not due to military actions and achievements, or to opposition and resistance to torture. Rather, it resides in Joan's alleged rejection of femininity. This is a forceful illustration of the natural law–like status that Rand ascribes to her own conceptions of the masculine and the feminine in sexual psychology.

Randian Alternatives to Rand's View of Gender

An obvious alternative interpretation of the sexual act, namely, that who conquers and who surrenders need not be predetermined either in fact or by gender, that the sexual power transactions may shift, change, and reconfigure themselves over time, is addressed neither by Rand nor by other Objectivists. The Randian version of erotic combat seems monotonous compared to the rich natural variation of expression in human sexuality.

The lack of awareness of alternatives may be rightly interpreted by feminists as an example of what Riane Eisler ([1987] 1995) calls "the dominator model" at work, whereby human interaction is always interpreted as instances of corresponding domination and submission. This is distinct from what Eisler calls "the partnership model," whereby human interaction is viewed as a voluntary exchange between equals (xvii). Replacing power hierarchies (especially gendered power hierarchies) with equality and choice has always been a major (perhaps, and ideally, *the* major) concern of feminism, and a discussion of this aspect of feminism is essential to our understanding of the tensions between Rand and feminism.

Interpreting Rand with Eisler's terminology, one may argue that Rand's general philosophy, as well as her heroic characters, upholds "the partnership model," which is the only moral basis for human interaction and transactions, what Rand calls "the trader principle." Yet, the literary images of human sexuality projected by Rand, as well as several of her explicit nonfiction statements, are written in the language of "the dominator model." This is an inherent contradiction in Rand's writing, and a feminist rereading of Rand must address and, if possible, resolve it.

There are three interaction-style alternatives to male conquest and the domination of women: "women conquering men," "switching between submission and conquest," and "equality without power-difference fetishism." Are these alternatives compatible with Rand's philosophy? Or does her philosophy contradict her own position on gender, which entails a restrictive and limited view of human psychology and sexuality?

The alternatives above are underemphasized in Rand's work because of her gender restrictions. Indeed, if Rand's gender-style preferences are viewed as universal gender-role prescriptions, the alternatives would be rejected in toto by any ardent Objectivist. This would indeed be a strange and tragic outcome for a philosophy that started out as a highly integrated vision of love, sex, self, and relationships.

Gender Lenses or Essences?

Sandra Bem (1993), a leading psychologist and researcher on gender and gender roles, identifies three "lenses of gender"—three main categories of deep, hidden cultural assumptions of gender that are embedded in cultural discourses, social institutions, and individual psyches:

> The first lens . . . is androcentrism, or male-centeredness. This is not just the historically crude perception that men are inherently superior to women but a more treacherous underpinning of that perception: a definition of males and male experience as a neutral standard or norm, and females and female experience as a sex-specific deviation from that norm. It is thus not that man is treated as superior and woman as inferior but that man is treated as human and woman as "other."
>
> The second lens is the lens of gender polarization. Once again, this is not just the historically crude perception that women and men are fundamentally different from one another but the more subtle and insidious use of that perceived difference as an organ-

izing principle for the social life of the culture. It is thus not simply that women and men are seen to be different, but that this male-female difference is superimposed on so many aspects of the social world that a cultural connection is thereby forged between sex and virtually every other aspect of human experience, including modes of dress and social roles and even ways of expressing emotion and experiencing sexual desire.

Finally, the third lens is the lens of biological essentialism, which rationalizes and legitimizes both other lenses by treating them as the natural and inevitable consequences of the intrinsic biological natures of women and men. (2)

While Rand was not a biological essentialist (even though several of her positions on gender would seem to require a basis in biological essentialism), she favored androcentrism and gender polarization, both incompatible with her Objectivist philosophy. In my view, Rand's Objectivism logically entails "metaphysical equality" of women and men (not androcentrism) and gender nonessentialism (not gender polarization). Nonessentialism, in the context of gender and social science, does not mean a denial of the identity of consciousness, as Rand's supporters might fear. It means a rejection of biological determinism—specifically, it means a rejection of the idea that biological sex alone determines or delimits human behavior. It means that environmental and cultural factors, as well as individual choice, will always be a part of the picture, and that they may override, direct, or redefine the expression of genetic or biological tendencies at any time. So the term "essentialism" means one thing in philosophy (a universal and immutable Platonic essence) and something quite different in the social sciences (where "essence" is translated into an assumption of a transcultural, transindividual biological determinism).

According to Rand and Objectivism, on the other hand, consciousness has a particular identity.[13] However, this identity is the same for men and women. (In fact, this is the only gender position compatible with Objectivism.) The idea of a gendered identity of consciousness is not only unsupported; there are many indications against it, including the empirical fact of human variety with overlap between men and women, such that no characteristic isolated to one sex has been found and the variety of characteristics within each sex is actually larger than it is between the sexes.[14] The idea of a gendered identity of consciousness is incompatible with one of Rand's key ideas, namely, that people are born tabula rasa, that is, without inborn ideas.[15] This means that all of an individual's ideas and actions are open to rational evaluation, and may be changed volitionally. The idea of a universal "gender essence" is a Platonic construct totally at odds with Objectivism.

Sex Versus Gender

Does a biological dichotomy of male and female exist, or do we need a corresponding psychological dichotomy of masculine and feminine?[16] The terms "masculine" and "feminine" presuppose that there is a similar psychological dichotomy on the same level of reality as the biological one, that is, something given and determined by nature. The implicit claim is that men normally are, or should conform to, an approved list of psychological characteristics perceived or defined as "masculine," and that women normally are, or should conform to, a complementary list of psychological characteristics perceived or defined as "feminine"—and, as an immediate and unavoidable implication of this, that the not-masculine man and the not-feminine woman are abnormal or immoral. The "gender-deviant" boy or girl may be subjected to psychiatric treatment against his or her will, including incarceration, drugs, and electroshock.[17] Such implications seem to be inherent in the terminology. But is there really a sex-gender link?

Sandra Bem (1971) demonstrates the existence of two widespread, fairly specific polarized stereotypes, or notions, of gender in our culture, assigned to men and women respectively and exclusively. This bipolar view of gender assumes that "masculinity" (M) and "femininity" (F) are opposite ends of a scale. However, this view is false. M and F are two independent variables. An individual may have much of one and little of the other (M) or little of the one and much of the other (F) or much of both (which is called "androgynous") or little of both (which is called "undifferentiated"). Since about 50 percent of men and women describe themselves as androgynous, gender stereotypes are wrong at least half the time and have poor predictive power.

In our culture, the good part of "masculinity" centers on "instrumentality" or mastery, for example, being strong, enduring, independent, verbally accurate, competent in making and using tools, persevering and excelling in one's activities and in the ability to organize and lead. In contrast, the bad part of "masculinity" includes being cold, emotionally repressed, focused on defeating others rather than on self-improvement (aggressive competitiveness), unable to admit and deal with doubt or failure, and compulsive in one's inclination to dominate and control others.

The good part of "femininity" centers on expressivity: being coopera-tive, easygoing, warm, loyal, playful, adept at nonverbal communication skills, and able to identify and express emotions and to listen and nurture. The bad part of "femininity" includes passivity, helplessness, submissive-ness, repression of "aggressive" feelings, and lack of self-assertion, of inde-pendent action, of systematic pursuit of goals, and of structure.

Western culture, however, often downplays feminine characteristics altogether, equating moral virtue with maleness. Walker (1983, 1051) notes, about virtue: "Latin *virtus* was derived from *vir*, 'man,' and origi-nally meant masculinity, impregnating power, semen, or male magic, like Germanic heill. Patriarchal thinkers defined manliness as good and wom-anliness as bad, therefore *virtus* became synonymous with morality or godliness along with other synonyms hinting at male sexuality: erectness, uprightness, rectitude, upstandingness, etc."

By contrast, the androgyny model challenges those who would privi-lege the masculine as virtue. More importantly, it sees no automatic link between maleness and "masculinity," or between femaleness and "femi-ninity." It assumes M and F are defined with wide differences in different cultures; a characteristic that is considered M in one culture is considered F in another. The grouping of characteristics into grab bags labeled M or F is arbitrary; it is the result of cultural invention, not natural law. In other words, androgyny seems to exempt or disconnect gender from sex.

It follows from this that the constituent characteristics of gender ste-reotypes are arbitrarily joined and assigned; they are not dictated by na-ture. One's psychological characteristics are not determined by one's reproductive system. Biology is not destiny. This suggests a need to en-courage males to acquire those characteristics (or rather the positive part of them) that our culture calls "feminine," not instead of, but in addition to, the masculine characteristics. And females need encouragement to acquire the best of "masculine" characteristics in addition to "feminine" characteristics (that is, the best of both worlds).

One effect of encouraging the best of the "masculine" and "feminine" characteristics in everybody, that is, promoting cultural, psychological and ethical androgyny,[18] is that androgyny counteracts the bad parts of both "femininity" and "masculinity." That is, the good parts of F drive out the bad parts of M, and the good parts of M drive out the bad parts of F. There are no "masculine virtues" and no "feminine virtues," only *human* virtues that should be encouraged in everyone. Hence, there are many morally neutral psychological characteristics that should be available to (i.e., socially permissible for) anyone inclined toward them.[19]

Being androgynous means having more options to choose from, because one is in touch with a bigger part of one's humanity. Androgyny also implies that one will be able—and permitted—to develop in directions chosen by oneself. Androgyny translates into freedom and gender individualism. It encourages integrated human character development, in contrast to the two incomplete half-humans of sex stereotyping.

For many, "femininity" and "masculinity" appear to be two vague and yet strangely limiting separate modes of being whose reconciliation is impossible. Consequently, women and men are viewed as so fundamentally different that they may as well have come from different planets. Replacing these two terms with more descriptive and objective ones like "expressivity" and "instrumentality" may be a step toward resolving such conflicts within and between individuals. Warren (1982, 184) notes: "What's artificial is the notion that *combining* these diverse characteristics is more difficult than *separating* them." This combination is the goal of feminist androgynists.

Beyond Androgyny

The concept of androgyny has been criticized for reproducing the same flaws inherent in "masculinity" and "femininity"—namely, the idea of metaphysically given gender essences (even if coexisting in the same body). If our goal is to liberate virtues and vices from arbitrary gender categories, why not abandon androgyny, along with femininity and masculinity?

There are two reasons to reject this line of reasoning: First, androgyny has served to undermine and expose the flaws of traditional gender views. Second, since it is unlikely that "femininity" and "masculinity" will drop out of popular usage, a strategy is needed to counteract their most damaging collectivist implications. Androgyny is that strategy; it is a concept of a process, the process of transcending the masculine-feminine duality.[20]

A problem in the historical and etymological connection between femininity and women and masculinity and men is that, in a Randian context, it may encourage the unwarranted and harmful conclusion that only men are worthy of hero worship, and only women are to be granted the privilege of hero-worshiping. Ideally, in the long run, we should abandon the terms "femininity" and "masculinity" altogether, as remnants of a collectivist past. Gender liberation or gender individualism encourages individuals to take pride in and develop their own unique gender identities. Perhaps most or all concepts of androgyny will make themselves superfluous through the creation of a "postandrogynous," or individualist, society.

Indeed, in terms of genetic variation and natural selection, one could argue that eradicating individual differences and variety, the function and purpose of gender-role collectivism, is opposed to our biological nature, since natural selection needs biological variation in order to work. This article, however, is written on the assumption that gender is an *ethnicity* (a cultural artifact), rather than a *temperament*—that is, that gender is defined primarily or ultimately by culture and by choice, rather than by biology.[21]

This approach means that we must reject Rand's description of a femininity that sees the object of a woman's worship to be specifically a man's *masculinity*, "not any human virtue she might lack" (Rand [1968] 1988, 268). Rand's claim is narrow in three ways: First, it posits masculinity as the only object worthy of hero worship, and second, it only permits women the privilege of hero worship, not men. But Rand's claim is wrong in a third way as well: in its tacit assumption that one can only admire or worship some aspect *other* than masculinity/gender in the other if one does *not* possess (at least not to the same degree) the trait or virtue in question. And if it is a basic character virtue that one lacks and therefore seeks to find in another person, the relationship must degenerate into Platonic love.[22]

But one can possess a virtue to the same degree as one's lover and still worship an expression of that virtue in a realm or through skills that one does not possess. For example, I may be as courageous as my lover, but lacking her physical skills and training; I can worship her courage as expressed through her abilities as a skydiver or kickboxer. The unique embodiment of virtues, skills, characteristics, preferences, experiences, gestures, ideas, beliefs, and so forth, constitute the flavor and style of a unique personality. It is this flavor and style that are the building blocks of a person's sense of life, which, according to Rand, is the main component of attraction in a person with whom one falls in love. Being in love implies that two persons' senses of life resonate.

So Rand posited an asymmetry between femininity and masculinity, and hence between men and women, and that was a mistake. However, there *is* an asymmetry here, one not properly addressed or explored by Rand. Being a hero (which, for Rand, means having a productive purpose, developing and using one's abilities and creativity to the fullest, and earning pride in the process)[23] is something that one can achieve for oneself. But hero worship requires *another*, one who is the object and recipient of worship.

This constitutes a fundamental asymmetry. On the one hand, developing a fully self-sufficient ego is a demanding task. Indeed, it is this task that is the very theme of *The Fountainhead*. Still, it involves primarily oneself and thus one self. It rests on factors that are, in principle, available to the individual in the first place, factors *within* the individual. Finding *another* self, however, that special other self with whom one has a great deal in common, developing and maintaining a relationship with this other resonating self, depends on many external factors that may be outside an individual's control. In other words, "finding oneself" is a *self-contained* task, so to speak, while finding another is not.

The need for hero worship is also outwardly directed. It is the need for connection, the crucial foundation for a love relationship. And since this connection emerges through a process of mutual psychological visibility, the need for a hero to worship, in a romantic-sexual context, speaks to the very essence of the relationship. One might say, in this context, that it is even more crucial than the need to be a hero.[24] What each hero needs from a relationship, then, is not primarily the recognition of his or her own heroism, but an outlet for the act of worshiping the other's heroism. Both need to be heroes in the first place, and both need an external source for hero worship.

A romantic relationship with only one hero and one hero-worshiper is dysfunctional; it would reduce the hero-worshiper to a kind of metaphysical parasitism. Rand can easily be read to support and uphold such a position. This is why Rand has never been popular with feminists; and it is certainly a strange position for her to hold, as an individualist.[25]

There must be an equality of worth and an equality of "soul trading" in a relationship, and the asymmetry between being a hero and worshiping a hero (between pride and admiration) destroys that equality, unless both lovers do both. However, since Rand equates masculinity with being a hero, and femininity with hero worship, she obscures our perception of the heroic in women.

I have argued for the mutuality, equality, and symmetry of these needs in all humans, regardless of gender. The paradox is that my case is based on inferences drawn from a rereading of Rand's own philosophy; it suggests that Rand's personal views of gender are at variance with that philosophy.

Love: Aristotelian Versus Platonic

Given this mutuality, this "Randian androgyny" of heroism and hero worship if you like, how different can two people be and still retain a relationship that is equal and mutual? What about Rand's heroes and heroines? Do they fall short of this standard?

Rand's heroic characters, in my view, when examined in isolation, "as individuals," are acceptable, because the author makes it clear that each person is and must be morally complete. The relationship must be its own goal and reward, not a means to some other "higher" end. The key concept here is "moral completeness" (an Aristotelian concept), or, in Randian terminology, "the self-sufficient ego." As Rand states through the character of Howard Roark, in order to say "I love you," one must first be able to say the "I" (Rand [1943] 1986, 377). Exploring this topic, Allan Gotthelf (1989), an Aristotelian scholar and an Objectivist, introduces the opposing concepts of "Aristotelian love" and "Platonic love":

> *Aristotelian love* is that conception of love according to which love of another human being (I) stems from a fundamental *completeness* of person—an achieved moral character and its consequence, an authentic self-love; and (II) is aimed at a heightened, and joyous, self-experience, as an end in itself, not a means to some greater end—because there is no greater end for a human being than his own happiness on earth, and such love is a source of profound happiness. *Platonic love* is that conception of love according to which love of another human being (I) stems from

a fundamental incompleteness of person, and (II) is aimed at some higher goal and value beyond the love relationship itself, through which the desired completeness is approached.

Gotthelf identifies six key aspects of the Aristotelian alternative to Platonic love. First, that there is nothing higher or more real than the individual. Second, that completeness of character (moral perfection) is possible. Third, that humans can achieve full virtues. Fourth, that humans take pride in this, and that this is profoundly good. Fifth, that love of others is an expression of love for self. And sixth, that love is an end in itself.

Gotthelf also identifies romantic love as a species of Aristotelian love. Rand was an Aristotelian in her conceptions of love and sex, building upon and enhancing foundations laid by Aristotle. Since all of Rand's heroes and heroines are (or come to be) morally complete, they practice Aristotelian love. However, if one considers their larger context, a gender-role pattern emerges. A rereading of the Randian canon reveals a pattern that reflects Rand's personal preferences, rather than a universal prescription to be inferred or derived from her philosophy.

Gender: Aristotelian Versus Platonic

For Rand, gender is metaphysical, not human-made. Rand is an advocate of what I call "Platonic gender." Platonic gender is the idea that there exist universal ideal forms of masculinity and femininity, forms that all men and all women respectively and separately either share by birth or ought to adhere to by choice. Rand suggests that gender must be chosen by the individual, in accordance with the individual's biological sex.[26] Hence, Rand appears at first glance to be a nonessentialist, insofar as she posits that individuals do not have an inborn gender identity.

However, Rand claimed that the woman who is or aspires to be the political leader or ruler of men will do damage to herself. This is an essentialist claim, since apparently the woman cannot choose away the alleged damage (resulting from her loss of femininity and her alleged psychological masculinization), a damage that cannot happen to a man. So on the one hand, gender is chosen, but on the other hand, it is not.

Rand's ideas of gender seem to be in conflict with her general philosophical ideas of free will, universal moral virtues, and women's equality.[27]

The idea of Platonic gender runs contrary to Rand's Aristotelianism. In particular, it is incompatible with Aristotelian love, which is the basis for Rand's theory of love. In contrast to Platonic gender, we can formulate an alternative concept: Aristotelian gender. Aristotle's concept of the personal daimon may serve as a basis for this concept: each person is conceived to be constituted of a "daimon," a unique personal identity that is the great sum of all an individual's characteristics (inborn, learned, or chosen—and comprising personality as well as character traits). The gender daimon is that part of this sum which is related to gender. The daimon concept emphasizes the individual and underscores the empirical fact of human variety. This places primacy on the individual context, rather than on the uniform enforcement of universal rules as suggested by Platonic constructs. Aristotelian gender is entirely unique to the individual. Implicit in this view is that one should not try to impose one's own gender daimon on someone else.

Hence, the concept of Aristotelian gender aims (1) to clarify the individuality and variety of gender, and (2) to thwart the uniform collectivism inherent in the traditional, "Platonic" conceptions of gender, masculinity and femininity. Aristotelian gender forms the basis for gender individualism. In a sense, both Aristotelian gender and psychological androgyny are aspects of the same reality. When we examine this reality from the vantage point of Rand and Aristotle, we may call it "Aristotelian gender." When we assume the vantage point of feminism, equality, psychology and cultural anthropology, we may call it "androgyny."

Gender as Human-Made

My point then, is that the ideas of contemporary feminism concerning the (non)relationship of gender and sex are compatible with Objectivism and individualism, unlike Rand's own personal views of gender. Moreover, these ideas are best supported by empirical findings, unlike research purporting to support biological essentialism, "research" that is usually biased, methodologically flawed, and conceptually ambiguous.[28]

So, gender is man-made, not metaphysical;[29] there are no universal gender forms of masculinity or femininity. Gender is Aristotelian; it is personal and unique to the individual. Gender and sex are two different things.[30] Hence, those who uphold Platonic gender, including Rand, commit the epistemological fallacy that Rand called "package-dealing"; they treat sex and gender as the same thing.[31] Platonic gender is in conflict with the idea of tabula rasa, that humans have no inborn ideas. Platonic gender is sex as destiny and sex as duty: a rationale for cultural and social enforcement of collectivist gender roles, and for other rules regulating the expression of gender and sexuality.

The idea of gender roles (and rules) is a form of collectivism, and is incompatible with individualism. The feminist claim that there is no connection, or a weak and breakable connection, between sex and gender[32] is thus not merely an empirical claim, but also a moral imperative. By removing the collectivist restrictions on gender, it becomes possible to treat people as individual humans first, thus liberating them to choose their own path. Ironically, many feminists hold a view on gender roles that is much closer to individualism than are the views of many Randians. When it comes to issues of gender, contemporary feminism is more "Randian" than Rand.

According to Rand, "Man is a being of self-made soul"—and so, of course, is Woman. So why should Man (or Woman) let tradition or other group thinking decide their gender expression or sexual preferences? People have a *right* to be anything they want to be, including a right to limit themselves with collectivist stereotypes. Rand developed and advocated a philosophy of enlightened self-interest, with an imperative to "be all you can be." But this striving for one's best self, this "moral ambitiousness," is irreconcilable with adherence to stereotypes, with reducing oneself to an interchangeable unit in a collectivist binary gender machine.

The Richness of Human Sexuality

Rand ([1968] 1988) tells us "that a properly feminine woman does not treat men as if she were their pal, sister, mother—or *leader*." But she is inconsistent with her own philosophy. Relationships go through dynamic shifts. They are not always about sex or lovemaking. Sometimes a relationship is about emotional support. For example, through a difficult moment, during stress or crisis, one or the other may temporarily assume a role like that of a sister, brother, mother, or father, a situation where sex would be inappropriate. And pal? Certainly friendship is a vital and necessary ingredient in any long-lasting romantic relationship. Often a long-lasting relationship begins as a solid friendship. A lover can be a good pal.[33] There are also such things as sexual friendships—friendships that take on a sexual component, without the assumption of a lasting romantic relationship, and without love in the strict sense.

Furthermore, sex and lovemaking are much richer and more complex realms than Rand seems to allow. Let us identify four different main categories of interaction in human sexuality: (1) male domination with active penile penetration; (2) female domination with active vaginal engulfment; (3) switching roles, sometimes one dominates, sometimes the other; (4) equality, with neither partner more active or dominating.[34] Since this is a conceptual categorization, the four roles may be combined in different ways, or used alternatively in the same sexual experience.

Sciabarra (1995, 200) describes an interpretation of the sexual act as portrayed by Dmitri Sergeyevich Merezhkovsky, a Russian Symbolist poet in the Silver Age era of Rand's youth: "Merezhkovsky had viewed the sexual act as the highest form of unity, since each body is interpenetrated by the other. For Merezhkovsky, true human being involves a synthesis of the womanly aspect in man, and the manly aspect in woman." Sciabarra further points out that this ideal of an indivisible androgyne goes beyond what Objectivists—so far—have accepted, even though some Objectivists reject many culturally induced gender stereotypes (at least in the intellectual and emotional realms).

There are two points that require comment here: First, the use of the word "interpenetration" is unfortunate because it is androcentric, evoking the image of penile penetration to the exclusion of vaginal engulfment. A better term might be, for example, "permeation." Second, while the idea of mutual interpenetration (or permeation) is an improvement over androcentric, one-sided, active male penetration/passive female reception, it is still problematic. The concept seems to hide a great variety in the reality it attempts to describe, ranging from complete female domination and active engulfment to complete male domination and active penetration. Just as the male penetration concept excludes the three other main interaction categories, the mutual interpenetration concept seems to overemphasize the "equal-roles" category (and perhaps male penetration as well, due to the choice of words).

All four sexual-interaction categories are compatible with the feminist "partnership model," as defined by Eisler, only when identified as equally valid personal preferences. None of them would be acceptable or compatible if enforced as a universal prescription.

The Female Hero: A New Synthesis of Rand and Feminism

In this article, I have argued that Ayn Rand laid the foundations for a revolution in our philosophical understanding of human sexuality, love, and relationships, but that her project has been prohibited from reaching its full potential because of flaws and inconsistencies in her notions of gender. The fundamental contradiction is that, in metaphysics, Rand is a gender nonessentialist (gender must be *chosen*), while in metaethics, ethics, and aesthetics, Rand is a gender essentialist (gender *must* be chosen *correctly*). The gender-role restrictions that Rand prescribes as normative universals, and their Platonic underpinnings, undercut the very individualism and revolutionary sexuality inherent in Rand's philosophy.

Because we live in a culture that is both androcentric (derived from its ancient Greek roots)[35] and misogynistic (derived from its Christian heritage), we are culturally deprived of symbols and myths of female power, female heroism. While it is equally important that men reclaim their emotional and nurturing sides ("feminine" virtues), cultural deprivation demands that we concentrate on women's reclamation of power and mastery ("masculine" virtues). This is where the heroic potential in Rand's philosophy meets feminism.

It is my belief that a feminist rereading of the Randian canon can energize and contribute to feminism, by nourishing its individualist aspects. What we need are symbols and myths that integrate female power and sexuality, strength and beauty, courage and grace. What we need is not "heroines" (who are usually reduced to passive prize objects/rewards for male heroes), but *female heroes* (active heroes who happen to be female). The term "heroine" serves to masculinize what can otherwise be an excellent term for a virtuous person—namely, "hero"—because it prevents women from being subsumed under the category of "hero." This is a prime example of how the male is defined as the norm, the human, and the female as a deviation from that norm or as "other" (see also Hofstadter 1987). So starved are we that we grope at any sign, any crumb, we can find of the female hero in popular culture.

As part of the feminist enterprise, archaeologists, historians, and cultural anthropologists (like Eisler) are rediscovering, reclaiming, and reinterpreting ancient images and myths of female power and female heroism. These images and myths of a "new ancient feminism" (Stone [1979] 1990) can be used as vehicles for assessing and interpreting the feminist potential in Rand's philosophy.

There is an archetype of female power and heroism that is known in all cultures and all times, even among the most androcentric and misogynistic ones: the Amazon.[36] Heroic Amazon traditions, ancient Greek mythology and philosophy (including androcentrism), and Rand's ancient Greece–influenced philosophy have a number of intriguing conceptual and historical interconnections. Rand compared one of her heroines to a Valkyrie, a powerful Amazon feminist symbol (see note 5). Is there a basis for an *Amazon feminist* interpretation of Rand,[37] and how would such an interpretation relate to the author's explicit androcentrism?

The Amazon archetype may be the most radical and subversive alternative to gender-role collectivism. The heroic image of a strong and proud woman undaunted in pursuit of her goals is an archetypical image of individualism. Such women, real or imaginary, are excellent role models—heroes—for girls and young women. The popular culture icon of the contemporary female action hero is a relatively new phenomenon in films, but an old trend in myths and literature. Popular culture provides many examples of how Amazon myths are rewritten in order to sunder female power and female sexuality.

Red Sonja, a 1985 Dino de Laurentis movie based on the character from Robert E. Howard's Conan stories, is one such example. She is a strong and capable Amazon warrior, and she has sworn not to make love to any man that has not beaten her in a sword fight. As a result of her prowess and ability, she is a virgin. This is an old idea; we also find it in Goethe's story about Siegfried and Brunhilde, where Brunhilde is far too strong to be conquered, and so Siegfried cheats her into believing that he has actually conquered her. But Brunhilde is chaste; she does not use her power to get a lover, as a man would do.

There are several ancient Greek myths with similar motifs, such as the myth of Atalanta, an Amazonian huntress and the best athlete in Calydon, who could outrun any man and would only marry a man who could outrun her. She was beaten when she was tricked into stopping to pick up three golden apples dropped by one of the suitors. The message remains that a woman must renounce her power if she is to have a lover or to exist as a sexual being.

The idea that Amazons are chaste or asexual beings stems from the conception of sexuality as an act of conquest by which an active male subdues a passive female and makes her surrender. In this context, the act of sex is always interpreted as penetration—and, hence, domination—even if it is initiated and led by a female giant interacting with a male dwarf. But a strong, autonomous, female hero is not submissive, and has not surrendered. Conventional wisdom tells us that such a female denies her own femininity and sexuality; she is virginal.

However, the original meaning of the term "virgin" is a woman who is whole unto herself, not controlled by a male (Naisbitt and Aburdene 1994). She has a self-contained identity, or, in Rand's terminology, a self-sufficient ego. Artemis and Athena were called virgins, even though they took lovers, because their myths are not defined by family members; theirs were self-contained identities.

The literal meaning of virginity is not sexual celibacy or abstinence, but the state of being unmarried. Larson (1995, 100) writes: "The virgin, because purity was a kind of freedom from the sexual claims of any man, was theoretically more free than the wife. This conceptual freedom was translated into the power of virgins in myth. Virgins were associated with the wild and untamed; hunters were often required to maintain chastity. The verb *damazo*, 'tame,' referred to the taking of a wife."[38] This is a powerful illustration of the cultural sundering of female sexuality and female power. In order to be a sexual being, a woman must be accessible to a man, available for conquest and penetration. If she is not, she cannot have a sex life, and a sexuality, because these are given to her by the man. She cannot take them on her own; she cannot herself win or conquer a man and take him into her, engulfing him—or so this mythology will have us believe. Hence, as a result of an overemphasis on the first sexual-interaction category, male domination and conquest, the powerful woman is widely imagined as virginal, and perhaps even sexless.

Rereading Rand's "Woman President" essay in this context is illuminating. Rand describes the woman in power as "totally depersonalized," "utterly selfless," "incommunicably lonely," "unfeminine," "metaphysically inappropriate," and "rationally revolting." In essence, Rand's formulation is part of an old, ignoble canonical tradition stretching back to the androcentric society of ancient Greece.

Men Are from Earth; Women Are from Earth

The pernicious combination of androcentrism and gender polarization has sundered female power and female sexuality, thus depriving us all of female heroes. This whole approach corrupts and degrades the female, in fact and on principle. The Western canon has for too long been starved for integrated symbols of female power and female sexuality. Dagny Taggart at her best is a glaring exception—a railroad-running Randian protagonist of Amazonian proportions. But Amazon myths, images, and stories have often been repressed, obscured, rewritten in an androcentric image. Still, they persist, return, and resurface.

At this time, a revival seems to be under way in popular culture. A few years ago, Wonder Woman, the Bionic Woman, Modesty Blaise, and Pippi Longstocking (for the younger ones) were rare examples of popular female action heroes. Today, however, there is an increasing interest in real-life female heroes who serve as lifeguards, firefighters, astronauts, and athletes. Women are gaining access to professions and positions traditionally associated with masculinity. In sports, in particular, female martial artists excel in power, skill, and self-confidence. Female bodybuilders, sculptors of living flesh, use the body as a vehicle to express determination, power, beauty, and sexuality, an integration of mind, body, and spirit (Dobbins 1994; Ian 1991). Such women are inherently feminist, insofar as they threaten not men, but male privilege and masculinity. They challenge and change the very assumptions of androcentrism and gender polarization. They constitute a new "Power Feminism for the twenty-first century," as advocated by the new feminists (Wolf 1993).

The cultural revival is expressed further in the explosive popularity of the larger-than-life TV-action-fantasy-series hero Xena, who has skyrocketed into the American consciousness (Crenshaw 1997). Xena is a role model for many American girls. Other cinematic examples can be found in the *Alien* movies, *Terminator 2*, and in the fantasy and science-fiction work of feminist writers in the heroic-fiction tradition.[39]

Perhaps the long winter is drawing to a close, as it is realized that female-hero deprivation in the culture is a problem for both girls and boys, women and men. Indeed, to the extent that men are responsible for androcentricity and gender polarization, they have also punished themselves. They deprive and drain their own existence of the inspiration, zest, and color that only a female hero can bring. A master-slave relationship among men and women entails mutual dependency. As Rand ([1943] 1986, 691) observed, "[A] leash is only a rope with a noose at both ends." A master may be as rigidly confined to his role as a slave. Both the master and the slave could benefit greatly from breaking out of a gender-role prison. They would lose their separate role perks, but they would collaborate in the process of dismantling the polarization that has crippled them.

This is the potential in Rand's vision—and in its synthesis with feminism. Rand limited herself to the task of projecting Man the Hero, the ideal man. The time is ripe for Woman the Hero, the ideal woman—woman as equal and woman as conqueror. Those who wish to carry forth Rand's legacy should take it upon themselves to uphold "Randian androgynes"—a fully realized heroism that extends to female and male heroes equally. It is a synthesis that clears Rand's philosophy of androcentric and Platonic gender ideals, while clearing feminism of any vestige of collectivism and victimology. The future belongs to the androgynes and postandrogynes.

Notes

1. I use the terms "Randian" and "Randianism" broadly to describe the philosophy and philosophers influenced by and building upon Rand (on a par with "Aristotelian," "Kantian," etc.). Hence "Randian" is a broader term than "Objectivist" (but narrower than "Aristotelian," if one agrees that Randianism is a tradition within Aristotelianism).

2. See Rand [1943] 1986, 219–21. I do not mean to suggest that these scenes imply or advocate rape. There is a distinction between rape and physical force, and the two must not be confused. The essential characteristic of rape is *nonconsensuality* (Amsden 1983b). The use of physical force need not be part of rape, because it can be consensual. Erotic combat is a valid and moral preference. If one of the lovers has a distinct physical prowess and "superiority," this can be a resource for sexual playfulness and a basis for hero worship in action. Just as there can be physical force without rape, there can be rape without physical force. Having sex with an unconscious person is rape. Sex coerced with threats is rape, even if no actual physical force is exerted.

3. One might argue that Dagny Taggart was mentally superior to Hank Rearden and that, in spite of this, they had a love affair. But this love relationship was a temporary one—it was over the moment that Dagny set eyes on John Galt. At that point, Galt became the center of Dagny Taggart's romantic-sexual life. Both Rearden and later Francisco d'Anconia immediately accept Galt as the winner of Dagny's love. Hence, the Rearden–Dagny Taggart relationship is not an exception to Rand's general ideal of male superiority, but a particular way of illustrating how this ideal is supposed to work.

4. Consider also Rand's reply to Peikoff concerning *Think Twice*: "Do you think that I would ever give the central action in a story of mine to anyone but the hero?" (1984, 333).

5. While Dagny Taggart is usually perceived to be the mature and most fully realized Rand

heroine, a case may be made that in the context of feminism, gender, and sexuality, Kira Argounova of *We the Living* may in fact be a better candidate. See Valérie Loiret-Prunet's essay in this volume. Since *We the Living* is an early work by Rand, the male hero has not yet gained primacy over the heroine. Kira is in fact stronger than both Andrei and Leo, and profoundly determines the course of their lives, even though she chooses the pose of submitting to them. The descriptions of Kira underscore her strength and power, her heroism (3, 4, and 26–37). She is contrasted both to her stereotypically feminine sister Lydia and to the masculine Communist Comrade Sonia, and she may in many ways be perceived as androgynous. She is also compared to a Valkyrie (27)—a symbol of female power and the conqueror of heroes. Dagny Taggart, on the other hand, is subject to the mature Rand's literary obsession with male primacy.

6. Rand [1943] 1986, 581: "She had the special faculty of making satin and perfume appear as modern as an aluminum table top. She was Venus rising out of a submarine hatch. Eve Layton believed that her mission in life was to be the vanguard—it did not matter of what. Her method had always been to take a careless leap and land triumphantly far ahead of all others. Her philosophy consisted of one sentence—'I can get away with anything.' In conversation she paraphrased it to her favorite line: 'I? I'm the day after tomorrow.' She was an expert horsewoman, a racing driver, a stunt pilot, a swimming champion."

7. Rand [1936] 1959, 51: "The young woman had broad shoulders and a masculine leather jacket; short husky legs and flat masculine oxfords; a red kerchief tied carelessly over short straight hair; eyes wide apart in a round freckled face; thin lips drawn together with so obvious and fierce a determination that they seemed weak; dandruff on the black leather of her shoulders."

8. Rand generously condemns the irrationality of Freudianism; yet one of the most bizarre consequences of Rand's views on gender is that she actually provides some rationalization for Freud's concept of "penis envy." After all, if a penis is required in order to be a powerful subject, a seducer, a sexual initiator and aggressor, and a hero, then surely it must be rational to want one?

9. One wonders whether a romantic liaison between a man and a physically stronger, bigger, or more energetic woman (or even a woman equal in these respects) would be considered abnormal or immoral; the formulations would seem to favor such a conclusion.

10. Rand divides philosophy into five disciplines: metaphysics, epistemology, ethics, politics, and aesthetics.

11. Actually, one need only consider Rand's *Playboy* interview (1964, 7) to see a contradiction with her general philosophy:

> *Playboy:* Do you believe that women as well as men should organize their lives around work—and if so, what kind of work?
> *Rand:* Of course. I believe that women are human beings. What is proper for a man is proper for a woman. The basic principles are the same. I would not attempt to prescribe what kind of work a man should do, and I would not attempt it in regard to women. There is no particular work which is specifically feminine. Women can choose their work according to their own purpose and premises in the same manner as men do.

This is Rand's general philosophy, and it directly contradicts what Rand says in her "Woman President" essay.

12. For a much more plausible and better-investigated interpretation of Joan of Arc, see Feinberg 1996, chap. 4, and Walker 1983, s.v. "Joan of Arc."

13. See Rand 1990, 75–82, 154–58, and 193–96, and Peikoff 1991, 48–52.

14. See, for example, Fausto-Sterling 1992; Tavris 1992; Caplan and Caplan 1994; Lenskyj 1987; Rothblatt 1995; Vetterling-Braggin 1982.

15. See Rand [1964] 1970, 28; 1975b, 190.

16. Even the assumption of a male-female duality is being challenged, by intersexuals and transgenders as well as by increasing historical and cultural anthropological data suggesting that several,

perhaps most, cultures operate with more than two sexes/genders. See, for example, Rothblatt 1995 and Feinberg 1996.

17. See Burke 1996 and Feinberg 1993.

18. By "ethical androgyny," I mean a moral imperative that identifies all virtues (and all vices) as *human* virtues (and vices). This rejects the idea of gendered (masculine or feminine) virtues (and vices). Ethical androgyny must not be confused with androgyny as a gender expression (androgynous looks, "unisex" clothing, etc.), since it assumes that all gender expressions are equally valid, as morally neutral options available to the individual.

19. See Trebilcot 1982.

20. In Randian terminology, we could say that androgyny is a concept of method.

21. Note however, that the sex-gender distinction follows from and depends upon the canon of Western ideas and culture. Other cultures (notably many Native American and African cultures), without a history of gender rigidity and oppression, without androcentrism, biological essentialism, and gender-sex dualism, depart from the duality. See Mead [1949] 1975 and Feinberg 1996, especially chap. 3.

22. In a Randian or Aristotelian context, Platonic love is unhealthy and undesirable for several reasons. First, Platonic love assumes that sex, as opposed to "pure love" (an example of the mind-body dichotomy), is impure and base. Second, it assumes that love has a "higher purpose" than itself, that is, that love is a means to some other goal, such as moral or religious improvement. Thus, love is not a goal in itself, but is demoted to a lower status. Third, the idea of Platonic love, based upon Plato's metaphysics, rejects the importance of the individual, and the possibility for completeness of character for which an Aristotelian ethics provides.

23. Interestingly, and unfortunately, neither "hero" nor "heroism" nor "masculinity" is explicitly defined in the Randian corpus, and none of these terms is to be found in the index of any of Rand's books or in *The Ayn Rand Lexicon*. Masculinity is, however, implicitly equated with being a hero, since femininity is defined as hero worship. But notice how this concept of masculinity contradicts Rand's general philosophy—where heroism is understood as a *human* character trait, as a sum and effect of *human* life-affirming and necessary virtues. Recently Andrew Bernstein (1998) has addressed the issue of heroism in an on-line article, discussed by Gramstad (1998).

24. It must be stressed, however, that these two needs are not to be conceived as dualistic opposites, but as relational and as mutually reinforcing, thus constituting an organic unity. Consider Gail Wynand's worship of Dominique in *The Fountainhead*: "It was a strange glance; she had noticed it before; a glance of simple worship. And it made her realize that there is a stage of worship which makes the worshiper himself an object of reverence" (Rand [1943] 1986, 509). In other words, the ability to worship is both an expression of a person's heroism and a causal factor in creating and establishing that heroism. In order to become heroic, one must first desire heroic being, and in order to desire this, one must value (or worship) the perceived heroism in another. So hero worship is more fundamental, but the fundamental and the derivative constitute a reciprocal, bicausal organic whole. For a discussion of the role and importance of organic unity in Rand's thought, see Sciabarra 1995, especially 17, 117, 128, 138, 145, 256, 269, and 403 n. 5. A relationship with one hero and one hero-worshiper would sunder organic unity and create dualistic opposition. This is why we talk of "opposite" sexes and the "war between the sexes." This feminist rereading of Rand stresses organic unity in its rejection of "opposite" sexes and the gender-role collectivist ideology associated with them.

25. The famous Russian filmmaker Andrej Tarkovskij has said that when the masculine world and the feminine world meet in a relationship, the feminine must give way and reorient itself according to the masculine. This attitude seems to be very common in Russia, taken for granted even by the Communists. Rand may have inherited this attitude from her environment (see Sciabarra 1995). It was a part of the Russian air she breathed, an aspect of the Russian culture of her youth, and may have been reinforced by Rand's childhood admiration of Hollywood.

26. See Rand [1968] 1988. See also notes 15 and 34.

27. See note 11.

28. See, for example, Fausto-Sterling 1992; Tavris 1992; Caplan and Caplan 1994; Lenskyj 1987; Rothblatt 1995; Vetterling-Braggin 1982.

29. Normally I would say "human-made," not "man-made." However, I use the term "man-made" at this juncture because "the metaphysical versus the man-made" is a central motif in Rand's philosophy (see her essay by that title in Rand 1982b). Furthermore, the androcentrism, misogyny, gender polarization, and biological essentialism in our culture are to a large degree *man*-made.

30. For a discussion of the different meanings of sex and gender, see the introduction to Vetterling-Braggin 1982. See also Burke 1996 and Bem 1993.

31. It is a curious parallel between Rand and Aristotle that they both were unable to overcome so many of the poor gender stereotypes of their respective ages, in spite of rethinking and innovating so many other areas of their contemporary thought. Even more curious is the fact that Plato was a gender egalitarian; he did not accept the low and restricted view of women of his day. Aristotle was the one who, in advocating male and female essences, applied Platonic forms to gender.

32. See Vetterling-Braggin 1982, pt. 4. See also Tavris 1992; Caplan and Caplan 1994; Lenskyj 1987.

33. Rand's novels have many instances of this. For example, Dagny was a pal to Frisco before their love affair ended; after they became "enemies," their relations retained elements of friendship. Hank and Dagny were friendly business associates.

34. There are other dimensions as well, concerning, for example, degrees of tenderness and of playfulness (Branden 1983). Yet another dimension is the type of activity, such as polymorphous (nongenital) sex. The idea of genital sex as the only worthy form of sex, while anything else is just "foreplay," is another result of the androcentric and gender-polarized view of human sexuality.

Moreover, since the gender of the lovers does not make any difference (there is no such thing as a gender role or a gender duty), the lovers need not be of different sexes. They may both be of the one sex, or the other sex, or one of each sex. Being heterosexual, I frame this whole essay in heterosexual terms, but I see no reason to assume that the arguments I make are not equally valid for a gay or lesbian couple. Quite the contrary, unlike many Objectivists, who exhibit antigay sentiment, I say that we don't need to know the developmental origins of homosexuality in order to evaluate its morality. The validity of homosexuality as a neutral moral option (neither a virtue nor a vice)—like heterosexuality—follows directly from two premises: (1) the "metaphysical egalitarianism" of women and men, and (2) the mutuality of pride and admiration in relationships, as I have described. This is in stark contrast to Rand, who perceived homosexuality as "immoral" and "disgusting," a result of "psychological flaws and corruptions" (Rand 1971). One might assume that she would have been most opposed to lesbianism, since that, by her own definition, supposedly cannot involve a hero. This assumption seems to be confirmed in Rand's expressed disgust with the Women's Lib movement: "[T]o proclaim spiritual sisterhood with lesbians, and to swear eternal hostility to men—is so repulsive a set of premises from so loathsome a sense of life that an accurate commentary would require the kind of language I do not like to see in print" (Rand 1975a, 175).

Rand's antigay sentiment has been softened somewhat by Peikoff (1994). Peikoff's statement is worth quoting at length:

> Romantic love is the status of one individual to another when that individual is irreplaceable in the person's life, a profound passion that was not necessarily sexual, but of a completely different order than friendship. . . . And [Rand] felt that this was a very profound need of man, to have relationships that have this deeper commitment. . . . Now, she did not see any reason why one man could not feel this for another, or for that matter, one woman for another. . . . Ayn Rand, as you know, was not a great admirer of women—and I asked her . . . if you had a choice, would you have wanted to be born a man? . . . And . . . she said . . . "Oh no, then I would have to love a woman.". . . And the idea for her as a woman and as a man-worshiper, having her love object as a woman was just too awful to be contemplated.

Now, therefore, she had great sympathy for the idea of Man as the hero and another man seeing that, particularly in a case like Wynand and Roark, where they're equals, and yet at the same time Roark has an edge of strength, and Wynand sees that this is what he could have become. It was a setup for two such passionate valuers, one to reply to the other. She told me she even had Roark nude, naked, in front of Wynand, when he . . . came out of the water, on the yacht, and Wynand says to him, "it should have been a statue of you." That's the closest she got to hinting, not that there was a sexual relation, but that Wynand was in love with this man so profoundly that he even had a special aesthetic pleasure from looking at his body.

Peikoff admits that "philosophy as such has [nothing] to say about sexual orientation," but he suggests that Roark and Wynand do not have a sexual relationship, because "essential" to sexuality is "conquest and surrender, or dominance and submission." Rand, he says, saw these roles not as arbitrary, but as having an "anatomical basis. There has to be a reason in the nature of the two bodies why one conquers and why one surrenders. Otherwise, she thought it was arbitrary, demeaning and irrational. . . . for that reason she believed that homosexuality was improper. Not immoral. . . . You could be completely moral and just trapped in an upbringing and conclusions that you didn't under-stand, but objectively wrong, in that, knowingly or not, it is a defiance of one of the conditions of a mature and healthy sexual relationship. But that is not the same thing . . . as this irreplaceable male love relationship," symbolized in the Roark-Wynand connection.

Given Rand's expressed disgust with homosexuality, and her view of romantic love as "an inte-grated response of mind and body, of love and sexual desire," as a "profound, exalted, lifelong *passion* that unites . . . mind and body in the sexual act" (1988, 54–56), it is clear that Peikoff has deviated from Rand's position—even while maintaining her Platonic view of gender.

35. It may be noted that ancient Greece had its share of strong women, exemplified in panthe-ons, myths, literature, theater plays, and so forth. But the range of choice, expression, and societal participation for women was severely limited. According to Larson (1995, 8): "As a general rule, only heroines who *lack* significant familial ties (i.e., husband or son) can stand alone"—and thus be independent female heroes.

36. The Amazons were a people who originally lived in Asia Minor and North Africa, among whom women were political and military leaders, and soldiers (Bell 1991; Stone 1976, [1979] 1990; Walker 1983). They are known from Greek legends; the Greeks feared them, and they were long believed to be invincible. The term has survived in the vernacular, usually referring to any tall and strong woman—or, more generally, referring to any woman who is vigorous, unafraid, outspoken. Women like this are known in all cultures. But androcentric societies disparage and debase them, and institutionalize social and cultural patterns that suppress and oppress such qualities in girls and women.

37. The soc.feminism terminology FAQ file presents this definition of "Amazon feminism": "Amazon feminism is dedicated to the image of the female hero in fiction and in fact, as it is expressed in art and literature, in the physiques and feats of female athletes, and in sexual values and practices. . . . Amazon feminism rejects the idea that certain characteristics or interests are inherently masculine (or feminine), and upholds and explores a vision of heroic womanhood" (http://www.cis.ohio-state.edu/hypertext/faq/usenet/feminism/terms/faq.html).

38. Modern texts about reclaiming "wild-woman" archetypes address the same situation. See, for example, Estes 1995.

39. For example: Joanna Russ, Marion Zimmer Bradley, Mercedes Lackey, Tanith Lee, and Anne McCaffrey.

References

Amsden, Diana Avery. 1983a. *An Index to Ayn Rand's "Atlas Shrugged."* Santa Fe: Diana Avery Amsden.

————. 1983b. *Some Observations on Ayn Rand and Her Work*. North Hollywood, Calif.
Pamphlet.

Bell, Robert E. 1991. *Women of Classical Mythology: A Biographical Dictionary*. New York:
Oxford University Press.

Bem, Sandra Lipsitz. 1971. The theory and measurement of androgyny. *Journal of Personality and Social Psychology* 37:1047–54.

————. 1993. *The Lenses of Gender: Transforming the Debate on Sexual Inequality*. New
Haven: Yale University Press.

Bernstein, Andrew. 1998. The philosophical foundations of heroism. http://www.mikem-
entzer.com/heroism.html.

Binswanger, Harry, ed. 1986. *The Ayn Rand Lexicon: Objectivism from A to Z*. New York:
New American Library.

Branden, Nathaniel. 1968. Self-esteem and romantic love (part 2). *Objectivist* 7, no. 1.
(Also published in *The Psychology of Self-Esteem: A New Concept of Man's Psychological Nature*. New York: Bantam, [1969] 1987.)

————. [1980] 1983. *The Psychology of Romantic Love*. New York: Bantam.

————. 1983. Love and sex in the philosophy of Ayn Rand. Washington, D.C.: Biocentric Institute. Audiotape.

————. 1996. Interview by Karen Reedstrom. *Full Context*, October.

Burke, Phyllis. 1996. *Gender Shock: Exploding the Myths of Male and Female*. New York:
Anchor Books.

Caplan, Paula J., and Jerry Caplan. 1994. *Thinking Critically About Research on Sex and
Gender*. New York: HarperCollins.

Chesler, Phyllis. 1994. *Patriarchy: Notes of an Expert Witness*. Monroe, Maine: Common
Courage Press.

Crenshaw, Nadine. 1997. *Xena X-posed: The Unauthorized Biography of Lucy Lawless and
Her On-Screen Character*. New York: Prima Publishing.

Dobbins, Bill. 1994. *The Women: Photographs of the Top Female Bodybuilders*. New York:
Artisan.

Eisler, Riane. [1987] 1995. *The Chalice and the Blade: Our History, Our Future*. San Francisco: Harper.

Estes, Clarissa Pinkola. 1995. *Women Who Run With the Wolves: Myths and Stories of the
Wild Woman Archetype*. New York: Ballantine.

Farrell, Warren. 1990. *Why Men Are the Way They Are*. London: Bantam.

————. 1994. *The Myth of Male Power*. London: Fourth Estate.

Fausto-Sterling, Anne. 1992. *Myths of Gender: Biological Theories About Women and Men*.
New York: Basic Books.

Feinberg, Leslie. 1993. *Stone Butch Blues*. Ithaca, N.Y.: Firebrand.

————. 1996. *Transgender Warriors: Making History from Joan of Arc to RuPaul*. Boston:
Beacon Press.

Gladstein, Mimi Reisel. 1986. *The Ayn Rand Companion*. Westport, Conn.: Greenwood
Press.

Gotthelf, Allan. 1989. Love and philosophy: Aristotelian vs. Platonic. Handout from
lecture delivered at the EuroCon Objectivist Conference in Amsterdam, 27 May.

Gramstad, Thomas. 1990. Sex vs. gender. The Mail-men electronic mailing list (October). Internet.

————. 1992. Red Sonja—a review. Amazons International 17. Internet.

————. 1998. Heroism: Rand's and Bernstein's. *Full Context* 10, no. 7:4–6.

Hite, Shere. 1987. *The Hite Report: Women and Love, a Cultural Revolution in Progress*.
New York: Penguin.

Hofstadter, Douglas R. 1987. *Metamagical Themas: Questing for the Essence of Mind and Pattern*. New York: Penguin.

Ian, Marcia. 1991. From abject to object: Women's bodybuilding. *Postmodern Culture* 1, no. 3.

Larson, Jennifer. 1995. *Greek Heroine Cults*. Madison: University of Wisconsin Press.

Lenskyj, Helen. 1987. *Out of Bounds: Women, Sport, and Sexuality*. Toronto: Women's Press.

Mead, Margaret. [1949] 1975. *Male and Female: The Classic Study of the Sexes*. New York: William Morrow.

Monaghan, Patricia. 1990. *The Book of Goddesses and Heroines*. St. Paul, Minn.: Llewellyn Publications.

Naisbitt, John, and Patricia Aburdene. 1994. *Megatrends for Women*. London: Arrow Books.

Nelson, Mariah Burton. 1991. *Are We Winning Yet? How Women Are Changing Sports and Sports Are Changing Women*. New York: Random House.

——. 1994. *The Stronger Women Get, the More Men Love Football: Sexism and the American Culture of Sports*. New York: Avon Books.

Peikoff, Leonard. 1991. *Objectivism: The Philosophy of Ayn Rand*. New York: Penguin Dutton.

——. 1994. *Eight Great Plays*. 9 lectures (18 audio tapes), tape 4, 2B. New Milford, Conn.: Second Renaissance Books.

Rand, Ayn. [1936] 1959. *We the Living*. New York: Random House.

——[1943] 1986. *The Fountainhead*. New York: Bobbs-Merrill.

——. 1957. *Atlas Shrugged*. New York: Random House.

——. [1961] 1968. *For the New Intellectual*. New York: New American Library.

——. 1964. *Playboy* interview with Ayn Rand: A candid conversation with the fountainhead of "Objectivism." *Playboy*, March, 35–43.

——. [1964] 1970. *The Virtue of Selfishness: A New Concept of Egoism*. New York: New American Library.

——. 1968. *Night of January 16th*. New York: New American Library.

——. [1968] 1988. About a woman president. In *The Voice of Reason: Essays in Objectivist Thought*, edited by Leonard Peikoff. New York: New American Library. Originally published in *The Objectivist*, December 1968.

——. 1971. The moratorium on brains. Oceanside, Calif.: Second Renaissance Books. Audiotape.

——. 1975a. The age of envy. In *The New Left: The Anti-Industrial Revolution*, 2d rev. ed. New York: New American Library.

——. 1975b. The comprachicos. In *The New Left: The Anti-Industrial Revolution*, 2d rev. ed. New York: New American Library.

——. 1975c. The goal of my writing. In *The Romantic Manifesto: A Philosophy of Literature*, 2d rev. ed. New York: New American Library.

——. 1982a. *Anthem*. Caldwell, Idaho: Caxton Printers.

——. 1982b. *Philosophy: Who Needs It*. New York: Bobbs-Merrill.

——. 1984. *The Early Ayn Rand: A Selection from Her Unpublished Fiction*. Edited by Leonard Peikoff. New York: New American Library.

——. 1990. *Introduction to Objectivist Epistemology*. 2d enl. ed. Edited by Harry Binswanger and Leonard Peikoff. New York: New American Library.

Rothblatt, Martine. 1995. *The Apartheid of Sex: A Manifesto on the Freedom of Gender*. New York: Crown Publications.

Sciabarra, Chris Matthew. 1995. *Ayn Rand: The Russian Radical*. University Park: Pennsylvania State University Press.

Stone, Merlin. 1976. *When God was a Woman.* San Diego: Harcourt Brace Jovanovich.
———. [1979] 1990. *Ancient Mirrors of Womanhood: A Treasury of Goddess and Heroine Lore from Around the World.* Boston: Beacon Press.
Tavris, Carol. 1992. *The Mismeasure of Woman: Why Women are not the Better Sex, the Inferior Sex, or the Opposite Sex.* New York: Simon & Schuster.
Taylor, Joan Kennedy. 1992. *Reclaiming the Mainstream: Individualist Feminism Rediscovered.* Buffalo, N.Y.: Prometheus Books.
Trebilcot, Joyce. 1982. Two forms of androgynism. In *"Femininity," "Masculinity," and "Androgyny": A Modern Philosophical Discussion,* edited by Mary Vetterling-Braggin. Totowa, N.J.: Rowman & Allanheld.
Vetterling-Braggin, Mary, ed. 1982. *"Femininity," "Masculinity," and "Androgyny": A Modern Philosophical Discussion.* Totowa, N.J.: Rowman & Allanheld.
Walker, Barbara G. 1983. *The Woman's Encyclopedia of Myths and Secrets.* New York: HarperCollins.
———. 1996. *Feminist Fairy Tales.* New York: HarperCollins.
Warren, Mary Anne. 1982. Is androgyny the answer to sexual stereotyping? In *"Femininity," "Masculinity," and "Androgyny": A Modern Philosophical Discussion,* edited by Mary Vetterling-Braggin. Totowa, N.J.: Rowman & Allanheld.
Wolf, Naomi. 1993. *Fire with Fire: The New Female Power and How It Will Change the 21st Century.* New York: Random House.
Wu, Qingyun. 1995. *Female Rule in Chinese and English Literary Utopias.* Liverpool: Liverpool University Press.

19

Fluff and Granite: Rereading Ayn Rand's Camp Feminist Aesthetics

Melissa Jane Hardie

I

Writing in 1978, in reply to Mimi Gladstein's proposition that Rand's work might be included on the women's studies syllabus, Judith Wilt commented: "I *could* wish that the cancer-causing cigarette were not the ultimate symbol of glowing mind-controlling matter in the book, I could wish that the rails which reflect the self-assertion of the heroine were not envisioned running to the hands of a man invisible beyond the horizon. . . . But yes, I agree with Mimi Gladstein, there is a feminist element in Ayn Rand's *Atlas Shrugged*, and it's on my ideal women's studies reading list too" (Wilt 1978, 333).[1] It is entirely appropriate to the argument of this paper that it opens by rearticulating a scholarly debate initiated over twenty years ago. Wilt's anxiety over the "cancer-causing cigarette" is shared by Gladstein (1984), for whom Rand's cancer demonstrated the difference between life and art: "The cigarettes that had served Rand effectively as a dramatic symbol served her ill in real life" (17).

In *Cigarettes Are Sublime*, Richard Klein (1993) extrapolates precisely this asymmetry of the cigarette; for him, it offers a negative experience that figures the paradox of the sublime: "Kant calls 'sublime' that aesthetic satisfaction which includes as one of its moments a negative experience, a shock, a blockage, an intimation of mortality. It is in this very strict sense that Kant gives the term that the beauty of cigarettes may be considered to be sublime. . . . The sublimity of cigarettes explains why people love what tastes nasty and makes them sick" (xi). For Klein, the defense of the indefensible is necessarily extravagant: "To say that cigarettes are sublime installs a ratio that allows one to conclude that they are not simply abysmal" (18). The argument of this paper follows a similar logic: to say that a return to Rand is useful to feminism offers one way to conclude that her work is not simply inimical to it. In their camp appeal and paradoxical readability—paradoxical because the novels are repetitious, didactic, excessively long, and formulaic—the Rand novels generate their own desiring economy.

The relationship between Ayn Rand and feminism is historically problematic: Rand's infamous proclamation that "the essence of femininity is hero worship" ([1968] 1988, 268) suggests a fundamental subordination of femininity to masculinity, as do the often violent heterosexual dynamics of *Atlas Shrugged* and *The Fountainhead*. Never one to mince words, in the 1970s Rand suggested that the understanding of sex offered by "Women's Lib" demonstrated "so repulsive a set of premises from so loathsome a sense of life that an accurate commentary would require the kind of language I do not like to see in print" ([1971] 1975, 175). Rand's critique of Women's Lib maintains that the claim of feminism is based on "weakness" (175). Though her trenchant vocabulary could hardly be reproduced, in her critique of a victim-based idea of feminism she prefigures the ambit issues that define a critique of equality feminism, one that has enjoyed some currency throughout the eighties and nineties. Sciabarra (1996, 533) notes that Rand observed that "the 'real warfare' of the neofascist 'mixed' economy is not between classes but within them"; Rand's work similarly may provide one unlikely way to contour the debates *within* feminism over the nature of representation *in* feminism. My argument uses Rand's own analyses of representation and identification to argue the value of camp as a reading strategy for feminist fans of Rand. It will focus on the cinematic realization of *The Fountainhead* in 1949, and the extended history of a Rand "cult" in Mary Gaitskill's 1991 novel, *Two Girls, Fat and Thin*, to explore a feminist interpretation of Rand.

In 1975, Susan Brownmiller described Ayn Rand as a "traitor to her own sex" (315).[2] Brownmiller's *Against Our Will*, at nearly five hundred pages itself a monumental text of Second Wave feminism, introduces its analysis of Freudian models of female masochism with a reminiscence and return to *The Fountainhead*:

> [W]hen I requested it at the library, I was faintly anxious that the search for Dominique's undoing amid the more than seven hundred pages of Rand's opus might take more time than I cared to spend. I seriously underestimated the universality of my interest. The library's copy of *The Fountainhead* opened itself to Dominique's rape. Hundreds of other readers had, in effect, indexed it for me. And I must say, the two-and-a-half-page scene was as torrid as I had remembered it—all the more remarkable in the light of present-day fiction since, the genitals of the two antagonists are not even mentioned. (315)

Brownmiller's account suggests a "universality" of interest not in *The Fountainhead* per se, but in the section for which she searches. Her move pursues the logic of the collective "our" of her title, a logic antithetical to that of Rand's career as antagonist of *"the great WE"* (Rand 1946, 14). For Rand, the substitution of the plural for the singular first person was the linguistic registration of collective tyranny. In her quest for material, Brownmiller locates a shared experience of reading, one that ties her nostalgic past to the experience of other readers: "*The Fountainhead* heated my virgin blood more than twenty years ago and may still be performing that service for schoolgirls today" (1975, 315). Her haste similarly reproduces past reading habits; reading for speed is a characteristic of the "adolescent reader," according to Matei Calinescu. Brownmiller's haste is not simply the symptom of an adult who, as critic and feminist, disdains her text, but also the professionalized version of that indexing process which identifies the pleasure of the adolescent reader: "[O]ne of the cardinal rules in their informal code of reading for pleasure seems to be speed" (Calinescu 1993, 98).

Brownmiller's anecdote of return, however, replaces the effect of the

other readers—their indexing of the excerpt—with an assumption of
what that reading might be: semipornographic, in that the passage both
"heats" the "virgin blood" and yet marks the time of its reading as "virgin," historical, vitiated in its pornographic potential by the present—by
current practices of "present-day fiction." Notwithstanding her agonistic
rehearsal of the scene, it provides corporeal as well as intellectual self-
recognition. The excerpt, in fact, may be regarded as metonymy for the
cult reader's particular relationship to the text, as I will argue. Brownmiller's anecdote stages her adversarial analysis of *The Fountainhead* as an
autobiographical moment of recognition: "The vivid picture I had carried in my memory for more than twenty years was surprisingly accurate"
(1975, 314). Aligning herself with the cult readership of *The Fountainhead*, Brownmiller allies her critique with the reading practices of Rand's
fans, in that she exhibits their same symptoms: return and repetition. In
a complimentary move, the text itself bears the effects of other hands,
the corporeal and intellectual work of reading and rereading: the text in
Brownmiller's account installs a passive reader as it "opens itself,"
through the services of readers who read before her.

The excerpt, of course, was a textual strategy adopted by Rand herself.
For the New Intellectual, for example, excerpts and glosses sections of
Rand's novels. The "new intellectual" might be regarded as the logical
antithesis of "virgin blood," where "virgin" stands for the historical, and
"blood" for the corporeal. The lines of my argument lie somewhere between each of these distinctions: on the one hand, between the old and
the new, or the modern and the historicized; and, on the other hand,
between the intellectual and the corporeal. Gladstein (1984, 25) refers
to Rand's agonistic phrasing of her project of cultural salvage through the
topos of the "antipodes," listing three:

Individualism versus Collectivism

Egoism versus Altruism

Reason versus Mysticism

My problematic ties two contentious issues in the elaboration of a
feminist rereading of Rand. Most ideas of culture are predicated on a
discourse of consensus—how might a consensus about individualism be
reached? This question I will address by addressing the construction of
cult as a corporate domain. The second issue relates to questions of repre-

sentation and questions of gender. Rand figures, in her own texts, and others', as a hard or unfeminine woman whose apparently affectless aban- donment of altruism earmarks her as the antithesis of traditional notions of femininity. In this persona, she is in the paradoxical position of being repellent both to conservative discourses of gender and to the altruistic, collective spirit of equality feminism, which celebrates an ethics of selflessness. Yet Rand's camp persona as ersatz movie queen borrowed broadly from melodrama and associated genres. She is both "fluff" and "granite."[3] Her romance plots assume the congruence of passion and epis- temology, and her apparent authorization of a discursive construction of subordinated femininity, almost inevitably described as masochistic, distinguishes her as a figure of hyperfemininity. Brownmiller (1975, 315) writes: "So this was grand passion! A masochistic wish by a superior woman for humiliation at the hands of a superior man!"

This quotation suggests one way to reconcile these apparent paradoxes: the subordinated superior woman offers, I will argue, a different way to think about masochism. Rather than map masochism as the likely exten- sion of heterosexual subordination of women, I reread Rand's masochistic scenarios, via the concept of corporate domain, to demonstrate the asym- metry of that apparently symmetrical pair of pairs: masochist/sadist; man/ woman. In Rand's hands, this asymmetry offers a potential site for the rearticulation of women's experiences.

Contemporary feminism, unable or unwilling to base its political prac- tice on the idea of essentialism—another registration of the plural—must formulate more complex models to understand a shared experience among women. As Chantal Mouffe (1992, 373) asks:

> If the category "woman" does not correspond to any unified and unifying essence, the question can no longer be to try and un- earth it. The central issues become: how is "woman" constructed as a category within different discourses? how is sexual difference made a pertinent distinction in social relations? and how are relations of subordination constructed through such a distinc- tion? The whole false dilemma of equality versus difference is exploded since we no longer have a homogenous entity "woman" facing another homogenous entity "man," but a multiplicity of social relations in which sexual difference is always constructed in very diverse ways and where the struggle against subordination has to be visualized in specific and differential terms.

Ironically, only three years after Brownmiller disdainfully paraphrases *The Fountainhead*, Gladstein (1978) advanced *Atlas Shrugged* as one of the texts on an "ideal" women's studies reading list. While acknowledging that the book contains "attitudes toward women and femininity . . . that are offensive" (685), Gladstein turns, like Brownmiller, to her past: "Examination of my reading experience led to the realization that my own move toward independence and liberation had been inspired by a popular novel. Pre-Friedan and pre-Millett, nascent feminism had been nurtured by the reading of *Atlas Shrugged*, published in 1957" (681). Borrowing a discourse of origin analogous to the one implicit in *The Fountainhead*, Gladstein calls the emancipatory potential of Rand's text "nascent"; Rand precedes, chronologically and politically, the feminist blockbusters of the sixties and seventies. Gladstein finds the suspicion with which *Atlas Shrugged* is viewed by "liberal feminists" paradoxical, noting that they "miss the positive implications it holds for women" (681). If liberal feminists have viewed Rand with suspicion, that was because they collapsed the idea of political representation (*Vertretung*) with the representations of aesthetic texts (*Darstellung*); in distinguishing between these two, Gladstein reads selectively to occlude those aspects of the "offensive" representation of women in her praise of Rand.

For Hunt (1984), the partial, feminist reading of Rand is full of error: the confusion of intellect and emotion. "Yet even at the 'rational,' mimetic level Rand works almost exclusively upon the reader's emotions. One important example can stand for many: a large number of intelligent young women, feminist by conviction and not conventionally right-wing, have read Rand closely and remember her works in detail (though their memories often conflate individual scenes from *The Fountainhead* and *Atlas Shrugged*)" (94). Reading closely, the feminist reader of Rand replaces the narrative logic of the two distinct texts with her own. Although Hunt sees emotion as the apparent contradiction of intellect, his example may be understood to represent another category: the cult reader. In particular, Hunt moves between generalization and idiosyncrasy—an idiosyncratic feminist politics becomes representative, not merely of feminist readers, but of the "emotional." Ironically, then, Hunt goes on to suggest that the appeal of these conflated and misremembered scenes is that they institute an ethics of affectlessness, the renunciation of "the emotional claims of parasitic friends and relatives" (94). For Hunt, the feminist reader understands the agency afforded by renunciation; the parasitic "second-hander" is differentiated from the reader herself through an identification with the "heroic." In what sense, however, is the emotional reader distinguished from the parasitic claimant: how might we theorize this practice of enabling misrecognition within the context of a cult readership?

Despite her opposition to the idea of a Rand "cult," Rand was a generous correspondent with her readers. Her collected letters describe various correspondences with faithful readers and fans, and Rand devoted many years of her life to a labor of exposition, one that, Gladstein (1984, 14) suggests, was prompted by the relationship she enjoyed with Nathaniel Branden, initiated by his "fan letter" full of "perspicacity."

If Brownmiller's rereading of *The Fountainhead* is framed by academic disdain, that is at least partly because she is distancing herself from the rereading of the fan, although, ironically, rereading might be precisely the habit that ties these two positions. The lack of serious analysis of Rand's texts within literary or philosophical studies may be partly traced to their popularity, but also to the existence of this body of serious but nonprofessional readers. The disparagement of a cult readership is often grounded in an understanding of its project as exegetical, and its interpretations as purely intentionalist, that is, as an endeavor to discover most exactly the author's intention as the best reading of a text. This model of reading is one readily critiqued within the almost uniformly anti-intentionalist models of literary theory currently available.

Rand's biographers and critics agree that her work is an extraordinary instance of the effect of aesthetic texts on their readers. In her biography of Rand, Barbara Branden (1987) devotes the final chapter of the book to describing the diverse readership of Rand's work, noting that the "story of the influence of a series of novels on philosophic thought is unprecedented in literary history; it is a saga worthy of an Ayn Rand novel" (422).

This story suggests that the analysis of popular culture must elaborate its own practice by locating the agency of popular audiences. Hunt (1984, 98) writes: "Clearly, our understanding of modern culture becomes distorted when critics ignore the books people want to read in favor of those they ought to read." Rand's nonfiction career, usually understood as a turn to philosophy, may also be understood as a long correspondence with her readership. Rand encouraged the development of a body of interpretation as integral to her project: her novels aim to sway, to persuade, and even to convert. Nathaniel Branden's memoir gives a graphic account of the development of her relationship with him as pedagogical fandom. Rand's close circle, "the children" or "the class of '43," read Rand's work in manuscript, and were the founders of the Objectivist movement, what Gladstein (1984, 14–15) describes as a "miniculture." Rand's circle, or "miniculture," represents a unique instance of popularity. Rand's texts were not mass but appealed to a specialized popular audience. In this sense, Objectivism represents the cult as an autotelic system of inquiry into this audience.

If disinterest is commonly understood to be a hallmark of the professional pedagogue, as well as of the self-styled "Objectivist," then the informal cult of disinterest is a novel proposition, for the discursive construction of the cult is one of pathological interest. The interested nature of the cult, for example, generates the most vituperative critique: upon spotting a notice for a Rand lecture on radio, Cook attempts to scrape it away, writing, "[N]o matter how I and my fellow liberals have scraped, scratched and picked away at her, Ayn Rand has clung to her dark corner, surrounded by her followers, as persistent as a plague of lichens" (1965, 119). The plague of lichens instantiates the praxis of Rand and her followers indifferently as secondary, opportunistic, and chronic, indexically marking the malaise of the space in which they are found as "her dark corner." If the corner is the architectural feature Rand would be least likely to choose, with its connotations of closure, cramping, and solitary infestation, Cook's metaphorics betray the paradox of the cult of the solitary as one malign formation of the selfishness of ego-based morality. Opportunistic, secondhand, cramped, and contingent, Cook's metaphor suggests a precise contradiction of the aesthetics of Rand's writings, which celebrate the sublime infinite in architecture, the originary, and the foundational—the Fountainhead.

Rand's analysis of political and ideological representation extends to her understanding of the relationship between a textual world and its audience: the "identification" of reader and text is a negotiation of textual meanings, rather than a simple process of reflection. Rand's writings critique a simple model of textual identification and representation; in particular, the essays collected as *The Romantic Manifesto* argue that textual meanings are negotiated. Rand ([1963] 1971) argues against realist ("naturalist") art because she sees its purpose as purely representational and didactic. She suggests instead that art is "the technology of the soul," a transaction between artist, artwork, and reader that requires particular and sophisticated interpretative labor (134). Similarly, Rand's antirepresentational politics—"representation without authorization is slavery embellished with fraud" ([1972] 1988, 238)—may be understood as a critique of singular or authoritative interpretations. As Sciabarra (1996, 523) notes, Rand's aesthetics interlace the "attributes" of a text to produce a sub-Aristotelian "whole." Rand's idea of the "organic unity" of the text may be as disreputable within contemporary literary theory as the idea of authorial intention, but it is in no way identical to it. On the contrary, her extraordinary didacticism is mitigated by the function of readerly persuasion and consent: Rand's libertarian philosophies, above all, suggest the interrogative participation of her reader in the formulation of her novels' complex rhetorics. In other words, it is in the surplus generated by the exchange between text and reader—in the effect that the text has beyond its polemic—that we may locate the uncanny appeal of the cult text.

Cook's metaphorics of the subterranean corner may be contrasted with Gladstein's assessment of *The Fountainhead* as "underground classic": "Though *The Fountainhead* has become a marvel of the publishing world, it was not an instant best-seller. Like *One Flew over the Cuckoo's Nest*, another underground classic, it grew by word of mouth, developing popularity that asserted itself slowly on the best-seller lists" (1984, 12). Cook's castigation of Objectivism warns against its substitution for "orthodox" spiritual practices. One of Rand's objections to the characterization of Objectivism as a cult rested precisely on the imputation of mystical value: mysticism, of course, forms one of the reviled subjects against which Objectivism constructs its indifference. Rand herself, in a letter to a fan, rejected the notion of obedience to authorial intention: "A blind follower is precisely what my philosophy condemns" (1995, 592). The "word-of-mouth" success story inverts a model of textual authority as passing from author to reader, substituting the figure of exchange between readers for the model of mass consumption by popular readership. It insinuates the blockbuster whose literally massive dimensions figure the bulk of the readership as the active participants in the public life of the text, from its points of subterranean origin.

Theories of rereading and of cult readership can contribute to a complex understanding of the work done by Rand's "cult" readers. A "cult" readership often has specific qualities, including (though not limited to) the practice of rereading, and the identification of a coherent and recognizable world system within its canonical texts—reading practices consonant with Rand's own project for the "philosophical novel." Umberto Eco (1986, 197–98) asks: "What are the requirements for transforming a book or a movie into a cult object? The work must be loved, obviously, but this is not enough. It must provide a completely finished world so that its fans can quote characters and episodes as if they were aspects of the fan's private sectarian world, a world about which one can make up quizzes and play trivia games so that the adepts of the sect recognise each other through a shared expertise." Consonant with both Rand's and Brownmiller's desire to excerpt, Eco notes the potential to be excerpted as a feature of the cult text: "I think that in order to transform a work into a cult object one must be able to break, dislocate, unhinge it so that one can remember only parts of it, irrespective of their original relationship with the whole. In the case of a book one can unhinge it, so to speak, physically, reducing it to a series of excerpts" (198).

Eco's emphasis on the materiality of the book can be read literally in terms of "bulk." Rand's novels are notoriously long; Hunt (1984, 82) describes *Atlas Shrugged* as "a novel, a monument, an artifact, a shibboleth." "The hardbound edition is an artifact of biblical length and heft; the paperback a thousand-page maze of eight-point type, its reading a pilgrimage of faith enacted on buses, subways, and park benches, a few pages at a time." Hunt borrows the discourse of evangelism to describe the reading practice of the cult audience, vivifying textual passage with a metaphorics of transportation, one that maps the intermittent action of transport onto the periodic reader, who is of necessity able to read only via excerpt, and whose reading thus duplicates in the text the "word-of-mouth" chain of the underground classic. Disentangling the opacity of the "maze" text through a practice of excerpting, the cult reader rearticulates not only the text, but also their position in relation to the text and its other readers, occupying a domain these twinned (though distinct) textual practices construct. The "repetitious" nature, then, of Rand's texts, their revisiting of certain issues and scenarios, may be understood as a topos for the revisited and recapitulated text—the text that promises reward upon return, and a pedagogy of repetition and connection. "The novel's bulk, which tends to subvert its value as entertainment, is actually an asset to its function as apologue. The reader is impressed, oppressed, and finally overwhelmed by the sheer width of the world according to Rand." Hunt sees this as coercive, suggesting that reading Rand's texts is "an emotional investment; only conviction (or at least openness) to the author's ideas can justify the effort. The act of reading is also a kind of sensory deprivation; *Atlas Shrugged* effectively shuts out all other literary and intellectual influences for a period of weeks or months." Hunt considers commitment to the text an inhabitation: "[R]eaders . . . remain . . . within the novel's fictive universe" (85). A discourse of authorial intention is replaced by a metaphorics of incarceration; Rand's readers are her characters, their own reading logic subordinated to the logic of her narratives.

Hunt suggests the weakening or alienation of the reader through the text's architecture, the sublime materiality of the textual universe located by and through the reader. Cook reads the excerpted text as blind spot—the corner displaces the blind reader as point of no return. The chain of readers instituted by the underground classic is the consequence of a transposition of the "story" of the text to the text's surrounding culture. "Who is John Galt?" is a question that operates initially at a phatic level in *Atlas Shrugged*. As a greeting and expostulation, it signals the connectedness of a word-of-mouth culture, rather than a question with significant semantic content. It opens the novel as a question whose import is screened from the reader (as Galt's Gulch is screened), and it develops as the motif of the novel's teleological organization. The "rhetorical question"—the blind question, the question misread, paradoxically becomes a question with an answer. Similarly, the limitlessness of the "maze" text or cult book installs the reader in a sublime, man-made landscape, screened like the answer to the question. The text, to return to Brownmiller, "opens itself" through the repeated operations of its readers.

A rearticulation of the text that offers an open horizon of potential rereading is a figure for the sublime text, and Rand's architectural edicts are true to a discourse of modernism as a site of the architectural sublime. *The Fountainhead* charts the progress and perversion of modernist architecture. Rand's seamless incorporation of arguments against revivalist architecture in *The Fountainhead* operates through a discourse of absolute individualism in the figure of Howard Roark, but also through the transplantation of modernist bromides, including Mies van der Rohe's dictum "form follows function" ([1943] 1968, 35). As Bender and Taylor (1987, 190) note, the verticality of the skyscraper pays homage to the capitalist corporation, whereas the civic building casts a horizontal silhouette. Rand negotiates the historically backward-looking architecture of New York City in her account of the career of Howard Roark, and the final sublime moment of *The Fountainhead* presents the prospect of the infinite verticality of the Wynand Building, a vertical shaft that does not recapitulate, but rather erases entirely the historical context of the building, while celebrating the historical circumstances of its creation. Hell's

Kitchen operates as the antipodean term to the "Fountainhead": the kitchen, like the fountainhead, is a domain of origin; hell, the metaphor of a judgment antithetical to the cool fountain. The building represents the antipodean registration of the contrary relation between Wynand and Roark, an articulation performed elsewhere by Dominique. Wynand entrusts Roark with the duty of building the last skyscraper, noting that "[d]ead things . . are only . . . financial fertilizer" ([1943] 1968, 676). Roark's and Wynand's identities, variously celebrated in the sublime prospect of the Wynand Building, are corporate identities. Dominique provides a space of sexual rendezvous for the two men, a space whose corporate domain becomes the vertical sublime of the skyscraper. For the architect and the publisher, each of whom in his profession prosecutes the interaction of aesthetics, texts, and aggregates of people, the building locates the domain in which shared experience, like the cult, can articulate singular subjects. "In addition to organising the building materials, the architect organises the inhabitants' lives within the structures, as well as organizing their perspectives on the world outside" (Gordon 1977, 704).

That location, however, suggests one way of theorizing the second-generation Rand text, from within the "stylized universe" (Branden 1989, 14) of Rand's novels. In particular, camp offers a fruitful way of theorizing the followers of Rand, and the historically attenuated connection between Rand's radical individualism and feminism.

II

Theories of "camp" suggest one model for a fruitfully disobedient cult readership, located within the architecture of Rand's texts. Camp, variously theorized since Sontag's seminal 1964 essay "Notes on Camp," may be understood as at once a strategy of celebration and one of critique or distance: with irony as its leading trope, camp proposes the possibility of disrespectful homage, or tribute, through a rereading or revival of texts. For Rand (1971), the errors of the present were expressed through a metaphorics of the historic as grotesque: in "Basic Principles of Literature," she describes the purveyors of contemporary aesthetics as "unfocused gargoyles" (63). The repression of history, or its sublation, may seem a curious point from which to argue the economy of camp. How can the idea of camp be used to animate an aesthetic like Rand's, which is so resolutely antihistoricist in its project? Isn't such an aesthetic the antithesis of a camp reading?

To reread Rand, and in particular to do so as a feminist strategy, corresponds to one of camp's most important functions: to liberate unexpected meanings from unorthodox materials. Andrew Ross (1989, 151) writes that camp "retrieves . . . the more unsalvageable material that had been picked over and left wanting by purveyors of the 'antique.' " The purveyor of the antique situates aesthetic quality in the historicism of certain aesthetic regimes; camp instead, according to Susan Sontag (1969), celebrates the modernity of artifacts released from their contemporary banality. As "the re-creation of surplus value from forgotten forms of labor" (Ross 1989, 151), camp locates the labor of the past as a source of value. Camp's aesthetic of unorthodox retrieval, offering a logic distinct from the celebratory aspects of neoclassicism, thus articulates intellectual labor as the site of surplus value, a restitution that may be uncannily aligned with John Galt's traced dollar sign at the end of Atlas Shrugged.

Ayn Rand borrowed from Hollywood discourses of extravagance and high seriousness to produce herself as a camp figure. Hollywood celebrates the potential of aesthetic texts to generate *income*, a potential often seen as inimical to serious aesthetic projects. For the immigrant Rand, acculturation as an American subject was a Hollywood narrative, not simply scripted by her own enjoyment and study of Hollywood products, but effected by joining the economy of Hollywood in various roles from early in her new life, including work in the studio of Cecil B. DeMille.[4]

In her text, as Hunt (1984) notes, she relies upon a cinematic register for the panoramic and exaggerated representation of feeling: "DeMille's most memorable imagery—roiling mobs, hulking muzhiks, spectacular train wrecks, and art deco orgies in a zeppelin moored over Manhattan— can all be traced in Rand's fiction" (92).

In her domestic environment, Rand married the streamlined aesthetic of modernism with camp identity, adopting many of the mannerisms and habits of the star. She lived, for example, in a house designed by Neutra for Marlene Dietrich, complete with "a bidet set down not in the bathroom, but in the bedroom; 'I believe that was Dietrich's contribution,' Ayn joked" (Branden 1989, 54–55).

Dietrich's displaced bidet represents the same structure of allegorical foregrounding that generates the perversity of many of the sexual scenarios of Atlas Shrugged and The Fountainhead. For Bennett Cerf (1977), her publisher at Random House, the "adulation" of Rand, which may be understood as a sign of her authority, actually made her dependent: "Ayn is a remarkable woman, but in my opinion, she was not helped by her sycophants. She's like a movie queen with her retinue, or a prize-fight champion who's followed by a bunch of hangers-on, or a big crooner and his worshippers. They all come to need this adulation. These people tell her she's a genius and agree with everything she says, and she grows more and more opinionated as she goes along" (250–51).

Rand's confection of populist literary conventions and high philosophical arguments produces another signal dissymmetry. In the inappropriateness of Rand's behavior, Cerf says, she resembles an entertainer; the popular intellectual, that apparent oxymoron, produces a discursive conflict whose faultlines are traced in the paradoxical submissiveness of the diva, Rand. Like the submissive dominant woman whose "needs" structure the female subject positions of Rand's novels, Rand, as portrayed by Cerf, suggests the displacement of the sadomasochistic dynamics of heterosexuality onto the dynamic of the cult and the cult figure.

Rand revised her novel for the screenplay of King Vidor's 1949 film, *The Fountainhead*. The film adopts the genre of melodrama (a genre that in Rand's terms might be understood as "romantic" or antinaturalistic), to dramatize cinematically the novel's aesthetics of skyscraper modernism and sadomasochistic sexuality. Melodrama, with its grammar of overstatement, exaggeration, and passion, is a curious vehicle to propose the integrity of sublime, abstract, ornament-free modernism. And it is precisely this curiosity that generates a camp reading of the film. A *generic* overstatement of the *thematic* of sincerity produces an effect of failed seriousness, an effect that is one common source of camp rereading. King Vidor, as the director of "women's films," offers an unusual orientation for the masculinist ethos of *The Fountainhead*. If the exaggerations and affect-laden scenarios of women's films are usually sustained through the elaboration of a story line oriented by private-sphere concerns, *The Fountainhead* transfers this affective and generic freight to the prosecution of a profession. In doing so, the film generates a complicated realignment of conventional gender mappings: the melodramatic masculine endeavor makes possible the sublime aspirations of a professional life. Patricia Neal's whip-wielding Dominique Francon signifies the potential conjunction of melodrama and seriousness within the aesthetic regime of the film, one that complicates its philosophical interests with paradoxical moments of camp humor. Despite its sometimes crude depictions of heterosexuality and affect—or perhaps because of them—the film has generated its own camp following as a second-generation text.

The film offers the fetish of the architect's maquettes as the miniatures that locate the "miniculture" of architecture as it frames the world. These are brandished by Roark (played by Gary Cooper) as the film proceeds, the material signifiers of a worldview largely stymied until the film's conclusion, offering an inset metaphor of the Roark mise-en-scène. In a complimentary gesture, the materiality of the book is represented in the film, which opens with a graphic representation of the book's cover as the film's "opening," and with an exhortation to read the book. Similarly, the conventional representation of time passing as a ruffle of calendar pages becomes an ironic recapitulation of the act of abridgment (or excerpting) required for the realization of this cinematic product. The Hollywood film offers the ideal context in which Rand could rehearse her own theories about Americanness. It represents her aesthetics in a manner unavailable in written texts, where bulk can only figure metonymically and through the operations of a readership, the mise-en-scène of Rand's worldview.

According to Ross, camp "liberates" texts from "disdain and neglect." Disdain is a powerful term in Rand's ethics of indifference. Sontag (1969, 280) notes that "[m]any examples of Camp are things which, from a 'serious' point of view, are either bad art or kitsch." As a relic of a "serious" art economy that apportions value unevenly, camp art often mirrors the high seriousness of the economy that excludes it. This uncanny mirroring translates the serious disdain implicit in the formation of canons, relocating that very aesthetics of disdain and seriousness as a quality of rejected texts: "In naive, or pure, Camp, the essential element is seriousness, a seriousness that fails. Of course, not all seriousness that fails can be redeemed as Camp. Only that which has the proper mixture of the exaggerated, the fantastic, the passionate and the naive" (285).

The relationship between irony and seriousness is camp and humorous; Rand, as Hunt (1984, 89) describes her, was "[impervious] to irony." She generates ironic humor in her texts precisely at the point of hyperbolic sincerity, and the excerpt ("Don't touch those levers, you fool!" [Hunt, quoting *Atlas Shrugged*]) operates to resensitize the reader to the text's camp potential. As Hunt notes, Rand's hyperbolic seriousness can lead to bathos, a variety of camp. Writing of *Atlas Shrugged*, he comments: "The torture device, a kind of footnote to the sound-ray generator, does no more than deliver calculated electric shocks, but Rand presents it as a major invention, with its own squat laboratory and hulking, brainless attendants" (90).

In *The Fountainhead* and *Atlas Shrugged*, Rand gives her heroic characters those ambitions that for Susan Sontag (1969) mark camp seriousness, in its collapse of individual effort with corporate enterprise: "[the] ambition on the part of one man to do what it takes a generation, a whole culture, to accomplish" (285). For many of Rand's skeptical readers, her prose fiction is ideally camp in its high seriousness, apocalyptic diction, fantastic scenarios, and narrative simplicity. Rand's high seriousness is implicit in her own description of her project:

> The motive and purpose of my writing is *the projection of an ideal man*. . . . Let me stress this: my purpose is *not* the philosophical enlightenment of my readers, it is *not* the beneficial influence which my novels may have on people, it is *not* the fact that my novels may help a reader's intellectual development. . . . My purpose, first cause and prime mover is the portrayal of Howard Roark or John Galt or Hank Rearden or Francisco d'Anconia *as an end in himself*—not as a means to any further end. Which, incidentally, is the greatest value I could ever offer a reader. (Rand [1963] 1971, 127)

Even in her italics, Rand registers the seriousness, exaggeration, and passionate naivete of her writing. While she claims the effect of her texts is purely incidental to her motivation and purpose, that *incidental* effect becomes "the greatest value." What is incidental, or casual and contingent, generates value, but does so in relation to the disinterested nature of the prose: what it is valuable for the reader to know is indexically related to the author's disinterest in the *potential* for value to the reader. This paradoxical ratio promotes the incidental over the didactic, mapping Rand's disdain for the effect she might have on her readers onto her solicitude for them. Disdain becomes a heuristic, even a kind of caring.

For Rand, indifference, or passionate disdain, may be understood as the ethical foundation of a laissez-faire narrative economy: it is the disinterested nature of Howard Roark, professionally and romantically, that generates the plot of *The Fountainhead*, as it is calculated disinterest that motivates the strike of the mind in *Atlas Shrugged*. The title of *Atlas Shrugged* offers a parable of disinterest, explained by Francicso d'Anconia:

"If you saw Atlas, the giant who holds the world on his shoulders, if you saw that he stood, blood running down his chest, his knees buckling, his arms trembling but still trying to hold the world aloft with the last of his strength, and the greater his effort the heavier the world bore down on his shoulders—what would you tell him to do?"

"I . . . don't know. What . . . could he do? What would *you* tell him?"

"To shrug." ([1957] 1959, 429)

Francisco's response answers the rhetorical question "What . . . could he do?" the indifferent question, with an interested, or "selfish," question. In *Atlas Shrugged*, the necessity to face need with indifference is metaphorized by Francisco as a "shrug." The strike of the brain is a gesture of indifference, a shrug, "so what?" phrased in the subjunctive "if" of science fiction.

Commonly understood as rhetorical, the question "so what?" orients the return to Rand; if the argument of this essay has been to find the potential for fruitfully disobedient rereading in Rand's work, the reorientation of the rhetorical question, a strategy I've located in Rand's work, may be one way to think of the relocation of Rand's indifference—to feminism, to femininity, to the claims of altruism. Indifference incites its own reply, whether Brownmiller's disdain or the innovative reworking of Rand's philosophy and motifs in Gaitskill's *Two Girls, Fat and Thin*.

The "sadomasochism" of Rand's representation of sexuality has been, for feminism, the most problematic aspect of her writing. Rand's predilection for highly choreographed scenarios of sexual violence has been read against her representation of women of integrity and intelligence, forgers of their own destinies. In their high theatricality, passages such as that for which Brownmiller castigates Rand may be read instead as ironic camp. The fetishistic nature of her sexual representations depends in part on an ironic reversal of passion and action, in which the contradictory logic of passionate indifference is played out. As a coda to the rape scene between Dominique and Howard, Rand theorizes: "They had been united in an understanding beyond the violence, beyond the deliberate obscenity of his action; had she meant less to him, he would not have taken her as he did; had he meant less to her, she would not have fought so desperately" ([1943] 1968, 206). According to Deleuze (1989, 134), there is "a masochism specific to the sadist and equally a sadism specific to the masochist, the one never combining with the other." Deleuze argues that it is only on the basis of "very crude and ill-differentiated concepts" (132) that one can speak of sadomasochism as a singular entity. As he notes, "a genuine sadist could never tolerate a masochistic victim . . . [n]either would the masochist tolerate a truly sadistic torturer" (40–41). Casting Dominique as the submissive, masochistic partner in her sexual trysts with Roark ironizes the perverse suggestion of her name without invoking a deeper irony, the complexity of exchange invested in her passionate scenes with Roark, which offer ritualistic scenes of reciprocal domination and submission: "She tried to demonstrate her power over him. She stayed away from his house; she waited for him to come to her. He spoiled it by coming too soon; by refusing her the satisfaction of knowing that he waited and struggled against his desire; by surrendering at once. She would say: 'Kiss my hand Roark.' He would kneel and kiss her ankle. He defeated her by admitting her power; she could not have the gratification of enforcing it" ([1943] 1968, 298). Instead, and as the encounters between Dominique and Howard demonstrate, the irreducible dissymmetry of their positions belies the idea of a sadomasochistic unit as a model of oppressive heterosexuality. Dominique's indifference to Roark is frustrated by his masochistic return to her. For Deleuze, sadism (as implied in Brownmiller's account) operates according to the institution of laws, while masochism operates in terms of contractual agreements; whereas Brownmiller's reading of the rape scene finds its sadistic reiteration of "laws" of sexuality, in Deleuze's terms Dominique and Howard are engaged in a masochistic ritual of contractual negotiation. Roark indoctrinates Dominique as sadist; in Deleuze's account of the masochistic male subject, he notes: "It is essential to the masochist that he should fashion the woman into a despot, that he should persuade her to cooperate and get her to 'sign' [the contract]" (1989, 21).

Dominique's "indifference" to Roark, her cruelty, generates the suspense of the sexual narrative, a narrative allegorically played out in the construction and demolition of the Stoddard Temple, with its enshrined figure of the statue of Dominique. This building marks the material site of masochistic suspense as its fate is debated in the courts. Here the narrative follows the logic of masochistic arrest: in the masochist's scenario, "moments of suspense . . . are the climactic moments . . . because the woman torturer freezes into postures that identify her with a statue, a painting or a photograph" (33). As the court case (the law) adjudicates the fate of the temple, Dominique's testimony for the prosecution, disavowing Roark's work, leads to the destruction of the building, the suspension of their love affair, of her marriage to Keating, then Wynand, and the eventual construction of a new temple to her, this time located in the private space of the marital home Roark builds for her and Wynand.

Whereas sadism is marked by repetition and apathy, Deleuze notes that masochism is marked by "coldness": "The coldness of the masochistic ideal has a quite different meaning: it is not the negation of feeling but rather the disavowal of sensuality" (52). Dominique's coldness is driven from the beginning of the novel by her desire to replace the sensual present with the abstract ideal; her destruction of the statue of Helios renders it an abstraction, removing its power over her ([1943] 1968, 135). Her coldness toward Keating makes her the symmetrical other of his passion. Keating "refused to accept the thought that a woman could remain indifferent to him" (168); Roark preempts the indifference of Dominique by accepting it. Dominique's indifference—that of "an utterly frigid woman" (170), as she describes herself—is negotiated by Roark not as his opposite but as an asymmetrical mirror of his own disdain. For Deleuze (1989, 55), "What characterizes masochism and its theatricality is a peculiar form of cruelty in the woman torturer: the cruelty of the Ideal, the specific freezing point, the point at which idealism is realized." Appropriate, perhaps, for a text that finds for its masochist the frozen figure of the sadistic woman in the marital home she shares with another man, this novel closes with a contract signed by lover and husband, with the collateral figure of woman in exchange. The function of women to articulate relationships between men suggests that there is a separate sexual contract negotiated in the text, between men. Roark's affect-laden relationships with a number of men are immortalized in his buildings, either through their commission and naming (Wynand, Enright) or their construction (Mike Donnigan, Steven Mallory). Baker (1987, 55) argues that between Roark and Wynand grows "a strange nonphysical homoerotic relationship." He writes that the relationship between the two men is "a love affair that dwarfs any heterosexual affairs in Rand's fiction." In a letter to Gerald Loeb, dated 3 June 1944, Rand (1995, 137) wrote: "[G]reater, I think, than any other emotion in the book, is Wynand's love for Roark. Wynand is in love with Roark—in every way except the physical. It is not a homosexual feeling—but it *is* love in the romantic sense and in the highest sense. Not just affection or admiration." Rand's "romantic" love, implicitly sexual between a man and a woman, is necessarily nonsexual once it describes the affection between two men. As

Sciabarra notes, though, Rand almost always reserves the term "roman-tic" for love that includes a sexual component, and her use of "romantic" here is both puzzling and intriguing.[5]

Eve Kosofsky Sedgwick's cultural analysis of masculine desire, *Between Men*, examines "the radically disrupted continuum, in our society, be-tween sexual and nonsexual male bonds" (1985, 23), finding homopho-bia to be the regulatory structure that differentiates such cognate practices as homosexuality (erotic action between men) and homosocial-ity (male-male sociality). Rand's repudiation of homosexuality may be understood in Sedgwick's terms as precisely the homophobic regulation of that distinction: to maintain the value of the homosocial, she finds it necessary to exclude homosexuality, while at the same time the similarity between the relation and an erotic relation is unmistakable.[6] Thus, Baker's paradoxical formulation—the "nonphysical homoerotic."

Similarly, Sedgwick's text describes the asymmetry of gender in terms of the triangulation of desire, where the relations between men are medi-ated by the exchange of women; after Girard, she writes: "[T]he bond between rivals in an erotic triangle [is] even stronger, more heavily deter-minant of actions and choices, than anything in the bond between either of the lovers and the beloved" (21). Homoerotic, but nonphysical, Wy-nand's unconsummated affection for Roark replaces the figure of arrested romance that Dominique augurs, with an eternally arrested homosexual relation between the two men, a contract whose collateral, and conduit, is the wife they share. In her *Journals*, Rand (1997) describes Wynand's feelings after Dominique confesses her love for Roark:

> After a sleepless night, the full force of the blow has come to Wynand. It is his last outburst of emotion. He goes to Domini-que's room, begs her, threatens her, offers her anything to remain with him; she can have all the lovers she wants, but not *that one!* She can even leave him, Wynand, if she insists, and go with any other man, but *not Roark*. Anything, but not Roark! (175)
>
> . . . Roark becomes Wynand's obsession. . . . [Dominique] is jealous of Wynand, of any feeling Roark might have in re-sponse to Wynand's adoration of him. It is a triangle—in which the husband and wife are both in love with the same man. (233)

Might the figure of the frozen women, then, be one way in which Rand's text animates the arrested figure of homoeroticism, a homoeroticism that is "nonphysical" or inexpressible?

III

As Elspeth Probyn (1996, 22) notes, "so what?" is the "dreaded question, that potential response to all cultural critique." As a heuristic it frames Gladstein's introduction to *The Ayn Rand Companion:* "The Companion's organization follows a logical heuristic: Who? What? and So what?" (1984, 5). "So what?" is a question that generates its own suspense; *The Fountainhead* ends with the sublime prospect of the Wynand Building, Roark and Dominique, and a future vista of suspended conjugality; in her rehearsal of the conventional closure of romance narratives, Rand points to the conjugal as a suspended future, a sublime or unrealized horizon of action.

But so what? Earlier, I suggested that Rand conceives the effect of her texts as valuable and incidental. Whereas a feminist analysis of Rand critiques her representational practices, perhaps such a heuristic suggests a new critique may be generated by examining instead the *incidental effects* of her work. I have suggested the model of camp, which proposes a fruitfully disobedient rereading practice, one that considers the contradictory ironic or transformative possibilities of Rand's aesthetics, in particular her incongruous participation in Hollywood codes of melodrama, and the development of a camp following for her texts.

Mary Gaitskill's novel *Two Girls, Fat and Thin* (1991) offers another way of thinking about the incidental contacts of Rand's work. Gaitksill's novel narrates the investigation of the members of Rand's inner circle by a freelance journalist, Justine Shade, focusing on her developing relationship with one member, Dorothy Never. As Justine's name allusively suggests, the novel explores at length the etiology and practice of sadomasochistic scenarios; Justine's encounters and interviews with Dorothy are punctuated by the achronological narratives of each woman's complex history of abuse and sadomasochistic sexual experience.

For Gaitskill, the indifference of antialtruism is metaphorized through the name of her Rand stand-in, Anna Granite. In the unlikely animation of the sculptural granite, Gaitskill recapitulates the monumental and sculptural figure of indifference that limns *Atlas Shrugged*, renamed *The Gods Disdained*. The sculptural body of the slender heroine in Rand's texts figures their indifferent aestheticism. As Gladstein (1984, 22) notes: "Her main female characters share certain characteristics: they have slender physiques, defiant stances, and inner calm." As if to distinguish between the scenarios of Rand's texts and the culture they incite, the title, *Two Girls, Fat and Thin*, foregrounds the distinctive physiques of its main characters; the solid Rand acolyte resembles less a Rand character than a cultist; the skeptical reporter, outside of and suspicious of the Objectivist culture (referred to as "Definitism") is a slender, Rand-like heroine. Although Justine's project is to expose the cultlike personalities of Anna Granite's circle, she is instead confronted with the solitary spectacle of the lone follower as the remainder of what once was; the community she forms in the course of the novel is with Dorothy.

The novel's interest in mise-en-scène, the spatial articulation of contact, is an elaborate homage to Rand's own practice. Initial contact between the two women is made via a bulletin board. Reading Justine's note, Dorothy finds it implies "a lone kook gripping a grimy sheaf of papers, philosophical tracts, and paperback books, her jaw clenched, her face unnaturally pale" (Gaitskill 1991, 12). While the note prompts Dorothy's reconsideration of the history of her life within the Definitist circle, the encounter between the two women is significantly delayed, at first through their incidental failure to contact each other, and then by a series of interposed narratives of personal history. For each woman, personal and cultural history both inhibits and generates the eventual contact and intimacy between the two. This intimacy concludes the novel as they finally touch and curl up together, in a scene that neither precludes nor specifically signals sexual contact.

Anna Granite haunts these encounters as an immaterial presence, realized through her inhabiting of the domains of personal experience. Dorothy enters her apartment to feel "the harsh splendour of Granite's presence arrayed through all my rooms. I had never forgotten her, of course. Her books were all upright on my shelves" (13). The book-lined room spatially organizes the singular experience of the circle; their disposition as the material relics of an immaterial circle, "arrayed" and "upright" in "harsh splendour": "This was the first time in years that I had felt the almost visceral sensation of the woman's presence, which was nothing short of a shimmering, diamond-studded aurora borealis. It was as if this star system had become hidden, bound in a thick skein of ordinariness, and that 'writer,' [Justine] with his/her innocuous request, had peeled off a corner of the binding, causing all that I had never really abandoned to come tumbling into my living room" (13). Dorothy's simile of the star system reminds us of the orbiting logic of the circle as a constellation of singular elements. If the organizing force of Granite produces a "visceral" sensation, this metaphorical melange works as well to convey the contradictory logic of the historical return of the cult; the circle, Dorothy's repressed history, returns, and in its turn initiates a narrative return to each woman's childhood.

Two Girls, Fat and Thin investigates the status of female masochism. When Justine objects to Granite's masochistic characters, Dorothy replies: "When the women in Granite's books submit, they do it out of strength, out of choice, as a gift" (35). Dorothy, in effect, grants Justine the gift of the interview. The interview becomes an exchange of gifts, which constitutes a contractual negotiation of masochism. Ironically, though appropriately, Dorothy's gift of the interview is received by an indifferent Justine. When Justine's article finally surfaces, it offers a generational account of the Granite circle titled "Yuppie Grandmother," and its leading metaphor is the cult as "bad novel" (281). Reading the story, Dorothy feels "insulted and yet seduced" (283). This penultimate negotiation over the valency of masochism in Granite's writing has its own irony; while Dorothy, the apologist for Granite, has suffered at the hands of sadistic sexual partners, Justine herself has been in the process of a masochistic engagement that recapitulates her own sadism in encounters with other children during her youth. Justine and Dorothy both exemplify the rereading of masochistic scenarios: in Dorothy's case, through the reinscription of contract and consent; in Justine's, through her ability to move between the polarities of sadist and masochist in a fashion that amplifies the Deleuzian notion of the masochist's sadist and vice versa. Dorothy offers Justine a horizon of possibility, to reanimate questions of dominance and submission outside the arena of sadistic heterosexuality—the novel finishes as Dorothy literally interrupts a potentially fatal sadistic scenario in which Justine finds herself. The "gift" of this coincidence forms her reply to the insult of the article.

In this melodramatic narrative, Young suggests that Granite "functions largely as *deus ex machina*": "It is a powerful book, albeit flawed. The Ayn

Rand figure functions very uncomfortably as device, as meeting-point. . . . The denouement is contrived" (1992, 180). Young's criticism actually suggests the relevance of Rand. The contrived denouement of *Two Girls, Fat and Thin*, reminiscent of the contrivance of the endings of both *Atlas Shrugged* and *The Fountainhead*, recapitulates the camp potential of the "bad novel" to instruct and redefine. The device, or "meeting-point," is hardly a trivial or ineffectual narrative device, but rather one that reanimates that negotiation of encounter, simultaneously incidental and valuable, which characterizes Rand's interpretation of her texts' impact on her readers. The function of Granite as *deus ex machina* describes her *incidental* ability to structure the negotiation of a variety of scenarios through the novel. Similarly, the novel offers a feminist rereading of the masochistic tendency of Rand's writing, rearticulating relationships between women in terms of the idea of exchange, gift, and indifference. Gaitskill exemplifies the practices of camp liberation. In Gaitskill's ironic recapitulation of the ethics and history of the Granite circle, Anna Granite offers a point of contact between women, even if her novels' orientation suggests the articulation of relationships between men.

As Klein (1993, 45) writes of the smoker's habit: "In a strange reversal of the temporality of desire and fulfillment of desire, cigarette smoking seems to run desire backward—as if the fulfilment were even more the desire than the desire it fulfils, as if what normally comes after, comes upon desire, comes before." Completion incites desire, rather than extinguishes it. Satisfaction creates the desire to return and replay, but this time in reverse: to incite the desire precisely by satisfying it. Fulfilling a desire is no longer adjunct to experiencing it: it simply is the experience of desire. So too with the practices of a cult readership, which invests in its own practices of return and recapitulation to renegotiate the text.

This essay has attempted to reread the reception of Rand in another generation, by proposing a reconsideration of the nature of cult readership, the recuperative potential of a camp reading, and finally through the critique of recent theorizations of sexuality and sexual practice as they relate to a second-generation Rand text. A reconsideration of Rand's work on the *labor* of representation and identification in the aesthetic domain provides a powerful model for a feminist rereading of her work. Hunt (1984, 80) writes, "Ayn Rand is a prophet whose time has come, gone, and come again." As Gaitskill's novel suggests, the value of a return of Rand in feminism offers the paradox of a sublime and yet contingent value.

Notes

Many thanks to Kate Lilley.

1. The Gladstein and Wilt essays from *College English* are reprinted in Part One of this volume.

2. The relevant material from Brownmiller 1975 is reprinted in Part One of the current volume.

3. One of the unlikely revelations of Peikoff's memoir is that Rand's husband's nickname for her was "Fluff" (Peikoff in Rand 1988, 352). In *Two Girls, Fat and Thin*, Mary Gaitskill renames Rand "Anna Granite."

4. After graduating from Leningrad University, Rand studied at the State Institute for Cinema Arts. She first published, in Leningrad and Moscow, a 2500-word monograph on the silent film actor Pola Negri, which was part of a series of three monographs on American actors. Later, she wrote *Hollywood: American Movie-City* (under the name A. Rosenbaum); this forty-three-page volume was a collection of essays, printed in Russia, without her permission, in 1926. It is clear that Hollywood's influence on Rand predates her arrival in America. My thanks to Chris Matthew Sciabarra for supplying this information, gleaned from the July 1995 and March 1996 issues of *Impact*, the newsletter of the Ayn Rand Institute.

5. Private correspondence. See also Sciabarra 1995, 421 n. 68. As Sciabarra notes, Rand had some unflattering things to say about gays and lesbians (200–201). In "The Age of Envy," "Women's Lib" is a particular target for proposing "spiritual sisterhood with lesbians" (Rand 1971a, 175).

6. In this connection, and with the masochistic motif in mind, Rand (1997, 171) states in her notes detailing the plot of *The Fountainhead:* "In the most spiritual sense only, without the slightest possibility of the merest hint of sexual perversion, Wynand is actually in love with Roark. There are no definite events, no concrete speeches in which this is displayed. It is there, nonetheless. It is an instance of Wynand's masochism, of which he has quite a taint. The torture of loving a man whom in many other ways he hates appeals to him. He hates him for everything that Roark is and he, Wynand, isn't."

References

Baker, James. 1987. *Ayn Rand*. Edited by Warren French. Boston: G. K. Hall.

Bender, Thomas, and William R. Taylor. 1987. Culture and architecture: Some aesthetic tensions in the shaping of modern New York City. In *Visions of the Modern City: Essays in History, Art, and Literature*, edited by William Sharpe and Leonard Wallock. Baltimore: Johns Hopkins University Press.

Branden, Barbara. 1987. *The Passion of Ayn Rand*. London: W. H. Allen.

Branden, Nathaniel. 1989. *Judgment Day: My Years with Ayn Rand*. Boston: Houghton Mifflin.

Brownmiller, Susan. 1975. *Against Our Will: Men, Women, and Rape*. New York: Simon & Schuster.

Butler, Judith, and Joan W. Scott, eds. 1992. *Feminists Theorize the Political*. New York: Routledge.

Calinescu, Matei. 1993. *Rereading*. New Haven: Yale University Press.

Cerf, Bennett. 1977. *At Random: The Reminiscences of Bennett Cerf*. New York: Random House.

Cook, Bruce. 1965. Ayn Rand: A voice in the wilderness. *Catholic World* 201:119–24.

Deleuze, Gilles. 1989. The cold and the cruel. In *Venus in Furs*, edited by Leopold von Sacher-Masoch. New York: Zone Books.

Eco, Umberto. 1986. Casablanca: Cult movies and intertextual collage. In *Travels in Hyperreality*, translated by William Weaver. London: Picador.

Gaitskill, Mary. 1991. *Two Girls, Fat and Thin*. London: Chatto & Windus.

Gladstein, Mimi Reisel. 1978. Ayn Rand and feminism: An unlikely alliance. *College English* 39, no. 6:680–85.

———. 1984. *The Ayn Rand Companion*. Westport, Conn.: Greenwood Press.

Gordon, Philip. 1977. The extroflective hero: A look at Ayn Rand. *Journal of Popular Culture* 10, no. 4:701–10.

Hunt, Robert. 1984. Science fiction for the age of inflation: Reading *Atlas Shrugged* in the 1980s. In *Coordinates: Placing Science Fiction and Fantasy*. Eds., George E. Slusser, Eric S. Rabkin, and Robert Scholes. Carbondale: Southern Illinois University Press.

Klein, Richard. 1993. *Cigarettes Are Sublime*. Durham, N.C.: Duke University Press.

Mouffe, Chantal. 1992. Feminism, citizenship, and radical democratic politics. In *Feminists Theorize the Political*, edited by Judith Butler and Joan W. Scott. New York: Routledge.

Peikoff, Leonard. 1988. My thirty years with Ayn Rand: An intellectual memoir. In Ayn Rand, *The Voice of Reason: Essays in Objectivist Thought*, edited by Leonard Peikoff. New York: New American Library.

Probyn, Elspeth. 1996. *Outside Belongings*. New York: Routledge.

Rand, Ayn. [1943] 1968. *The Fountainhead*. New York: Bobbs-Merrill.

———. 1946. *Anthem*. New York: New American Library.

———. [1957] 1959. *Atlas Shrugged*. New York: New American Library.

———. 1961. *For the New Intellectual The Philosophy of Ayn Rand*. New York: New American Library.

———. [1963] 1971. The goal of my writing. In *The Romantic Manifesto: A Philosophy of Literature*. New York: New American Library. Originally published in *The Objectivist Newsletter*, October–November 1963.

———. [1968] 1988. About a woman president. In *The Voice of Reason: Essays in Objectivist Thought*, edited by Leonard Peikoff. New York: New American Library. Originally published in *The Objectivist*, December 1968.

———. [1971] 1975. The age of envy. In *The New Left: The Anti-Industrial Revolution*, 2d rev. ed. New York: New American Library. Originally published in *The Objectivist*, July–August 1971.

———. 1971. *The Romantic Manifesto: A Philosophy of Literature*. New York: New American Library.

———. [1972] 1988. Representation without authorization. In *The Voice of Reason: Essays in Objectivist Thought*, edited by Leonard Peikoff. New York: New American Library. Originally published in *The Ayn Rand Letter*, 17 July.

———. 1975. *The New Left: The Anti-Industrial Revolution*. 2d rev. ed. New York: New American Library.

———. 1988. *The Voice of Reason: Essays in Objectivist Thought*. Edited by Leonard Peikoff. With additional essays by Leonard Peikoff and Peter Schwartz. New York: New American Library.

———. 1995. *Letters of Ayn Rand*. Edited by Michael S. Berliner. Introduction by Leonard Peikoff. New York: Dutton.

———. 1997. *Journals of Ayn Rand*. Edited by David Harriman. New York: Penguin Dutton.

Ross, Andrew. 1989. Uses of camp. In *No Respect: Intellectuals and Popular Culture*. New York: Routledge.

Ross, Shelley. 1978. Reply to Mimi Gladstein. *College English* 40, no. 3:333, 337.
Sciabarra, Chris Matthew. 1995. *Ayn Rand: The Russian Radical.* University Park: Pennsylvania State University Press.
———. 1996. Ayn Rand. In *American Writers: A Collection of Literary Biographies, Supplement IV, Part 2: Susan Howe to Gore Vidal,* edited by A. Walton Litz and Molly Wiegel. New York: Charles Scribner's Sons.
Sedgwick, Eve Kosofsky. 1985. *Between Men: English Literature and Male Homosocial Desire.* New York: Columbia University Press.
Sontag, Susan. 1969. *Against Interpretation and Other Essays.* New York: Dell.
Wilt, Judith. 1978. Reply to Mimi Gladstein: On *Atlas Shrugged. College English* 40, no. 3:333–37.
Young, Elizabeth. 1992. Library of the ultravixens: Tama Janowitz; Mary Gaitskill; Catherine Texier. In *Shopping in Space: Essays on American "Blank Generation" Fiction,* edited by Elizabeth Young and Graham Caveney. London: Serpent's Tail.
Young, Elizabeth, and Graham Caveney. 1992. *Shopping in Space: Essays on American "Blank Generation" Fiction.* London: Serpent's Tail.

Selected Bibliography

Since virtually every article in this volume includes a reference list, the following selected bibliography is designed to highlight primary and secondary sources of most interest to feminists in pursuit of Rand studies. In certain instances, we highlight essays of relevance to feminist inquiry within particular works. It should be noted, however, that many of the secondary sources cited are not written from feminist perspectives. Since the current volume constitutes the first—and definitive—collection of essays on Rand and feminism, our bibliography should be used as a more general guide to research.

There are a plethora of URLs, usenet groups, and moderated discussion lists on-line that deal with the philosophy of Ayn Rand. And there is a growing number of undergraduate, graduate, and doctoral theses devoted to her thought (some of which we note below). In addition, several associations promote the study of Objectivism: the Ayn Rand Institute (which includes an archival library) in Marina Del Rey, California; the Institute for Objectivist Studies in Poughkeepsie, New York; and the Ayn Rand Society, an affiliate of the Eastern Division of the American Philosophical Association. Some of Rand's manuscripts and personal papers are in the Library of Congress.

Much of the Objectivist canon can be found on audio and video; we note some taped courses below. Many of these courses are available through Second Renaissance Books, in New Milford, Connecticut. Additional materials dealing with Rand are available through Laissez-Faire Books, San Francisco. Rand's estate has promised to publish more from their archives, including an authorized biography gleaned from interviews with Rand, and transcriptions of courses taught by Rand and by her associates.

Selected Works by Ayn Rand

Works of Fiction

[1933] 1968. *Night of January 16th.* New York: New American Library.
1936. *We the Living.* New York: Macmillan; 2d ed. New York: New American Library, 1959.
[1937] 1946. *Anthem.* New York: New American Library.
1940. The unconquered. Typewritten play manuscript, unpublished. Adaptation of *We the Living.* First New York production, Biltmore Theatre, 13 February.

[1943] 1993. *The Fountainhead*. 50th anniversary ed. Afterword by Leonard Peikoff. New York: Bobbs-Merrill.

[1957] 1992. *Atlas Shrugged*. 35th anniversary ed. New York: Dutton.

1984. *The Early Ayn Rand: A Selection from Her Unpublished Fiction*. Edited by Leonard Peikoff. New York: New American Library.

Works of Nonfiction

1944. The only path to tomorrow. *Reader's Digest,* January 1944, 88–90.

[1958] 1986. *Lectures on Fiction-Writing*. Oceanside, Calif.: Lectures on Objectivism. Twelve-tape lecture series (audio). (Available from Second Renaissance Books.)

1961. *For the New Intellectual: The Philosophy of Ayn Rand*. New York: New American Library.

[1962–65] 1982. *The Objectivist Newsletter*. Edited by Ayn Rand and Nathaniel Branden. Vols. 1–4. Palo Alto, Calif.: Palo Alto Book Service (now published by Second Renaissance Books). Included in this collection is Edith Efron's review of Betty Friedan's *Feminine Mystique* (July 1963).

1964. *The Virtue of Selfishness: A New Concept of Egoism*. New York: New American Library.

[1966–71] 1982. *The Objectivist*. Vols. 5–10. Palo Alto, Calif.: Palo Alto Book Service (now published by Second Renaissance Books). Edited by Ayn Rand and Nathaniel Branden, January 1966–April 1968, then by Rand, May 1968–September 1971. This collection includes Ayn Rand's essay on the abortion debate, "Of Living Death" (October 1968), and her "Answer to Readers (About a Woman President)" (December 1968).

[1966–67] 1990. *Introduction to Objectivist Epistemology*. 2d enl. ed. Edited by Harry Binswanger and Leonard Peikoff. New York: New American Library. This volume includes in an appendix excerpts from the epistemology workshops, and an additional essay, "The Analytic-Synthetic Dichotomy," by Leonard Peikoff.

1967. *Capitalism: The Unknown Ideal*. New York: New American Library. This anthology includes Robert Hessen's essay "The Effects of the Industrial Revolution on Women and Children."

[1971–76] 1979. *The Ayn Rand Letter*. Vols. 1–4. Palo Alto, Calif.: Palo Alto Book Service (now published by Second Renaissance Books). This collection includes "A Last Survey" (from vol. 4, nos. 2–3), with further reflections by Rand on the issue of abortion.

1975. *The New Left: The Anti-Industrial Revolution*. 2d rev. ed. New York: New American Library. This volume includes Rand's essay "The Age of Envy," which deals partially with the "Women's Lib" movement.

1975. *The Romantic Manifesto: A Philosophy of Literature*. 2d rev. ed. New York: New American Library.

1982. *Philosophy: Who Needs It*. Introduction by Leonard Peikoff. New York: Bobbs-Merrill.

1989. *The Voice of Reason: Essays in Objectivist Thought*. Edited, with additional essays by Leonard Peikoff. New York: New American Library. This volume includes reprints of Rand's discussion of the abortion debate ("Of Living Death"), her "Woman President" article, and "Through Your Most Grievous Fault," an obituary-tribute to Marilyn Monroe, originally published in 1962 in the *Los Angeles Times*.

1991. *The Ayn Rand Column*. Introduction by Peter Schwartz. New Milford, Conn.: Second Renaissance Books.

1995. *Letters of Ayn Rand*. Edited by Michael S. Berliner. New York: Penguin Dutton. A most provocative look behind the scenes. In one letter, Rand responds to T. A.

Robertson of King Features Syndicate, who had asked her to do a piece on the home of tomorrow, and to be "completely feminist" in her approach. Rand wired Robertson back, saying: "Am not a feminist and would be no good at doing article from woman's angle." She explained that she'd be unable "to write a feminine piece on the home. . . . That is not my specialty, I know nothing about it and care less, being the worst housekeeper on earth. . . . of all writers on earth I'm the worst one to pick for an article aimed at women from the angle of women. I just *ain't* that kind of writer" (219).
1995. *Ayn Rand's Marginalia: Her Critical Comments on the Writings of Over 20 Authors.* Edited by Robert Mayhew. New Milford, Conn.: Second Renaissance Books.
1997. *Journals of Ayn Rand.* Edited by David Harriman. Foreword by Leonard Peikoff. New York: Penguin Dutton. A companion volume to *Letters*, this book provides crucial material on Rand's literary and philosophical development. It includes notes on all her works, architectural research for *The Fountainhead*, research for a movie on the atomic bomb, unpublished nonfiction essays, and Rand's testimony before the House Un-American Activities Committee dealing with "Communist Infiltration of the Motion Picture Industry." In his review in the *New York Times Book Review* (5 October 1997), David Brooks suggests that "there is a current of misogyny throughout" the journals (38). Readers can decide for themselves.

Rand-Influenced Publications

The following publications show the wide range of Rand's influence—in epistemology, aesthetics, psychology, ethics, politics, and philosophy of history.

Aristos: The Journal of Esthetics. Vols. 1–8. Edited by Louis Torres (July 1982–September 1991) and by Louis Torres and Michelle Marder Kamhi (since January 1992).
Binswanger, Harry. 1990. *The Biological Basis of Teleological Concepts.* Los Angeles: Ayn Rand Institute.
Branden, Nathaniel. [1969] 1979. *The Psychology of Self-Esteem: A New Concept of Man's Psychological Nature.* Los Angeles: Nash Publishing.
The Intellectual Activist. Vols. 1–12. Edited by Peter Schwartz (October 1979–September 1991), Linda Rearden (November 1991–May 1994), Robert W. Stubblefield (July 1994–May 1995), Paul Blair (July 1995–September 1996), and Robert Tracinski (November 1996 to the present). Peter Schwartz's "Wages of Sex," dealing with "comparable worth," appears in the 1 September 1981 issue of *The Intellectual Activist* (vol. 2, no. 9). "Ayn Rand's Letters-to-the-Editor" appears in the March 1966 issue (vol. 10, no. 2).
Kelley, David. 1986. *The Evidence of the Senses: A Realist Theory of Perception.* Baton Rouge: Louisiana State University.
———. 1990. *Truth and Toleration.* Verbank, N.Y.: Institute for Objectivist Studies.
———. 1996. *Unrugged Individualism: The Selfish Basis of Benevolence.* Poughkeepsie, N.Y.: Institute for Objectivist Studies.
———. 1998. *A Life of One's Own: Individual Rights and the Welfare State.* Washington, D.C.: Cato Institute.
The Objectivist Forum. Vols. 1–8. Edited by Harry Binswanger (1980–87). This publication includes "The Age of Mediocrity" (June 1981), with further reflections by Rand on the issue of abortion.
Peikoff, Leonard. 1982. *The Ominous Parallels: The End of Freedom in America.* New York: Stein & Day.

————. 1983. *Understanding Objectivism*. Oceanside, Calif.: Lectures on Objectivism. Twelve-tape lecture series (audio). (Available from Second Renaissance Books.)

————. 1991. *Objectivism: The Philosophy of Ayn Rand*. New York: Dutton.

Walsh, George. 1998. *The Role of Religion in History*. New Brunswick, N.J.: Transaction.

Bibliographies and Reference Guides

Binswanger, Harry, ed. 1986. *The Ayn Rand Lexicon: Objectivism from A to Z*. New York: New American Library. This is a very useful guide to Rand literature, with entries on "abortion," "femininity," "man-worship," "marriage," and "sex." There are, however, no specific entries on "feminism," "masculinity," or "women."

Gladstein, Mimi Reisel. 1984. *The Ayn Rand Companion*. Westport, Conn.: Greenwood Press. Expanded edition, 1999.

Perinn, Vincent L., comp. 1990. *Ayn Rand: First Descriptive Bibliography*. Rockville, Md.: Quill & Brush.

Biographical and Critical Studies

The following publications include relevant books, chapters in books, articles, reviews, theses, and other references to Rand. We would like to thank Matthew Stoloff for providing us with some of the more obscure references to Rand in this literature.

Baker, James T. 1987. *Ayn Rand*. Edited by Warren French. Boston: G. K. Hall.

Barnes, Hazel E. 1967. Egoistic humanism: Ayn Rand's Objectivism. In *An Existentialist Ethics*. New York: Alfred A. Knopf.

Branden, Barbara. 1986. *The Passion of Ayn Rand*. Garden City, N.Y.: Doubleday.

Branden, Nathaniel. 1978. Thank you Ayn Rand, and goodbye. *Reason*, May, 58–61.

————. 1983. Love and sex in the philosophy of Ayn Rand. Washington, D.C.: Biocentric Institute. Audiotape.

————. 1984. The benefits and hazards of the philosophy of Ayn Rand: A personal statement. *Journal of Humanistic Psychology* 24, no. 4:39–64.

————. 1989. *Judgment Day: My Years with Ayn Rand*. Boston: Houghton-Mifflin.

Branden, Nathaniel, and Barbara Branden. 1962. *Who Is Ayn Rand? An Analysis of the Novels of Ayn Rand*. New York: Random House.

Clapper, Thomas Heman. 1983. American conservative utopias. Ph.D. diss., University of Oklahoma.

Cox, Stephen. 1986. Ayn Rand: Theory vs. creative life. *Journal of Libertarian Studies* 8, no. 1:19–29.

————. 1987. It couldn't be made into a really good movie: The films of Ayn Rand. *Liberty* 1, no. 1:5–10.

————. 1993. The literary achievement of *The Fountainhead*. In *The Fountainhead: A Fiftieth Anniversary Celebration*. Poughkeepsie, N.Y.: Institute for Objectivist Studies.

Crass, Julianne Elizabeth. 1996. *The Tiger and the She-Wolf: The Individualisms of Thomas Hobbes and Ayn Rand*. Wellington: Victoria University of Wellington.

Current Biography. 1982. Ayn Rand. New York: H. W. Wilson.

Den Uyl, Douglas J. 1999. *The Fountainhead: An American Novel*. New York: Twayne Publishers; Macmillan Library Reference.

Den Uyl, Douglas J., and Douglas B. Rasmussen, eds. 1984. *The Philosophic Thought of Ayn Rand*. Urbana: University of Illinois Press.

De Renzo, Denise. 1988. The view from outside the prison: Themes of dominance and subservience in Ayn Rand's fiction. M.A. thesis, Villanova University.

Ellis, Albert. 1968. *Is Objectivism a Religion?* New York: Lyle Stuart.

Ephron, Nora. 1968. A strange kind of simplicity. *New York Times Book Review*, 5 May, 8ff.

Erickson, Peter. 1997. *The Stance of Atlas: An Examination of the Philosophy of Ayn Rand.* Portland, Oreg.: Herakles Press.

Fletcher, Max E. 1974. Harriet Martineau and Ayn Rand: Economics in the guise of fiction. *American Journal of Economics and Society* 33, no. 4:367–79.

Gladstein, Mimi Reisel. 1981. Ayn Rand. In *American Women Writers: A Critical Reference Guide*, vol. 3, edited by Lina Mainiero.

———. 1989. Ayn Rand—sidelights. In *Contemporary Authors*, New Revision Series 27. Detroit: Gale Research.

———. 1995. Ayn Rand. In *The Oxford Companion to Women's Writings in the United States*, edited by Cathy N. Davidson and Linda Wagner-Martin. New York: Oxford University Press.

———. 2000. *Atlas Shrugged: Manifesto of the Mind.* New York: Twayne Publishers; Macmillan Library Reference.

Glennon, Lynda M. 1979. *Women and Dualism: A Sociology of Knowledge Analysis.* New York: Longman.

Gotz, Ignacio L. 1995. *Conceptions of Happiness.* Lanham, Md.: University Press of America.

Greenberg, Paul. 1993. *Resonant Lives.* Foreword by Irving Kristol. Washington, D.C.: Ethics & Public Policy Center.

Haley, Alex. 1993. *The Playboy Interviews.* Edited by Murray Fisher. New York: Ballantine.

Hamblin, Dora Jane. 1967. The cult of angry Ayn Rand. *Life* 7 (April): 92–102.

Heider, Ulrike. 1994. *Anarchism: Left, Right, and Green.* Translated by Danny Lewis and Ulrike Bode. San Francisco: City Lights Books.

Hellman, Lillian. 1976. *Scoundrel Time.* Introduction by Gary Willis. New York: Bantam.

Heyl, Jenny A. 1995. Ayn Rand (1905–1982). In *Contemporary Women Philosophers*, vol. 4, edited by Mary Ellen Waithe. Boston: Kluwer Academic Publishers.

Hook, Sidney. 1961. Each man for himself: Review of Rand's *For the New Intellectual.* *New York Times Book Review*, 9 April, 3, 28.

Hospers, John. 1990. Memoir: Conversations with Ayn Rand, part one. *Liberty* 3, no. 6:23–36.

———. 1990. Memoir: Conversations with Ayn Rand, part two. *Liberty* 4, no. 1:42–52.

Jelinek, Estelle C. 1978. Anaïs Nin: A critical evaluation. In *Feminist Criticism: Essays on Theory, Poetry, and Prose*, edited by Cheryl L. Brown and Karen Olson. Metuchen, N.J.: Scarecrow Press.

Johnson D. Barton. 1995. Nabokov, Ayn Rand, and Russian-American literature or, the odd couple. *Cycnos* 12, no. 2: 101–8.

King, Billie Jean. 1976. Interview. *Playboy*, March, 55–70, 194–96.

King, Florence. 1992. Our lady's juggler shrugged on the installment plan. In *With Charity Toward None: A Fond Look at Misanthropy.* New York: St. Martin's Press.

Landrum, Gene N. 1994. *Profiles of Female Genius: Thirteen Creative Women Who Changed the World.* Buffalo, N.Y.: Prometheus Books.

Lennox, James G. 1976. Fletcher's oblique attack on Ayn Rand's economics and ethics. *American Journal of Economics and Sociology* 35, no. 2:217–24.

Lepanto, Paul. 1971. *Return to Reason.* New York: Exposition Press.

Machan, Tibor. 1999. *Ayn Rand.* New York: Peter Lang.

Merrill, John Calhoun. 1994. *Legacy of Wisdom*. Ames: Iowa State University Press.

Merrill, Ronald E. 1991. *The Ideas of Ayn Rand*. LaSalle, Ill.: Open Court.

Nozick, Robert. 1971. On the Randian argument. *Personalist* 52 (spring): 282–304.

Olster, Stacy. 1997. Something old, something new, something borrowed, something (red, white, and) blue: Ayn Rand's *Atlas Shrugged* and Objectivist ideology. In *The Other Fifties: Interrogating Midcentury American Icons*, edited by Joel Foreman. Urbana: University of Illinois Press.

O'Neill, William F. [1971] 1977. *With Charity Toward None: An Analysis of Ayn Rand's Philosophy*. Totowa, N.J.: Littlefield, Adams.

Parker, Sara Kristin. 1985. Ayn Rand, female misogynist: A study of androgyny in *Atlas Shrugged*. M.A. thesis, Longwood College.

Patai, Daphne. 1982. When women rule: Defamiliarization in the sex-role reversal utopia. *Extrapolation* 23, no. 1:56–69.

Paxton, Michael. 1998. *Ayn Rand: A Sense of Life*. Layton, Utah: Gibbs Smith. Based on the Academy Award–nominated documentary of the same name.

Pierpont, Claudia Roth. 1995. A critic at large: Twilight of the goddess. *New Yorker*, 24 July, 70–81.

Plasil, Ellen. 1985. *Therapist*. New York: St. Martin's Press.

Pruette, Lorine. 1943. Battle against evil: Review of *The Fountainhead*. *New York Times Book Review*, 16 May, 7ff.

Quinto, Emerita. 1986. *Three Women Philosophers: Arendt, Rand, Beauvoir*. Philippines: National Printing Co.

Ridpath, John B. 1976. Fletcher's views on the novelist's aesthetic purpose in writing. *American Journal of Economics and Sociology* 35, no. 2: 211–17.

Riggenbach, Jeff. 1979. In praise of decadence. *New York Times*, 24 June, E21.

———. 1982. The disowned children of Ayn Rand. *Reason*, December, 57–59.

Robbins, John W. 1974. *Answer to Ayn Rand: A Critique of the Philosophy of Objectivism*. Washington, D.C.: Mount Vernon.

———. 1997. *Without a Prayer: Ayn Rand and the Close of Her System*. Hobbs, N.M.: Trinity Foundation.

Sayre, Nora. [1973] 1996. *Sixties Going on Seventies*. 2d ed. New Brunswick, N.J.: Rutgers University Press.

Sciabarra, Chris Matthew. 1995. *Ayn Rand: The Russian Radical*. University Park: Pennsylvania State University Press.

———. 1996. Ayn Rand. In *American Writers: A Collection of Literary Biographies, Supplement IV, Part 2: Susan Howe to Gore Vidal*, edited by A. Walton Litz and Molly Wiegel. New York: Charles Scribner's Sons.

———. 1998. A renaissance in Rand scholarship. *Reason Papers*, no. 23 (fall).

Secrest, Meryle. 1992. *Frank Lloyd Wright*. New York: Alfred A. Knopf.

Smith, George H. 1979. *Atheism: The Case Against God*. Buffalo, N.Y.: Prometheus Books.

———. 1991. *Atheism, Ayn Rand, and Other Heresies*. Buffalo, N.Y.: Prometheus Books.

Stricker, Barry Arthur. 1987. The life and thought of Ayn Rand: The roots of Objectivism. Ph.D. diss., Golden Gate Baptist Theological Seminary.

Torres, Louis, and Michelle Marder Kamhi. 1999. *What Art Is: The Esthetic Theory of Ayn Rand*. LaSalle, Ill.: Open Court.

Tuccille, Jerome. [1972] 1997. *It Usually Begins with Ayn Rand*. 25th anniversary ed. Foreword by David Friedman. New York: Stein & Day.

Walker, Jeff. 1999. *The Ayn Rand Cult*. LaSalle, Ill.: Open Court.

Wheeler, Kathleen M. 1997. *A Guide to Twentieth-Century Women Novelists*. Cambridge, Mass.: Blackwell Publishers.

Whissen, Thomas R. 1992. *Classic Cult Fiction: A Companion to Popular Cult Literature*. New York: Greenwood Press.

Contributors

BARBARA BRANDEN is a writer and lecturer. She earned her M.A. in philosophy, and authored a thesis on free will, under the direction of Sidney Hook at New York University. She was Ayn Rand's intimate friend and colleague for eighteen years, and a close friend of the members of the "Rand Circle." She was Managing Editor of *The Objectivist*, a philosophical journal, and Executive Vice-President of Nathaniel Branden Institute in New York. At NBI, she conceived and presented a popular course on the nature of efficient thinking. In 1986, Doubleday published her best-selling and critically acclaimed biography, *The Passion of Ayn Rand*. This biography has spawned two adaptations: a Showtime television movie, written by Howard Korder, and a stage version, written by Julian Barry, to be presented by Sir Peter Hall, former head of the British National Theatre, at the Old Vic in London.

NATHANIEL BRANDEN is a graduate of New York University (M.A.), the California Graduate Institute (Ph.D.), and a pioneer in the field of self-esteem. He is a psychologist in private practice, and a corporate consultant. He was Ayn Rand's closest associate for eighteen years, until their break in 1968. His books include *The Psychology of Self-Esteem* (Nash, 1969), *The Psychology of Romantic Love* (Bantam, 1980), *Judgment Day: My Years with Ayn Rand* (Houghton Mifflin, 1989), *The Six Pillars of Self-Esteem* (Bantam, 1994), *Taking Responsibility* (Simon & Schuster, 1996), *The Art of Living Consciously* (Simon & Schuster, 1997), *A Woman's Self-Esteem: Struggles and Triumphs in the Search for Identity* (Jossey-Bass, 1998), and *Self-Esteeem at Work: How Confident People Make Powerful Companies* (Jossey-Bass, 1998).

DIANA MERTZ BRICKELL has a B.A. (magna cum laude) in philosophy from Washington University in St. Louis. In 1997, she received the Nishi Luthra Prize in Philosophy from Washington University. Diana currently resides in Los Angeles, where she works as a computer programmer and continues to write on philosophy and feminist issues.

SUSAN LOVE BROWN is a political and psychological anthropologist who received her bachelor's degree from Regents College, State University of New York, in 1984. She subsequently earned her master's degree in anthropology from San Diego State University in 1987, followed by her doctoral degree in anthropology from the University of California, San Diego, in 1992. Currently an associate professor of anthropology at Florida Atlantic University in Boca Raton, she teaches a course in gender and culture and serves as a member of the women's studies faculty. She has done fieldwork in the Bahamas and the United States, and is currently working on her book *Solidarity and Individualism in an Archipelago State* and an edited volume tentatively titled *Communalism and Community*.

SUSAN BROWNMILLER is the author of many books and essays, including *Against Our Will: Men, Women, and Rape* (Bantam Books, 1975), *Femininity* (Linden Press, 1984), *Waverly Place* (Grove Press, 1989), and *Seeing Vietnam: Encounters of the Road and Heart* (HarperCollins, 1994).

MIMI REISEL GLADSTEIN, co-editor of *Feminist Interpretations of Ayn Rand*, is a Professor of English and Theatre Arts at the University of Texas at El Paso, where she is currently Associate Dean of Liberal Arts. She was the first Director of the Women's Studies Program at her university. She has chaired the English Department twice, was the Executive Director for the University's Diamond Jubilee Celebration, and Director of the Western Cultural Heritage Program. She is the author of *The Ayn Rand Companion* (1984) and *The Indestructible Woman in Faulkner, Hemingway, and Steinbeck* (1986). She has won international recognition for her work on John Steinbeck: the John J. and Angeline Pruis Award for Steinbeck Teacher of the Decade (1978–87) and the Burkhardt Award for Outstanding Contributions to Steinbeck Studies in 1996. She has been a Fulbright Professor in Venezuela (1990–91) and Spain (1995). Currently, she is working on a second edition of *The Ayn Rand Companion* and a volume on *Atlas Shrugged* for the Twayne Masterworks series.

THOMAS GRAMSTAD is a "digital nomad": a freelance writer, teacher, and conference organizer with a primary focus on interactive cyber- and multimedia, virtual communities, and computer art. His work focuses on the intersection of feminism, gender liberation, and multiculturalism. He is the creator of more than thirty interactive group forums on the Internet, including alt.feminism.individualism, alt.tv.xena, and the Amazons International Newsletter. He is the author of "The Edison Galaxy: Text Beyond the Oral/Literary Dichotomy," in T. Julsrud and J. W. Bakke's *Digital Nomad* (Oslo: Spartacus), and of numerous articles and essays. He can be contacted at thomas@gramstad.no.

MELISSA JANE HARDIE teaches English, cultural studies, and women's studies in the English Department, University of Sydney. Her Ph.D. was awarded at the University of Sydney in 1994. She is currently completing her book, *Camp Quality: Women, Popular Culture, Queer Aesthetics*. Her recent publications include "'I Embrace the Difference': Elizabeth Taylor and the Closet," in *Sexy Bodies: The Strange Carnalities of Feminism*, ed. Grosz and Probyn (Routledge, 1995), and "Restless: Paglia v. Sontag," in *American Feminist Studies* (1997). Future projects include work on liberation and nostalgia.

BARBARA GRIZZUTI HARRISON is the author of many books and essays, including *Unlearning the Lie: Sexism in School* (Liveright, 1973), *Visions of Glory: A History and a Memory of Jehovah's Witnesses* (Simon & Schuster, 1978), *Off Center: Essays* (Dial Press, 1980), *The Astonishing World: Essays* (Ticknor & Fields, 1992), and *An Accidental Autobiography* (Houghton Mifflin, 1996).

VALÉRIE LOIRET-PRUNET is Agrégée Professor of Linguistics and Literature. She earned her degree at the University of Paris, and teaches courses in text analysis, grammar, and philosophy. Her current project is "Rediscovering the 'I' in Discourse and Grammar: Modern Enunciative Linguistics and Objectivism." She serves as Vice-President of the French Ayn Rand Society.

WENDY MCELROY is the author of *XXX: A Woman's Right to Pornography* (St. Martin's Press, 1995) and *Sexual Correctness: The Gender-Feminist Attack on Women* (McFarland, 1996). She is the editor of the anthology *Freedom, Feminism, and the State* (Cato Institute, 1982), now in its third edition. She is a freelance writer whose articles have appeared in publications as diverse as *National Review* and *Marie Claire*. She is a feminist lecturer, most recently at the International Congress on Prostitution sponsored by the California State University, Northridge, and at the Wisconsin Scholars' Society, University of Madison.

KAREN MICHALSON holds a Ph.D. in English from the University of Massachusetts at Amherst. She is a full-time writer and musician. She is the author of several novels, book reviews, scholarly articles, and one scholarly book, *Victorian Fantasy Literature: Literary Battles with Church and Empire*. She has taught at Worcester Polytechnic Institute and the University of Connecticut at Storrs. She is also the President of Arula Records and the bassist-vocalist of her rock band, Point of Ares, whose debut CD, *Enemy Glory*, is based on her literary fantasy trilogy of the same title, due to be released by TOR Books in fall 2000. Her URL is: http://www.ultranet.com/~ares.

CAMILLE PAGLIA is Professor of Humanities at the University of the Arts in Philadelphia. Her books include *Sexual Personae: Art and Decadence from Nefertiti to Emily Dickinson* (Yale University Press, 1992), *Sex, Art, and American Culture* (Vintage Books, 1992), and *Vamps and Tramps: New Essays* (Vintage Books, 1994).

SHARON PRESLEY received her Ph.D. in social psychology from the City University of New York. She has taught psychology of women and other gender-related courses at California State University, Iowa State University, the College of Wooster, and Weber State College. Her published research includes a study of political resisters to authority, historical papers on women resisters, and a study of Mormon feminists. She is Executive Director of Resources for Independent Thinking, a nonprofit educational organization, and is working on two books: an edited collection of essays by nineteenth-century individualist feminist Voltairine de Cleyre and *Is Gender in Our Genes?* a research-based critique of popular concepts of gender.

CHRIS MATTHEW SCIABARRA, co-editor of *Feminist Interpretations of Ayn Rand*, is Visiting Scholar in the Department of Politics at New York University. At NYU he earned a B.A. (magna cum laude) in history (with honors), economics, and politics, an M.A. in politics, and a Ph.D., with distinction, in political theory, philosophy, and methodology. He is the author of the forthcoming *Total Freedom*, his third book in the trilogy that began with *Marx, Hayek, and Utopia* (State University of New York Press, 1995) and continued with *Ayn Rand: The Russian Radical* (Penn State Press, 1995). In his exploration of the nature of political radicalism, he integrates libertarian social theory and dialectical method. His URL (http://www.nyu.edu/projects/sciabarra) features many of the debates that his work has provoked.

ROBERT SHEAFFER is the author of *Resentment Against Achievement* (Prometheus Books, 1988) and *The Making of the Messiah* (Prometheus, 1991). He received B.A. and M.A.T. degrees from Northwestern University. He has contributed articles and reviews to *Reason*, *Liberty*, the *Humanist*, *Scientific American*, *Free Inquiry*, and other publications. He works in California's Silicon Valley as a data communications engineer.

JOAN KENNEDY TAYLOR is the author of *Reclaiming the Mainstream: Individualist Feminism Rediscovered* (Prometheus Books, 1992) and has contributed numerous articles to periodicals and books. She has been senior editor of the *Libertarian Review*, publications director for the Manhattan Institute, and a radio commentator for the Cato Institute's syndicated "Byline." Currently, she is the national coordinator of the Association of Libertarian Feminists and is also active in the anticensorship organization Feminists for Free Expression. Her article "Protecting Minors from Free Speech" was in the fall 1977 *Journal of Information Ethics*, and she is working on a book about sexual harassment for New York University Press.

BARRY VACKER is an assistant professor in the Center for Communication Arts at Southern Methodist University in Dallas, Texas. He earned his doctorate in philosophy, law, and communication at the University of Texas at Austin. He is the author of several scholarly articles, including the lead essay on "pursing beauty" for a special edition of the journal *Psychology and Marketing*. His forthcoming book, entitled *Chaos at the Edge of Utopia*, is an extension of his dissertation, and it explores how utopian visions emerge from the reciprocal relation of science, aesthetics, politics, and media technology. He has presented papers before the

American Society for Aesthetics and has taught courses on "media and society," "aesthetics and culture," and "the cyber age."

JUDITH WILT is professor of English, former chair of the department, and founding director of the Women's Studies Program at Boston College. She teaches and writes in the fields of British and American fiction, popular culture, women's studies, and religion and literature. She has written books on George Meredith, Sir Walter Scott, and the Gothic novel and English fiction. Her most recent book is *Abortion, Choice, and Contemporary Fiction: The Armageddon of the Maternal Instinct* (1991). Her current work is on English novelist Mary Arnold Ward.

Index